TILTED MIRRORS

MEDIA ALIGNMENT WITH POLITICAL AND SOCIAL CHANGE

A Community Structure Approach

TILTED MIRRORS

MEDIA ALIGNMENT WITH POLITICAL AND SOCIAL CHANGE

A Community Structure Approach

John C. Pollock

The College of New Jersey

HAMPTON PRESS, INC.
CRESSKILL, NEW JERSEY

I dedicate this book to my parents,
John Crothers Pollock, Jr., (1915–) and Jane Reib Pollock (1920–),
whose encouragement has made my educational journey a joyful
pilgrimage, and whose love I shall always treasure

CONTENTS

SECTION II FIVE UMBRELLA HYPOTHESES AND CASE STUDIES

List of Figures

List of Tables

ACKNOWLEDGMENTS

I wish to express my appreciation to the many reviewers and colleagues who examined the case studies when they were submitted or accepted for presentation at refereed scholarly conferences of the National Communication Association, Eastern Communication Association, the Association for Education in Journalism & Mass Communication and International Communication Association. Most of the case studies in this book represent a joint composite: My own and the efforts of several generations of undergraduates at The College of New Jersey. I wish to extend my profound thanks to these student collaborators for their excellent work in data collection and data entry, data analysis or outlines/initial drafts of several sections of a variety of case studies, which include the following:

Chapter 3: Buffer Hypothesis

Coverage of Anita Hill's testimony: Karen Killeen

Coverage of physician-assisted suicide: Primarily Spiro Yulis for earlier and multiple drafts, but also Melissa Steiger, Patricia Montane and Ellen O'Hara

Coverage of embryonic stem cell research: Daniella Gratale, Christina Steer, Aimee Fisher, Matt Donaruma, Keli Steuber

Chapter 4: Violated Buffer Hypothesis

Coverage of the tobacco Master Settlement Agreement: Michael J. Miller, Kristen Caldwell and Justin Langlois

Coverage of efforts to regulate privacy on the Internet: Adam Ehrenworth, Robert Hunsicker and Sean Collins

Coverage of Bush v. Gore "stopping the counting" decision by the US Supreme Court: Devin Dino, Katie Elia, Lauren Borrone

Chapter 5: Vulnerability Hypothesis

Coverage of capital punishment: Charles Auletta, Adrian Castillo, Susan Haderer, Michael Bobal

Coverage of a Patients' Bill of Rights: Adrian Castillo, Adam Solomon, Kathy Griffiths

Chapter 6: Protection Hypothesis

Coverage of NAFTA: Jodi Giannattasio and Brian Siano,

Coverage of the handover of Hong Kong to the People's Republic of China: Michael C. Johnson, James Sverapa IV, Christopher Jensen and Alyssa Clark

Chapter 7: Stakeholder Hypothesis

Coverage of gun control efforts since Columbine: Kelly Johnson, Erica Geiman, Megan Riddell, as well as Jeff Fogliano and Jason Geipel

Coverage of drilling in the Arctic National Wildlife Reserve: Daniel Salimbene and Matthew Marhefka

Coverage of trying juveniles as adults: Charles Auletta, Elizabeth Hartwick, Gina Brockenbrough, and Renee Carpentier

Chapter 8: Coverage of Those with HIV/AIDS Over Time

Jerry Autobelli and Ginger Hall, both graduates of the College of New Jersey, for help in data collection and data analysis. Other students who contributed to data collection, data analysis or initial drafts of coverage of specific years or celebrities include , for the Magic Johnson materials, Mary Jane Awrachow, William J. Kuntz, Jacqueline Valentino, Bernard Zuccarelli and Christine Thibodeau. Gratitude is also offered Kelly McNeil, Lisa Pizzatello, Amanda Donovan, Erin Hiner, Maureen Grillo, Patricia Shields, Alice Griffin, Alan Hollander, Melissa Petterson, Jennifer Fowler, Jamie Garbowski and Meg Huggins.

Chapter 9: Coverage of Homosexuals in the Boy Scouts of America

Angela M DuRoss, Jill E. Moscatello and Christine A. O'Rourke

A group of students contributed a great deal not only to individual case studies, but also to the entire community structure research enterprise, functioning as advanced "research commandos," even teaching assistants, helping to assist and generate excitement among other students (Pollock, in press). Along with some of their achievements and contributions to the communication field, they include:

- Jonathan Peck, the first winner of a Marshall Scholarship in the field of communication studies, for two years of study in the United Kingdom.
- Elvin Montero and Jessalynn Kearney, both of whom worked on studies of coverage of the Internet in the mid-90s. Elvin became a Master's candidate at the Annenberg School for Communication at the University of Pennsylvania. Jessalynn earned a MPA from the Maxwell School at Syracuse.

- Ichiro Kawasaki, master's in communication, Newhouse School, Syracuse.
- Tiffany Tanner, who earned a MPA from the Maxwell School, Syracuse.
- Gustavo Dantas, M.A., the Annenberg School at the University of Pennsylvania.
- Spiro Yulis, who earned a MHS degree from Johns Hopkins in public health.
- Adrian Castillo, MA in advertising from the University of Texas.
- Charles Auletta, MA in advertising from the University of Texas.
- Melissa Mink, who earned a MPA from the Maxwell School, Syracuse.
- Jennifer Puma, who earned a MPA from the Maxwell School, Syracuse.
- Stefanie Loh, who earned a MPA from the Maxwell School, Syracuse.
- Katie Elia, who earned a MPA from the Maxwell School, Syracuse.
- Daniella Gratale, who earned a master's in public affairs, George Washington U.
- Yvonne Lachmann, who earned a master's in public health at Johns Hopkins.
- Jean Lutkenhouse, Ph.D. candidate, the Annenberg School for Communication at the University of Pennsylvania.
- Laura deZutter, who earned a master's in communication at Rutgers.
- Jaclyn Kupcha, who earned a MPA at the Maxwell School, Syracuse U.
- Stefanie Gratale, master's candidate in public affairs, George Washington U.
- Alissa D'Amelio, master's candidate in health communication, George Mason U.
- Tom Hipper, master's candidate in health communication, Penn State U.
- Dana Eisenberg, master's candidate in health communication, Ohio State U.
- Brittany Hammer, master's candidate in media studies, University of Texas.
- Jill Nash, master's candidate in communication studies, University of Delaware.
- Allison Rosinski, Katie Pagliara, Jonathan Smyth, Katherine Dokus, Jennifer Hagert, Caitlin Gaughan, Amanda Griffiths, Kendall Anderson, Pam Braddock, Kristine LaPlant, Samantha Schumacher, Lindsey Oxley, Lindsey Borda, Victoria Cullen, Jason Katz, Brigitte McNamara, Connor Buttner, and Elyse Mitchell, all of whom presented papers at scholarly conferences.

Montero, Dantas, Yulis, Castillo, Lachmann, Lutkenhouse, Anderson and Hipper have all exercised national leadership responsibilities in communication studies. Each of the eight was elected to a one-year term as national president of the national undergraduate honor society in communication studies, Lambda Pi Eta (LPE). Pam Braddock and Brittany Hammer were elected vice president of LPE for 2005-2006 and 2006-2007, respectively. Laura de Zutter was elected national secretary of Lambda Pi Eta for 2004-2005.

In addition, several students who have made contributions far beyond class expectations include: Ginger Hall, Valerie Nisi, Amie Huebner, and Kim Atwood. I wish to thank the College of New Jersey for offering the equivalent of one course of release time for most of the years I have taught there. Among colleagues, Gary Woodward at The College of New Jersey has offered thoughtful encouragement many times, as have Gary Kreps of George Mason University, K. "Vish" Viswanath of the Harvard School of Public Health, Jorge Schement of Penn State and Larry Frey of the University of Colorado. My mentors at Stanford, Richard Fagen, Robert Packenham, Richard Brody, Sidney Verba and the late Gabriel Almond all helped convey the joy of research in the social sciences, as did Irving Louis Horowitz, Rutgers emeritus. Ron Rice, James Katz, David Demers, Tom Patterson, Wolfgang Donsbach, David Paletz, Gary Gumpert and Lewis Donohue have all offered helpful advice at different points in my intellectual journey, as have several colleagues at Rider University: Frank Rusciano, Robin Rusciano, Jonathan Mendilow, Bosah Ebo, Minmin Wang and Jonathan Millen. I want to thank Robin Cutler for her loyal support in the final stages of this project. I also wish to thank collectively my colleagues in the New Jersey Communication Association and the New York State Communication Association for their collegiality and support over many years, as well as many colleagues in the International Communication Association and National Communication Association, especially those in the health communication divisions, as well as colleagues in the Association for Education in Journalism & Mass Communication. Series editor Lee Becker of the University of Georgia and publisher Barbara Bernstein of Hampton Press have been extraordinarily patient.

The author wishes to thank Taylor & Francis for permission to reprint some pages from an articles that appeared in *Journal of Health Communication,* 9(4), 281-307, and the Association for Education in Journalism and Mass Communication for permission to reprint material published in *Mass Comm Review,* 22, 166-177.

I wish to recognize my magical sons, Christopher Frasier Pollock and Maxwell Crothers Pollock, for their enduring understanding, as well as my sisters, Mary Pollock Shilling and Amy Pollock Morse, for their lifelong support.

Finally, I dedicate this book to my parents, John Crothers Pollock, Jr., and Jane Reib Pollock, whose encouragement has made my educational journey a joyful pilgrimage, and whose love I shall always treasure.

ABOUT THE AUTHOR

John C. Pollock, Professor in the Communication Studies Department, The College of New Jersey (TCNJ), received his BA from Swarthmore (political science), M (I) PA from the Maxwell School at Syracuse (international public administration) and PhD from Stanford (political science/international relations/comparative politics). He also studied at the Johns Hopkins School of Advanced International Studies as a PhD candidate. His current teaching and research interests include health communication campaigns, international communication, mass communication and research methods. He has taught at Rutgers University and the City University of New York (Queens College) and has conducted research in India and Latin America (Colombia), serving as director of the Latin American Institute at Rutgers. He serves on several editorial boards, has authored *The Politics of Crisis Reporting: Learning to be a Foreign Correspondent* (Praeger) and coauthored two other books. He has published scholarly and professional articles in *Journalism Quarterly, Journal of Health Communication, Communication Research Reports, Society, Newspaper Research Journal, Journal of International Communication, Mass Communication Review* and *Communication Yearbook IV*, as well as *The New York Times, The Nation, Industry Week* and the *Public Relations Journal*. Former president of the national public opinion research subsidary of a leading public relations firm, he is the recipient of a Silver Anvil, the "Oscar" of the Public Relations Society of America. He has also appeared on the *Today* show and *Nightline* and has testified before congress on the results of his surveys. Former president of the New Jersey Communication Association, he has received grants from the Social Science Research Council, National Cancer Institute and the United Nations Foundation for research on media coverage of critical issues. He also received the 2003 national "Advisor of the Year" award from the National Communication Association for his work with the TCNJ Chapter of Lambda Pi Eta, the national communication student honor society. His current research focuses on international media coverage of critical health issues, especially AIDS in sub-Saharan Africa.

INTRODUCTION

JOURNALISTS' CHOICES
AND COMPETING NEWS FRAMES

How do journalists make decisions when reporting on critical political and social events? Encountering emerging issues, how often do reporters rely on established professional conventions and norms, and how often do they consider other factors, in particular the characteristics of the communities in which they work and typically live? These questions are central to this exploration of media alignment with political and social change.

When reporting on proposals to challenge established customs or laws, journalists face significant choices among competing news frames. News framing by journalists is the activity of organizing events into a coherent story, presenting some perspectives as more reasonable than others. Expressed more formally by Robert Entman (1993b), framing is the: "selection of some aspects of a perceived reality (to) make them more salient in a communicating context, in such a way as to promote a particular problem, definition, causal interpretation, moral evaluation and/or treatment recommendation" (p. 53) (see also Entman, 1991, 1993a; Entman & Page, 1994).

In reporting on proposed legalization of physician-assisted suicide, for example, reporters can choose to write about that activity primarily from the perspective of the way that procedure challenges traditional medical ethics or alternatively from a perspective of dignity and rights accorded senior citizens. Similarly, journalists can choose to frame the Master Settlement Agreement banning tobacco advertising to minors primarily as a triumph for public health or perhaps as an infringement on freedom of (corporate) expression or even as a financial windfall for state treasurers, tying their budget expectations to the fortunes of tobacco giants. In parallel fashion, do journalists frame the proposal to drill for oil in the Arctic National Wildlife Reserve (ANWR) primarily as a way to add to vital oil reserves or primarily as an emblem of environmental callousness and insensitivity? Of course, journalists may make careful efforts to balance competing frames. Often, however, deadlines and scarce news hole space, along with the imperative to tell a coherent story, impel journalists to make alternative framing choices when reporting on critical events.

Examining the process that leads to these and related framing decisions is no mere academic exercise. The level of media support for physician-assisted suicide, opposition to tobacco advertising to children, or opposition to drilling in previously protected environments can have a profound impact on both public and policymaker perspectives on these issues. As a result, because so much is at stake, the search for factors that affect journalist framing of critical events takes on special urgency and purpose.

Consider some recent research on the power of journalists' framing choices. Political communication scholar Thomas Patterson documented the growing intrusiveness of media in the political process, gathering evidence that media have usurped that process by substituting the judgments of journalist-commentators for the opinions of political parties, leaders, and elected officials. Since the presumed political "reforms" of the McGovern era, earlier and more nearly simultaneous presidential primaries increase media influence on the presidential election process (Patterson, 1995). In another study, Patterson (2002) argued that "media bias" toward negative reporting on both liberal and conservative political campaigns is a major factor promoting voter disengagement from politics. (A more optimistic assessment is offered by Pippa Norris, 2000, in *A Virtuous Circle*, a cross-national assessment suggesting that attention to the news media does not diminish but gradually reinforces civic engagement, and vice versa.) Related arguments documenting the enormous influence of media on the political process are marshaled by other communication scholars. Jamieson and Waldman (2002) contend that media "framing" had a substantial effect on the 2000 presidential election, generally framing Bush as "not too bright" and Gore as "untrustworthy," perhaps rendering Bush the safer, less venal choice. In coverage of foreign policy, Bennett and Paletz (1994) document the way reporting frames legitimized the political and military buildup to the first Gulf War. In consistent fashion, Iyengar and Kinder (1987) provide extensive evidence that television newscasts powerfully affect public opinion.

A seminal study confirms the power of framing. According to Iyengar (1991), television news is often reported in the form of specific events or particular cases of "episodic" news framing, distinct from "thematic" coverage putting political issues or events in broader context. These alternative frames matter a great deal, since Iyengar's own experimental research suggests that viewers of thematic frames tend to attribute causes and solutions to broad social, party or government policies, whereas those exposed to episodic framing tend to assign blame for social problems to individuals. Because television news emphasizes episodic framing, in Iyengar's (1991) view, it deflects political accountability away from government. Other studies on the consequences of news framing for audiences confirm that issue frames can have substantial influence, with a new frame cognition driving out old frames in what Price, Tewksbury, and Powers (1995) call a "hydraulic" pattern, or master frames serving as motivators for individuals to support social movements (Entman & Rojecki, 1993; Klandermas, 1997; Klandermas, Kriesi, & Tarrow, 1988).

Of course, the connection between media and public opinion or policy-makers may be somewhat indirect. Media may function, for example, as "accomplices" of society (or parts of it) or as "indicants" of public opinion for various audiences. Consider, for example, perspectives on the power of media asserted by Timothy Cook (1998):

> The news media are commonly recognized as wielding political power. Instead of arguing over whether the media do so, we should turn our attention to the more important question of what kind of power is wielded and to what effect. We must also remember that the American news media rarely work in isolation. The journalist Tom Rosenstiel has acutely noted, "The press, contrary to common mythology, is rarely if ever a lone gunman. More often, it is society's accomplice" (Rosenstiel, writing in the *Los Angeles Times* Calendar Section, November 27, 1988, p. 25). Even then, we might wish to amend this insight by asking: To which part of society are the news media an accomplice? . . . Most crucially, we need to be able to gauge who wins and who loses as a result of the routine production of American news, and to figure out how to respond. (pp. 191–192)

Similarly, media may be linked to public opinion less as a force exercising direct impact than as an indirect indicator of opinion for particular audiences. In the view of Schöenbach and Becker (1995), in an international evaluation of media roles media may be especially effective less as direct molders of public opinion than as "indicants" of public opinion for their audiences, in particular elite audiences. Politicians, for example, often take cues from what media report public opinion to be on specific issues.

Although the influence of journalists' choices is increasingly apparent, how those choices are made remains something of a mystery. Many explanations turn to professional norms, news-gathering routines, or newsroom social validation. Others may turn to media markets or "imagined communities" or real or potential sources. Often overlooked are the social and political contexts of particular communities, the metropolitan areas or cities where many journalists work and live. It is my conviction that "community structure"—demographics, city characteristics—surrounding journalist decision making has a great deal to do with reporting on social and political change. In one of the first studies targeting a national cross-section sample of newspapers, this book defines and documents the power of that perspective: the community structure approach.

FROM PROFESSIONAL "OBJECTIVITY" TO VARIATIONS IN REPORTING PERSPECTIVES

The journalists' ethic of media fairness or objectivity has long suggested that the judgments and reporting of media professionals are not supposed to be influenced by "outside" forces. This worthy goal served journalism well in the late 19th and earlier part of the 20th centuries and was an effort to insulate journalism from the arbitrary pressures of powerful economic and political interests (see Schudson, 1978). But today's media professionals and audiences alike are well aware that media are quite capable of portraying people and events in ways that set the stage for audiences to view certain features as more important than others, framing events so that some outcomes appear more likely or reasonable than others.

Memorable examples include the abundance of conspiracy theories to explain the explosion of TWA's Flight 800 over Long Island; the persistent pejorative reporting on the parents of JonBenet Ramsey (the child beauty queen who was murdered in Boulder, Colorado); or the savage, destructive reporting on Atlanta's Richard Jewell, who was falsely accused of planting a bomb at that city's 1996 summer Olympic games. Reporting the Bill Clinton/Monica Lewinsky/Linda Tripp/Kenneth Starr exchanges became a textbook example of unprofessional journalism. Critiqued as much by media professionals themselves as by the public, it was an example that consistently violated cherished canons of journalistic objectivity or fairness.

Indeed, political communication scholar Larry Sabato (1991) labeled this kind of growing tendency among even mainstream journalism to act like tabloid-mongers *junkyard dog* journalism, apparent since 1974 (in contrast to *lapdog* journalism from 1941 to 1966 and *watchdog* journalism from 1966 to 1974). In more recent work, Sabato and colleagues extended the argument, suggesting that a politician's private life should be liable to public scrutiny only in special circumstances, for example, regarding health or use of public funds, not concerning internal family matters or past sexual activity (Stencel, Lichter, & Sabato, 2000). In response to such charges, fairness in journalism was the subject of a multiyear investigation by the Freedom

Forum, a national nonprofit organization devoted to upholding the highest standards of journalism.

The media have a great deal of influence on individual opinions and perspectives, and media can also be affected by surrounding political and social conditions (Nisbet et al., 2002; Shanahan, Nisbet, Diels, Hardy, & Besley, 2005). As a set of ethical principles to guide professionals, "objective" journalism has many advantages. As a descriptive or explanatory system, however, objective journalism is inadequate in accounting for a great deal of news coverage of critical events. As researchers we must reach beyond critiques of journalists, beyond concerns about the demise of objective reporting, to ask whether new trends or patterns are emerging. If the traditional model of objective reporting is less useful in helping researchers understand major questions about possible close, significant links between media reporting and social change, what models (or expected blueprints) might help us explore that relationship? Is it really as simple as some experts suggest, that the growing competition between rapidly mushrooming news channels and outlets has led to a rush to judgment and tabloidization of even the most dignified media in an effort to gain competitive advantage? In other words, is market competition, in itself, driving reporting on social change issues? Although I agree that market competition might affect the speed and accuracy of public affairs reporting, I do not believe that the competitive explanation is satisfactory in accounting for the systematic ways different media report on issues that illuminate social change.

ASKING THE RIGHT QUESTIONS

Communication scholars can ask three broad questions that explore reporting patterns, specifically: (a) How much variation exists in reporting on issues of social or political change; (b) Are there consistent patterns in that reporting on change; and (c) If variation does exist, why? Over the past few years, many students and I have conducted joint research on the first two questions (Pollock, 1999), and although the investigation is ongoing, we can report provisional results that illuminate several consistent patterns as media report on political and social change. The third question, asking "why" variation exists, is addressed in chapter 10 and in the epilogue.

This study focuses on newspapers for three major reasons: First, newspaper databases for a wide range of cities nationwide are more readily available than are radio or television databases. Second, analysis of newspapers accesses most of what newspaper readers see (e.g., placement, headline size, article length, visuals). For television, by contrast, the number of variables that might affect a viewer are far larger, embracing not only text but also vocal tone and pace, facial expressions, body movement, color, set design, and a wide array of variables considered in the study of media ecology. Analyzing newspaper text, by contrast, maximizes the correspondence between the material coders analyze and what readers encounter, reducing the extraneous influence of multiple ecological variables, thereby increasing the external validity of the media analysis. An analysis of newspaper articles on specific topics can focus on a finite set of factors that affect audience or reader perceptions.

A third reason to focus on newspapers is their capacity to act as agenda-setters for other media. Local television and radio schedulers frequently refer to daily newspapers in deciding which topics to cover or emphasize. Newspapers often function as "primary" agenda-setters for other channels of communication.

This examination compares a cross-section of issue coverage from many major newspapers and cities from throughout the United States, from the *San Francisco Chronicle* to the *Boston Globe*, from the *New Orleans Times Picayune* to the *Detroit Free Press*, and several other papers as well. Multiple nationwide community structure surveys of newspaper reporting have explored a wide range of topics and have been presented in more than 80 scholarly papers at regional, national, or international conferences. The illustrative case studies selected for inclusion in this study fall into four broad categories: human rights issues, health care issues, economic issues, and quality-of-life issues. Each of these concerns illustrates a critical issue linked to proposals for political or social change. Examples of each of these issue categories are elaborated throughout this book, but they are organized according to five major hypothesis "patterns" outlined elsewhere.

A SEARCH FOR PATTERNS IN THE VARIATION

After several years of collecting and analyzing newspaper coverage of myriad issues representing efforts at political or social change, it was clear that for essentially all of these topics, there was widespread variation in the "direction" or degree of favorable or unfavorable coverage in newspapers throughout the United States. After mapping substantial differences in directional coverage of human rights, health care, economic, and quality-of-life concerns, a second question emerged: Are there any patterns in this variation? Seeking answers to this question is a major challenge and can be addressed by forwarding four subquestions:

1. *Professional Question*: How much reporting is the product simply of individual reporting decisions, professional norms, or organizational decisions, and how much reporting is linked to larger contextual, especially community-based factors?
2. *Theoretical Question*: What can a "community structure" approach add to existing theories of reporting on political and social change? What level of analysis—individual, organizational, or community—is most productive (and perhaps most overlooked) in the search for reporting patterns?
3. *Methodological Question*: Is there a way to measure the amount of attention an issue attracts in a newspaper by going beyond simple measures of salience or prominence, on the one hand, and on the other, framing "direction" (favorable, unfavorable, balanced/neutral)? Is there a systematic way to combine several sensitive measures into a single, combined newspaper "score"?
4. *Empirical Question*: How much can we learn from piecing together geographically and methodologically distinct case studies, and how feasible is it to conduct nationwide studies using comparable sample designs, methodologies, and data collection techniques in order to pursue studies that reveal the functioning of nationwide "patterns" in reporting on political and social change?

Regarding the professional question about the best way to understand what affects variations in reporting on political and social change, several sources have probed differences in individual reporters, in the way news organizations are operated, or in newspaper readership "markets." Most of these possible explanations are unlikely to be associated with reporting variation. According to nationwide studies, individual reporters and editors generally come from similar educational and economic backgrounds and are unlikely to manifest substantially different perspectives on social change. Neither do separate newspapers organize their newsgathering operations in substantially different ways, so that newsroom organization differences are unlikely to account for reporting variation. Nor do readership audiences or markets differ much from one newspaper to another because papers are typically read by relatively well-educated, higher income citizens.

What does vary from one city to another is something that has become the focus of a search for satisfactory explanations: differences in city demographics or characteristics that might be plausibly linked to differences in reporting on social change. Because other scholars have generally chosen not to test these connections systematically in a national context, this study explores uncharted terrain, addressing the second, or significant theoretical issue: What can a study linking city characteristics or "community structure" add to existing theories about the functioning of media generally? A wide range of city characteristics can be examined in this study: privilege (measuring different levels of family income, education, percent with professional status in each city); vulnerability (percent unemployed, poverty levels); access to health care (e.g., number of physicians, nurses, and hospital beds per 100,000 citizens); and, depending on the issue under study, different stakeholders (e.g., the proportion of different age or ethnic groups, families with children of different ages, percent voting Democratic or Republican). Several of these characteristics proved important across many of the case studies of critical events, confirming hunches and guesses that city characteristics are significantly related to media coverage of social change.

From the perspective of media theories, confirming the importance of variations in community structure linked to reporting on change draws attention to relatively "macro" constructs associated with reporting, distinct from a substantial body of theory focusing on "micro" constructs such as the attitudes, norms, or incentives of journalists; the uses and gratifications of media use for individual readers or audience members; or even the "imagined communities" of journalists. (For a discussion of different levels of analysis frequently used to study journalism, see Shoemaker & Reese, 1996.) Community structure theory is not incompatible with any of the more widely used theories, exploring especially individual attitudes and behavior and norms of journalists, theories that yield valuable results. In addition to complementing other approaches, the community structure perspective, like other theories, can be used not only to explain the past, but also to propose prospective hypotheses for the future, discussed in the epilogue. The community structure perspective deserves a place at the table of legitimate approaches and theories taken into account when explaining reporting on critical issues.

A methodological contribution also merits attention. In order to test any links between community structure and reporting, it is useful to do two things simultaneously: be sensitive to as many variations in article attention or "prominence" (e.g., placement, headline size, article length, number of graphics) as possible, and yet also take into account the way an issue is "framed" overall in each article (funneled in this study into the three constructs of favorable, unfavorable or balanced/neutral). Several studies pay attention separately to tabulations of attention/prominence or types of framing, but it is unusual to combine both prominence and framing measures in a single study. The methodology proposed in this study does combine those distinct measures and provides evidence for a new measure of issue "projection."

The fourth contribution of this study is empirical. Most studies using structural approaches examine only a few communities, one state, or a few states located near one another. This study undertakes an ambitious, nationwide sample of newspapers in major U.S. cities. This national sampling frame facilitates innovative comparisons.

It is reasonable to expect that reporting on critical national issues might differ among newspapers from distinct regions. Northeastern newspapers such as the *Boston Globe* or the *Philadelphia Inquirer* might have different perspectives on embryonic stem cell research or cloning than do midwestern papers such as the *Omaha Herald* or the *Kansas City Star.* Western papers such as the *Denver Post* or the *Seattle Times* might be expected to display different viewpoints about tobacco advertising directed at children compared to southern papers such as the *Charlotte Observer* of North Carolina or Tennessee's Memphis *Commercial Appeal.*

In parallel fashion, reporting on critical issues might differ not only among regions, but also across cities themselves. Newspapers in cities with higher poverty levels or proportions of teenagers may present different perspectives on the death penalty or trying juveniles as adults than do newspapers in cities with lower poverty levels or lower proportions of families with teens. Newspapers with different proportions of those voting Republican or Democratic in presidential elections may reflect different viewpoints on gun control or the Supreme Court's decision to "stop the counting" in Florida during the 2000 presidential election, a decision that may have proved decisive in the selection of George W. Bush as president of the United States. Similarly, newspapers with different proportions of the population "at risk" from biological threats or threats to a cherished way of life—whether from HIV/AIDS or legalization of physician-assisted suicide, or with different "stakes" in issue outcomes, for example, in drilling for oil in the ANWR— may report differently on issues that some consider "threats." In summary, given the diversity found in distinct cities, different newspaper viewpoints are certainly to be expected across the United States.

Existing studies on communities and newspaper coverage have focused on a few selected cities (see Stamm, 1985) or primarily on one state, Minnesota, an area with a relatively homogeneous population, and as such, not completely representative of the nation as a whole (see various studies by Tichenor, Donohue, & Olien, 1973, 1980). These explorations contain a variety of fascinating findings for the cities sampled and many excellent theoretical propositions and empirical findings (Demers, 1998; K. A. Smith, 1984), yet they do not put those propositions to an empirical test across several major cities throughout the nation.

Moreover, several studies have focused on the "uses and gratifications" of newspaper reading for individuals rather than more broadly on newspaper perspectives on social change. Because so many journalists and policymakers agree that newspapers are crucibles for debates on social policy and social change, it is surprising that so few scholars have come forward to compare newspapers systematically nationwide.

Several newspaper studies adopt perspectives that examine the individual viewpoints or training of journalists on the one hand, or the organizational incentives of newspapers as institutions on the other, seeking "similar explanations for newspaper "behaviors" or outcomes. The findings typically illustrate what newspapers have in common. However, newspaper or reporting differences may be as important as their similarities.

THEORY: VIEWING NEWSPAPERS
AS COMMUNITY INSTITUTIONS

This study, by contrast, is an effort to address long ignored or overlooked issues: to compare systematically newspaper coverage of significant social issues in major papers throughout the United States, and to explore a wide range of city or community structure characteristics associated with that coverage, testing which ones are most closely associated with perspectives relatively "receptive" or "unreceptive" to social change. This community structure approach to newspaper reporting makes it possible to explore which aspects of a city's characteristics—demographics, economic circumstances, city size, ethnic composition, occupational distribution, quality of life, and so on—are most closely linked to newspaper perspectives accommodating or resisting social change.

With the growing abundance of one-way and interactive electronic media, newspapers are one of the few remaining "local" or "community" media institutions in the United States. City newspapers are often considered forums where social and political issues are raised and, in effect, "discussed" (Tichenor et al., 1980). Curiously, however, despite the longevity and importance of newspapers not simply as "businesses," but rather as vibrant institutions or forums where "community" discussions and perspectives on social change could occur, *no systematic cross-sectional national study has yet been conducted on newspapers and social and political change.*

EFFICACIOUS GROUPS AND COMMUNITY NORMS:
THE IMPORTANCE OF EXAMINING PRIVILEGED GROUPS

Most studies on media agenda-setting start with media content analysis as the point of departure and then test the association between media coverage and either public opinion or public policy. The key question is usually: how much do media agendas "set" the agendas found in public opinion or public policies? A 1995 study, for example, concluded that press coverage does have an impact on social beliefs regarding HIV transmission (Hertog & Fan, 1995). The studies on this topic are important because they help us understand just how much impact media agendas have on agendas in other domains.

Curiously, however, although media themselves are often viewed as the "first cause" or "causal" agent in the chain of agenda-setting, a previous question is seldom asked: Who or what influences the agenda-setters? Scholars occasionally focus on that question, asking, for example, how much the biographical histories of journalists might reveal about their perspectives on reporting (see Johnstone, Slawski, & Bowman, 1976; Pollock, 1981; Weaver & Wilhoit, 1988, 1996). Or how much do journalists mirror the interests of influential elites, functioning perhaps less as "watchdogs" skeptical of official pronouncements than as "guard dogs" for established interests (see Olien, Donohue & Tichenor, 1995)? This interest in what happens "prior" to agenda-setting allows researchers to move from asking how media influence public opinion or policy to queries about how media themselves are influenced. From whom or what do media agenda-setters take their cues about the significance and direction of news events?

The new attention to influentials who may affect journalists' perspectives on social change has yielded specific scholarly interest among health communication researchers. For example, in a study of newspaper agenda-setting and HIV/AIDS Dearing and Rogers; (1992) urged that: "Mass media organizations are far from autonomous actors in the determination of which issues become news. . . . Research on media agenda-setting should conceptualize the output of mass media organizations as being closely responsive to the *perceived attitudes and values* held by *efficacious groups* of people within their relevant environment" (p. 191, italics added).

These scholarly recommendations deserve serious examination, but to engage in a study of sufficient magnitude and scope to yield conclusive results, thousands of research dollars and years of careful data collection and analysis are desirable. Prior to substantial funding, is there anything small teams of scholars on limited budgets can accomplish to test the association between "efficacious groups" on the one hand and coverage of critical issues such as HIV/AIDS victims on the other? This study represents an effort to illuminate that question using a modest but highly targeted research design.

A FOCUS ON CITY CHARACTERISTICS

Specifically, without the resources to deploy a substantial series of questionnaires toward large populations over time, or to map the perspectives of journalists toward "efficacious groups," this study focuses on aggregate data at the city level, or "city characteristics," as indirect indicators of "efficacious groups." For example, some city characteristics measuring proportion of "privileged"—such as percent in professional occupations, percent with college educations, or percent with somewhat high incomes—are relatively stable over time. The percentages of the population in each of these categories do not vary greatly from year to year for each city. These indicators, or similar ones, may be used to tap the influence of efficacious groups, collectivities likely to be relatively stable in size over time.

It is reasonable to assume that, in the aggregate, efficacious groups are relatively well-educated, relatively affluent and likely to belong to high-status professional occupations. It is also reasonable to assume that these efficacious groups, in the aggregate, are likely to have a great deal to do with the creation or maintenance of community norms because it is precisely those groups that are most likely to become involved in public affairs (to discuss politics with others, to vote, to write letters, to help organize campaigns, even to run for office). In summary, aggregate data in the form of city characteristics are useful "indirect" indicators of both community norms and the perspectives of efficacious groups. Studying newspapers as "mirrors" or "reflectors" of significant groups surrounding them as they report on a crisis addresses a concern articulated by several scholars.

CRITICAL ISSUES AND EVENTS OFTEN OVERLOOKED BY COMMUNICATION SCHOLARS

With aggregate data serving as indicators of significant independent variables, what indicators help measure newspaper perspectives on political and social change? A suggestion made in the 1970s by Steven Chaffee and others helps answer that question. This perspective asks that media scholars look at "critical events" (political) coverage as an indicator of key coverage choices newspapers make (Chaffee, 1975; see especially, Kraus, Davis, Lang & Lang, cited in Chaffee, 1975; Rivers, Miller, & Gandy, cited in Chaffee, 1975). Instead of focusing on the routines of party politics and elections, for example, an exploration of significant committee hearings, civil disturbances, court cases, referenda, communication policy formation (Graber & Smith, 2005), major crises such as 9/11 (Coleman & Wu, 2006), or recessions (Wu et al., 2002) can reveal a great deal about the ways newspapers function as gatekeepers and agenda-setters. Adopting a "critical event" perspective, previous studies have found that certain city population characteristics measuring the proportion of relatively privileged (efficacious) groups in a city can be linked to relatively favorable or unfavorable reporting on the 1973 U.S. Supreme Court decision on abortion (*Roe v. Wade*), Cuban political refugees or Dr. Kevorkian's physician-assisted suicide activities (Pollock, Robinson, & Murray, 1978; Pollock, Shier, & Slattery, 1996; Pollock, Coughlin, Thomas, & Connaughton, 1996). A related measure, city poverty level, is also linked to coverage of a 1971 prisoner uprising at Attica; reporting on a referendum to revoke homosexual rights regarding housing discrimination in Dade County, Florida; and coverage of a conflict between Caribbean-Americans and Orthodox Jews in Crown Heights, Queens, New York City. (Pollock & Robinson, 1977; Pollock & Whitney, 1995).

This book examines nationwide coverage of "critical events" for evidence about the way newspapers make decisions about coverage, focusing on some broadly defined critical issues that communication scholars have largely neglected (except for Anita Hill and HIV/AIDS), issues that deserve systematic study, including:

- Coverage of workplace rights and health-related rights (Anita Hill's testimony at the Clarence Thomas hearings, physician-assisted suicide, embryonic stem cell research, the tobacco Master Settlement Agreement, and those with HIV/AIDS).
- Coverage of Internet privacy issues, voting rights and rights of association (restrictions on Internet use, the Bush vs. Gore decision of the US Supreme Court to 'stop the counting" in Florida in the 2000 election, and homosexual membership in the Boy Scouts of America).
- Coverage of recently emerging or re-emerging "survival" issues focusing on "distributive justice" (the death penalty and proposals for a Patients' Bill of Rights).
- Coverage of new economic/political initiatives that raise questions about equitable treatment of workers or access to markets (the North American Free Trade Agreement [NAFTA] debate in congress and the handover of Hong Kong to the People's Republic of China).
- Coverage of "stakeholder" concerns (gun control since Columbine, proposals to drill for oil in the ANWR, and trying juveniles as adults).

The community structure approach draws attention to the power not just of newspaper "markets" defined as newspaper "circulation" demographics, but more broadly, of city structures and demographics as factors clearly associated with reporting variation on critical events. If newspapers are institutions where new and significant community issues are displayed and discussed, then it is reasonable to expect that newspaper coverage of critical events will be associated not simply with markets, but also with some of the major forces and distributions of influence in their communities. For example, systematic comparisons of newspaper coverage nationwide with comparisons of city demographic and other aggregate data characteristics—focusing on such HIV/AIDS "events" or people as Ryan White, "Magic" Johnson, Arthur Ashe, and Greg Louganis—would help us understand why some newspapers may be more alert to this health threat than others. This book does that by comparing systematically, and using the same methodology to study health communication issues as well as each of the other issues mentioned.

SECTION I

COMMUNITY STRUCTURE APPROACH
AND MEDIA ALIGNMENT

1

THE COMMUNITY STRUCTURE
APPROACH AND NEWSPAPER FRAMING
OF CRITICAL EVENTS

INTRODUCTION:
THE IMPORTANCE OF MEDIA "FRAMING"
AND "FRAME-BUILDING"

Journalists use well-established, professional newsmaking routines when reporting on a wide range of conventional occurrences. When "critical events" erupt, however, or when something happens that is widely viewed as almost or altogether unprecedented, journalists are compelled to reach beyond the comfort of expected rhythms and commonplaces that guide daily reporting. At these unusual and sometimes momentous junctures, journalists must select dominant "frames" or value contexts that give perspective to opportunities for political or social change. This study explores the way newspaper frames are "built" by focusing on the communities that surround news organizations (see Scheufele, 2000; Shoemaker & Reese, 1996).

Framing in news media refers to the way journalists organize news stories that provide meaning to related events (Gamson, 1989). But framing does more than simply provide meaning in a general sense. As Pan and Kosicki (1993) noted, news media framing views "news texts as a system of organized signifying elements that both indicate the advocacy of certain ideas and provide devices to encourage audience processing of the texts" (pp. 55–56). Indicating advocacy and providing devices for audience processing are two functions of framing that reveal the capacity of journalists' choices to impact public opinion and policy formation.

For example, Nelkin (1987) noted that people assimilate media information about health-related issues in ways that depend on their previous experience, and media framing is important as it coalesces isolated incidents into coherent public issues (pp. 980-986). Andsager (2000), reviewing the recent literature on framing, suggests that "Through their representation of news stories, journalists suggest attitudes and opinions for the public" (p. 579). Quoting McCombs, Einsiedel, and Weaver, Andsager asserts that although "people actively construct their pictures of reality, they are *constrained* (emphasis added) by the information available to them from the mass media and other sources" (McCombs, Einsiedel & Weaver, 1991, p. 12, cited in Andsager, 2000, p. 580). Paraphrasing Pan and Kosicki, Andsager concluded that "framing research suggests that the media go beyond telling the public what is important and newsworthy; rather they also tell the public what opinions, interpretations and definitions of a controversial issue are most valid" (Pan & Kosicki, 1993, p. 70, cited in Andsager, 2000, p. 580).

The selection of frames may not be explicit or self-conscious. As documented by Susan Herbst (1998), journalists may not generally articulate formal, sophisticated themes of public opinion or audience formation in order to make educated guesses about prevailing perspectives on political or social change. Yet journalists' choices about value frames in news making can have important links to public opinion, for example in public perspectives on foreign policy (Rogers & Dearing, 1998; Rusciano, 1998) or protest groups (McLeod & Detenber, 1999). Framing choices can have special significance when the consequences for public opinion and policymaking are far reaching, as in the issues that rise to the level of congressional debates, bills or laws; legal cases reaching higher courts and presidential contests.

In the language of Stephen Reese (2001), framing refers to "the way events and issues are organized and made sense of, especially by media, media professionals and their audiences" (p .7). Framing helps media studies move beyond a narrow concern with "bias"—deviation from an objective standard—to a more productive view of "the ideological character of news, thoroughly structured in its content, practices and relations with society" (Reese, 2001, p. 9; see also D'Angelo, 2002; McCombs & Ghanem, 2001; Scheufele, 1999, 2000). Reese drew attention to the capacity of framing to illuminate the antecedents of news, examining the way issues are framed "as a result of social and institutional interests" (p. 9). As a result, framing approaches can draw the attention of researchers to the social, political, and corporate contexts of media patterns in reporting on political and social change.

The (value) framing of critical events, as used in this analysis, reaches beyond the level of newsroom decision making by journalists or editors.

For example, a study might focus on criteria for making judgments about new or unprecedented issues at the organizational or professional level. One research effort suggests that editors, confronting unprecedented issues such as the Pentagon Papers or Starr Report, must make intuitive judgments about how to report on so much material so quickly, and that these judgments can be aggregated into different decision-making "clusters." One recent study, for example, uses factor analysis to illuminate such clusters as Maverick Populist, a perspective that values both good stories and democracy, and Unfettered Professional, more concerned about pleasing readers than about newspaper ad revenue (Reber, Beaudoin, & Sanders, 2000).

It is the thesis of this study that reporting on critical events can be studied effectively not simply by examining newsroom or news making routines, but rather by adding a special macro focus: examining directly the demographic characteristics of communities where media messages are produced and transmitted. Specifically, this study urges the adoption of a "community structure" approach to illuminate the links between relatively enduring community characteristics—such as proportion of economically or educationally privileged citizens, or percent with access to healthcare or percent community "stakeholders" on a particular issue (such as senior citizens or working women or gays)—and reporting on political and social change. Before elaborating the community structure approach further, it is useful to focus on some of the critical events and the types of framing decisions journalists encounter as they try to fashion intelligible stories out of recently emerging issues.

This chapter outlines some of the critical framing choices faced frequently by journalists, explores the special utility of the community structure approach in a modern information society and illuminates theoretical, methodological, and empirical contributions. This chapter also demonstrates the broad assistance a community focus can offer in filling research gaps in studies connecting newspapers, public issues, and public policy; and balances the abundant literature on audience research with research on the community context and "antecedents" of newsmaking. Furthermore, this chapter attempts to rekindle excitement about some of the larger questions that gave birth to the modern communication field in the 1920s in the United States, paying special attention to national variations in reporting on political and social change, urging scholars to explore a wide range of city characteristics potentially linked to that variation. Finally, this chapter offers several linked propositions that summarize the argument for the effectiveness of the community structure approach in measuring accurately newspaper perspectives on political and social change.

CRITICAL "FRAMING" CHOICES ARE FACED FREQUENTLY BY JOURNALISTS

When reporting on "critical events," journalists' choices are not simply a matter of judgments about professional routines or newsmaking conventions about stories most likely to merit placement on the front page. In critical circumstances, reporters must select perspectives that connect newsmaking routines with social and political issues in a way that is comprehensible for readers or viewers. Although it is not argued that journalists reduce significant events to polarized stereotypes, simplistic choices between one extreme viewpoint or another, evidence from empirical studies on several critical events undertaken in recent years can illustrate the importance of the framing choices journalists face. Based on multiple studies, the following categories emerge:

1. *"Human Rights" Issues.* Consider some recent efforts to address human rights issues. Anita Hill's testimony at the Clarence Thomas judicial confirmation hearings could have been presented primarily as the efforts of a disgruntled former employee to derail a worthy nominee, or by contrast, the justified testimony of an employee who had suffered workplace discrimination. Efforts to legalize physician-assisted suicide could be viewed by media primarily as medical/ethical issues regarding preservation of human life or rather mostly as representing protection of the rights and dignity of seniors. Proposals to engage in embryonic stem cell research could be framed primarily as issues raising religious/ethical concerns or as opportunities for scientific innovation and medical breakthroughs advancing the rights of those with degenerative diseases. In each of these cases, journalists faced or continue to face choices that stretched beyond newsgathering routines to reflect significant concerns about human rights.

2. *Ominous Issues: Threats to Biological Existence or Cherished Customs.* This set of issues illuminates concerns about potential threats either to biological existence or to a cherished way of life. When Magic Johnson announced his HIV condition in 1991, journalists could choose perspectives that emphasized primarily empathy for those with the condition or, by contrast, fear of contagion. When efforts were made, under the tobacco Master Settlement Agreement (MSA), to reduce or eliminate tobacco ads targeting children, reporters could emphasize primarily threats to first amendment guarantees of unfettered communication, or

by contrast, the health threats to children unable to appreciate fully the biological consequences of their actions. When proposals were made to introduce restraints on censorship of the Internet, journalists could emphasize the privacy concerns of families or classic freedom of speech issues. Regarding the Supreme Court's decision in *Bush v. Gore,* effectively awarding the presidency to George Bush, reporters could emphasize the longstanding tradition of judicial supremacy in our political system or the willingness of judges to reach into the sanctity of the voting process.

3. *Redistributive Justice Issues.* This set of issues can reveal journalists' perspectives on innovative legal and medical concerns that reach far beyond either traditional "markets" for media or organized "interest groups" advocating clearly articulated public policies, especially when such issues reflect a concern with "redistributive justice," an effort to level historically uneven opportunity playing fields for vulnerable populations. Regarding legalization of capital punishment, journalists can write narratives emphasizing primarily a "punitive" perspective, or by contrast, one emphasizing unequal access to fair representation and procedural fairness in the legal system. With efforts to pass a "Patient's Bill of Rights," journalists can illuminate perspectives concerning economic ramifications of this bill category, or by contrast spotlight the profound dilemmas of those denied access to health care.

4. *Economic Issues.* Examining economic issues, consider North American Free Trade Agreement (NAFTA) or the transfer of Hong Kong to mainland China. With NAFTA, journalists could frame policy debates and outcomes primarily as threats to the U.S. workforce or more often as opportunities for a more efficient division of labor among U.S. and other manufacturers throughout the hemisphere. The transfer of Hong Kong to China could have been presented primarily as the restoration of a colonial enclave to Chinese sovereignty, or as an economic risk or loss for established global financial markets. To be sure, neither professional journalists nor their reporting can be summarily reduced to bipolar caricatures, delivering news in the form of obvious stereotypes. Journalists, do, nevertheless, have important choices to make as they create narratives about social and political change. The perspectives chosen for emphasis can fall more clearly into some frameworks than others most of the time.

5. *New Stakeholders.* This category focuses on key issues that clearly affect specific population segments. Previous community

structure studies have illuminated stakeholder choices faced by journalists. With Dr. Kevorkian's activities, journalists could reflect primarily the concerns of those over age 75, or by contrast offer more conventional perspectives on medical advancements to maintain life. With efforts to legalize same-sex marriage, reporters could emphasize traditional perspectives on marriage, for the most part, or reflect newer perspectives on gay efforts to normalize personal relationships. Regarding the trial of the British nanny who killed a young boy in her care, journalists could emphasize the risks of working women leaving children with others, or highlight the reasonableness of working mothers trusting others with their children.

In this study, journalists covering efforts at gun control could report primarily from the perspective of traditional views of the Bill of Rights or from the viewpoints of victims or potential victims of gun-related violence. Regarding proposals to drill for oil in the Arctic National Wildlife Reserve (ANWR), journalists could emphasize economic benefits or, by contrast, risks to a vast range of environmental stakeholders. Examining proposals to try juveniles as adults, reporters could emphasize the activities of younger criminals or the dangers of hardening young people into lifelong criminal lifestyles by sentencing young people as adults. In each case, how much do reporters take into account different stakeholders such as families with young children, the environment or political party support?

In each of the preceding issue categories, journalists have confronted many choices about the frames they used to help make information about critical events intelligible to those who access media. Although reporters fashioned stories in ways far more complex than simple dichotomies can suggest, the presentation of substantially different ways of viewing critical events illustrates the dilemmas journalists face when making decisions on how to write about emerging issues. Emerging issues, of course, offer few previous guidelines for reporters and more plasticity in their possible interpretations. In these circumstances, journalists and their institutions have many choices to make about how they present or build frames for new material, far more choices than would be available when reporting on more established issues.

USING A COMMUNITY STRUCTURE APPROACH IN THE INFORMATION SOCIETY

The community structure approach, or variations of it, has been used successfully to associate elements of community structure, especially community size—where larger communities, usually more diverse, are considered more structurally "pluralistic"—with reporting on social and political events. Based on classic sociological theories of Durkheim and others, the community structural pluralism studies of Tichenor, Donohue, and Olien at the University of Minnesota have pioneered a research paradigm and nurtured generations of graduate students and scholars in the conviction that macrosocial forces play a key role in journalists' coverage of critical events, especially those affecting the interests of local political and economic elites (see Tichenor et al., 1973, 1980, 1995; Donohue, Olien, & Tichenor, 1985, 1989; Jeffres et al., 2000).

The *community structure approach* can be defined as "a form of quantitative content analysis that focuses on the ways in which key characteristics of communities (such as cities) are related to the content coverage of newspapers in those communities" (Pollock, cited in Frey, Botan, & Kreps, 2000, p. 238). The initial Minnesota "structural pluralism" studies were elaborated by Demers (1996a, 1996b), Demers and Viswanath (1999), Hindman (1996, 1999), and Hindman, Littlefield, Preston, and Neumann (1999) among others. Tested in nationwide studies by Pollock and Robinson (1977), Pollock, Robinson, and Murray (1978), and Pollock et al. (1995–2005), the community structure approach studies the connection between city structure characteristics in major U.S. cities and newspaper reporting on critical events.

The community structure perspective represents an effort to accomplish at least three tasks: First, this approach focuses on the "antecedents" of newspaper content, a topic that has received relatively little attention in the scholarly communication studies or journalism literatures (Riffe, Lacy, & Fico, 1998). Second, the community structure approach also seeks to go beyond media-centric descriptive approaches of traditional content analysis in order to connect theory with data collection, an activity that has been infrequently practiced among scholars using content analysis methodologies (see Riffe & Freitag, 1996; Shoemaker & Mayfield, 1987; Shoemaker & Reese, 1990, 1996).

Third, the community structure approach has traditionally illuminated the relationship of media to social and political "control," but it can also be used effectively to explore the relation of media to social and political change. Sociology of communication scholars have viewed newspapers as being linked, in many ways, not only to the readers, but also to the communities that they serve. In a structural-functionalist paradigm long popular in the social sciences, "the media may be viewed as prominent subsystems within the larger social systems of the community; thus, they tend to reflect the values and concerns of dominant groups in the community they serve" Smith, 1984b, p. 260). From the viewpoint of Tichenor et al. (1980), newspapers are "mechanisms for community social control that maintain the norms, values, and processes of a community, and . . . their functions necessarily fit into a pattern that varies predictably according to size and type of community" (pp. 102-103).

The guard dog hypothesis of Olien et al., for example, is a clear metaphor underscoring the view that local media often function less as watchdogs alert to the misuse of power than as guard dogs, sentinels protecting the very interests of elites whose political overreachings media are presumably (and professionally) charged with exposing. This perspective does not suggest media are simple lap dogs, catering reflexively to the interests or wishes of individual elites. Rather, the Minnesota researchers suggest that city media function to preserve the interests of city elites collectively by maintaining a vigilant view of leadership interests, prepared to punish and ostracize those elites who betray or embarrass those interests. This might mean punishing by severe criticism any who deviate so greatly from the pursuit of collective elite interests that they invite public anger at political, economic or social elites generally. Doggedly pursuing those charged with corruption (e.g., ENRON) is one way that media function as guard dogs, portraying those who betray the public trust as not "belonging" to a world of privilege and respect (Donohue, Tichenor, & Olien, 1995; Olien et al., 1995). This seminal work has been extended by a variety of distinguished scholars, applying it to such issue domains as corporate control of newspapers and their effects (Demers, 1996a, 1996b), community structure and reporting on environmental risks (Griffin & Dunwoody, 1995), local control (Hindman, 1996), ethnic conflict (Hindman, Littlefield, Preston, & Neumann, 1999), and the superb edited collection by Demers and Viswanath (1999).

This pioneering work represents a foundation on which some innovative scholarly architecture can be erected that extends previous work to match modern society's rapidly changing information patterns. The community structure approach to reporting on political and social change cannot help but be affected by changes brought about by transformations often labeled the emerging *information society*. Although community structure is likely to retain its potency as an explanatory framework, the processes and timeframes associated with that pattern of influence may be altered. Indeed, the shifts through what Hindman (1999) called the "community control era" through the "mass society era" to the "information era" provide impetus for adapting earlier community structure approaches to fresh research perspectives.

At least four characteristics of the new information society can have an impact on structural approaches to media content. Summarizing observations by Hindman (1999), they include the following:

1. In an information society, mass media may be more likely than in previous eras to be viewed as potential agents of social change, due in part to new media's capacity to bypass structural barriers

of previous eras. The information era has created a unique potential for "many-to-many" communication that is the instantaneous linkage of individuals with similar interests (Rheingold, 1993). This pattern is obviously different from traditional mass communication, with its relatively small number of (often professional) opinion givers and large number of opinion receivers.

2. In an information society, newspapers may serve a role as stimulators of discussion and debate about civic issues, a forum to link community members into discussions of mutual concerns.

3. In an information era, media can monitor audience choices and preferences far more closely than ever before. "In an increasingly pluralistic social and economic environment, firms maintain profits by continuously monitoring demand for products and by limiting supplies accordingly" (Hindman, 1999, p. 110). As financial transactions become more common over the Internet, sponsors are able to compare various media outlets in terms of efficiency in producing sales. The "ability to closely monitor online commerce allows retail and manufacturing firms greater control over consumer demand and puts greater pressure on media organizations to produce content that maintains the attention of groups likely to buy the sponsors' products" (Hindman, 1999, p. 111). One of the major functions of media in the information society is therefore surveillance of consumers, interest groups or stakeholders interested in a variety of concerns.

4. From an audience or consumer perspective, the information society appears to improve the capacity for choice. In a "broadcasting model," useful in describing the mass society era, there was an emphasis on transmission of information and programming to audiences. In the information society, by contrast, there is greater potential for greater selectivity and wider choices, making media use more efficient from the perspective of the consumer (Hindman, 1999). Especially with the advent of online newspapers, audiences and consumers can access more choices more quickly than ever before.

Whether through the multiplicity of many-to-many communications, functioning as surveillance or matching functions, or serving as a forum for discussion of emerging issues, the political and social roles of media, in particular newspapers, are transformed by the information era. Three key aspects of that transformation deserve special attention.

1. *Acceleration of adjustments.* Due to advances in communication technologies, shifts in information collection at the supermarket

and personal computer levels and advances in targeted marketing, media can facilitate almost instantaneous adjustments to new
information on a cornucopia of issues. This capacity for immediacy suggests that links between community structure and media
coverage of critical events can be made quickly both by journalists and marketers in the marketplace.

2. *Precise measurement of audiences.* As the cable industry has
made clear, it is possible to "narrowcast" to quite small audience
segments. Targeting precise audiences, seen in the newspaper
development of special newspaper sections and sidebars, is made
possible by improved techniques of audience segmentation and
feedback. That feedback can be offered by traditional market
surveys or focus groups, or by more modern, online versions of
surveys and focus groups.

3. *Alignment with a wide array of publics.* Both accelerated adjustments and precise audience measurements permit media to align
their content with a wide array of audiences. It is worthwhile
noting that the information now available to media reaches far
beyond classical definitions of media "markets" or even "organized "interest groups" to encompass all those categories that
might be considered issue "stakeholders," whether or not they
access media on a regular basis as a "market" or organize in any
clear fashion as an identifiable "interest group." Citizens over
age 75 or women in the workforce, for example, are not necessarily "markets" or organized "interest group" categories, but
they may nevertheless be "stakeholders" for distinct critical
issues. The information society now permits media to access the
concerns not only of media audience markets or interest groups,
but also of any social or statistical category that might be affected by a critical event.

This is not to suggest that modern, especially digital media will automatically create vibrant "publics" or a thriving, Habermasian "public
sphere." Rather, the emergence of an information society does suggest that
newspaper roles may be altered substantially. As Hindman (1999) noted,
"The promise of information technologies to increase participation and to
allow for the decentralization of bureaucracies does not address basic issues
of the imbalance of power and wealth that inevitably lead to inequities in
knowledge" (p. 111). Nevertheless, the information era changes the ways
community structures are linked to the production of media messages.
Consequently, as critical events arise, media professionals and communication scholars alike, aware of these changes, can expect the connection
between structure and media content to be swift, precise and richly varied in

the multiplicity of audiences—media users, interest groups and stakehold-ers—whose concerns are linked to concrete issues.

A MODERN STUDY OF COMMUNITY STRUCTURE AND REPORTING ON CHANGE: THEORETICAL, METHODOLOGICAL, AND EMPIRICAL INNOVATION

These shifts driven by the information society will affect the study of com-munity structure and media reporting on political and social change on three different levels: theoretical, methodological, and empirical.

Theoretical Shift: Focus on Social Change, Newspapers as Forums

A great deal of the literature on community structure and media has empha-sized that "mainstream mass media are agents of social control for dominant institutions and value systems" (Demers & Viswanath, 1999, p. 419). Illuminating the role of newspapers as change facilitators rather than inhibitors would represent a distinct focus, even a theoretical shift. Rather than regarding newspapers inevitably as essentially vehicles for the preser-vation of the status quo, a "facilitating" perspective would examine the con-ditions under which newspapers generally support or oppose political and social change. A willingness to explore the circumstances surrounding news-paper support for social change would lead researchers to consider newspa-pers not simply as guard dogs for privileged interests, but rather as possible forums for the exchange of views or playing fields where a variety of view-points compete for attention.

Methodological Shift: Beyond Local or Regional to Nationwide Focus; Beyond One-Shot Case Studies to Systematic Comparative Analysis; Beyond Cross-Sectional Observation to Longitudinal "Process"

At the methodological level, the almost "boundariless" transmission of information in the modern era diminishes several distinctions among local, regional and national issues and transforms them all into potentially "national" issues. A focus on "nationwide" perspectives on issues is a depar-ture from the local, state, or regional focus of most previous research using the community structure approach.

At the methodological level, the national scope and wide range of struc-tural indicators envisioned in a revitalized approach to community structure and reporting on social change requires a methodology that permits the comparison of a wide range of critical events. An appropriate, consistent methodology would allow researchers to compare issues as disparate as economic policies and human rights, social risks, newly emerging issues and stakeholder concerns. Searching for a content analysis methodology that maximizes the opportunities to compare distinct events in a systematic way is a meritorious endeavor in an information society that conveys so many messages so quickly to so many.

The same systematic methodology that permits comparisons of multiple, diverse issues at a single point in time, or cross-section studies, can facilitate studies over time as well. Studies on early newspaper coverage of those with HIV/AIDS or the first reports on the Internet may be intriguing. But a systematic methodology yielding clearly comparable results for newspaper coverage of the same issues over time can pinpoint trends and allow researchers to draw conclusions about changes in coverage of the same types of issues "longitudinally," at several points in time (coverage of HIV/AIDS over several years in the early 1990s is explored in chap. 8). The community structure approach can move analysis beyond retrospective observations connecting city characteristics and reporting frames to forward-looking projections. In particular, some cities with particular sets of demographics can be expected to manifest reporting patterns accommodating social change "earlier" as new issues emerge than do other cities. (For a discussion of these "frame diffusion" projections, see the epilogue.)

Empirical Shift: Broader Range of Community Structure Indicators

At the empirical level, recognition of the transforming nature of the information era suggests the wisdom of searching for a broad set of reliable quantitative indicators of community structure, ones linked to a diverse array of critical events, comparable nationwide and perhaps cross-nationally as well. Much of the previous research has focused on relatively few indicators of community structure that can be compared systematically across cities throughout the United States.

The very "boundariless" information transmission that defines the new information society, however, simultaneously enlarges community structure theory to embrace a wider set of structural dimensions. These newer indicators of variation in community structure reach beyond levels of "structural pluralism" (often associated with the population sizes of different communities) to include categories that may not fit clearly into "markets " or "elite" or "non-elite" designations, for example: newly emerging stakeholders such as women in the workforce, people over age 75, gays, or families with young children.

GAPS IN STUDIES OF THE NEWSPAPERS, PUBLIC ISSUES, AND PUBLIC POLICY

A modern community structure approach is more than a scholarly innovation. It is useful in filling a gap in studies of newspapers, public issues and public policy. It is curious that communication studies scholars generally pay little attention to the way communities interact with media. It is especially curious in the case of newspapers, because newspapers, along with radio, are among the last bastions of community focus, containing not only news of interest to community residents, but also the wide range of bulletin board activities—from lists of community functions and advertisements to births, weddings, and obituaries. Yet until recently, journalists and communication scholars alike have explored patterns of newspaper use and influence that focus either on newspapers themselves—as institutions or collections of professionals—or on individual newspaper readers as consumers of news or as recipients of certain news perspectives filtered through a range of uses and gratifications. The characteristics of communities in which newspapers are located have been given relatively little attention.

Yet those same community characteristics have commanded substantial interest in other disciplines, in particular in the social sciences. In political science there is a commonplace that "all politics is local." In sociology, the characteristics of different communities help define the quality of social existence. Urban studies, by definition, are concerned with the quality of urban life. The reason for this fascination with community and city characteristics is that they are seen as having great bearing on the quality of life community residents experience. A community that exhibits a strong sense of solidarity and Gemeinschaft, for example, a community that is "for" itself, is quite different from a community that is simply a community because of the existence of a number of people and structures co-existing in close proximity, a community "in" itself, or Gezellschaft.

Indeed, this very concern with the quality of community life has inspired modern scholarship on "social capital," of which Putnam's "Bowling Alone" essays are a representative sample. Communities low in "social capital" are unlikely to be as capable as communities high in that resource to assist one another, to engender the conditions that reduce crime, to pursue projects in the public interest, or even, in the extreme case, to resist threats from the outside (Putnam, 2000). The quality of community life has fascinated scholars from many disciplines for a long time, and the scarcity of attention to this area of inquiry in the communication discipline stands out rather sharply.

There may be reasonable historical and professional explanations for this lack of curiosity on the part of communication scholars. Part of the lack of attention to community context may be the professional norms and ideology of journalists, in which editors and reporters are supposed to be "objective," somewhat immune to the influences of community forces in their efforts to deliver accurate information. The historical reasons for that norm of objectivity are certainly understandable, an effort to insulate journalists from the pressures of powerful economic and political interests. As an ethical goal, the effort to detach the profession of journalism from specific community contexts is reasonable, even laudable. As an explanatory inquiry, however, the norm of objectivity fails to account for a great deal that happens in reporting on political and social change.

It is odd that some of the basic questions about the quality of life in communities that fascinate other scholars are rare or minimal among a wide range of scholars in a field and a medium that has a great deal to do with how communities view themselves. It is possible, as well, that one of the reasons the communication discipline has such difficulty gaining the acceptance other disciplines enjoy either in academic institutions or among the public at large is that the communication field sometimes avoids dealing with issues in a way or at a level that can be easily understood. For all these reasons, an examination of the interaction among communities and newspapers is a worthwhile endeavor, whether to synthesize previous research, to test prevailing wisdom, or to open new areas of inquiry.

PUBLIC OFTEN ON THE RECEIVING END OF MEDIA INFLUENCE; COMMUNITY CONTEXT MINIMIZED

For many years, models of media influence have suggested a rather linear view of media acting on viewers or readers as essentially "recipients" of media input. McLuhan's "magic bullet" theories, suggesting a direct "injection" of media messages into individuals, are admittedly an extreme case. But even the more sophisticated two-step or multistep flow models and uses and gratifications approaches, although allowing for individual variation in access and interest in media, still tend to view media as the basic starting point of analysis. Agenda-setting research, for example, suggests that although media may not tell people what to think, media can certainly suggest a menu of options for people to think about. Some agenda-setting research has even suggested that personal experience and local newspaper reading are almost antithetical. The concept of *obtrusive contingency* has been used to describe research indicating that the richer and more varied someone's personal experience with an issue in a given community, the less local newspapers are read, suggesting that experience is somehow quite different from, and mutually exclusive of media access. In this view, personal experience is a functional substitute for mass-mediated messages (Demers, Craff, Choi, & Pessin, 1989; Palmgreen & Clarke, 1977; Winter & Eyal, 1981).

This one-way street perspective on media influence has been challenged in recent years by some researchers. On both theoretical and empirical grounds, several researchers have found that personal experience may reinforce or invigorate rather than reduce media effects (see Erbring, Goldenberg, & Miller, 1980). This proposition, as described by Demers, (1996b) suggests that conditions in a person's environment sensitize, or prime, the individual's attention to an issue (p. 305). Erbring et al., for example, found that agenda-setting effects for unemployment are stronger among people who are unemployed and who have a union member in the family. Iyengar and Kinder (1987) found that senior citizens are more likely than younger viewers to consider social security an important issue facing the country after media exposure to the issue. The capacity of media messages to reinforce a personal experience or interpersonal discussion, or the "consonance" between media messages and personal experiences, has also been documented by Demers et al. (1989), lending further support to the "priming" hypothesis.

Personal experience may not only reinforce media agenda setting (the "cognitive priming" hypothesis), it may also, in its own right, contribute to increased media use. Researchers focusing on community attachment or community ties, in particular, have found a strong connection between community involvement (such as memberships in religious organizations, sports teams, nonprofits) and community identification (self-described or based on residential and commuting patterns) and newspapers, in particular, local newspaper use. Historically, Park (1922) and Janowitz (1952) documented this connection. More recently, others have found strong relationships (see Finnegan & Viswanath, 1988; Stamm, 1985; Stamm & Fortini-Campbell, 1983). Demers (1996) took this research further by finding that there is evidence of "social priming," in which personal experience, in particular connections with a community, stimulate needs for information that can be satisfied through reading of the local newspaper.

Although attention to cognitive priming has a scholarly history, a focus on social priming is relatively recent (Demers, 1996) in media research generally. The attention to cognitive and social priming as contextual constraints on media use and newspaper use in particular is also rather selective in its focus on relatively few variables that might lead some individuals to access newspapers more often than others. Why there has been such limited interest in expanding the range of contextual factors affecting newspapers is unclear, because several segments of communication scholars focus a great deal on social demographics.

The literature on public communication and social marketing campaigns, for example, reveals a wide range of contextual influences, all studied in an effort to understand the way those in high-risk categories can be persuaded to change their high-risk behavior. In his chapter in the Rice and Atkin edited volume, *Public Communication Campaigns*, on "Theoretical Foundations of Campaigns," for example, William McGuire (2001) recommended collecting information on receiver "demographics" and "lifestyle" (p. 45). Similarly, in his discussion of "audience segmentation," Douglas Solomon (1991) acknowledged the importance of studying the way different audiences are likely to view the same (or distinct) messages (pp. 96–97) Other examples can be cited, but the general point is clear: Newspaper research uses social demographic and lifestyle categories only rarely, whereas public health communication researchers use such categories routinely and automatically. Why this discrepancy exists among communication researchers is puzzling, but it is especially curious that researchers studying newspaper use have not taken advantage of research on the social context of media use readily available in other parts of the communication discipline.

LARGER QUESTIONS BYPASSED; CONTENT OF REPORTING SUBORDINATE TO READERSHIP QUANTIFICATION

A wide range of studies printed in *Journalism & Mass Communication Quarterly* and other academic outlets identify as their outcome or dependent variables some highly quantifiable yet extremely narrowly focused concepts. One of the major outcomes is "media use," in the case of newspapers, frequency of newspaper reading. This kind of outcome is the product of a question that is indeed useful and important for the newspaper profession and industry: How to increase or maintain readership in an era of increasing competitive media. The fascination with quantifying use and readership, however, may have diminished the attention scholars and media professionals alike pay to other significant questions that connect media with society at large.

To ask important questions about the relation of media to the quality of life in communities is not to introduce a set of queries foreign to the study of media influence. If anything, connecting media more explicitly with the policies and programs of communities and cities is a return precisely to the questions that launched the study of communication in the United States earlier in this century. Prior to the quantitatively sophisticated work of the more recent founders of the communication discipline (Lasswell, Lewin,

Lazarsfeld, and Hovland), Park, at the University of Chicago, posed research questions in his 1922 book, *The Immigrant Press and Its Control,* that are both important and widely overlooked today (E. Rogers, 1993). As summarized by Rogers, those questions include the following:

- How does media content influence public opinion? (the agenda-setting process)
- How are mass media influenced by public opinion?
- Can the mass media bring about social change? (E. Rogers, 1986, p. 79)

Reviewing these questions, media scholars have paid a great deal of attention to the first question, testing the agenda-setting perspective in a variety of contexts, but the second and third questions have received far less attention.

There may be perfectly understandable reasons why media profession-als largely ignore the second and third questions. To suggest that mass media are influenced by public opinion or that mass media, in themselves, bring about change, is to challenge directly the deepest canons of traditional pro-fessional journalism, which is supposed to be "independent" of public opin-ion and to report "impartially" on events without favoring one side or the other of a social issue. The reasons for the development of this approach to professional journalism are well documented in the historical literature on the growth of modern journalism (Schudson, 1978). Although avoiding these questions helped distance professional journalism from the more sen-sational, muckraking forebearers, the baby may have been thrown out with the bath. In the name of professional journalism some of the most important questions that journalists and media scholars can pose have been eclipsed or overshadowed. To ask questions about public influences on journalists may be construed to suggest that journalists can be swayed by the passions and prejudices of the moment, what de Tocqueville warned about as the "tyran-ny" of democracy. To make inquiries about the relation of media to social change is to hint that journalists or newspapers have a "position" on social issues that infuses their writing, a perspective at odds with professional claims to dispassion and reporting "without fear or favor."

This is not to suggest that professional journalists or media scholars are craven hypocrites, willfully misrepresenting what they do or what they study. Indeed, a concern for media independence and First Amendment pro-hibitions lies at the heart of any democratic endeavor. But it is precisely because media are so important in shaping, framing and priming public opinion, and because media content is so important in that process, that the way that content is formed deserves sustained attention from media profes-sionals and scholars alike. It is in this context that a call for more attention is justified, more attention not just to the frequency of readership, but to the themes and frames that are put forth in media accounts of critical events, and to the ways those themes and frames correspond to variations in community characteristics.

It is crucial that the concept of "variation" be underscored when describing both community characteristics and the content of reporting. Just as communities vary in their composition—regarding education levels, occupational distributions, media saturation, quality of life, and so forth, so too can media be expected to vary in the content of their reporting, in particular reporting on social change. Every politician knows that communities vary in the kinds of issues and changes they will accept, reject, or ignore. Responsible community media, with all their access to sources of public opinion formation, are certainly aware of the types of issues and issue variation. Variations in the content of media reporting on social change, therefore, are a significant topic for all those interested in asking some of the important questions posed by Park: How does the public influence mass media, and can media bring about social change?

This effort to explore media variation in reporting on social change is different from some of the significant efforts to explore journalistic behavior that look for commonalities across different media institutions. Several systematic studies have sought and found common patterns to explaining reporting patterns in: the biographic backgrounds of journalists (Johnstone, Slawski, & Bowman, 1976; Pollock, 1981; Weaver & Wilhoit, 1986, 1996), the "incentive structure" of regular beats (Sigal, 1973), or the organizational structure of newsrooms (Tuchman, 1978). This search for patterns common to all journalists, however, does not go far enough in helping to answer questions about the relation of journalism to social change. In particular, comparing the way different communities report on social change requires a research perspective asking questions about variations in both community composition and the content of reporting on critical issues. Recently, scholars have begun examining factors affecting coverage within the structure of journalism, comparing, for example, public and private chain ownership and its effect on reporting (see Summer [1996] issue of *Journalism & Mass Communication Quarterly*). But this interest in connecting variations in the context of news production with reporting on social change is nevertheless recent and exploratory.

It should be noted at this juncture that the questions about the public and media, as posed by Park, were made in the context of an ameliorative effort to help cities adapt successfully to social change, in his case rapid urbanization. Successful adaptation to change suggests an effort to accommodate social change within a democratic political framework, a framework that encourages political access within a system of legitimate political institutions—governments, political parties, interest groups and associations of various kinds. It should also be noted that Park did not ask "whether" the public influenced mass media. He took it as understood that the public exercised such an influence and sought to study that influence. He also took it as understood that the media played some role in social change, and that this role merited scholarly attention.

The study of the content of media variation in reporting on social change has been limited until recent years not simply by the scarcity of questions targeting that issue directly, but also by the difficulty in comparing media coverage from different media outlets. Recent advances in databases, however, now make it possible to collect data from several media sources so that systematic comparisons of several media covering a specific event at one point in time can now be made quickly and efficiently.

Recovering some of the original questions that ignited the formation of communication studies as a discipline in the United States helps fashion research questions about media and social change. Departing from dependent variables that focus tightly on amount of interest or amount of readership, these research questions direct attention not just to amounts of coverage but to the content of that coverage, asking whether some issues are framed or primed more consistently than others. Fashioning direct questions about issue content places researchers in a strong position to address serious questions about the relation of the public to media reporting and about the relation of media to social change.

EMPOWERING THE PUBLIC: CONVERGING PERSPECTIVES

Several scholarly perspectives connecting media and society suggest either that communities or cities are excellent levels of analysis and that the content of media reporting on social change is as important as the amount of that reporting. Each of these perspectives suggests a clear, strong link between distinct communities or community structures and media perspectives on change.

From a historical perspective, one of the questions posed by Park, asking about the influence of the "public" on media in the twenties, acknowledged the connection between the social process of rapid urbanization and media reporting on that process. From the viewpoint of one of the key founders of the communication discipline in the United States, it would be completely reasonable, indeed intelligent, to examine the link between indicators of social change or social structure in a city and reporting on social change.

From a professional perspective, journalism professors and journalism schools have moved in parallel with this concern about the connection between media and community change. Challenging the established canons of traditional journalism as espousing an ethic that is too value neutral and value free to acknowledge the powerful impact of today's journalists, a growing number of journalism professors and practicing professionals are calling for a "public journalism," one that holds itself responsible for the broad social and political consequences of reporting that simply quotes what reliable sources say. In his recommendations for what practitioners of public journalism might do at future political conventions (in light of what happened in the 1996 political conventions), Davis Merritt (1996), editor of *The Wichita Eagle*, and the author of *Public Journalism and Public Life: Why Telling the News Is Not Enough*, wrote:

> . . . (T)he style of political reporting that has developed in the past two decades . . . has systematically driven Americans away from public life, spread hopelessness and cynicism and turned citizens into spectators at an event, an audience to be entertained rather than a public to be involved.
>
> Voters are not interested in being mere spectators. And last week (during the Republican presidential convention) they simply clicked off to some other channel, a dangerous act for democracy.
>
> It doesn't have to be this way when we do this again in the year 2000. If TV journalists were to imagine a broader purpose than simply telling the news (by whatever definition), the public would have an incentive to tune in.

That broader purpose would be to tell news in ways calculated to get people involved in the political process rather than to drive them away. For instance, networks could focus on how well each party was addressing the nation's problems as defined by real people rather than on how each party was addressing tactical problems as defined by politicians and journalist (Davis Merritt, "Unconventional Wisdom," *The New York Times*, August 23, 1996, p. A27).

A belief that voters want political coverage minimizing cynicism and conflict, and maximizing opportunities for constructive collective activity, is central to the thrust of the new "public journalism." What is central for the purposes of this discussion is that the journalism community is beginning to acknowledge some connection between the ethics of journalism and the quality of public/city life, a connection that Park and other scholars of the Chicago School asked researchers to study. It is a connection that has been overshadowed in professional journalism until recently by the admonition to maintain a reporting posture that owes allegiance only to the norms of professional, dispassionate journalism, not to any concern with the consequences of that reporting. Today, the concrete consequences of reporting in metropolitan media on the quality of life (including interest in community affairs and politics) in city after city fascinates journalists who have seen too many citizens (and presumably journalists, too) turned away from civic involvement by a reporting modality that upholds criticism and conflict as essential approaches to reporting on public affairs.

USING THE "COMMUNITY STRUCTURE APPROACH" TO LINK CITY CHARACTERISTICS WITH REPORTING ON POLITICAL AND SOCIAL CHANGE: SEVERAL PROPOSITIONS

Both empirical work and theoretical reviews of literature in the field of communication studies lead to a focus on several distinct propositions that guide this inquiry.

1. There is a clear need for research on media's interaction with society that is more holistic and less media centric.

The case for more holistic approaches to communication studies has been made with extraordinary clarity by one of Europe's foremost media scholars and by some leading scholars from the United States as well:

> The study of media effects and, above al, content analysis may be presented as examples of the narrow specialism of the discipline, which has created a sort of *media centrism,* in which attention and the results of the analysis have quite often had an essentially *self-referential range,* concentrating on one hand on the critical discussion of the instruments used and on the other on the subject of mass media seen in its different aspects. *What has proved lacking or incomplete is the connection with other problems of society that are influenced by the mass media and with the sciences or approaches that analyze them.* In short, only rarely have the instruments of mass communication and their different problems been analyzed as one of the many and different components of social change and therefore within the system of relationships between its components. (Mancini, 1993, p. 103, italics added)

Closer to the U.S. experience, others agree. This call for "connection" between instruments of mass media and "problems of society" and "social change" is echoed in research by Carey (1992, 1995), Gitlin (1978) and Blumler and Gurevitch (1987). The last call for "multiple approaches capable of dealing with the problem of characteristics that may significantly shape and constrain media performance, including its implications for other institutions and individuals" (Blumler & Gurevitch, 1987, cited in Mancini, 1993, p. 103).

2. A community structure approach, focusing on communities or cities as units of analysis and generators of news issue interest, is a logical extension of audience research extolling the importance of both cognitive and social priming, and in particular, social ties.

Research calling attention to constraints on the capability of media to affect publics has pointed the way to a serious focus on communities or cities as valuable units of analysis. Beyond the early work of Tonnies and Simmel in Germany on community structure, through the work of Park and later Janowitz at Chicago, to Stamm (1985) with his elaborate studies on newspaper use and social ties, and the work on community structure and size and newspaper reporting on political conflict undertaken over many years by Tichenor, Donohue, and Olien—all draw attention to the importance of community as a level of analysis worthy of serious attention. More recently, Dunwoody and colleagues examined the link between community characteristics and reporting on environmental issues in Wisconsin (Dunwoody & Griffin, 1999), whereas Demers (1996) examined the role of structure—both in communities and in news institutions—as significant concomitants of reporting variation. Hindman (1996) drew connections between community newspapers and local conflict and ethnic pluralism (Hindman et al., 1999). Other recent studies of local media influence have also documented the significance of *Community Media in the Information Age* (Jankowski & Prehn, 2002) and *Community Radio and Public Culture* (Fairchild, 2001).

3. Media scholars have used macro analyses, especially city or county characteristics, to study media as instruments of "social control," but little attention has been given to media as instruments of "social change."

Despite the historical emphasis on mainstream mass media as instruments of "social control," social actors—and this study would add social and political "stakeholders"—have also demanded or been receptive to changes over time for such groups as women, labor, minorities, environmentalists, and gays (Demers & Viswanath, 1999). The traditional emphasis in community structure research on media as instruments of social control therefore needs to be leavened with more research on the role of mass media in social change. As Demers and Viswanath (1999) explained it, "We in the communication field . . . need to give more consideration to processes of social change, especially secular social change and public policy. Only then will it be possible to initiate structural or cultural changes that will enable mass media to be more responsive to the needs and goals of disadvantaged and repressed groups" (p. 424). Similarly, Carragee and Roefs (2004) argued that there has been a:

> failure to examine framing contests within wider political and social contexts . . . (in particular) issues of political and social power . . . (and that) framing research can contribute to an understanding of the interaction between social movements and the news media (p. 214)

4. Comparing cities nationwide is a systematic way to test the connection between newspapers as community-bound institutions and reporting on social change.

A range of studies has focused on reporting in one, two, or a few communities and some characteristics of their communities. What this collection of somewhat unconnected studies seldom provides, however, is sufficient empirical consistency—comparable questions and methodologies—to permit a systematic focus on communication and social change that encourages replication, cumulative knowledge aggregation and theory-building. Indeed, theory-building is an activity given far too little attention in the field of content analysis (Shoemaker & Mayfield, 1987).

Given the diversity found in distinct cities throughout the nation, different newspaper viewpoints are certainly to be expected across the United States. Existing studies on communities and newspaper coverage have focused on a few selected cities (see Stamm, 1986) or on one state, Minnesota (Tichenor et al., 1973, 1980). That state has a relatively homogeneous population and is relatively unrepresentative of the nation as a whole. Although these studies contain a variety of fascinating findings for the cities sampled, and many excellent propositions, they do not put those propositions to an empirical test across several major cities throughout the nation. Moreover, most studies have focused on the uses and gratifications of newspaper reading for individuals rather than on the way newspapers frame perspectives on social change. Because so many journalists and policymakers agree that newspapers are crucibles for debate on social policy and social change, it is surprising that so few scholars have come forward to compare newspapers systematically.

Several newspaper studies adopt perspectives that examine the individual viewpoints or training of journalists on the one hand, or the organizational incentives of newspapers as institutions on the other, for explanations of similar newspaper "behaviors" or outcomes. The findings typically illustrate what newspapers have in common. This study, by contrast, is an effort to address long ignored or overlooked issues: to compare systematically newspaper coverage of significant social issues in major papers throughout the United States, and to explore a wide range of "city structure" characteristics associated with that coverage, testing which ones are most closely associated with perspectives relatively "receptive" or "unreceptive" to social change. No study of national scope has yet been mounted that compares systematically the characteristics of multiple cities associated with different newspaper perspectives on social change.

5. Mapping city characteristics can reveal the relative strength of a wide range of factors potentially linked to reporting perspectives.

A "city characteristic" approach to newspaper reporting makes it possible to explore which aspects of city structure—demographics, economic circumstances, media saturation, city size, ethnic composition, occupational distribution, quality of life, and so on—are most closely linked to newspaper perspectives accommodating or resisting social change. It is worthwhile calling attention to the power not just of newspaper "markets" defined as newspaper "circulation" demographics, but more broadly, of city structures and demographics as factors clearly associated with reporting variation on critical events. If newspapers are institutions where new and significant community issues are displayed and discussed, then it is reasonable to expect that newspaper coverage of critical events will be associated not simply with markets, but also with some of the major forces and distributions of influence in their communities.

Modern scholars such as Dearing and Rogers, in their study of media-agenda setting regarding the AIDS issue, call for the study of the way different influentials and elites all influence media agendas on that issue. But we have not yet seen systematic comparisons of AIDS coverage in different media linked to different aspects of city structure—aspects such as percent of municipal budget devoted to health care, physicians or nurses per 100,000 population, the rate of increase of reported cases of HIV/AIDS, minority distribution, and so on. Systematic comparisons of newspaper coverage nationwide with comparisons of city demographic and other aggregate data characteristics would help us understand why some newspapers may be more alert to this health threat than others, and why reporting on specific issues over time can shift significantly.

6. Focusing on coverage of "critical events" is a valuable way to measure reporting on political and social change.

Kraus, Davis, Lang, and Lang (1975); Bennett (1993); and others inter-ested in political and social communication have long called for taking a "critical-event" or "issue-situation" approach to the study of political and social issues, looking beyond traditionally studied activities such as political party efforts or elections. Instead, they suggest looking at U.S. Supreme Court decisions, congressional committee work on key issues, city and county referenda or recalls, resignations and some of the less well publicized activities that may actually be excellent bellweathers of political and social change. Indeed, the Langs have suggested that modern databases allow us to compare the impact of "festivals, public disorder, the outbreak of war and disasters on populations in different media environments" (Lang & Lang, 1993, p. 97). This book adopts this approach by comparing systematically, and using the same methodology to study, such issues as human rights, health concerns, economic interests, and quality-of-life issues.

This analysis also follows a major issue over time in a cross-section of national newspapers, reporting on victims of the modern plague of HIV/AIDS, undertaken by focusing both on patterns of coverage through-out selected years from 1990 to 1995, as well as on such critical issues as reporting on Ryan White, Magic Johnson and Arthur Ashe. Additionally, to illustrate the range of research opportunities the community structure approach offers, analysis of reporting on the U.S. Supreme Court's decision allowing the Boy Scouts of America to exclude homosexuals is included. That case study extends the community structure approach to multiple methodologies, reaching beyond Pearson correlations and regression coeffi-cients to factor analysis and comparisons among newspaper issue "projec-tion," public opinion and ownership patterns.

2

MEASURING MEDIA ALIGNMENT

The Challenges of Nationwide Samples, a Single Score "Media Vector" and Key Umbrella Hypotheses

KEY FEATURES OF NEWSPAPER CONTENT ANALYSIS LINKED TO REPORTING ON POLITICAL AND SOCIAL CHANGE

Newspapers are an Excellent Indicator of Community Change; Modern Databases Allow Reporting Variation To Be Measured Systematically

Newspapers, along with radio stations, remain among the most vibrant crucibles for the expression or exchange of community opinion in the United States. Except for papers with a national reach such as the *Christian Science Monitor*, *USA Today* and the *Wall Street Journal*, most newspapers target local or regional markets and are presumably somewhat responsive to those markets. Local newspapers are such reliable indicators of new trends that an entire business was founded by John Naisbitt based on the systematic tracking of local news coverage. Those results were published in such books as *Megatrends 2000* and *Megachallenges* (respectively, Naisbitt, 1982, 1999).

Until recently, coverage of several cities or several events has been difficult because researchers have found it difficult to collect a substantial amount of press coverage of a specific event in a reasonable amount of time. Modern databases such as the newspaper database found on the DIALOG Computer Instruction Program and Lexis-Nexis make it possible to compare coverage easily in many different papers and regions. Indeed, using innovative databases and time series analysis, David Fan (2002) employed content analysis to creative predictive equations that associate precise variations in press coverage with variations in self-reported cocaine use, resumption of smoking by quitters (smoking recidivism), percent of gay/bisexual men reporting high risk sexual behavior, and calls to the hotline of the Centers for Disease Control (CDC).

From a methodological perspective, this analysis can help reveal how findings focused on local or statewide studies in the newspaper and community structure literature can be modified or expanded when adapted to a national context. This study is one of the first to apply community structure hypotheses systematically to *national cross-section* samples of newspapers, samples made possible by modern databases.

A Focus on Critical Events Can Illuminate Decision Making

Some of the literature on newspaper reporting focuses either on what news professionals as individuals are likely to believe or do most of the time, whether in domestic reporting (Johnstone et al., 1976) or foreign affairs reporting (Pollock, 1981). Another segment of newspaper literature focuses on what news organizations are likely to do most of the time (e.g., Sigal, 1975; Tuchman, 1978).

Yet, often at critical moments, when a variety of values and resources are at stake and perhaps in conflict, key editorial decisions must be made that reveal the ways newspapers are connected to the communities they serve. As mentioned previously, Kraus, Davis, Lang, and Lang (1975), Lang and Lang (1993), and Bennett (1993) have all called for a focus on critical events or issue situations as a way of building scientific communication propositions from the ground up (rather than expecting so much from a grand, unified theory that encompasses most situations most of the time). Consistent with those recommendations, this study's methodology focuses on critical events as a way of measuring the circumstances under which newspapers accommodate or resist change.

The Community Structure Approach Complements Other Approaches; Excellent at Exploring Reporting Variation

Other scholars have used selected aspects of the community structure approach to ask questions about newspaper readership uses and gratifications. These studies have typically included surveys that collect data at the individual level of analysis and then draw conclusions about community or city-level aggregates. Pioneering studies include those conducted in Minnesota by Tichenor et al. (1980), who asked questions about size (community and circulation) and media saturation or multiplicity (number of newspapers and whether community or regionally focused) to ask how individuals used newspapers in cities that varied according to those characteristics. The Tichenor et al. series of studies also asked individuals questions about reading patterns in the context of several critical local or regional issues in Minnesota. Another pioneering study by Stamm (1985) explored the community structure literature thoroughly and used readership surveys in order to understand how much communities affect newspaper coverage versus how much news coverage may affect or define a sense of community. These empirical studies are limited to a few selected communities.

The community structure approach proposed in this book uses far more indicators than those used in previous works and tests their association with coverage of a wide range of issues across a multiplicity of newspapers across the nation. Comprehensive marketing and market research as well as U.S. Census data are available, making it possible to compare many more aspects of community structure today than was possible in the past.

Content Analysis Is an Effective, Reliable Way to Make Comparisons; Compares Favorably With Survey Research

Content analysis of coverage of critical events permits researchers to measure some enduring aspects of community values that single-shot surveys do not. As the former officer of a national opinion research firm in New York City, the author has a high regard for the power of surveys to measure public opinion on a wide range of issues. But snapshots of public opinion are not necessarily good barometers of relatively enduring community concerns. To tap long-held or deeply held values underlying current attitudes or opinions, expensive and time-consuming longitudinal studies would be required, operations that are often beyond the reach of most researchers.

Content analysis of news coverage is an excellent alternative because newspapers typically have long histories of interaction with the communities they serve and can be assumed, over time, to in some sense "represent" or "reflect" major elements of community opinion. In particular, the media vector content analysis measurement tool, described here, can be used effectively to arrive at a sensitive single "score" for each newspaper covering a specific issue. The media vector allows newspapers and cities to be compared and ranked along a variety of structural characteristics to test for any associations.

INNOVATIVE METHODOLOGY: MEASURING "PROJECTION" USING A "MEDIA VECTOR"

A typical chapter in this volume collects from 300 to more than 900 articles printed on a critical event during a time frame of maximum coverage, mostly using the DIALOG Classroom Information Program newspaper database and more recently, beginning in Spring 2002, the Lexis-Nexis database available to college libraries. The DIALOG database began losing newspapers after a 2001 U.S. Supreme Court decision allowed reporters to collect royalties for multiple uses of their reports and stories, resulting in several papers dropping off the database. Case studies written during the Spring 2002 academic semester used a combination of DIALOG, Newsbank and Lexis-Nexis databases. Case studies written in the Fall 2002 semester and thereafter primarily used Lexis-Nexis. Furthermore, other databases were employed in literature reviews of the communication literature on each topic, including ComIndex, CIOS, and ComAbstracts. Additionally, content-specific databases were explored as well, including Social Sciences Index and Public Affairs Information Service.

Newspapers were generally selected from large cities in four major U.S. regions: east, south, midwest and west.[1] Most of the case studies sample a similar list of newspapers. There is some variation, however, because some papers did not give extensive coverage to particular issues or critical events, impelling researchers to select alternative papers. In each case, the "leading" paper (defined by age or circulation or stature) in each city was chosen unless unavailable on a database. In rare cases where two papers had similar circulation levels, either might be used (e.g., the *Denver Post* or the *Rocky Mountain News*), depending on availability in a database Typically, all articles of 150 words or more were selected from each newspaper in order to increase the validity of statistical procedures comparing city demographics and newspaper scores. Because length is considered one indicator of importance by editors, the longest articles in each newspaper were chosen in order to compare those articles considered most significant by each newspaper.

Case studies typically sampled articles in a range of 14 to 21 newspapers, in part because prior experience suggested that range yielded sufficient numbers of articles to test significant differences in city characteristics. Additionally, given time and responsibility constraints, it would have been difficult for teams of two to three undergraduates to collect, code, and analyze data, as well as draft multiple sections of papers for class projects had students been expected to sample larger numbers of newspapers in the space of a single semester.

Sometimes, one or two newspapers were excluded from the sample during the analysis phase. For example, in chapter 6 the *Detroit Free Press* was excluded from the analysis of reporting on NAFTA because, regardless of

---

[1]Leading city papers (primarily in terms of circulation, but sometimes in terms of stature) were selected for analysis, comparing each city's characteristics with the coverage in a major newspaper. Comparisons of coverage and other papers in major cities are difficult to justify as methodologically useful (or valid), because most secondary papers in major cities have far smaller circulation figures, and are less likely to represent a wide range of publics, than are the leading papers.

city demographics, the paper had historically generally favored the perspectives of labor, which was opposed to NAFTA. In a case study published in *Newspaper Research Journal,* the *Denver Post* was excluded from analysis of coverage of China's bid for the 2000 Olympics because Colorado was perhaps the only state in the United States (or anywhere else, for that matter) to pass a popular referendum rejecting its (Denver's) selection as an Olympic site because of enormous expenses to taxpayers. Because Denver had historically experienced an upswell of public opinion opposing the Olympics, it appeared wise to exclude that city's leading newspaper from a cross-section analysis of city characteristics and reporting on an Olympic selection issue (Pollock, Kreuer, & Ouano, 1997).

The text of news stories and feature stories were examined in order to test any issue "direction," which is one of the purposes of this study. Editorials and op-ed pieces were excluded because these newspaper items are already assumed to contain a "directional" slant. In all but two case studies, *The New York Times, The Washington Post,* and *The Los Angeles Times* were excluded from analysis because these papers are often considered, in many ways, "national" newspapers reflecting the views of national decision makers as well as local concerns.

Coders were undergraduates, mostly communication studies seniors trained personally by the author to conduct library and online research on city demographics and content analysis of newspaper databases. Although coders were aware of a wide range of hypotheses, they understood that the author had no particular interest in validating any particular hypothesis. Indeed, given the algebraic formula used to calculate each newspaper's media vector (described later), as well as the wide range of demographic data used to operationalize the independent variables, there is no clear way an individual coder could predict the influence of a discrete coding decision on the outcome of a specific hypothesis.

Although coders were asked to code an entire article as a unit of analysis, they were asked to pay particular attention to the headline and first five paragraphs. This focus on the initial portions of articles is consistent both with the "inverted pyramid" style that guides journalists in putting what they consider to be most important information at the beginning of articles, including in the headline, as well as with research on readership patterns. Both a standard journalism school textbook and recent research suggest that most newspaper readers do not read far beyond an article's first five paragraphs, underscoring the importance of an article's initial reporting perspectives. (Fedler, Bender, Davenport, & Drajer, 2001; Fico & Cote, 2002).

Most of the case studies in this book replicate several previous studies. The case studies therefore often represent similar findings by several "generations" of undergraduates, sometimes sampling different time frames and mixes of newspapers. Similarity in findings among different students studying the same topic increases confidence in both the reliability of the coding measures—the "prominence" score and the Media Vector—as well as the validity of substantive findings and patterns.

All articles on each case study's critical issue or critical event usually sampled newspapers representing a geographic cross-section of the United States, typically collecting articles between periods of news "inflection," for example, from a month coverage increases noticeably to a month after which coverage diminishes noticeably. A paper on Dr. Kevorkian's activities, for instance, sampled: *The Albany Times-Union, The Baltimore Sun, The Boston Globe, The Charlotte Observer , The Chicago Tribune, The Detroit Free Press, The Houston Post, The Los Angeles Times, The Miami Herald, The New Orleans Times-Picayune, The Orlando Sentinel, The Phoenix Gazette. The Pittsburgh Gazette, The Philadelphia Inquirer, The Seattle Times,* and *The St. Louis Post-Dispatch.* These are all large or medium-sized cities.

Comparison of coverage between large and smaller cities is a major characteristic of "structural pluralism" theory and research, in which it is expected that larger city papers will display more varied coverage in conditions of social and political conflict because of the greater variety of public, stakeholders and interests in larger cities. Recent research by Joseph Harry (2001), however, suggests several reasons why this traditional distinction is less relevant as new trends continue:

1. As news professionalism rises among the general reporting community, more critical conflict coverage will result.
2. As relatively small communities suburbanize, news media in these communities will begin to perform more like their fellow newspapers in metropolitan environments.
3. As new electronic information and newsgathering sources become generally available, news media of all sizes will be influenced by this content and will tend to use it to effect a generally more critical level of coverage.
4. To the degree to which community sentiment in small towns is perceived as fragmented and highly contested toward a given conflict issue, local medias will tend to project this fragmentation in coverage that, rhetorically, reflects a similar tension between opposing sides. (p. 436)

Measures and Dependent Variables

Measuring Projection: Calculating a Media Vector

Articles collected from each newspaper can be coded in two different ways, one focusing on the amount of attention or "prominence" an article receives in a newspaper, the second focusing on the "direction" or "perspective" of the article's content regarding the specific issue studied. Then the two scores are combined employing a formula used previously by psychologists, the Janis-Fadner Coefficient of Imbalance (Janis & Fadner, 1965), to yield a media vector.

This study calls the results a *media vector* because the measure combines two properties typical of vectors as they are defined in the dictionary and as they are used in the study of physics. The two properties of a vector are the strength or magnitude of a variable (in this case, "prominence"), and its "direction": a vector combines both concepts to yield a measure of "thrust" or "projection." For newspaper articles in this study, a media vector measures the combined impact of the strength or "prominence" of an article and its "direction" (favorable, unfavorable, or balanced/neutral toward an issue). The media vector concept therefore goes beyond traditional single dimension measures of frequency or placement to record a more sensitive composite of issue "projection." The media vector can be described in more detail.

Article "Prominence." Each article can be read and given two scores. The first, reflecting editorial decisions about how much prominence to give an article, is an attention or display score, which is a total numerical rating from 3 to 16 points based on the following criteria: placement (front-page prominent, front-page nonprominent, inside prominent or other), headline word count, length of article word count, and number of graphics. This research method measures editorial judgments about the appropriate prominence of an article based on the way it is displayed in the newspaper publication. The higher the number of assigned points, the more "prominence" the article received.

Article "Direction." The second, or "direction" score is derived from evaluation of article content. The nominal measurements of favorable, unfavorable, or balanced/neutral toward a predetermined issue, activity, or person are assigned to each newspaper article. Consider again a previous exploration of coverage of Dr. Kevorkian. A major challenge for this content analysis method was to ensure that "favorable" articles did indeed legitimize Dr. Kevorkian, "unfavorable" articles did indeed criticize Dr. Kevorkian. Carefully crafted definitions of each concept were derived from article content, for example:

- Coverage *favorable* to Dr. Kevorkian included articles describing him as an "avant-garde thinker," "hero," "angel of mercy, and the like." Additionally, those articles containing lengthy discussion of patients' support from their families, quotes from actual patients, and so on, were also coded as favorable.

TABLE 2.1 Prominence Score for Coding Newspaper Databases[a]

	CODING SCORE			
DIMENSION	4	3	2	1
Placement	Front page of first section	Front page of inside section	Inside first section	Other
Headline size (in number of words)				
Length (in number of words)	1,000+	750–999	500–749	150–499
Photos/graphics	Two photos or graphics	One photo or graphic		

[a]Copyright John C. Pollock 1994–2007.

- Coverage *unfavorable* to Kevorkian included articles containing such phrases as "Dr. Death," "serial killer," "ethical outlaw," and so on. Unfavorable articles also tended to focus on laws prohibiting Kevorkian's actions, to describe the poisoning as the type used at Auschwitz, or to supply quotes from other medical professionals denouncing Kevorkian's methods.
- *Balanced/neutral* coverage either contained material that made no effort to legitimize or delegitimize Kevorkian's activities, or it contained an approximately equal proportion of both favorable and unfavorable material (Pollock, Coughlin et al., 1996).

To test evaluation reliability with this threefold classification, coefficients of intercoder reliability can be calculated. The two measures of prominence and direction are then combined and aggregated in order to transform article scores into a single Media vector score. The resulting statistic, which can vary between +1.00 and –1.00, permits quantitative comparisons of each newspaper's coverage of the critical event being studied.

In the past, communication studies using this or a related method of content analysis have explored a wide range of issues, for example: cross-national coverage of Nixon's resignation (examining microfilm copies of newspaper articles); coverage of prison disturbances; a referendum on housing discrimination against homosexuals; coverage of the *Roe v. Wade* decision; international coverage of a coup; an election; a civil disturbance in the Third World

TABLE 2.2 Calculating the Media Vector[a]

- f = the sum of the prominence scores coded favorable
- u = the sum of the prominence scores coded unfavorable
- n = the sum of the prominence scores coded neutral/balanced
- r = f + u + n

If f > u (the sum of the favorable prominence scores is greater than the sum of the unfavorable prominence scores), the following formula is used:

FAVORABLE MEDIA VECTOR: (Answers lie between 0 and +1)

$$FMV = \frac{(f^2 - fu)}{r^2}$$

If f < u (the sum of the unfavorable prominence scores is greater than the sum of the favorable prominence scores), the following formula is used:

UNFAVORABLE MEDIA VECTOR: (Answers lie between 0 and −1)

$$UMV = \frac{(fu - u^2)}{r^2}$$

---

[a]Media vector copyright John C. Pollock, 2000–2007

and the activities of Dr. Jack Kevorkian (see, respectively, Hurwitz, Green, & Segal, 1976; Pollock & Robinson, 1977; Pollock et al., 1978; Pollock & Guidette, 1980; Pollock, 1995; Pollock, Coughlin et al., 1996).

AN OVERVIEW OF FIVE UMBRELLA HYPOTHESES: BUFFER, VIOLATED BUFFER, VULNERABILITY, PROTECTION, AND STAKEHOLDER

Although the 15 case studies selected for this book initially appeared to fall into four general topics—human rights, health care, economic interests, and quality of life—systematically testing relations between city characteristics and reporting on change yielded five broad "umbrella" hypotheses or patterns organized somewhat differently than initial observation suggested.

For each of the five umbrella hypotheses, this analysis attempts to identify those city characteristics most closely associated with "accommodating" or "resistant" reporting in the case of the four hypotheses connecting city characteristics and reporting on political or social change, and with "protective" reporting, in the case of the economic protection hypothesis. Each umbrella hypothesis is the topic of a separate chapter. In each case, empirical indicators have been selected on the basis of their enduring capacity to yield significant correlations across a wide range of studies carried out over a period of more than 10 years. The five umbrella hypotheses are distilled from this multi-year data collection effort involving more than 600 undergraduates enrolled in basic and advanced research methods courses.

The five umbrella hypotheses do not correspond with the four "natural" topic categories offered in the introduction: human rights, health care, economic, and quality-of-life issues. Rather the empirically derived hypothesis clusters appear to segment case study topics into five somewhat overlapping categories that can be labeled as follows:

1. "Human rights" issues that draw attention to social injustice;
2. "Ominous" issues that threaten either the long-term biological existence of some population segments or a cherished way of life;
3. "Redistributive justice" issues that represent a renewed effort to ensure equal access to benefits historically unevenly available to those with few economic resources and also to ensure survival;
4. "Protection" issues that can strongly affect the economic interests of the financially privileged; and
5. "Stakeholder" issues that clearly and directly affect a particular population segment.

Each of the linked hypotheses and topic categories can be elaborated.

The "Buffer" Hypothesis

Regarding some human rights issues, the greater the proportion of privileged city residents, the more likely a city's major newspaper is to report favorably on several human rights "claims," for example, Anita Hill's testimony about her treatment by Clarence Thomas (see chap. 3) or legalization of physician-assisted suicide (Chapter 3; Pollock, Coughlin et al., 1996). A related finding links a very specific measure of privilege—greater availability of medical care (e.g., number of physicians per 100,000 residents)—to more support for the "right" to engage in innovative and potentially life-saving research on embryonic stem cell research. Corroborating studies have found that the higher the level of privilege in a city, the more favorable the coverage of the "right" to engage in cloning, or the "right" of Cuban refugees to enter the United States (Pollock, Dudzak, Richards, Norton, & Miller, 2000; Pollock, Shier, & Slattery, 1995).

This pattern linking precise levels of privilege in cities to precise levels of favorable or unfavorable reporting on human rights claims is so persistent that it can be called a Buffer Hypothesis. The buffer hypothesis proposes that the greater the proportion of a city's population that is privileged or "buffered" from financial and occupational uncertainty, the more receptive or "accommodating" a city's major paper is likely to be to claims for moral attention by those who are less privileged, or by those making "human rights" claims. (*How* this pattern works is a matter for speculation and is addressed in chap. 10.)

The "Violated Buffer" Hypothesis

Curiously, the antithesis of the buffer hypothesis is encountered when examining "ominous" issues. For these topics, the greater the proportion of city residents who are privileged, the less favorable (or perhaps more fearful or "resistant") the reporting in a city's major newspaper (e.g., reporting on the Master Settlement Agreement [MSA] with large tobacco companies—thus limiting tobacco ads toward children, or on proposals to "censor" or reduce privacy on the Internet, both found in chap. 4). Consistently, a related study found that the higher the education level (or the larger the number of college students) in a city, the less favorable the newspaper reporting on a new and potentially disruptive technology, the Internet, which was increasingly capable of distributing information previously available only to an educated elite to as many people as could access computers (Pollock & Montero, 1998).

This pattern is so marked that it can be called the Violated Buffer Hypothesis. The violated buffer hypothesis proposes that issues viewed as imperiling either privileged groups or a relatively stable, secure way of life will be regarded as threatening by privileged sectors and will be associated with relatively "resistant," unfavorable reporting. For example, one study encountered relatively unfavorable coverage of a country's government widely perceived as violating human rights: After the repression in Tiananmen Square, China's bid for the 2000 Olympics (Pollock, Kreuer, & Ouano, 1997). Similarly, Magic Johnson's announcement dramatized the reality that even relatively successful, wealthy citizens could be vulnerable to HIV/AIDS (see chap. 8). Children everywhere exposed to tobacco ads or women eligible for combat roles (Pollock, Mink, Puma, Shuhala, & Ostrander, 2001) are examples of threats to long-established viewpoints that children and women should be protected from obvious danger. The reasons for these patterns are still being explored, but the pattern is clear. The greater the proportion of privileged citizens in a city, the more unfavorable newspaper reporting is likely to be on issues framed as "ominous," hazardous to physical safety or a secure, predictable way of life.

The "Vulnerability" Hypothesis

For selected issues, a Vulnerability Hypothesis appears reasonable. A strict "market" perspective on reporting would expect links between the proportion of relatively well-educated, economically comfortable citizens in a city (the most likely readers of newspapers) and coverage generally mirroring their interests. The community structure approach, however, envisions media coverage that might reflect the interests of a wide range of groups and concerns, including the least economically advantaged.

Some previous research confirms that expectation. For example, the higher the poverty level in a city, the more favorable the coverage of *Roe v. Wade* during the time of the Supreme Court decision legalizing abortion in 1973. Higher city poverty levels also corresponded with higher levels of abortions performed in cities after legalization took effect (Pollock et al., 1978). Similarly, the higher the poverty level, the more favorable the coverage of issues of concern to prisoners (a prison revolt), those seeking abortions (a 1976 Supreme Court abortion decision) and homosexuals—regarding a Dade County (Miami), Florida referendum rescinding housing protections for homosexuals (Pollock & Robinson, 1977). These and the issues investigated in this study—eliminating capital punishment and passing a Patients' Bill of Rights—share a common concern with "redistributive justice," providing more equitable opportunities and freedom from injustice to those who have been historically, in particular, economically disadvantaged. Both capital punishment and a Patients' Bill of Rights also focus directly on issues of physical survival. Specifically, it is expected that the higher the poverty levels in a city, the more unfavorable the coverage of capital punishment and the more favorable the coverage of a patients' health rights.

The "Protection" Hypothesis

Regarding economic issues, it is reasonable to expect that the higher the proportion of city residents who are "privileged" (the higher the proportions with college educations or working in the "professions" or enjoying family incomes of $100,000 or more annually), the more favorable a newspaper's reporting is likely to be toward economic developments that buttress privileged interests (e.g., favoring the creation of NAFTA), or the more unfavorable a newspaper's reporting is likely to be toward economic developments that challenge those interests (e.g., opposing the handover of Hong Kong to China). A related study found that cities with relatively "fewer" economic interests to protect regarding privatization of social security—those cities with larger proportions of younger residents ages 18–35, are also the cities with papers most likely to favor some privatization of social security (Pollock, Tanner, & Delbene, 2000). Accordingly, city characteristics measuring economic interests can be associated with reporting that is relatively "protective" of those interests.

Olien et al., (1995) relied on surveys conducted in Minnesota to call this pattern—linking privileged economic interests to reporting favoring those interests—the Guard Dog hypothesis. Examining nationwide reporting on selected economic issues, our research confirms for two case studies what these scholars expected to find in their state: Newspaper reporting can frame economic perspectives in ways that are directly associated with the proportion of privileged groups in a city.

A "Stakeholder" Hypothesis

Some efforts to explain the connection between city characteristics and reporting on social change cannot be easily contained or categorized by buffer, violated buffer, vulnerability, or protection hypotheses. Some explanations resemble traditional "interest group" or "stakeholder" politics. For example, one nationwide study of newspaper reporting on the proposed legalization of same-sex marriage concluded that the greater the proportion of gay-owned or gay-marketed businesses or cultural institutions in a city (those groups with a "stake" in legalization), the more favorable the newspaper coverage of same-sex marriage legalization (Pollock & Dantas, 1998). Similarly, another study found that the higher the proportion of citizens over age 75 in a city, the more favorable the newspaper reporting on Dr. Kevorkian's physician-assisted suicide activities (Pollock, Coughlin et al., 1996). Once again, the relative percentages or numbers of those with the greatest "stake" in the issue, those over age 75, were linked with precise levels of favorable reporting on a topic that directly concerns that age group.

In this study, it is expected that the greater the proportion of families with teenagers in a city, the greater the perceived stakeholder "risk," and the less favorable the coverage of gun control. Similarly, it is expected that cities with higher proportions of Democrats will be associated with that party's relatively stronger concern for environmental issues and therefore with reporting favoring environmental protection. Because we do not have polling or attitude survey data from each city on this or most other issues, we can only speculate at this point about the different perspectives of distinct groups. In any case, from a stakeholder perspective, we hypothesize that the larger a group's presence or influence in a city, the more likely media are to treat it and its concerns with dignity and respect. A visual representation of the potential influence of the five umbrella community structure hypotheses is found in Fig. 2.1.

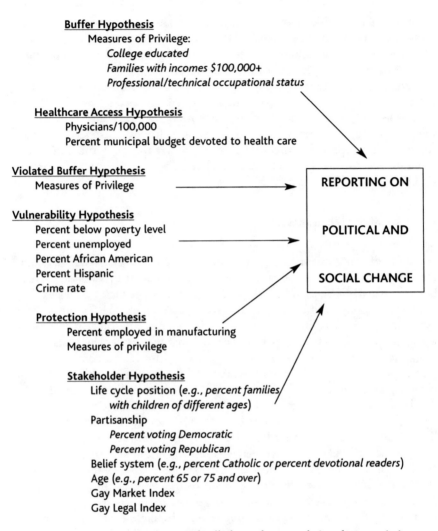

Buffer Hypothesis
    Measures of Privilege:
        College educated
        Families with incomes $100,000+
        Professional/technical occupational status

Healthcare Access Hypothesis
    Physicians/100,000
    Percent municipal budget devoted to health care

Violated Buffer Hypothesis
    Measures of Privilege

Vulnerability Hypothesis
    Percent below poverty level
    Percent unemployed
    Percent African American
    Percent Hispanic
    Crime rate

Protection Hypothesis
    Percent employed in manufacturing
    Measures of privilege

Stakeholder Hypothesis
    Life cycle position (*e.g., percent families*
        with children of different ages)
    Partisanship
        Percent voting Democratic
        Percent voting Republican
    Belief system (*e.g., percent Catholic or percent devotional readers*)
    Age (*e.g., percent 65 or 75 and over*)
    Gay Market Index
    Gay Legal Index

REPORTING ON

POLITICAL AND

SOCIAL CHANGE

Fig. 2.1. Community structure umbrella hypotheses and city characteristics.

Shifting Perspectives Over Time

These proposed connections between certain city characteristics and reporting on critical issues are not necessarily "fixed" permanently, linking one particular hypothesis, always a buffer or violated buffer hypothesis, for example, with a specific issue. Examining reporting on HIV/AIDS from 1986 to 1994 revealed relatively buffered, sympathetic reporting toward those with HIV/AIDS in 1990, then violated buffer, fearful reporting after

Magic Johnson's HIV announcement in 1991, and a return to buffer reporting sympathetic to those diagnosed with the condition in 1994 (see chap. 8). Clearly, reporting perspectives on a particular group or condition can change, but it is important to note that, in each of the examples and years cited throughout the study of HIV/AIDS coverage, the relative proportion of privileged groups in each city was the dominant factor associated with either relatively unfavorable reporting (in the case of Magic Johnson) or relatively favorable reporting (both before and after Magic Johnson's announcement). The proportion of privileged groups in a city is clearly a major axis about which news reporting favorable or unfavorable to social change can turn, but the strongest hypotheses linking city characteristics and accommodating reporting can shift over time.

Links to Public Opinion, Public Behavior, and Public Policy

One of the most powerful tests of the utility of any media theory is how well it connects media to society. In this endeavor, the community structure approach connects relatively enduring city characteristics with media coverage of critical issues. The media vector's measures of issue "projection" can also be linked to other measures of social and political change, including regional measures of public opinion, city-level measures of behavior or clusters organized by level of policy regulation of a particular topic (e.g., tobacco use). Employing multiple methodologies, a case study examining media coverage of the Supreme Court decision allowing the Boy Scouts of America to exclude homosexuals illustrates ways the community structure approach and media vector can be linked to public opinion, public policy and media ownership patterns (see chap. 9).

SECTION II

FIVE UMBRELLA HYPOTHESES
AND CASE STUDIES

3

THE BUFFER HYPOTHESIS

Privilege Linked to Favorable Reporting on Human Rights Claims

A great deal of the literature on macrosocial characteristics and media focuses on the way media align themselves with the status quo. A prevailing research perspective suggests that media often reinforce the existing social order (see, Tichenor et al., 1980; and assorted chapters in Demers and Viswanath, 1999). As previously explained, Tichenor et al., see newspapers as "mechanisms for community social control that maintain the norms, values and processes of a community, and . . . their functions necessarily fit into a pattern that varies predictably according to size and type of community" (pp. 102–103).

Yet media are compelled to react to social change, and such phenomena as the civil rights and women's movements, to name only two, have changed social norms and the way journalists think about those issues as well. Certainly, since the 1960s, leading U.S. papers such as *The New York Times* and *The Washington Post* have not portrayed issues affecting minorities and women in a classically "objective" or "neutral" way, but rather as legitimate grievances illuminating historical injustices.

It is thus reasonable to expect, in a nation exhibiting as much social, political, and regional variation as the United States, that media coverage should exhibit substantial variation as well. One way to approach explanations for that variation is to focus on the concept of relative privilege: Some cities, compared to others, have higher percentages of high-income families or college graduates or workers in professional occupations. It is reasonable to expect, whether from a sense of noblesse oblige, regal sympathy, education level, or sense of being relatively "buffered" from economic uncertainty, that cities with relatively large proportions of privileged groups may be linked to relatively sympathetic media coverage of groups or group representatives making rights claims.

According to Keith Stamm (1985), in his pathbreaking theoretical and empirical work collected in *Newspapers and Community Ties: Toward a Dynamic Theory*, amenity-rich environments, those with higher quality-of-life measures, are those most likely to attract knowledgeable, educated citizens and to have the best prospects for prosperity. This expectation is broadly consistent with urban planner Richard Florida's (2002) work on *The Rise of the Creative Class: And How It's Transforming Work, Leisure, Community and Everyday Life*. Florida suggested that professionals are attracted to city environments rich in creative energy, where there are multiple opportunities for dynamic cultural participation, homosexuals, music and other indicators of creativity and acceptance of diversity. Furthermore, Florida marshalled effective evidence confirming that such culturally rich environments are linked closely to "hard" indicators of economic success such as economic vitality and growth (Florida, 2002).

By extension, the more "lifestyle advantage" a city enjoys, the more likely a city paper is to be open to reasonable efforts to change or be able to evaluate proposed changes less in terms of immediate economic scarcity or uncertainty than in terms of long-term values and gains. This might be called a "buffer" hypothesis. The more individuals in a city who are "buffered" from scarcity and uncertainty, the more likely they are to accord legitimacy to those who articulate their concerns in human rights frames.

This chapter examines three critical controversies that contained human rights claims as major dimensions: Anita Hill's claims and treatment during the Clarence Thomas hearings in the U.S. Senate; efforts to legalize physician-assisted suicide; and ongoing political, social, and moral exchanges surrounding embryonic stem cell research. Each of these issues has been framed by at least one of the "sides" as expressing human rights claims, and each permits a test of the expectation that relatively "buffered" populations are likely to grant some measure of legitimacy to such claims. Furthermore, it is expected that more buffered cities are likely linked to media coverage relatively sympathetic to such claims

ANITA HILL'S TESTIMONY
AT THE CLARENCE THOMAS HEARINGS

Introduction: The Issue

The Clarence Thomas–Anita Hill hearings are widely thought to have illuminated gender discrimination in the workplace. Articles written in the aftermath of the hearings employed that event as a touchstone for feminist and even more general public anger at the insensitivity of policymakers toward an issue that has concerned many women. In retrospect, the event has been seen as a wakeup call, even a "gender quake" for women to become more involved in politics and was given partial credit for subsequent impressive showings by women senatorial candidates in California, Washington, Illinois, and Pennsylvania.

This retrospective appreciation, however, may not accurately depict how well media presented citizens with a wide range of perspectives at the time. A key question is: How much wisdom did the presentations of news media introduce into the democratic process at the time? How well did media "frame" or "cue" events so that mere facts being reported were given attention and broader meanings (Bennett & Manheim, 1993)?

In their Gulf War report, Bennett and Manheim (1993) argued that "the public defines an issue as it is cued by media, and the media as they are cued by policy elites" (p. 332). The authors also argued that unless policy elites debate matters early and vehemently in the course of a developing news story, opportunities to cue the public may be lost.

Perhaps, as in the Gulf War, the introduction of Anita Hill's testimony in the confirmation process occurred too late to permit a thorough airing of opinions about workplace discrimination among policy elites. Furthermore, Hill's testimony may have lasted too short a period to yield a substantial debate on discrimination. And perhaps the past conduct of some senators in itself inhibited a lively discussion of the issues raised by Hill's charges. Opportunities to cue and frame events for a public discussion of workplace harassment clearly seem to have been lost.

Media nevertheless had important choices to make in their coverage of the Thomas–Hill hearings. It is clear from *Wall Street Journal*/Gallup polls taken at the time of the Hill–Thomas hearings and then some time later, that although most of the public believed Thomas (and disbelieved Hill) at the time the hearings occurred, by 1 year later most of the public believed the law professor's testimony (McAneny, 1992). The media doubtless played a key role in the evolution of that opinion shift.

But to the extent media could have played a more educational role earlier, what held them back? Why were opportunities for public education missed? And did some papers perform better than others in cuing and framing issues so that discussion of the discrimination issue could play a considered role in the confirmation process of Judge Thomas? Two questions drive this case study: How much variation existed in reporting on the Thomas–Hill hearings? If substantial variation is found, what city characteristics are most closely linked with news reporting differences?

The Literature on Sexual Harassment in the Media: A Recent Concern

Coverage of the Thomas–Hill hearings ignited an outpouring of newspaper coverage concerned with both individuals' motives and the issue of sexual

harassment. At the time of the Thomas hearings, however, there was a paucity of literature in the communications field focusing on sexual harassment in
the workplace.

Some studies in the *Journal of Communication*, for example, focused
broadly on the concept of gender and its centrality as an organizing perspective for research on gender "systems" (Rakow, 1986); gender as a primary
category of social organization (Dervin, 1987; Tuchman, Daniels, & Benet,
1978); the way gender politics produced a "socially structured silence" in the
information society (Jansen, 1989); and development communication and
the challenge of feminism (Steeves, 1993). Other studies focused more
specifically on concrete instances of gender distortion, illuminating, for
example, the attitudinal effects of filmed violence against women (Linz,
Donerstein, & Penrod, 1984), the persistence of female stereotypes in the
way success for women is defined in books (Bate & Self, 1983), the depic-
tion of women in music videos (Brown & Campbell, 1986), in magazine
photographs (Sparks & Fehlner, 1986), in children's literature (Moore &
Mae, 1987), in microcomputer training (Brunet & Proulx, 1989), and in television advertising (Myers & Biocca, 1992).

Yet, few studies focused concretely on sexual workplace harassment and
the way that issue was communicated in the media, or the relation between
that coverage and audience or community characteristics. Sexual violence,
harassment, and sexual activity on television and in movies had been
explored (Larson, 1991; Peterson, 1991; Smith, 1991; Smith, Fredin, &
Nardone, 1989; Weaver, 1994). Some communication studies did focus on
harassment, from the broad concept of "street harassment" (Kissling, 1991)
to recognizing and managing sexual harassment in the workplace; recognizing levels of "immediacy"; gender differences in perceptions of what constitutes harassment (Booth-Butterfield, 1989; Johnson, Stockdale, & Saal, 1991;
Sheffey & Tindale, 1992); nonverbal behaviors (Richmond, 1991); the inef-
fectiveness of victims' "stop" messages (Bingham & Burleson, 1989); and
educational programs using interpersonal communication messages
(Bingham, 1991). And some studies dealt directly with sexual harassment or
persistent gender inequities in the journalism profession itself (Konrad,
1986; Pomerantz, 1989; Schweitzer & Miller, 1991; Smith, Fredin, &
Nardone, 1989). In general, however, little was written about the way sexual workplace harassment was covered in mass media.

Regarding articles on the Thomas hearings themselves, the general
scholarly literature included some examples illuminating sexual workplace
harassment: an article in *PS* on defeats and victories for women (Palley &
Palley, 1992); an article in *Social Work*, titled "It Was Not Our Finest Hour
(Hartman, 1992, pp. 3-4); an article by Sheldon Stark (1992) on "Sexual
Harassment in the Workplace, Lessons from the Thomas-Hill Hearings," in
Trial explaining why Anita Hill waited 10 years to report Thomas; and a

1992 collection of articles about the aftermath of Justice Thomas' confirmation, produced by *The Black Scholar*, titled *Court of Appeals*, containing several articles unfavorable to Thomas. Even in this group, few scholarly critiques of media coverage are apparent. An exception was M. J. Boyd's (1991) "Collard Greens, Clarence Thomas and the High-Tech Rape of Anita Hill," a critique of the way Hill was portrayed on television.

Accusations of Media Bias in the Thomas–Hill Hearings

Scholars apart, some journalists did examine critically the role of journalists in reporting the Thomas–Hill hearings. In one important respect, the very presence of Anita Hill at the Clarence Thomas nomination hearings was due to media influence. According to several news sources, Nina Totenberg, a journalist with National Public Radio, discovered an affidavit that Hill telefaxed to the Senate Judiciary Committee. Totenberg's revelations related to that document lit a major spark that initiated the Hill controversy and testimony (Boot, 1992). Yet, available evidence does not confirm conclusively that media generally adopted either a pro-Hill or anti-Hill stance during the Thomas hearings. Evidence can be marshaled to support both perspectives.

The Center for Media in Public Affairs in Washington, DC, for example, after studying 220 network news broadcasts and newspaper articles, concluded that four out of five individuals quoted in news stories supported Thomas (Boot, 1992). Consistently, Peter Dykstra (1991), writing in *The Progressive*, urged that some journalists had reason not to be sympathetic to Hill's allegations. Dykstra suggested that two people who diminished Hill's credibility, Juan Williams of *The Washington Post* and John McLaughlin of *The McLaughlin Group*, had themselves been accused of sexual harassment either contemporaneously or in the past.

Yet, other opinions differed sharply, suggesting that reporters were out to block Thomas by exploiting a news leak. Writing in the *Columbia Journalism Review*, William Boot (1992) reported that many conservatives were convinced of the media's pro-Hill bias, a position articulated by Brent Baker's Media Research Center. And as Boot pointed out, the *Wall Street Journal* accused *The Washington Post* and *The New York Times* of "taking a 'politically correct' pro-Hill approach to the issue" (p. 9).

With media playing such a critical and controversial role in the inception and evolution of the Thomas–Hill hearings, events that were to achieve the status of a sea-change in gender politics in the United States, the precise direction of media coverage and the environmental or structural factors associated with coverage variation clearly deserve attention. Yet, no research had been found examining systematically the content of Clarence Thomas–Hill newspaper coverage in relation to the communities the newspapers serve.

The evidence presented thus far suggests that individual perspectives of reporters and editors may produce specific, idiosyncratic views on sexual harassment. But the larger context remains unmapped. Initial inspection of newspaper coverage of Hill's testimony suggests that the articles accomplishing the most in "framing" or "cuing" readers about workplace sexual harassment—presenting Hill's charges in historical or legal context—also tended to present Hill and her testimony as credible and a reasonable account of challenges women face in the modern workplace. Did some newspapers clearly favor Hill more than others, displaying distinct patterns in legitimizing or delegitimizing her charges? Did those patterns correspond to specific characteristics of cities where each newspaper is published?

Hypotheses

A review of the theoretical and empirical literature on ties between community structure and newspaper reporting yields five clusters of hypotheses in this exploration of reporting on Anita Hill during the Clarence Thomas hearings, concerning quality-of-life/lifestyle advantage (occupational status, education, income), poverty levels, ethnic identity, gender variation, and political partisanship.

Quality-of-Life/Lifestyle Advantage: The Buffer Hypothesis

According to the buffer hypothesis, the more "lifestyle advantage" a city enjoys, the more likely a city paper is to be open to reasonable efforts to change or be able to evaluate proposed changes less in terms of immediate economic scarcity or uncertainty than in terms of long-term values and gains. Regarding women's rights, the more individuals in a city who are "buffered" from scarcity and uncertainty, the less likely they are to hold tightly to traditional political values and social values that have denied women access to political and economic influence.

Privilege: Occupational Status. In Anita Hill's circumstances, one aspect of lifestyle advantage that characterizes cities deserves special attention: the proportions of professionals who live there. For example, individuals employed in professional jobs may not experience the same type of job uncertainty felt by blue-collar workers. Professional employees are often more secure in their positions; prolonged education makes them especially prepared and knowledgeable in their fields. Therefore they may feel less threatened by change (such as the emergence of large numbers of women professionals) than are those who lack the education and knowledge necessary for professional careers.

Conversely, one aspect of lifestyle disadvantage might be characterized by the proportions of nonprofessionals or nonexecutives who live in a city. Cities with a greater percentage of blue-collar workers, workers whose positions can be eliminated through new technologies or exporting of jobs abroad, may be less likely to accept change.

In general, the higher the proportion of professionals (or executives, or white-collar workers) in a city, the more likely that city's reporting is expected to favor Anita Hill. It might be suggested that occupational status is not likely to predict reporting perspectives for or against Anita Hill because both Hill and Thomas are professionals (lawyers). Yet it is precisely because they are both professionals that other professionals are likely to sympathize with Hill's dilemma.

A profession is defined as an occupation with a long period of training in abstract knowledge, rigorous requirements such as examinations for admission to the profession, and a clear code of ethics that are enforced (e.g., medical doctors can lose their licenses and lawyers can be disbarred). People who consider themselves "professionals" view their occupations—and the requirements they passed to enter those careers—as different from other occupations.

The code of ethics, in particular, sets a professional apart from people who simply work at a "job." It is the code of ethics, for example, that helps someone decide whether to obey the orders of an employer of the moment, when ethical decisions must be made, or to consider overriding the code of ethics of one's profession, loyalty to which is supposed to transcend the immediate concerns of any particular employer.

From this perspective, Hill's charges against Thomas are especially reprehensible, because they suggest not simply that Thomas may have taken advantage of his position as supervisor to abuse Hill, but also that in so doing he violated a profoundly respected set of professional guidelines about the way professionals are supposed to treat clients, direct reports, and other employees. To a professional, therefore, Hill's charges against Thomas are especially troublesome not only because they suggest insensitivity to a lawyer's code of ethics in particular, but also to an insensitivity to a presumed steadfast sense of propriety associated with the exalted position of justice of the U.S. Supreme Court.

The charges are unsettling also because the accusations against Thomas throw into question, in a public forum, the sense of propriety and high purpose claimed and esteemed by all professionals everywhere. All professionals in all professions were hurt by the public accusations against Thomas, and it would be reasonable to expect some sympathy with Hill as a result. Accordingly (with data sources placed in parenthesis after each hypothesis):

H1: *The higher the percentage of professionals or executives/managers in a city, the more likely a paper is to display favorable* *perspectives on Anita Hill.* (Source: County and City Extra, 1991)

Education (16 Years+). The higher the percentage of people with 16 or more years of education (at least college graduates) in a city, the more likely the coverage will favor Anita Hill. It is predicted that the presence of citizens with this many years of education will encourage appreciation for a wider scope of experiences and a willingness to consider unexplored topics, as well as support for educational and occupational opportunities for women specifically. Therefore:

H2: *The higher the percentage of citizens with 4 or more years of college in a city, the more favorable the coverage of Anita Hill.* (County and City Extra, 1991)

Income. The higher the proportion of families or those with incomes over $100,000 in a city, the more likely the coverage will legitimize Anita Hill. It is predicted that cities with more people earning higher incomes will be highly sensitive to the quality of the workplace environment; and therefore to sexual harassment in the workplace. Or, from a more narrow economic—buffer hypothesis—perspective, families who are more financially secure may not feel as threatened by affirmative action as are families who are not as economically fortunate. Similar to privilege in the form of education and professional status, economic privilege is generally hypothesized to be buffered from economic dislocation and therefore available for sensitivity to human rights issues (Pollock, Shier, & Slattery, 1995). The concept of the *upper class liberal*, exemplified in the presidencies of Franklin Roosevelt and John Kennedy, are examples of this expectation.

H3: *The higher the proportion of city residents with annual family incomes of $100,000 or more, the more likely a city newspaper is to display favorable reporting on Anita Hill.* (Lifestyle Market Analyst, 1994)

Vulnerability: Poverty Levels

Hypotheses linking poverty levels to news coverage are essentially the inverse of the hypothesized relation between higher income and coverage of Anita Hill. Because higher income is associated with an appreciation of workplace diversity and sensitivity to workplace discrimination, less abundance or "buffering" in the form of relatively high poverty levels is predicted to be associated with coverage delegitimizing Hill.

Hill's testimony appeared to harm Thomas' chances for upward mobility. Cities with relatively high percentages of citizens below the poverty level may display news coverage at least skeptical, if not disapproving of someone who is a comfortable professional interfering with someone else reaching for a desired occupational goal. Thomas was viewed as someone who had worked hard to advance himself. As Grahm (1992) noted in *1992 Current Biography Yearbook*, "Leola Thomas held the family together, by picking crabmeat and working as a housecleaner, until their house burned down when Thomas was seven" (p. 567).

Presumably, in cities with a higher proportion of people in poverty, there is a high likelihood of coverage delegitimizing Hill because there would exist widespread disapproval of last-minute efforts to halt a hard-working, upwardly mobile individual from reaching a prestigious position. Accordingly:

> **H4:** *The higher the proportion of citizens with incomes below the poverty level, the less likely a paper will display favorable perspectives on Anita Hill.* (County and City Extra, 1991)

Stakeholders

Ethnic Identity. It is predicted that cities with greater proportions of Blacks will register resentment against Hill for not supporting a member of her own racial/ethnic group. Although editors and publishers of African-American newspapers were anti-Thomas, polls taken at the time revealed that African-American people (the public) were clearly pro-Thomas (Lambro, 1991). Leroy Thomas, a Black cabbie and TV talk show host in Georgia opposed Thomas's judicial philosophy but said, "I'm against what she did. . . . I don't think anyone looking out for the race would have done what Anita Hill did" (Dawson, 1992, p. 1E). Conversely, the lower the percentage of Blacks in a city, the more likely coverage will legitimize Hill.

> **H5:** *The higher the percentage of Blacks in a city, the less favorable the coverage of Anita Hill.* (County and City Extra, 1992)

Percentage of Women in the Workforce. Workforce presence is an indicator of economic influence in family matters and in purchasing power, and is one index of the relative economic influence and authority of women in a city. Therefore:

> **H6:** *The higher the percentage of women in the workforce, the more likely pro-Hill coverage.* (County and City Extra, 1992)

Political Partisanship: Media presentations of remarks by members of the Senate Judiciary Committee questioning Thomas and Hill, in particular electronic media depictions, suggested a high level of political partisanship in the interrogations. Predictably, Republicans, especially Senator Arlen Spector of Pennsylvania, appeared to challenge Hill's assertions sharply and to display support for President Bush's nominee, Clarence Thomas. By contrast, Democrats showed skepticism toward Thomas' qualifications or character and appreciation for Hill's testimony. Accordingly:

> **H7:** *The higher the percentage of citizens who vote for Democrats in a city, the more likely a city's major paper is to legitimize Anita Hill.* (The Election Data Book, 1993)

Because not every city held senatorial elections in 1991, the election date chosen for comparative purposes was the 1992 presidential elections, for which all citizens were eligible to vote. Specifically, if partisanship is important, the higher the percentage of a city's citizens who voted Democratic in the 1992 presidential elections, the greater a city paper's expected support for Anita Hill.

Sample and Coding Categories

A total of 463 articles printed from October 7, 1991, when Anita Hill first testified, through December 31, 1992, after which article frequency dropped off sharply, were measured and evaluated using the DIALOG Computer Information Program newspaper database available to college libraries. All articles on Hill's testimony or its implications more than one paragraph in length printed in the stated time period were sampled in 23 newspapers representing a geographic cross-section of the United States (see Table 3.1.).

After "prominence" scores were calculated, "direction" scores were derived from evaluation of article content.

Coverage *favorable* to Hill included articles praising Hill's credibility ("she has nothing to gain," "bravery"); or criticizing Hill's treatment in the hearings (as "sickening," "adversarial," and generating a "backlash"). Articles were also considered favorable to Hill if she was praised in the context of disparaging Thomas (as "idiot," "sexually out of control," "unstable"); disparaging men generally (as "preoccupied with sex"). An article that simply attacked Thomas would not be considered a pro-Hill article.

Coverage *unfavorable* to Hill included articles denigrating Hill (as "venomous" or "mudslinging," attempting to "smear" Thomas, "ridiculous," or creating a "complete fabrication"); and belittling the hearings (as "catastrophic," "unfair," a "fiasco" or a "political sham"). Articles legitimizing Thomas as "honorable," "wise," or "decent" were not necessarily viewed as anti-Hill because it was possible for journalists to praise or criticize both celebrities simultaneously.

Balanced/neutral coverage demonstrated concern for the fairness of the hearings and the reputation of the Senate Judiciary Committee and the judicial selection process, including "harassment from both sides," a "hostile environment," a "sharply divided" judiciary committee, "racism," and a potential "constitutional conflict."

After evaluating article direction with this threefold classification, a systematic subsample of half the articles was coded by two researchers and yielded a Holsti's coefficient of intercoder reliability of .87. Each article's attention score and its directional score (favorable, unfavorable, or balanced/neutral) were then used to calculate the media vector.

TABLE 3.1 Anita Hill Media Vectors

NEWSPAPER	MEDIA VECTOR
The Washington Post	.320
San Francisco Chronicle	.257
Boston Globe	.190
Seattle Times	.178
Philadelphia Inquirer	.110
Albany Times-Union	.090
New Orleans Times-Picayune	.087
Houston Post	.085
Arizona Republic (Phoenix)	.071
Orlando Sentinel	.067
Oregonian (Portland)	.062
Buffalo News	.0548
Lexington Herald-Leader	.0547
Los Angeles Times	.032
Chicago Tribune	.016
Atlanta Journal-Constitution	.013
Detroit Free Press	.011
St. Louis Post-Dispatch	.009
Charlotte Observer	.004
Dayton Daily News	−.013
Pittsburgh Post-Gazette	−.020
Commercial Appeal (Memphis)	−.063

Results

All but three of the media vectors are positive, suggesting that major newspapers throughout the nation were at least somewhat sensitive to the position of Anita Hill. Yet there was sufficient variation to pose the question:
What city demographics and structural characteristics are associated most
and least strongly with that variation?

*Occupational and Educational Status Strongly Associated With Pro-
Hill Coverage.* Correlation analysis documents the importance of occupational and educational categories as key factors associated with reporting
relatively favorable to Anita Hill (see Table 3.2).

Consistent with evidence that the presence of professionals in a city is
associated with relatively favorable reporting on Hill ($r = .78; p = .000$) is the
finding that cities with higher proportions of college graduates are more
likely to be associated with coverage legitimizing Hill ($r = .73; p = .000$).
Congruently, the statistical association linking the proportions of professionals and college educated residents in a city is quite high ($r = .92; p =
.000$). Curiously, family income over $100,000 is not linked to reporting perspectives on Anita Hill.

Economic Circumstances Have Limited Relation to Reporting on Hill.
Only one indicator measuring economic vulnerability in a city is significantly associated with coverage of Hill. Percent below the poverty level is negatively associated with coverage of Hill ($r = -.44; p = .0363$), whereas percent with family income of $100,000+ is not linked significantly to coverage
of Anita Hill. Gross economic indicators, aggregate factors, are not as powerful as the specifics of occupational and educational categories—status categories more clearly "earned" than is economic wealth—in their association
with reporting legitimizing or delegitimizing Hill.

TABLE 3.2. Anita Hill Coverage Pearson Correlations

HYPOTHESIS	CORRELATION	SIGNIFICANCE[a]
Percent professionals	.78	.000
Percent college educated	.73	.000
Percent below the poverty level	−.44	.036
Percent women in workforce	.40	.058

[a]Only correlations significant at about the .05 level or better are reported.

Women in Workforce only Modestly Associated with Coverage of Hill.
The association between percent of women in the workforce and coverage
favoring Hill is only marginally important ($r = .40$; $p = .058$). The finding
that professional and educational accomplishment matter more than gender
accomplishment suggests that coverage of Anita Hill was of concern not
only to working women, but also to a larger audience of relatively well-educated, professionally accomplished citizens generally, both women and men.
This finding is consistent with Hill's own subsequent statements thanking
both men and women for support, as well as voting results in California,
Washington and Illinois, where women senators were subsequently elected
by voters of both genders.

*Percent African-American and Political Partisanship, Contrary to
Expectation, Have Little Relation to Coverage Favoring or Disfavoring
Anita Hill.* Percent Black had essentially no correlation at all with coverage
favoring Hill, a null finding. Suggesting there was no automatic, consensual
"Black" view on the Thomas–Hill hearings is consistent with the view that
there are many different political and social perspectives present among
African Americans today (see, e.g., Gates, 1994).

Political partisanship, likewise, had a weak relation to reporting favoring or opposing Anita Hill. Despite the conventional wisdom that the hearings were highly partisan, there was little evidence that percent voting
Democratic in a city had any significant relation to reporting favoring or
opposing Hill.

Multiple regression analysis confirms what the correlations have suggested, that percent professionals in a city is by far the most powerful variable associated with coverage favoring Hill. (No other variable yielded as
much as 5% of the variance.)

The key variable is percent professionals, accounting for 71% of the
variance. By reducing drastically the predictive power of the educational
variable, regression analysis suggests that professional and educational
accomplishment are essentially measuring similar dimensions and that education in this case may be a "mask" for professional achievement.

TABLE 3.3 Anita Hill Regression

HYPOTHESIS	CORRELATION	R-SQUARE	R-SQUARE CHANGE	F	PROBABILITY
Percent professionals	.84	.71	.71	25.95	.000

Conclusion and Implications for Further Research: The Anita Hill–Clarence Thomas Hearings May Have Been as Much a Professional and Educational Issue as a Gender or Political Issue

The extremely high correlation between percent of professionals in a city and coverage favoring Anita Hill (r =.78; p =.000), as well as the regression analysis finding that percent professional is the single most powerful factor predicting variation in coverage of Anita Hill, accounting for 71% of the variance, confirm that this factor, percent professionals in a city, is the pivotal dimension associated with differences in coverage of Anita Hill.

An additional finding reveals that percent of working women in a city is only marginally related to variations in coverage of Hill. For newspapers, the key dimension of the Thomas–Hill hearings may not have been the gender quake that it was widely perceived to represent, but rather a "professional quake" of major proportions. The proportion of professionals and college-educated residents in a city are excellent predictors of coverage favoring Hill.

This finding suggests that men as well as women may have been disturbed by the Thomas–Hill hearings, among the group considered "professionals." And perhaps that "professional" group, not women alone, had a great deal to do with the subsequent election of women senators in California, Washington, and Illinois, and the near election of a senator in Pennsylvania. To the extent this finding is confirmed through further research on other workplace discrimination critical events, It suggests that workplace discrimination is not simply a women's issue: it is an issue that profoundly concerns men and women everywhere who consider themselves professionals.

Community Structure Can Be Strongly Associated With Important Variations in Reporting on Critical Events. The power of one key variable in a community—percent professionals—to account for 71% of the variation in coverage of the Thomas–Hill hearings is a clear indicator that the community structure approach outlined in this study is valid and useful. It suggests that the cuing and framing engaged in by newspapers in coverage of critical events may be embedded in some relatively stable characteristics of the communities where those newspapers publish.

The community structure approach also suggests that relatively changeable factors, such as the politics of gender and the politics of partisan election campaigns—issues tied to electioneering issues or the immediacies of political loss and gain—may be less important than some of the enduring structural characteristics of communities that constrain reporting when critical events arise. A community structure perspective provides a framework that complements the theories and approaches that emphasize news outcomes as the product of newsgathering conventions (e.g., Danzger, 1975; Manoff & Schudson, 1987; Tuchman, 1978) on the one hand; and on the other hand, approaches that emphasize some of the more frequently cited "structural" forces at work in the media marketplace (Ginsberg, 1986; Merriam, 1989). Comparing different approaches allows scholars to reach beyond the view that media simply "mirror" reality to a more complex vision of news making as a complex process in which "the news represents an ongoing struggle among various competing social interests over the meaning of modern life and the definition of modern problems" (Wasserman, Stack, & Reeves, 1994, p. 65).

NATIONWIDE NEWSPAPER COVERAGE OF PHYSICIAN-ASSISTED SUICIDE

Introduction

Physician-assisted suicide, which involves a physician administering or writing prescriptions for lethal drugs when a patient has a terminal illness and wishes release from further pain, has created an ethical controversy worldwide. Yet it is also an issue of growing importance and popularity as more people are diagnosed with HIV/AIDS, cancer, and other terminal illnesses involving immense suffering. The debate escalated in political and media arenas when Oregon implemented an act to make physician-assisted suicide legal under certain specifications. After 3 years of appeals, the Death With Dignity Act became effective on October 27, 1997.

Despite opposition by the Drug Enforcement Administration (DEA), which suggested that Oregon physicians engaging in physician-assisted suicide would violate the Controlled Substances Act, Attorney General Janet Reno's Department of Justice ruled in June 1998 that physicians who engaged in physician-assisted suicide under compliance with Oregon law would not be prosecuted. The debate surfaced again with the implementation of President Bush's new administration. On November 26, 2001, Attorney General John Ashcroft ordered DEA agents to prosecute physicians who prescribed under the Death With Dignity Act. The court battle is far from over and the debate continues to be covered by newspapers nationwide.

The Death With Dignity Act ensures that the patient is of sound mind, has less than 6 months to live, has a mandatory second opinion by a qualified physician, makes a request orally and in writing followed by a 15-day waiting period, and has two doctors (an attending physician and a consulting physician) who concur that the patient's decision is not made out of depression. These measures serve as "safeguards, written into the law, to ensure that the patient is protected and is in control of the process" (Oregon Death With Dignity—Respect the Will of the People, 2002, paragraph 1). As a result, some believe that physician-assisted suicide allows a suffering patient to die with dignity and is protected under these safeguards. In fact, "doctors not only seek to preserve and restore the health of their patients but seek to alleviate their pain, comfort them when this is not possible, and (perhaps) aid them in their effort to have the kind of death that they would prefer" (Dworkin, Frey, & Bok, 1998, p. 13). In addition, Percy Williams Bridgman, a well-known physicist who committed suicide in an advanced stage of cancer, once said, "It isn't decent for society to make a man do this thing himself" (Dworkin et al., 1998, p. 11).

However, some view physician-assisted suicide as completely objectionable and morally intolerable. Some consider it a violation of the law of nature. Thomas Aquinas believed that "the desire to be put to death is not only an unnatural inclination, but also irrational, mad" (Dworkin et al., 1998, p. 100).

Media can play an important role in debates about the legalization and acceptance of physician-assisted suicide. The media serve as agenda-setters by telling people what issues to consider (cited in Biagi, 1999). As Viswanath and Finnegan (2002) documented in a study of dynamic secular trends accompanying studies on ways to reduce coronary disease, media can be a formidable force in public health campaigns, increasing the public salience of issues and helping to mobilize resources. Newspapers in particular often set agendas for other media and may accumulate more revenue than most other media, thus exercising substantial influence (Biagi, 1999). As discussed previously, one of the ways newspapers, like other media, exert influence is through the "framing" of critical events. News frames, in turn, can influence individual perceptions of a critical issue, and a city's demographic characteristics may affect the way issues are framed by journalists. A masterful decade-long overview of health content in the media underscores the importance of sociocultural context, in particular the capacity of privileged interests to "gain acceptance of a particular narrative or perspective without overtly comparing competing voices" (Kline, 2006, p. 49).

Using the community structure approach, it is expected that media coverage of physician-assisted suicide will be more favorable in cities with higher levels of privilege as well as media and health care access as a result of readiness to support social change. Furthermore, coverage is expected to be less favorable in cities with certain age and belief system "stakeholders," for example due to apprehension among senior citizens that they will be pressured into physician-assisted suicide or the Catholic Church's disapproval of suicide.

Literature Review

Legalized physician-assisted suicide has been debated worldwide since the rejection by the British Parliament of a proposal in 1935 to permit voluntary euthanasia for those adults suffering from illnesses (*The Providence Journal*, 1997). Media coverage became more prevalent in 1950 when Dr. Herman Sander was acquitted of engaging in physician-assisted suicide by ending the life of a terminally ill cancer patient with an injection of air, even though the physician acknowledged doing it. Another pivotal event in the right-to-die movement included the "Declaration of Euthanasia" issued by Pope John Paul II opposing mercy killing but permitting a patient to refuse life-sustaining methods. In 1990, the media revealed Dr. Jack Kevorkian as the physician who used a "suicide machine" to enable Janet Adkins, who was suffering from Alzheimer's disease, to kill herself.

While several other cases involving Dr. Kevorkian were revealed and Pope John Paul II continued to condemn euthanasia and physician-assisted suicide, state governments were facing attempts at legalization. On November 6, 1991, an initiative to allow physician-assisted suicide for terminally ill patients was rejected by Washington state voters. California voters rejected a similar proposal 1 year later. However, in November of 1994, Oregon voters approved a proposal allowing doctors to prescribe lethal drugs to terminally ill patients wishing to end their lives. Before the law took effect, a judge struck it down. Finally, in 1997, after the Northern Territory of Australia became the first jurisdiction to allow doctors to assist terminally ill patients in their quest to die, Oregon passed the Death with Dignity Act permitting physician-assisted suicide. As a result, the prominence of physician-assisted suicide in the media soared to new heights.

Although media and some scholars have devoted considerable attention to the controversy surrounding physician-assisted suicide (Hyde, 1993), a search of several communication databases revealed little research on physician-assisted suicide in the communication field. However, communication scholars have completed research studies concerning other related issues, such as euthanasia and suicide, in relation to media coverage.

A study conducted by Wasserman, Stack, and Reeves (1994) about the number of suicide stories published on the front page of *The New York Times* between 1910 and 1920 concluded that the number of articles escalated not as a result of an increase in suicide in New York City or the nation but rather because of institutional and human factors. As an institution, *The New York Times* was organized so that certain "editorial gatekeepers" who possessed a huge amount of power and morally opposed suicide, tried to use the newspaper as a way to publicize the names of suicide victims as a deterrent. This was done at the height of the progressive era when social and moral reform was at a high, and there were significant concerns about these issues. It also seemed that the editors were acting as "moral entrepreneur(s) with an agenda that transcended the objective facility of routine journalism" (Wasserman et al., 1994, p. 64).

Similarly, Kalwinsky (1998) studied the framing of life and death in *The New York Times* between 1991 and 1996 when Dr. Kevorkian's name was foremost in media coverage. Those frames changed in the early 1990s from Dr. Kevorkian's portrayal as a "modern Dr. Frankenstein with 'suicide devices created' to engage in 'murder'" (p. 99), to, by 1995–1996, a view that physician-assisted suicide was an aid in dying, not murder, dealing with "fundamental human dignity, freedom of choice and protection of privacy" (Kalwinsky, 1998, p. 104).

The wide spectrum of morals and attitudes held by the aged, the terminally ill, and the general public in response to physician-assisted suicide has been explored by scholars in fields other than communication studies. In a study of residents of Denton, Texas, Worthen and Yeats (1998) found that people who practice their religion, believing that "life belongs to God" and that "physician-assisted suicide is murder," were very much against the idea of physician-assisted suicide.

Since 1997, a variety of articles have been published in *Time* and *Cancer Weekly* magazines as well as journals such as the *Georgetown Journal of Gender & the Law* to illustrate varying public opinions toward physician-assisted suicide. For example, Henderson (2000), in *Cancer Weekly*, described an instrument in which the most "true" answers, receiving 46% of respondents, regarded dying as comforting. Some scholars argue that public opinion changes toward physician-assisted suicide when it involves homosexual men infected with HIV (Spindelman, 2000). According to researchers, homosexual men infected with AIDS/HIV are a sexual threat to other men in their community. Therefore, those people who would ordinarily oppose physician-assisted suicide for anyone else would somehow be more approving of its use if the terminally ill patient were homosexual.

Additionally, a variety of studies have explored the influence of religious affiliation and ethnicity on attitudes toward physician-assisted suicide. Braun, Tanji, and Heck (2001) examined the influence of adult attitudes toward physician-assisted suicide on plans for death among five ethnic groups in Hawaii: Caucasian, Chinese, Filipino, Native Hawaiian, and Japanese. "Those likely to advocate discussing/documenting wishes were Catholic and had more years of education" (Braun et al., 2001, p. 55). Those of Filipino or Hawaiian ancestry were less likely than the others to support physician-assisted suicide (p. 55). Another study found that, compared to Catholic physicians, Jewish physicians were more likely to approve of lethal injection, as were physicians who did not pray frequently (Meier et al., 1998). Although scholars in fields outside communication studies have addressed the controversy surrounding physician-assisted suicide, few studies have been conducted on the coverage of physician-assisted suicide by the media.

Hypotheses

Twelve community structure hypotheses could be categorized in four cluster groups: the buffer hypothesis, health care access, vulnerability, and stakeholders (age, belief system, and disease prevalence). Each of these clusters links city demographics and coverage of physician-assisted suicide throughout the country.

Privilege: The Buffer Hypothesis

The buffer hypothesis suggests that privileged individuals in a community who are "relatively 'buffered' from conditions of poverty and uncertainty, and newspapers in such cities, have proved to be relatively supportive of human rights claims." Therefore, cities with families with incomes greater than $100,000, cities with a greater percentage of college-educated students or cities with higher percentages of those with professional/technical occupational status are more likely to have newspapers that place favorable emphasis on physician-assisted suicide (see previous case study on Anita Hill).

In a related study, Pollock and Yulis (2004) sampled newspapers nationwide in the mid-1990s, finding that some measures of privilege (high family income, percent computer users) in a city are associated with relatively favorable coverage of physician-assisted suicide. This result confirmed the hypothesis that larger privileged populations buffered from uncertainty are associated with more favorable coverage of human rights issues. Therefore:

H1: *The greater the percentage of families with incomes over $100,000+, the more favorable the coverage of physician-assisted suicide.* (Lifestyle Market Analyst, 2000)

H2: *The greater the percentage of college-educated students (4 or more years completed) in a city, the more favorable the coverage of physician-assisted suicide.* (Lifestyle Market Analyst, 2000)

H3: *The higher the percent with professional/technical occupational status in a city, the more favorable the coverage of physician-assisted suicide.* (Lifestyle Market Analyst, 2000)

Health care Access

Decisions about the right to die are made every day in hospitals and long-term care facilities. According to Pollock and Yulis (2004), "most physicians are still trained to be against physician-assisted suicide according to the Hippocratic Oath" (p. 283). However, although prestigious medical boards and associations, such as the American Medical Association, continue to readily oppose physician-assisted suicide, the medical community has begun to lean more favorably toward physician-assisted suicide.

In 1995, public attitudes toward the right-to-die issue were the subject of a national poll by the Times Mirror Center for the People and the Press. The attitudes of health care workers were compared with the attitudes of the general American public on right-to-die issues. Among the participants were nurses, certified nurse assistants, and medical technical specialists. The study found that health care staff were significantly more likely than the general public to "agree that there are circumstances in which a person should be allowed to die, that people do have the right to make their own decisions about receiving life-sustaining treatment . . . and that they approve of the right to die legislation" (Walker, 1997, p. 341).

As stated in the literature review, Meier et al. found in 1998 that in 1,902 completed questionnaires, "eleven percent of the physicians reported that under current legal constraints, there are circumstances in which they would prescribe a medication for a competent patient to use with the primary intention of ending his or her own life" (Meier et al., 1998, p. 1195). Furthermore, the study showed that out of 320 physicians who had received a request to engage in physician-assisted suicide, 16% reported that they had written a prescription for a lethal dose of medication (Meier et al., 1998). Consistent with the perspective that the cities with the greatest lifestyle advantages are most likely to accommodate new choices, those cities with the greatest abundance of health care facilities or abundance of physicians should manifest favorable coverage of physician-assisted suicide suicide. Accordingly:

H4: *The larger the number of health care centers in a city, the more favorable reporting on physician-assisted suicide.* (County and City Extra, 2000)

H5: *The greater the number of physicians per 100,000 residents in a city, the more favorable reporting on physician-assisted suicide is expected to be.* (County and City Extra, 2000)

Vulnerability: The Unbuffered Hypothesis

Those in society who live a life with economic struggles and financial insecurities may fear illness because of social and economic marginality as well as an inability to easily obtain information about medical science. This may be associated with concerns that decisions are being made *about* less privileged citizens rather than *by* them (Pollock & Yulis, 2004). It is possible that some of the underprivileged may fear physician-assisted suicide, viewing it as an opportunity for physicians to end prematurely the lives of the poor or those lacking medical insurance. Considering the concerns of these "unbuffered" citizens:

> **H6:** *The higher the unemployment level, the less favorable news coverage of physician-assisted suicide.* (Lifestyle Market Analyst, 2000)

> **H7:** *The higher the percent below the poverty level, the less favorable news coverage of physician-assisted suicide.* (County and City Extra, 2000)

Stakeholders

The presence of stakeholders in a given community may alter the coverage of certain controversial issues in all facets of media. Thus, it is clear that the prevalence of key stakeholders can be linked to media coverage of controversial issues. The presence of these stakeholders also contributes to varying coverage in cities nationwide. The stakeholders in the physician-assisted suicide debate are categorized under the following subdivisions: age, ethnicity, and belief system.

Age. Researchers have indicated that the greater the proportion of citizens over 75 years of age in a city, the more supportive the newspaper coverage of Dr. Kevorkian's efforts to fulfill the concerns of older citizens, according to a nationwide study of news coverage of Dr. Kevorkian between 1990 and 1993 (Pollock, Coughlin et al., 1996). Yet, regarding actual "legalization" of physician-assisted suicide, the perspectives of America's seniors may differ sharply. For example, Morris (1997) conducted a study among the elderly (ages 60 to 97) from the Muncie/Delaware County, Indiana area, known as Middletown, USA, and found that five major groups of people oppose physician-assisted suicide: physicians, ethicists, advocates of the mentally ill, religious organizations, and the elderly. In addition:

> In a recent study conducted at Duke University Medical Center, a sample of 168 elderly patients were surveyed on their views regarding physician-assisted suicide. The results of the study reported that only 39.9 percent of the patients surveyed favored physician-assisted suicide. This figure stands in contrast, however, to the 59.3 percent of the same patients' relatives who supported physician-assisted suicide in the same poll. (Levine, 1997, n.p.)

The activities of a disability civil rights group called "Not Dead Yet!", when they "invaded" an e-mail list operated by the Euthanasia Research and Guidance Organization, confirm the vehemence of some senior opponents of physician-assisted suicide (Hyde & Rufo, 2000). Therefore:

H8: *The greater the percentage of residents age 75+ in a city, the less favorable the coverage of physician-assisted suicide.* (Lifestyle Market Analyst, 2000)

Ethnicity. Other vital facets of physician-assisted suicide that merit assessment are variations in reporting related to ethnicity. Only on rare instances in communication literature has the presence of racial or ethnic minorities been considered an indicator of community structure that is related to community "pluralism" (Gandy, 1996, 1999; Goshorn & Gandy, 1995). Available data do suggest that African-Americans commit suicide at a rate less than that of the non-African-American population. Out of 29,109 suicides in the United States in 1999, only 1,950 were by African Americans (Hoyert, Arias, Smith, Murphy, & Kochanek, 2001, p. 38). Therefore, although African Americans represent about 12.5% of the population, they only account for about 6.7% of suicides. The *World Almanac* also confirms that for previous years, similar low percentages of Blacks chose suicide as a way to end their lives (*World Almanac*, 1996). Similar considerations may apply to Hispanics. Consequently, it is reasonable to infer:

H9: *The greater the percentage of African Americans or Hispanics in a city, the less favorable the coverage of physician-assisted suicide.* (County and City Extra, 2000)

Belief System. Religious beliefs may also impact coverage of highly critical issues. For example, it has been found that there is less favorable newspaper reporting on *Roe v. Wade* (1973) in cities with higher percentages of Catholics (Pollock et al., 1978). According to the Catechism of the Catholic Church, euthanasia and physician-assisted suicide are morally unacceptable. "Thus an act or omission which, of itself or by intention, causes death in order to eliminate suffering constitutes a murder gravely contrary to the dignity of the human person and the respect due to the living God, his creator" (Catechism of the Catholic Church, 1997, p. 2277). Therefore, it is reasonable to assume that many devout Catholics also condemn physician-assisted suicide. Previous research also suggests that practicing Catholics may not look favorably on physician-assisted suicide because it is believed to go against God's commandments and plan for one's life (Braun et al., 2001). As a result, newspapers reporting on physician-assisted suicide in cities with high proportions of Catholics are assumed to be relatively unfavorable. Therefore:

H10: *The greater the percentage of Catholics in a city, the less favorable the coverage of physician-assisted suicide.* (Catholic Almanac, 2001)

Terminal Illness: AIDS and Cancer. The proportion of terminally ill patients living in a community also merits consideration. Patients dealing with terminal illnesses such as cancer could understandably favor physician-assisted suicide. For example, Wilson et al. (2000) conducted a survey from 1996 to 1998 consisting of 70 participants, 51 of whom favored limited access to euthanasia or assisted suicide. These respondents listed some of their reasons for favoring physician-assisted suicide as being, "individual's right to choose, pain, and diminished quality of life" (Wilson et al., 2000, p. 2456).

However, patients with cancer are not the only ones in favor of physician-assisted suicide. A large majority of patients with AIDS are also very much in favor of assisted suicide. In September 1997, Lavery, Boyle, Dickens, Maclean, and Singer (2001) conducted a qualitative study of 32 people with HIV-1 or AIDS. These participants were all interviewed face to face by researchers. The most important discovery of the study was that patients with AIDS "desired euthanasia or assisted suicide because of disintegration and loss of community, which combined to create a perception of loss of self. . . . Euthanasia and assisted suicide were seen as limiting the loss of self" (p. 365). Presumably:

H11, H12: *The larger the number of residents in a community who have died from the terminal illnesses cancer (H11), or AIDS (H12), the more favorable the reporting of physician-assisted suicide.* (Health and Healthcare in the US: County and Metro Data, 2000)

Methodology

This study investigated newspaper coverage of physician-assisted suicide across a national cross-section of 27 U.S. cities. All articles of at least 150 words or more (343 total) were collected over 5 years, from January 1, 1997 to January 1, 2002, representing all of the longest articles printed in that time frame in the sampled papers. During this time period, Dr. Kevorkian and the legalization of physician-assisted suicide became "continuing big stories" in newspapers due to the implementation of the Death With Dignity Act in Oregon and as other states began to consider legalization. Using Lexis-Nexis, Newsbank, and DIALOG Classroom Information Program newspaper databases, articles from 27 newspapers were collected (See Table 3.4.).

TABLE 3.4 Physician-Assisted Suicide Media Vector Coefficients

TCH NEWSPAPER	MEDIA VECTOR
San Francisco Examiner	.763
San Diego Union Tribune	.444
Seattle Post-Intelligencer	.311
Denver Post	.161
The Commercial Appeal	.062
Deseret News (Salt Lake City)	.022
Dayton Daily News	.008
Orlando Sentinel	−.002
Philadelphia Inquirer	−.017
Lexington Herald-Leader	−.031
Detroit Free Press	−.040
The Hartford Courant	−.043
Milwaukee Journal Sentinel	−.051
Chicago Sun-Times	−.061
Tulsa World	−.087
St. Louis Post-Dispatch	−.099
Arizona Republic/Phoenix Gazette	−.112
Houston Chronicle	−.130
Fresno Bee	−.163
Baltimore Sun	−.180
The Times Union (Albany)	−.183
The Boston Globe	−.220
Austin-American Statesman	−.252
Richmond Times Dispatch	−.285
Pittsburgh Post-Gazette	−.319
Buffalo News	−.338
The Tampa Tribune	−.360

Measures and Dependent Variables

All articles were coded and assigned two scores: a prominence and a directional score.

Favorable Coverage. Articles were coded as "favorable" if they contained content that was determined to be positive coverage of the legalization of physician-assisted suicide. This included articles that portrayed physician-assisted suicide as a positive way to exert control over the way to die. These articles also suggested that the right to die in comfort should be more important than opposing Dr. Kevorkian or legislation such as the Death With Dignity Act. Furthermore, these articles saw a ban on physician-assisted suicide as discrimination against terminally ill patients who are not on life support and therefore cannot choose fatal withdrawal of treatment as an option.

Unfavorable Coverage. Articles were coded as "unfavorable" if they opposed the legalization of physician-assisted suicide by providing negative coverage of the Death With Dignity Act or Dr. Kevorkian. "Unfavorable" articles also emphasized the religious ramifications of physician-assisted suicide and compared the act to suicide, sometimes questioning whether physician-assisted suicide was ethical or "morally acceptable." Hence, many of these articles targeted the ethical dilemmas of physician-assisted suicide rather than the choice of a patient to do as they wished. "Unfavorable" articles also criticized doctors for not following guidelines for euthanasia and physician-assisted suicide and sometimes presented opinions of doctors who opposed the act. Some articles also presented depression as the only reason why those suffering from terminal illnesses would consider physician-assisted suicide. Furthermore, some articles expressed the fear that physician-assisted suicide would become standard medical care if legalized, generating pressure on the ill to accept the option.

Balanced/Neutral Coverage. Articles were coded as "neutral" if they reported on physician-assisted suicide without direction. Several perspectives of the physician-assisted suicide debate were included in these articles, including roughly equal information on the Death With Dignity Act, Dr. Kevorkian, religious beliefs, the right to choose, and the ethical debate generally. These articles sometimes contained coverage of both those who oppose and support bills designed to legalize physician-assisted suicide, at times presenting opposing points of view of physicians. After assigning directional scores, Holsti's intercoder reliability coefficient was calculated at .983.

Results

Media vectors, Pearson correlations, and regression analyses were used to test hypotheses. Media vectors varied widely from favorable to unfavorable, ranging from +.763 to –.360, illustrated in Table 3.4. Most vectors (20 of 27) were unfavorable. Five of the highest six media vectors emerge in the western United States, with the top three scores in states of the Pacific Coast.

To explore the relationship between city characteristics and variation in coverage of physician-assisted suicide, Pearson correlations were also calculated (Table 3.5).

Buffer Hypothesis Supported; Vulnerability Hypothesis Also Supported

The buffer hypothesis expected more favorable coverage of physician-assisted suicide among cities in direct proportion to the percentage of citi-

TABLE 3.5 Physician-Assisted Suicide Pearson Correlation Results

HYPOTHESIS	PEARSON CORRELATION	SIGNIFICANCE LEVEL
Percent family incomes of $100,000+	.694	.000
Poverty level	–.519	.003
Percent college-educated	.460	.008
Physicians per 100,000	.405	.020
Percent professionals	.304	.069
Percent Hispanics	.220	.135
Deaths from AIDS	.144	.236
Unemployment level	.133	.255
Health care centers	.135	.260
Percent Catholic	–.121	.278
Deaths from cancer	–.112	.289
Percent African Americans	–.102	.306
Residents 75+	–.108	.465

zens who are more privileged economically and educationally. Results confirm that the greater the percentage of families with incomes over $100,000, the more favorable the coverage of physician-assisted suicide ($r = .694; p = .000$). These families are more likely to have access to better health care and therefore information on the issue. Additionally, higher education status is also linked to favorable coverage of physician-assisted suicide ($r = .460; p = .008$). The well educated could be more aware of ways in which physician-assisted suicide could improve the quality of life when suffering from illness. Curiously, percent professionals was not significantly linked to physician-assisted suicide coverage. Additionally, the vulnerability or unbuffered hypothesis was also supported, finding that the greater the percent below the poverty level, the less favorable the news coverage of physician-assisted suicide ($r = -.519, p = .003$).

Health Care Access Hypothesis Supported, Remaining Hypotheses Not Supported

Likewise, it was expected that more favorable coverage of physician-assisted suicide would be found in cities with a high number of physicians per 100,000 residents. The Pearson correlations confirmed this hypothesis ($r = .405; p = .020$). As is the case with economically advantaged and educated individuals, a greater density of physicians in a city can be associated with a wide range of health care options. Not supported in their link with physician-assisted suicide were ethnicity, belief system, age and the incidence of specific diseases.

Regression Analysis

A multiple regression revealed that three variables accounted for 71% of the variance in their association with the media vector: percentage of families with incomes over $100,000, number of physicians per 100,000 residents, and percent residents over the age of 75. More specifically, the percentage of families with incomes over $100,000 has a correlation of .69, which accounts for 47% of the variance and illustrates the strongest relationship (Table 3.6).

Conclusion and Implications for Future Research

After the legalization of physician-assisted suicide by Oregon with the Death With Dignity Act in 1997, physician-assisted suicide was prominent on national media agendas. The issue resurfaced with the presidential election of 2000, the new Bush Administration and the debate raised by Attorney General John Ashcroft. Consequently, many articles were found during the

January 1, 1997– January 1, 2002 time period. Pearson correlations from this
sample show that greater percentages of families with incomes over $100,000,
greater percentages of college-educated residents, and greater numbers of
physicians per 100,000 residents strongly correlated with favorable coverage.
On the other hand, higher percentages of people below the poverty level
strongly correlated with unfavorable coverage. Additionally, the percentage
of families with incomes over $100,000, the number of physicians per 100,000
residents, and the percentage of residents over the age of 75 account for 71%
of the variance in association with the media vector.

Future research on this topic should explore new hypotheses including
the influence of physicians age 45+ on newspaper coverage of physician-
assisted suicide. Meier et al. (1998) concluded that age is a significant predicting factor for both physician willingness to provide assistance under current law and the receipt of a request for assisted suicide. According to the
study, "Doctors 45 years of age or older were more willing to give a lethal
injection under current legal constraints and were more likely to have
received such requests than younger doctors" (Meier et al., 1998, p. 1199).
These results are not surprising because a doctor with more experience
would logically be more trusted by his or her patients than a younger, less
experienced doctor.

Although a correlation exists between the aforementioned city characteristics and the coverage of physician-assisted suicide, this chapter does not
assert causality. Even though patterns link city characteristics with reporting
on critical events, the reasons for these patterns should be explored further,
as they are in chapter 10.

TABLE 3.6 Physician-Assisted Suicide Regression Analysis

MODEL	R (EQUATION)	R SQUARE (CUMULATIVE)	R SQUARE CHANGE	F CHANGE	SIGNIFICANCE OF F CHANGE
Income $100,000+	.689	.474	.474	18.944	.000
Income $100,000+, Physicians per 100,000	.789	.622	.148	7.808	.011
Income $100,000+, Physicians per 100,000, Residents age 75+	.844	.712	.091	5.986	.024

EMBRYONIC STEM CELL RESEARCH

Introduction

Embryonic stem cells hold enormous potential for research purposes and for the treatment of various diseases. Therapeutic cloning can help scientists more fully understand cell division and human development, which could help treat cancer, a disease resulting from abnormal cell specialization and division. Moreover, experimental drugs could be tested on stem cells before they are tested on animals or humans. Finally, embryonic stem cells could be stimulated to develop into specialized cells that would replace cells and tissues as part of the treatment of various diseases, including Parkinson's and Alzheimer's diseases, spinal cord injuries, strokes, burns, heart disease, diabetes, osteoarthritis, and rheumatoid arthritis (National Institutes of Health, [NIH], 2000a).

Because of potential benefits offered by embryonic stem cells, on August 9, 2001, President Bush announced his decision that federal funding could be allotted for research on already existing embryonic stem cell lines (Gibbs & Duffy, 2001). Bush stipulated that only those stem cells derived from embryos created for reproductive purposes (through in vitro fertilization) and obtained with informed consent, without monetary inducements, would be eligible for federal funding (NIH, 2001b).

Bush's decision generated controversy about the ethics of stem cell research. Some believe that experimenting on the human embryo is completely objectionable and accuse scientists and politicians of "playing God" (Gibbs & Duffy, 2001). In fact, "religious conservatives argue that using those stem cells means deriving benefit from the destruction of human embryos—fertilized eggs in the early stages of development—in their eyes no less a crime than abortion" (Lacayo, 2001, p. 17). Congressmen Dick Armey, Tom Delay, and J. C. Watts issued a joint statement: "It is not pro-life to rely on an industry of death" (Lacayo, 2001, p. 22). These opponents of embryonic stem cell research favor increased funding for research on adult stem cells and a complete ban on embryonic research. However, in reference to adult stem cells, the NIH cautions, "There are some significant limitations to what we may or may not be able to accomplish with them" (NIH, 2000a).

Because embryonic stem cells seem to have more potential than adult cells, others advocate increasing federal funding for this type of research. Rejecting the idea that fertilized eggs are human beings, some believe that God has not yet breathed life into these cells, so experimenting on them does not violate an ethical code. Others say that any type of embryonic stem cell research is pro-life, for the research could help find cures for various diseases. In addition, some agree with James Thomson, among the first to isolate human stem cells in 1998, who believes that because the embryos from which the stem cells are derived are slated for destruction, "I could not see that throwing them out was better" (Golden, 2001, p. 27). Those who support stem cell research believe that Bush's decision did not go far enough, especially because the 64 cell lines presumably eligible for federal funding may not be accessible because of legal issues and the high demand for the cells (Begley, 2001).

Clearly, a dichotomy of viewpoints has emerged regarding stem cell research. As a result, media have reported extensively on this topic, and this coverage merits exploration for many reasons. As observed by Weaver and Wilhoit, the media set the news agenda by telling the people what issues to consider (cited in Biagi, 1999). Furthermore, as George Gerbner theorized, media have the power to mainstream divergent viewpoints, thereby homogenizing opinion (Biagi, 1999). Using the community structure approach, it is expected that media coverage of embryonic stem cell research will be more favorable in cities with higher levels of privilege, healthcare access, and certain stakeholders, but will be less favorable in cities with other stakeholders.

Literature Review

After President Bush made his speech regarding federal funding of this research, embryonic stem cell research generated a great deal of coverage during the summer of 2001. Articles about stem cells have appeared in magazines such as *Newsweek*, *Time*, and *People*. Moreover, for the past few years, scholars in various disciplines, including biology, nursing, and sociology, have published articles about embryonic stem cells. However, little is found on the topic in communication studies journals.

In the field of biology, scholars have written a plethora of articles about stem cells, some focusing on the potential health benefits offered by embryonic stem cells (Marwick, 2001; McKay, 2000; Odorico, Kaufman, & Thomson, 2001; Perry, 2000). Friedrich (2000) explained the legal and moral controversies surrounding embryonic research. Similarly, Defrancesco (2001) focused on the way medical advances resulting from stem cell research could improve the quality of life of those battling Parkinson's disease. However, he also raised the question of whether cell therapy should be undertaken with humans (Defrancesco, 2001). Although biologists generally support the continuation of embryonic stem cell research, they also recognize complex moral questions such research generates.

The nursing field has also focused attention on stem cell research, although no consensus has been reached about moral acceptability. "Research on the cells could provide insights into fundamental questions that have puzzled embryologists for decades" (Pederson, 1999, p. 73). White (2000) delineated the legal and ethical controversies of this research, concluding that "there is no one moral stance in nursing about the status of the human embryo. . . . Individual positions vary on whether it has the status of a person from the moment of conception and whether it should be a source of stem cells" (p. 116).

Ethical issues raised by stem cell research have also been discussed by sociologists. Marc Lappe (1991) questioned the morality and acceptability of any type of research involving embryos. More recently, Irving (1999) pondered the key question of whether life begins at conception. Irving made a distinction between the origin of a human being, which she determined is an embryological question, and the origin of a human person, a matter of philosophy (Irving, 1999). Eberl (2000) takes the view that "Ensoulment (the instantiation of a human intellective soul in biological matter) does not occur until the point of implantation (of the zygote in the uterus)" (p. 134). Although they came to different conclusions, Lappe, Irving, and Eberl explored the moral dilemmas raised by conducting embryonic stem cell research.

Although the popular press and several scholarly disciplines have devoted attention to embryonic stem cell research, a search of the databases CommIndex, CommSearch, and CIOS, *Communication Abstracts,* as well as numerous other scholarly journals, reveals that the communication field has published little scholarly literature to date on media coverage of stem cell research or cloning, another controversial health topic. A notable exception is an article by Nisbet, Brossard, and Kroepsch (2003) on "Framing Science: The Stem Cell Controversy in an Age of Press/Politics." Others have drawn attention to public opinion and stem cell or cloning research (Nisbet, 2004, 2005).

However, communication scholars have explored media coverage of scientific or technology or other health topics (Nisbet et al., 2002). In 1989, for example, Payne, Ratzan, and Baukus (1989) found that there were significant differences in the amount of coverage, headlines, topics, sources, and critical commentary among newspapers that covered the Harvard Medicare Project (Ratzan & Baukus, 1989). Similarly, Fico and Soffin (1995) examined newspaper coverage of health topics such as abortion, using a content-based technique of assessing fairness and balance of newspaper coverage of controversial issues, finding that newspaper stories "favored pro-choice sources by a wide margin" (p. 627). In effect, this study showed that newspapers do not always present issues in a balanced fashion, but rather may articulate a particular perspective.

Whereas Fico and Soffin focused on the variation in coverage from one newspaper to another, and Payne et al. concentrated on the balance in a newspaper article's coverage, other researchers have investigated why these differences in coverage exist. Swisher and Reese (1992) examined the way newspaper coverage of health topics, such as tobacco-related issues, can be linked to the economy of the sample newspaper's region. Similarly, studying newspaper coverage of silicone breast implants from 1992 to 1996, before and after Dow Corning's (the implant manufacturer) public relations campaign, researchers found that the way in which the media frame an issue can be influenced by the lobbying efforts of manufacturers (Powers & Andsager, 1999). Similarly, in 2000 Andsager examined media coverage of the late-term abortion debate of 1995–1996 and concluded that special interest groups help shape the way that the media frame health issues).

It is evident that communication scholars have conducted important research about media coverage of health topics. However, the field has fallen behind other disciplines such as biology, nursing, and sociology in focusing on current, controversial issues, including cloning and embryonic stem cell research. Because newspapers are agenda-setters that frame issues but at the same time can be influenced by special interest groups and regional economies, it is important that communication scholars map variations in newspaper coverage of health policies.

Hypotheses

Hypotheses pertaining to media coverage of embryonic stem cell research can be linked to the following three cluster groups: the buffer hypothesis, health care access hypotheses, and stakeholder hypotheses.

Buffer Hypothesis

A previous study confirmed a related buffer hypothesis: The higher the proportion of privileged groups in a city, the more favorable the newspaper coverage of human cloning (Pollock, Dudzak et al., 2000). Because embryonic stem cell research could advance human rights by providing treatments for numerous diseases, it is reasonable to assume that many privileged individuals, when privilege is measured by income, education, or occupational status, will be in favor of embryonic stem cell research. Furthermore, the higher the proportion of such privileged groups in a city, the more sympathetic the expected media coverage. Specifically:

H1: *The larger the percentage of college-educated residents in a city, the more favorable the reporting on embryonic stem cell research.* (Lifestyle Market Analyst, 2001)

H2: *The larger the percentage with professional/technical occupational status, the more favorable the reporting on embryonic stem cell research.* (Lifestyle Market Analyst, 2001)

H3: *The larger the percentage of families with annual incomes of $100,000+, the more favorable the reporting on embryonic stem cell research.* (Lifestyle Market Analyst, 2001)

City size may also be correlated with favorable coverage of embryonic stem cell research. Stamm (1985) found that cities with higher quality-of-life measures are the most likely to attract educated citizens, and newspapers in these cities are more likely to evaluate issues from a plurality of viewpoints. These findings are consistent with those of Tichenor et al. (1980) in *Community Conflict and the Press*, concluding that larger communities are believed to display a greater number of group interests and perspectives than is the case with smaller communities. Because media coverage in larger cities has been shown to reflect a more diverse spectrum of viewpoints, one can speculate that city size will be correlated with relatively favorable coverage of embryonic stem cell research.

H4: *The larger the size of a city, the more favorable the newspaper coverage of embryonic stem cell research.* (http://www.census.gov/population/ estimates/metro-city/ma99-01.txt)

Health Care Access

Health care access can be measured by the proportion of the municipal budget that a city spends on health care, in addition to the availability of hospital beds and physicians. The nursing and biology disciplines as well as the NIH have published a significant amount of literature on embryonic stem cell research. Clearly, this issue is salient to health care professionals. This chapter's previous case study found a positive correlation between access to health care (physicians per 100,000 residents) and favorable newspaper coverage of physician-assisted suicide. Because availability of medical care is one index of city support for medical efforts to reduce suffering, it is reasonable to assume that coverage would be more favorable in cities with a higher percentage of healthcare access.

H5: *The greater the number of physicians per 100,000 people in a city, the more favorable the coverage of embryonic stem cell research.* (County and City Extra, 2001)

H6: *The greater the number of hospital beds per 100,000 people in a city, the more favorable the coverage of embryonic stem cell research.* (County and City Extra, 2001)

H7: *The larger the proportion of the municipal budget spent on health care, the more favorable the coverage of embryonic stem cell research.* (County and City Extra, 2001)

Stakeholders

Clearly, the presence of stakeholders can influence media coverage of critical events. (See chap. 7 for fuller development of the "stakeholder" hypotheses.) The stakeholders in the embryonic stem cell controversy can be categorized under the following subdivisions: political affiliation, individuals who are Catholic, and individuals who engage in devotional reading.

Political Partisanship. There may be a link between the voting patterns of the residents of the city and newspaper coverage of critical events. For example, Pollock, Tanner, and Delbene (2000) found that the higher the percentage of individuals voting Republican in the 1996 presidential election, the more favorable the coverage of the privatization of social security. Newspapers in cities with larger populations voting Democratic in 1996 also displayed more favorable coverage of the Master Settlement Agreement reducing tobacco advertising, whereas newspaper in cities with a higher Republican population displayed more negative coverage of the agreement (chap. 4). Similarly, researchers found more favorable coverage of the Patients' Bill of Rights in populations with a higher proportion of Democrats and more negative coverage in cities with higher proportions of Republicans (chap. 5). Other community structure studies found more favorable coverage of trying juveniles as adults in cities with a higher proportion of Republicans, whereas newspaper coverage was less favorable in cities with a higher proportion of Democrats (chap. 7). Thus, media framing seems to be linked to the political perspectives of the majority of the citizens in a particular area. Because, according to an ABC News-Beliefnet poll, 76% of liberals support embryonic stem cell research, whereas only 44% of conservatives are in favor, it is reasonable to assume that newspaper coverage will reflect these differences (*Pittsburgh Post-Gazette*, 7/15/01).

> **H8:** *The greater the proportion of those voting Democratic in the 1996 presidential election, the more favorable the newspaper coverage of embryonic stem cell research.* (County and City Extra, 2001)

> **H9:** *The greater the proportion of those voting Republican in the 1996 presidential election, the less favorable the newspaper coverage of embryonic stem cell research.* (County and City Extra, 2001)

Belief System: Catholics and Devotional Reading. A previous study using the community structure approach found that the higher the percentage of Catholics in a city, the lower the newspaper support for elective abortion (Pollock, Robinson & Murray, 1978). The Catholic Church is vehemently opposed to abortion (Hurst, 1993), and Pope John Paul II urged President Bush to reject embryonic stem cell research, stating, "A free and virtuous society, which America aspires to be, must reject practices that devalue and violate human life at any stage from conception to natural death" (Yang, 2001). Therefore, it would be reasonable to assume that many Catholics condemn embryonic stem cell research, and newspaper reporting in cities with high proportions of Catholics could vary accordingly.

> H10: *The greater the proportion of Catholics in a city, the less favorable the newspaper coverage of embryonic stem cell research.*
> (Catholic Almanac, 2003)

Individuals who engage in frequent devotional reading can be expected to hold relatively traditional views regarding the origins of life. Accordingly, they and the newspapers they read may be opposed to embryonic stem cell research.

> H11: *The greater the proportion of individuals engaged in devotional reading in a city, the more negative the newspaper coverage of embryonic stem cell research.* (Lifestyle Market Analyst, 2001)

Disease Stakeholders: Deaths From Alzheimer's Disease and Cancer. Family members of those who died from Alzheimer's Disease or cancer, among a number of aliments, are most likely very concerned about their own prognosis because these diseases have a strong hereditary component. Not only are these individuals candidates for the disease themselves, but they have also endured the suffering of watching loved ones die. Nancy Reagan, a pro-life supporter, is an example of someone who might not have been in favor of embryonic stem cell research if her husband, former President Ronald Reagan, had not died from Alzheimer's, a disease that stem cell research could potentially cure. It is reasonable to assume:

> H12: *The higher the number of deaths from Alzheimer's disease in a city, the more favorable the coverage of embryonic stem cell research.* (Health and Healthcare in the United States, 2000)

> H13: *The higher the number of deaths from cancer in a city, the more favorable the coverage of embryonic stem cell research.* (Health and Healthcare in the United States, 2000)

Methodology

This study investigated the time period following the date President Bush made his speech, August 9, 2001, through March 31, 2002, after which the frequency of coverage dropped noticeably. Using the Lexis-Nexis database, a national cross-section of all articles containing at least 150 words or more were collected from 15 U.S. newspapers, yielding 199 articles (see Table 3.7 for newspaper names).

Measures and Dependent Variables

After "prominence" scores were calculated for all articles, each article was evaluated for "direction"

Favorable Coverage: Articles were coded favorable that offered positive coverage and supported Bush's decision regarding federal funding of embryonic stem cell research. Coverage of this kind also promoted potential health benefits and discussed diseases and/or disorders that may be cured as well as urging expansion of the research.

TABLE 3.7 Embryonic Stem Cell Research Media Vectors

TCH NEWSPAPER	MEDIA VECTOR
Capital Times (Madison, WI)	.314
San Francisco Chronicle	.270
Pittsburgh Post-Gazette	.250
Milwaukee Journal-Sentinel	.246
Denver Post	.235
Boston Globe	.191
Telegraph Herald (Dubuque)	.148
Cincinnati Post	.122
Houston Chronicle	.117
Plain Dealer (Cleveland)	.072
Virginia Pilot (Norfolk)	.060
Commercial Appeal (Memphis)	.040
Baltimore Sun	.018
St. Louis Post-Dispatch	.000
Omaha World Herald	.000

Unfavorable Coverage: Articles were coded unfavorable if they failed to mention any health benefits of embryonic stem cell research. Unfavorable content offered no support for research and instead discussed the ethics and morality of the debate.

Neutral Coverage: Articles were coded as neutral if they appeared to report on stem cell research without a particular direction. This coverage is clearly unbiased. If there is a mention of health benefits attention is also drawn to the ethical debate. Articles that only gave background on Bush's speech or stem cell research itself were also coded as neutral.

After the articles had been given directional scores by researchers, Holsti's coefficient of intercoder reliability was measured at .87. Combining both prominence and direction scores, media vectors, Pearson correlations, and multiple regression correlations were calculated.

Results

All embryonic stem cell research newspaper media vectors were favorable or neutral and ranged from 0 to +.314. Southern papers sampled were found in the least favorable half of the total list of media vectors.

Newspapers were individually ranked according to their media vectors. Pearson correlations were calculated to explore the link between city characteristics and coverage variations. Of the 15 correlations, 6 were negative. Table 3.8 details this summary.

Buffer Hypothesis Supported

According to the buffer hypothesis, cities with higher proportions of economic, educational, and professional privilege are expected to yield more favorable coverage of embryonic stem cell research. As the Pearson correlations revealed ($r = .617$; $p = .009$), proportion of college graduates proved significant at the .01 level. Perhaps higher level education instills an appreciation of the contributions of scientific methods and their link to improved public health. However, although college proved a significant factor, the proportions of families with incomes over $100,000 and of people with professional occupational status did not prove significant in the Pearson correlations ($r = .250$; $p = .194$ and $r = .376$; $p = .013$, respectively). These findings were somewhat surprising because there are high correlations among college education, family income, and professional/technical occupational status.

TABLE 3.8 Embryonic Stem Cell Research Pearson Correlations

HYPOTHESIS	PEARSON CORRELATION	SIGNIFICANCE LEVEL
Percent college educated	.617	.009**
Percent devotional reading	−.556	.019*
Percent voting Republican	−.481	.046*
Percent voting Democratic	.471	.048*
Physicians per 100,000	.450	.052*
Percent professional	.376	.103
Percent Catholic	.361	.102
Percent family income $100,000+	.250	.194
Cancer deaths	−.207	.230
Alzheimer's deaths	−.135	.316
Percent municipal budget on health care	−078	.391
Hospital beds per 100,000	−.002	.498
City size	.001	.499

*Significant at .05 level; **Significant at .01 level

Stakeholder Hypotheses Supported: Devotional Reading, Political Partisanship, Physicians

It was anticipated that the higher the percentage of specific stakeholders in a city, the more favorable the media coverage of that group's interests would be. Pearson correlations confirmed this expectation for three stakeholder hypotheses focusing on devotional reading, political partisanship, and physician density.

The most significant stakeholder correlation found that the greater the proportion of individuals engaged in devotional reading in a city, the more negative the newspaper coverage of embryonic stem cell research ($r = -.556$; $p = .019$). Perhaps more devout readers are likely to believe that the embryo is already human and therefore deserves protection afforded human life. Such a traditional view might be uncomfortable with the possibilities that embryonic stem cell research could provide. (The number of Catholics in a city, however, did not register significance.)

The proportion of those voting Republican ($r = -.481$; $p = .048$) and those voting Democratic ($r = .471$; $p = .052$) were also significant in predicting that political partisanship in a city is linked to newspaper coverage. Among all of the health care access or disease stakeholder hypotheses, only one was found significant. As predicted, the number of physicians per 100,000 people was linked positively with favorable coverage of embryonic stem cell research ($r = .450$; $p = .046$). Presumably, the more support a community gives to physicians, the more comfortable it is with the explorations or emerging medical technologies. Other indicators of medical access that did not prove significant included the number of hospital beds per 100,000 in a city as well as percent of municipal spending on health care. Similarly, the number of deaths directly related to Alzheimer's disease as well as cancer did not prove significant at the .05 level ($r = -.135$; $p = .316$ and $r = -.207$; $p = .230$). This may be attributed to the circumstance that embryonic stem cell research has not yet shown concrete cures for these diseases in humans, and that it may be some time before they do.

Regression Analysis: College Education is Key Characteristic

After running a multiple regression of variables to measure their variance in association with the media vector, only percent college educated remained significant, with a correlation of .603, accounting for 36% of the variance. Regression analysis strongly reinforces the buffer hypothesis linking in particular one measure of privilege, education, with newspaper support for embryonic stem cell research (Table 3.9).

Conclusion and Implications for Future Research on Coverage of Embryonic Stem Cell Research

Media coverage of embryonic stem cell research was substantial during the period sampled. Although there was limited coverage prior to President Bush's August 9 speech, the president's words may have awakened the nation at large to this emerging health issue. Results from Pearson correlations point to the significance of privilege (in particular college education),

TABLE 3.9 Embryonic Stem Cell Research Regression Analysis

MODEL	R (EQUATION)	R-SQUARE CUMULATIVE	R-SQUARE CHANGE	F CHANGE	SIGN. OF F CHANGE
College	.603	.364	.364	5.721	.038

political partisanship and physician density. In the regression analysis, percent college educated proved the most powerful variable, yielding 36% of the variance. One of this study's limitations deserves acknowledgment. Newspaper searches were limited to examining only those large city papers available on Lexis-Nexis and Dialog. Access to other databases might have enabled researchers to sample a wider variety of newspapers, in particular newspapers from more medium-sized and smaller cities.

Finally, although there may be a correlation between the specified city characteristics and coverage of this topic, this analysis does not assert causality, discussed in Chapter 10. Although any combination of factors could have contributed to variation in newspaper coverage of embryonic stem cell research, there is a clear link between city characteristics and newspaper coverage of this issue.

4

THE VIOLATED BUFFER HYPOTHESIS

Privilege Linked to Unfavorable Reporting on Threats to Existence or a Way of Life

Although the buffer hypothesis helps explain the link between levels of privilege in a city and reporting on human rights claims, a complementary proposition, the violated buffer hypothesis, helps explain the link between levels of privilege in a city and reporting on "ominous" issues: Those that contain biological threats or threats to a cherished way of life. Such issues can include topics that represent literal concerns about mortality and death, illustrated in the community structure study finding that the higher the percent of families with annual incomes of $100,000 or more in a city, the markedly less favorable the reporting on allowing women in combat positions, linking privilege and reporting framing women in combat negatively as a threat to a cherished way of life ($r = -.962; p = .000$) (Pollock, Mink et al., 2001). Similar "violated" perspectives are found in coverage of disease, such as reporting on HIV/AIDS—for example, Magic Johnson's HIV announcement (Pollock, Awrachow, & Kuntz, 1994); banning tobacco use among children; or efforts at gun control since the massacre at Columbine High School in Littleton, Colorado.

Ominous issues can also refer to imminent challenges to a traditional or predictable way of life. For example, new technology such as the Internet can imperil existing social and educational privileges because Internet use gives far more direct access to information to many more people than any technology has ever provided before. This perception was confirmed in a nationwide study of newspaper coverage of the Internet from 1993 to 1995, finding that the higher the proportion of educated citizens in a city, the less favorable the newspaper coverage of the then emerging Internet phenomenon (Pollock & Montero, 1998).

The following three case studies illustrate the relation between relative privilege in a city and less favorable (or unfavorable) coverage of individuals or issues threatening existing social and political arrangements: disease (the Master Settlement Agreement [MSA] banning tobacco ads targeting children); proposed Internet censorship; and the Supreme Court decision in the 2000 presidential election stopping the vote counting in Florida, effectively substituting judicial judgment for majority rule.

NATIONWIDE NEWSPAPER COVERAGE OF THE 1998 TOBACCO MASTER SETTLEMENT AGREEMENT

Introduction

In November 1998, the attorneys general from 46 states, Washington, DC, and five U.S. territories signed the MSA with five major tobacco companies. Worth $206 billion over the next 26 years, the agreement imposed some restrictions on tobacco advertising, marketing, and promotion, as well as providing payments to the states based on approximated tobacco-related Medicaid expenditures and the number of smokers in each state. However, the MSA does not specifically propose or restrict how states spend the money. Four other states, Florida, Minnesota, Mississippi, and Texas, individually settled with the tobacco industry for more than $40 billion.

Although each state will spend its part of the settlement differently, the majority of states have allotted a portion of their funds for health-related concerns. One of the central concerns about these different spending patterns is that the federal government may try to recover some of the money to cover Medicaid expenditures instead of using the funds for anti-tobacco and other public health programs. State governors and attorney generals would naturally be opposed to federal oversight of their funds, preferring instead to decide for their own states how money can best be appropriated.

To measure the outcome of systematic efforts to reduce smoking, one evaluation component has been the mapping of media coverage of smoking regulation. Analyzing the content of media coverage has drawn attention for at least two reasons, one related to media agenda-setting, the other to public understanding and involvement. In 1991, the American Stop Smoking Intervention Study (ASSIST) was initiated to prevent and reduce tobacco use primarily through policy-based approaches to alter the sociopolitical environment, such as encouraging policies and legislation or increasing coverage of tobacco-related issues in the media. One of the goals of the ASSIST program has been to develop a "media advocacy score" to evaluate how successful groups interested in tobacco control have been in persuading media to place tobacco issues high on media "agendas" (Stillman et al., 2001).

A second reason media coverage has received increasing attention is associated with concerns about health consciousness and community participation (Dutta-Bergman, 2004) and the accessibility and salience of tobacco issues for media audiences. Previous research has confirmed the failure of media to present health-related issues in ways the public can use. Jamieson and Capella (1995) documented the media focus on "horserace" or "strategic" concerns about health care legislation in the early 1990s, paying relatively little attention to substantive health issues. Also focusing on health care legislative issues in 1993, Walsh-Childers et al. (1999) conducted a content analysis of major national and regional papers and concluded that relatively little information was presented that consumers, health professionals or business owners could use. A specific paper analyzing nationwide newspaper coverage of the MSA revealed a missed opportunity for public health involvement for citizens. Newspapers mostly covered legislative and litigious aspects of the MSA, seldom showing the direct relevance of the proposed agreement to public health concerns (e.g., regulation of youth access to tobacco or banning vending machines; Stillman et. al., 2001).

This case study seeks to further efforts to understand media coverage as a "surveillance" tool, moving beyond the "mapping" of content analysis patterns to test how closely media coverage is "linked" to social and political contexts, specifically a wide range of city demographics that might help shape journalists' perspectives on tobacco. Using a community structure approach, it is expected that cities with higher levels of college graduates would be associated with relatively favorable news coverage of the MSA because of more widespread concern about tobacco's harmful effects. Other city characteristics typically explored include income, physician access/availability, and the relative strength of a variety of "stakeholders," for example, families with children.

Literature Review

It is clear that media can play varied, influential roles in "framing" critical public health issues of any kind, documented in studies of coverage of Magic Johnson after his November 7, 1991 HIV announcement (Payne & Mercuri, 1993), the Harvard Medicare Project (Payne et al., 1989), controversial issues including abortion (Fico & Soffin, 1995), the 1994 health care reform debate (Jamieson & Capella, 1995), "Mad Cow Disease" (Ratzan, 1997, 1998, 2001), and efforts at tobacco control (Clegg Smith et al., 2002). Indeed, exploring issue "framing" is now an established subfield in communication research, an alternative to viewing reporting bluntly polarized as either "biased" or "objective" (Reese, 2001).

Regarding the MSA in particular, although newspapers and magazines seem to have covered the issue, studies published in research journals are scarce. A thorough examination of the databases CommIndex, CommSearch, and CIOS, *Communication Abstracts*, and numerous other journals turned up only a few articles relevant to the MSA. There does exist a substantial amount of research conducted on related issues, such as public opinion and smoking, tobacco regulation, tobacco and public relations, tobacco and the media, and so on. An article from the 1997 volume of the *Journal of Social Issues* described the legislative and regulatory history of tobacco control efforts, introducing a puzzle that is central to the debate over tobacco control. The article states that "the principal conundrum is how to regulate a product that is lethal when used as intended, but remains legal for most people over eighteen years of age" (Anderson, Jacobson, & Wasserman, 1997, p. 75).

Several major positions on the MSA emerge. Some are content with the MSA because it is reallocating tobacco profits to help pay for medical expenses. Others are disappointed because the MSA bestows power on the tobacco companies to withhold money if a particular state attempts to raise a cigarette tax. In addition, still others criticize the MSA for being unconstitutional, as it punishes the makers of cigarettes despite the circumstance that cigarettes are a legal product.

Given the variety of positions available, it is reasonable to expect different media frames or perspectives on the MSA in different areas of the nation. A study published in the 1992 volume of *Journalism Quarterly* specifically addressed how newspaper coverage from different regions varies in support of tobacco, focusing on the correspondence between tobacco involvement in the local economy and the type of coverage given to tobacco-related issues. The major findings in this article reveal slight headline slant in support of tobacco in highly tobacco-involved economies and in "use of tobacco industry sources in major smoking-related stories" (Swisher & Reese, 1992, p. 987).

Targeting specific audience demographics is explored in other articles. A study in a 1991 volume of *Health Communication* tracks the ways tobacco companies target their products to selected audience demographics. A content analysis of 10 popular magazines demonstrated that Black- and youth-oriented publications have received an increasing number of tobacco advertisements since 1965 (Basil et al., 1991). Bergen and Caporaso's (1999) article in the *Journal of the National Cancer Institute* suggests links between varying demographics and local city paper coverage of the MSA. For example, "Current smoking in the United States is positively associated with younger age, lower income, reduced educational achievement, and disadvantaged neighborhood environment" (p. 1365). Additionally, a study quoted in an April 1996 issue of *Marketing News* pointed out certain demographics of smokers; specifically, children between the ages of 10 and 18 account for about 90% of new smokers in the United States (Pollay et al., 1996).

Another article in the 1991 volume of *Health Education Research* further supports these themes. After analyzing 901 billboards in San Francisco commercial neighborhoods, the number of cigarette and alcohol billboard ads found in Black/Hispanic neighborhoods was found to be significantly higher than those found in white or Asian neighborhoods (Altman, Schooler, & Basil, 1991).

Similarly, an article in the 1991 volume of *Public Opinion Quarterly*, titled "Self-Interest and Public Opinion Toward Smoking Policies: A Replication and Extension" confirms an inverse relationship between support for smoking restrictions and cigarette consumption. By contrasting the categories of "Smoke status" versus "Smoke bother," it was concluded that "both measures of self interest clearly and significantly relate to attitudes toward smoking restrictions and tobacco sales tax" and also "self-interest is a factor influencing opinions on smoking policy" (Dixon, Lowery, Levy, & Ferraro, 1991, p. 241).

The 1997 volume of the *Journal of Social Issues* contains an article titled "Tobacco Farming and Public Health: Attitudes of the General Public and Farmers," explaining how tobacco farmers and tobacco farming communities have "become a key factor in opposition to public health policies" (Altman, Levine, Howard, & Hamilton, 1997, p. 113). The article also lists states that are top producers of tobacco in the country.

It is obvious that over the years, different groups have held varied views on tobacco regulation. According to conventional wisdom, this would suggest that the latest regulation, the MSA, should also be a crucible for contrasting media viewpoints. Because our nation's congress has not created a statute completely banning cigarettes to protect its citizens, yet is willing to limit advertising for cigarettes and increase taxes on the industry, and because states are willing to accept $206 billion from the industry, the MSA is an issue that definitely evokes differing opinions. This case study measures systematically newspaper coverage of the MSA in a cross-section of several major cities throughout the United States.

Hypotheses

Several hypotheses concerning the MSA can be categorized into the following three clusters: privilege (violated buffer hypotheses), vulnerability, stakeholders (including life-cycle position, political partisanship, and ethnic identity) and health care access.

Privilege: Violated Buffer Hypotheses

One nationwide study on the coverage of tobacco and tobacco-related issues suggests that as the proportion of privilege in cities increases, news reporting concerning tobacco advertising targeting children becomes less favorable (Pollock, Nisi et al., 1999). In the language of this collection of community structure studies, this represents a violated buffer hypothesis, an instance where privileged groups in a community may believe that their own lifestyles or children's health (indeed, the health of all children of every socioeconomic status) are threatened. To the extent that newspapers mirror the concerns of privileged groups, reporting perspectives should be less favorable to the tobacco industry. Because the MSA deals with the threat of tobacco, it is believed that the higher the proportion of privileged groups in cities (when privilege is measured by income, education or occupational status), the more favorable the news coverage of the MSA.

A similar study conducted on coverage of Magic Johnson's HIV announcement, revealing striking health vulnerability for even economically successful Americans, linked relative privilege in a city to less favorable coverage of the basketball star (Pollock et al., 1994). Consistently, a nationwide newspaper coverage study of the Internet confirmed the "violated buffer" hypothesis, using education level as a measure of privilege, and linking it with less favorable coverage of the Internet in its early years, 1993–1995 (Pollock & Montero, 1998). Accordingly, it is expected that those with the privilege of higher education have the same relationship to coverage of the MSA as those who are economically and professionally privileged.

> **H1:** *The higher the proportion of city residents with annual family incomes of $100,000 or more, the more likely a city newspaper is to report favorably on the MSA.* (Lifestyle Market Analyst, 1998)

> **H2:** *The larger the percent with a higher level of education (college graduates of 4-year programs), the more favorable the reporting on the MSA.* (Lifestyle Market Analyst, 1998)

> **H3:** *The larger the percent with professional occupational status, the more favorable the reporting on the MSA.* (Lifestyle Market Analyst, 1998)

Vulnerability: Unbuffered Sectors

In contrast to those who have a high level of privilege are those who struggle to survive despite unemployment. Normally, newspapers do not target these groups, as they are not substantial newspaper readers. Yet, related community structure studies have also found links between one measure of vulnerability, poverty level, and nationwide variations in coverage of *Roe v. Wade* (favorable coverage) and coverage of ethnic conflict in Queens,

New York City (less inflammatory) (Pollock et al., 1978; Pollock & Whitney, 1997).

Those who are unemployed and/or dealing with poverty may fear the effects tobacco has on their bodies and could therefore be in favor of the MSA, which provides substantial aid to those afflicted with tobacco-related diseases. From another perspective, however, a study by Bergen and Caporaso (1999) indicates that one of the current patterns is for people with lower incomes to smoke. From a "stakeholder" perspective, this suggests that the higher the percentage of people with low income in a given city, the more favorable the coverage of tobacco. People who smoke may not want their access to tobacco to be limited via regulations on tobacco advertising or other restrictions. Conventional wisdom hints that many people live in the present and would therefore focus more on the tobacco they are using now rather than their potential health problems in the future. Accordingly:

H4: *The higher the percent unemployed in a city, the less favorable the newspaper coverage of the MSA.* (County and City Extra, 1998)

Stakeholder Hypothesis

Three "stakeholder" perspectives are forwarded, concerning life-cycle position, political partisanship, and ethnic identity.

Life-Cycle Position. In addition to reflecting a city's economic well being, a newspaper is also likely to accommodate the life-cycle responsibilities of citizens. If a city contains many families with children, it seems reasonable that the city's newspaper would give relatively favorable coverage to the MSA, which has reduced the tobacco industry's advertising and also allotted money for public anti-smoking campaigns to deter children from starting the habit. Nationwide studies using the community structure approach have found that the proportion of stakeholders in a community is often linked to relatively favorable coverage of their interests or concerns: The higher the percent of a city's population that is self employed, the less favorable the coverage of the 1997 UPS strike (Pollock, Dudzak, Spina, & Lemire, 2000) and higher percents of women in the work-force, a stakeholder category, are linked to relatively favorable newspaper coverage of human cloning and of the Eappens, the parents of the child shaken to death by the "British nanny" (Pollock, Dudzak et al., 2000; Pollock, Citarella, Ryan, & Yulis, 1999).

In the case of the MSA, families with children are likely to be concerned about tobacco companies aiming advertisements toward children. Although all families with children are presumed to be stakeholders for the MSA, families with children at considerable risk of smoking (families with children ages 12–18) are considered especially strong stakeholders and are according-ly assigned a specific hypothesis. Therefore:

H5: *The higher the percentage of families with children under 13 in a city, the more favorable the coverage of the MSA.* (Lifestyle Market Analyst, 1998)

H6: *The higher the percentage of families with children ages 12–18 in a city, the more favorable the coverage of the MSA.* (Lifestyle Market Analyst, 1998)

Political Partisanship. Political partisanship has been confirmed in another nationwide community structure study as associated with reporting on political change. The higher the percent voting Republican in the 1996 presidential election, the more favorable the newspaper coverage both of privatization of social security (Pollock, Tanner, & Delbene, 2000) and of trying juveniles as adults (chap. 7). The MSA and similar tobacco agreements have proven potent political issues for both Democrats and Republicans. Republicans have traditionally opposed tobacco settlements, whereas Democrats have typically been in favor of these agreements, a pattern found later in efforts by the U.S. Food and Drug Administration (FDA) to regu-late nicotine. Coverage of the Supreme Court's 2000 denial of FDA author-ity in that endeavor was aligned precisely with party voting strength in each city, in predictable directions (Caamaño, Virgilio, Lindstrom, & Pollock, 2001). Therefore:

H7: *The higher the percentage of Republican voters in a city, the less favorable the coverage of the MSA.* (Country and City Extra, 1998)

H8: *The higher the percentage of Democratic voters in a city, the more favorable the coverage of the MSA.* (Country and City Extra, 1998)

Ethnic Identity. Another important aspect of MSA coverage is report-ing associated with ethnicity. Bergen and Caporaso's 1999 article on trends in tobacco usage points out that smoking is on the rise among Blacks, Whites, and Native Americans. A Surgeon General's 1998 report on smok-ing and health published in the *Journal of the American Medical Association* found that cigarette smoking prevalence increased in the 1990s among African Americans and Hispanics after several years of substantial decline (US Surgeon General's Report, 1998). It seems plausible that those who smoke most might not be in favor of the MSA, as they might not wish a symbolic part of their lifestyles challenged. Therefore:

H9: *The higher the percentage of African Americans in a city, the less favorable the coverage of the MSA.* (Country and City Extra, 1998)

H10: *The higher the percentage of Hispanics in a city, the less favorable the coverage of the MSA.* (Country and City Extra, 1998)

Health Care Access

It seems reasonable that cities with a high regard for citizen health would print more articles relatively favorable to the MSA. This could be measured by looking at city characteristics such as the proportion of the municipal budget spent on health care, and availability of hospital beds and physicians. The higher the proportion of any of these indicators of access to health care, the more favorable the expected coverage of the MSA because the MSA is one more way of protecting the health of citizens. Observing this, conventional wisdom hints that a city with high access to health care would report news concerning the MSA favorably. Specifically:

H11: *The greater the proportion of the municipal budget devoted to health care, the more favorable the coverage of the MSA.* (Country and City Extra, 1998)

H12: *The higher the number of physicians per 100,000 people in a city, the more favorable the coverage of the MSA.* (Country and City Extra, 1998)

H13: *The higher the number of hospital beds per 100,000 people in a city, the more favorable the coverage of the MSA.* (Country and City Extra, 1998)

Methodology

Sample Selection

This study examined coverage of the MSA systematically in 14 major newspapers representing a geographical cross-section of the United States (see Table 4.1). All of the longest articles (more than 150 words in length) printed in each of the papers were sampled from the period of January 1, 1997 through April 1, 2000, for a total of 281 articles. January 1, 1997 through November 1998, when the MSA was signed, was a period of substantial debate over the issues raised by the MSA. Additionally, because it is important to explore the effects the MSA has had, articles up to 18 months

TABLE 4.1. Tobacco MSA Media Vectors

NEWSPAPER	MEDIA VECTOR
The Seattle Times	.278
St. Louis Post Dispatch	.168
The Philadelphia Daily News	.155
Star Telegram (Fort Worth)	.148
The Times-Union (Albany)	.129
Rocky Mountain News (Denver)	.035
The Phoenix Gazette	.016
The Plain Dealer (Cleveland)	–.009
The Atlanta Journal/ Constitution	–.064
The Times-Picayune (New Orleans)	–.097
Charlotte Observer	–.101
Democrat (Tallahassee)	–.172
The Wichita Eagle	–.178
Lexington Herald-Leader	–.222

after the signing of the MSA were examined. The articles were collected via the DIALOG Classroom Information Program newspaper database available in college libraries.

Measures and Dependent Variables: Article Prominence and Direction

Each of the articles was assigned a "prominence" score and a "direction" score. Recent content analysis research has yielded a multiplicity of tobacco-related "frames" displayed in media (Clegg Smith et. al., 2002). This analysis, however, reduces framing options to one of three choices, specifically:

Favorable. Articles were coded as "favorable" if they exhibited content that was determined to be generally positive coverage of the MSA. These articles included praise of lawyers during the settlement, descriptions of benefits of the settlement (e.g., money for health care), money for anti-smoking campaigns, reduced youth smoking, reduced persuasive advertising aimed at teens, and so on. Articles that described the money from the MSA as being allocated toward weaning tobacco farmers off of their current occupation and articles that accentuated the lies and deception of the tobacco industry and tended to describe the MSA as a solution for the future were also considered "favorable."

Unfavorable. Articles coded as "unfavorable" commonly omitted positive aspects of the MSA and included attributes that are negative. Examples of negatively coded articles included those that accentuated the MSA's ambiguity, and those that described the lack of mandating where state governments should allocate the new money. Other "unfavorable" articles satirized the MSA by suggesting that states sued the tobacco industry for health care costs and now can use the money for highways, prisons, environmental cleanup, or anything else not intrinsically related to the debate. Articles accentuating the clause included in the MSA stipulating that if tobacco companies go bankrupt or if tobacco companies become less profitable then states receive less money were considered "unfavorable." Additionally, coded "unfavorable" were articles proposing that the MSA could be unconstitutional because tobacco is a legal product, and government efforts to protect people should ban it altogether instead of reducing its advertising rights further and extracting money from the tobacco industry.

Other examples of unfavorably coded articles were those that highlighted the mayhem of political arguments or ambiguity in the MSA surrounding the possible uses of this money windfall for states. Any articles noting that overseas tobacco import profits, earned by hurting the health of foreigners, will only now translate into health care for domestic patients underscored an unfairness imbedded within the MSA and were thus coded as "unfavorable" as well.

Balanced/Neutral. Articles that reported on the MSA debate evenhandedly were coded as "balanced/neutral." These articles did not stray from the facts in the debate and allowed the reader to come to his or her own conclusions. Facts that aid the arguments of several differing camps of thought regarding the MSA were fully represented in balanced/neutral articles, including the perspectives of tobacco farmers, politicians, or everyday citizens. After one of three directional codings was assigned to each article, Holsti's coefficient of intercoder reliability was calculated at .87.

Results

After media vectors were calculated, Pearson correlations and regression analyses were run. Newspaper coverage of the MSA during the period of January 1997 to April 2000 varied considerably, with media vectors ranging from +.278 to −.222. Table 4.1 displays the media vector variations, with least

TABLE 4.2. Tobacco MSA Pearson Correlations

HYPOTHESIS	PEARSON CORRELATION	SIGNIFICANCE LEVEL
Percent families with annual incomes of $100,000+	.634	.007**
Percent of population with a college education	.574	.016*
Percent of people who voted Democratic	.434	.060
Percent of people who voted Republican	−.428	.064
Percent professional	.420	.067
Percent city finances spent on health and hospitals	−.368	.098
Hospital beds per 100,000 people	−.323	.130
Percent African American	−.320	.133
Percent unemployed	.304	.145
Percent Hispanic	.234	.210
Percent families with children 12 to 18	−.222	.223
Number of physicians per 100,000 people	.079	.394
Percent of families with children under 13	−.007	.490

* Significant at .05 level, one-tailed.
** Significant at .01 level, one-tailed.

favorable coverage of the MSA overwhelmingly found in the southern part of the nation, the region with the largest economic dependence on tobacco.

The newspapers were ranked according to each city's media vector, and then Pearson correlations were run to explore the association between city characteristics and variation in reporting on the MSA (Table 4.2).

Violated Buffer Hypothesis Supported

The violated buffer hypothesis expected more favorable coverage of the MSA among cities in direct proportion to the percentage of citizens who are more privileged economically, educationally, and professionally. Although tobacco use can affect citizens of every resource level, results indeed show that higher percentages of a population with income over $100,000 correlates with more favorable newspaper coverage of the MSA ($r = .634$; $p = .007$). Additionally, there was a similarly positive correlation between the percent population with a college education and favorable coverage of the MSA ($r = .574$; $p = .016$). Consistently, percent of professionals yielded a directional correlation ($r = .420$; $p = .067$). Although coverage was linked significantly to measures of privilege, it was not associated with a measure of underprivilege. Testing the unbuffered hypothesis, newspaper coverage did not become more negative with an increase in percent unemployed ($r = .304$; $p = .145$). Political partisanship revealed only nonsignificant, "directional" (though predicted) results. Democratic voting corresponded with directionally favorable coverage ($r = .434$; $p = .060$), Republican voting with directionally negative coverage ($r = -.428$; $p = .064$).

Regression Analysis

A regression of the variables revealed that percent with family income greater than $100,000 and percent African American were significant at the .05 level or better and together account for 58% of the variance in their association with the media vector. In particular, the percentage of families with income greater than $100,000 has a correlation of .63, accounting for 40% of the variance, illustrating the strongest relationship, as shown in Table 4.3.

Conclusions and Implications for Future Research

Pearson and regression correlations strongly confirm the violated buffer hypothesis: The higher the proportion of privilege (especially income and education) in a city, the less positive the expected media coverage of biological threats or threats to a cherished way of life. Because tobacco use is now

TABLE 4.3. Tobacco MSA Regression Analysis

MODEL	R EQUATION	R SQUARE (CUMULATIVE)	R SQUARE CHANGE	F CHANGE	SIGNIFICANCE OF F CHANGE
Income $100,000+	.634	.401	.401	8.046	.015
Income $100,000+, Republican	.713	.508	.107	2.384	.151
Income $100,000+, Republican, Percent African American	.827	.683	.175	5.530	.041

seen as threatening the children of the privileged as well as the nonprivi-leged, negative coverage of the tobacco industry and relatively favorable coverage of the MSA are expected. That is precisely what was found. The enduring potency of "privilege" throughout correlation and regression analysis procedures reinforces confidence in the validity of the violated buffer hypothesis.

That hypothesis parallels the assertions of the guard dog hypothesis articulated by Olien et al. (1995), asserting that media function less often as watchdogs against abuses of power, or even as lap dogs totally subservient to the wishes of dominant elites, than as "guard dogs," alert to challenges to the position or privilege of dominant elites, even willing to embarrass or criticize some powerful interests that, through their actions, could discredit the presumptive legitimacy of dominant elite coalitions. The tobacco indus-try's stonewalling and withholding of evidence has discredited the assertion that corporations are necessarily willing to act in the public interest. Because the tobacco industry's behavior is an embarrassment to corporations in gen-eral, according to the guard dog hypothesis, media are willing to challenge that industry's statements and intentions in the interests of guarding the authority and reputation of prevailing dominant groups.

In the language of this study, when a "critical event" (e. g., far-reaching tobacco ads targeting children) reaches violated buffer proportions, media—in this case newspapers—give themselves permission to criticize the corpo-ration or group that has brought discredit on an entire sector or industry. It would be productive if future research were to explore the conditions under which corporations or leading institutions are not only scrutinized by media, but also pursued with enormous investigative zeal (e.g., as in the case of ENRON). In this way, it might be possible to specify "threshold points" beyond which media turn from the modesty of critical inquiry to a crusad-ing fixation on whatever an industry might do that is insensitive or harmful to the public interest.

NATIONWIDE NEWSPAPER COVERAGE
OF PRIVACY ON THE INTERNET

The Issue

The Internet has grown enormously since it was originally introduced to the public for use at home in the late 1980s. As a result, many businesses found it lucrative to move into this new medium as a means of attracting new cus-tomers and improving the accessibility of their products or services, thus creating one of the Internet's primary uses: e-commerce. However, as this e-commerce rapidly increased, the question of user privacy came to the forefront. Internet privacy involves the access and availability of personal information over the World Wide Web (WWW). This information can include home addresses, phone numbers, credit card data, e-mail addresses, social security numbers, and so on. Computer users worldwide fear this information falling into the wrong hands and being used improperly. This anxiety is the result of a myriad of computer "evils" such as electronic mass mailings (spamming), telemarketing, credit card theft, and viruses. These abuses of privacy on the Internet are growing daily.

Different opinions exist about ways to prevent these types of problems from occurring. Some believe that the problems can be remedied through the addition of new rules. Such regulations would help govern the use and transmission of information over the WWW, primarily centering on consumer privacy, the main focus concerning "cookies." *Cookies* are defined as small pieces of information sent by a web server to store on an individual computer to be accessed at a later time. It is useful for storing specific types of information such as logins and passwords, Web site preferences, and purchasing information on a commercial site. Access to these bits of data can have staggering repercussions if they fall into the possession of pernicious predators.

In contrast, others argue that information on the Internet should not be restricted. For these individuals, the current state of the Internet is acceptable. Access to information, whether personal or commercial, is not subject to government control. They consider it an individual's right to use the Internet as a tool for gathering information for personal and commercial use. They simply see personal information as a part of the greater whole. To some extent, these people are less concerned about the ramifications of improper retrieval of sensitive material than they are about universal access.

It is highly probable that the Internet privacy issue will receive varying newspaper coverage from city to city based on computer usage and demographics. The demographic areas likely to be linked to differences in coverage include income level, age, education level, and occupational status. Computer usage can refer to types of tasks that the Internet is used for, as well as others. Differences in age demographics linked to coverage variations are likely because nearly 80% of children using the Internet will divulge personal information without first consulting with their parents or another adult (Teinowitz, 1998).

In summary, Internet privacy is a significant issue because the entire nation as a whole is rapidly becoming increasingly computer-dependent. With this dependency, the idea that information is available, and at times easily accessible, fosters a two-sided debate over whether regulation is necessary to control the Internet's misuse. Some are threatened by the prospect of invasion of their lives, worried that their personal information is accessible to millions. However, others are less concerned with these issues, viewing the Internet more as a valuable tool for exploring different ideas. In order for this tool to function properly, they believe regulation must be kept to a minimum.

A Review of Communication Literature

As an important contemporary information highway, the Internet is missing essential features of reliability, functionality, confidentiality, and integrity, and it is also threatened by various security attacks (Fischer-Hubner, 1998). If the proper safeguards and programs are not in place, many risks are associated with providing a site with personal information. These risks have caused a split in the computer community, spawning a heated debate among its users.

The main focus seems to be whether or not regulation is necessary for the Internet truly to be considered a safe medium. It seems evident that this issue has received a substantial amount of mass media coverage. However, investigation of various communication journals suggests limited concern for the issue of Internet privacy in the scholarly communication field. Although numerous articles focus on the Internet itself, few tend to include the issue of personal privacy linked to Internet use. A search of the keywords *internet and privacy*, using the online index EbscoHost and scans of various communication journals, yielded only two results. Entering the same search criteria using the Communication Institute for Online Scholarship's (CIDS) *Communication Abstracts* database, only five articles were located. These five articles included topics ranging from Internet privacy in a "global information society" (Fischer-Hubner, 1998) to the "embedding of identity issues in a more commercial Internet," but none linked Internet privacy and media.

Broadening the search parameters on *Communication Abstracts* to include all articles with the word *Internet* was useful in gauging the topic's prevalence. This strategy returned 204 articles, however the majority failed to cover any aspect of Internet privacy or the security risks of online data transfer. For example, one article from the *Journal of Broadcasting and Electronic Media* discussed factors that affect Internet use (Papacharissi & Rubin, 2000) and another focused on links among internet satisfaction and community participation (Dutta-Bergman, 2005), yet it failed to concentrate on the privacy issue. Additionally, even fewer focus on the Internet and links to newspaper coverage. A survey conducted by Stempel, Hargrove, and Bernt (2000) dealt with levels of Internet use and their association with a decline in television audiences and newspaper circulation, but this examination did not mention the element of Internet privacy.

One article dealing with Internet privacy (Lyon, 1998) explored different aspects of Internet surveillance such as employee monitoring, policing and security, and marketing. It focused on some technologies associated with Internet privacy including Cookies and Spiders, but the article lacked information on *media coverage* of privacy. Allard (1999) discussed the framework for national and international policies relating to Internet privacy but did not link the concept to media coverage. Yet another article studied "the extent to which heavy users of the Internet and other non-traditional media differ from heavy users of traditional media in their knowledge of the issue stances of Bill Clinton and Bob Dole" in the 1996 presidential campaign (Johnson, Braima, & Sothirajah, 1999, p. 99). Although this article illuminated the issue of the Internet's connection to other media coverage, it lacked the component of personal privacy on the WWW. A noticeable pattern in the communication field emerges: Internet privacy is an important and critical issue, but there is little interest among communication scholars regarding Internet privacy and its links to media coverage.

Exploring other literatures on media coverage of *Internet* privacy, several journals were examined in business, marketing, law, technology, and government. As expected, many articles dealt with the specific topic of Internet privacy. A second search on EbscoHost, reading beyond communications journals, with the keyword *internet*, returned more than 5,000 hits. A more refined search, *Internet and privacy*, displayed 62 hits. Another search on the Wilson Web Database, searching a spectrum of peer-reviewed literature, using the keywords *Internet and privacy*, yielded more than 100 articles. Although the majority of these pieces did not take into account media coverage of the issue, the prevalence of this topic confirms widespread interest in Internet privacy.

From a business/marketing standpoint, this issue seems clearly pertinent. A case study in the *Journal of Interactive Marketing* concerns how the Federal Trade Commission (FTC) alleged GeoCities had "engaged in unfair or deceptive practices under Section 5A of the Federal Trade Commission Act" by disclosing customers' personal information to advertisers and others (Roberts, 2000, p. 70). In a related article, the online book retailer Amazon.com "revamped its privacy policy, eliminating users' ability to block the 'e-tailer' from sharing data about their purchases and browsing patterns with others" (Borrus, 2000, p. 54).

In the area of government, there is substantial interest in Internet privacy. Presently, the FTC is responsible for attempts to regulate the Internet, and some articles focus on legislation and regulations in progress. An article in *Congressional Quarterly Weekly* (Ota, 1999) discussed the FTC's proposal for legislation requiring online firms to protect the security of any online information they gathered. Another regulatory article in *The Economist* noted that many individual states have already passed or in the process of passing privacy legislation, alarming many Internet companies "who fear they will have to deal with different standards set in each different state" ("Privacy on the Internet," 2000, p. 65).

The technology field yields abundant articles on Internet privacy, ranging from guidelines established by the Clinton administration (*IEEE Spectrum*, 1999) to the development of security methods on the web (Rubin & Geer, 1998). An article in *IEEE Technology & Society Magazine* discussed a specific Internet privacy technology, the "key escrow encryption system" (Davis, 2000). Most technological journal articles explained the risks and possible consequences directly associated with personal privacy on the Internet. Two articles in the *Communications of the ACM* explained how disclosing personal information affects every type of Internet user, from students in school (Weinstein & Neumann, 2000) to online shoppers (McGinty, 2000). Examining a wide spectrum of journals, it is evident that more research is needed on media coverage of Internet privacy.

Hypotheses

Community structure hypotheses concerning Internet privacy can be organized into two distinct clusters: violated buffer and stakeholders (life cycle position, personal computer [PC] use and political partisanship).

Violated Buffer

Taking into account indicators of privilege such as percentage of the population with professional/technical occupational status, the proportion of families with incomes $100,000 or more, it is possible to postulate a relationship between these city characteristics and newspaper coverage of Internet privacy. The privileged, in the case of Internet privacy, may consider government control of Internet privacy a potential threat to their personal access to information. Although the government contends it is securing personal information, the more educated may perceive the government as having too much control. Consequently, this supports a violated buffer hypothesis because privileged groups are at great risk, threatened with the loss of a cherished way of life if personal information falls into unwanted hands. Therefore, it is believed that high proportions of professionals, as well as families with incomes of $100,000+ in a city, will be linked to relatively negative coverage of Internet privacy regulation. Consistently, media coverage of Magic Johnson's HIV announcement confirmed the violated buffer pattern, in which his announcement created a new perceived vulnerability for Americans with high economic status (Pollock et al., 1994).

Research concerning early nationwide newspaper coverage and the Internet reinforced a similar violated buffer hypothesis, using education level as a measure of privilege (Pollock & Montero 1998). It is expected that the educationally privileged have the same relationship to coverage of Internet privacy as the economically and professionally privileged.

H1: *The higher the percentage of families with incomes of $100,000 or more, the less favorable the coverage of Internet privacy regulation.* (Lifestyle Market Analyst, 2000)

H2: *The higher the percentage of people with four years of college education the less favorable the coverage of Internet privacy regulation.* (Lifestyle Market Analyst, 2000)

H3: *The higher the percentage of people with professional or technical occupations, the less favorable the coverage of Internet privacy regulation.* (Lifestyle Market Analyst, 2000)

Stakeholders

At least three stakeholder measures, life-cycle position, PC use, and political partisanship, can be linked to media perspectives on Internet privacy.

Life-Cycle Position.

Families With Children of Different Ages

Individuals of families with different levels of responsibility for children occupy distinct positions in the life cycle. Compared with others, families with children have special responsibilities, including protecting children from external danger, in particular the hazards of Internet use. Children are relatively willing to divulge sensitive or personal information online (on consumer Web sites, in chatrooms, etc.). Protective parents may welcome legislation guarding children, especially younger ones, from pernicious external influences, as well protecting the privacy of personal information.

H4: *The higher the percentage of families with children, the more favorable the coverage of Internet privacy regulation.* (Lifestyle Market Analyst, 2000)

H5: *The higher the percentage of families with children ages 5 to 7, the more favorable the coverage of Internet privacy regulation.* (Lifestyle Market Analyst, 2000)

H6: *The higher the percentage of families with children ages 8 to10, the more favorable the coverage of Internet privacy regulation.* (Lifestyle Market Analyst, 2000)

H7: *The higher the percentage of families with children 11 to 12, the more favorable the coverage of Internet privacy regulation.* (Lifestyle Market Analyst, 2000)

H8: *The higher the percentage of families with children ages 13 to 15, the more favorable the coverage of Internet privacy regulation.* (Lifestyle Market Analyst, 2000).

H9: *The higher the percentage of single-parent families, the more favorable the coverage of Internet privacy regulation.* (Lifestyle Market Analyst, 2000)

Senior Citizens

Another factor included in this cluster is senior citizens, more specifically those over the age of 75. A study of nationwide newspaper coverage of Dr. Jack Kevorkian between 1990 and 1993 found that the greater the proportion of individuals over the age of 75, the more supportive the news coverage of Dr. Kevorkian's efforts to publicize the physical concerns of older citizens (Pollock, Coughlin et al., 1996). Those in this age category are likely to have less Internet savvy and be more concerned about their loss of privacy on the Internet. A study of articles printed between 1993 and 1997 showed a correlation between this age group and less favorable newspaper reporting on legalization of physician-assisted euthanasia (Pollock & Yulis, 2004). Accordingly:

H10 *The higher the percentage of people age 75+, the more favorable the coverage of Internet privacy regulation.* (Lifestyle Market Analyst, 2000)

PC Use. Most computer owners are aware of risks and dangers of today's computer technology. Computers sold back as far as the mid-1990s have come pre-installed with modems and trials to online subscription services, allowing direct access to the Internet. With this technology, the door is open for personal information to be "broadcast" across the WWW. Increasingly, computer users for the most part can be assumed to have some Internet capabilities.

Internet-based merchandising has emerged in the last few years and continues to gain popularity. The concept of being able to order essentially any item from practically anywhere from the comfort of your home has revolutionized the way people purchase products. This new technology brings with it various risks concerning the access to a customer's personal information (i.e., credit card data, social security numbers, address, phone numbers, etc.). Internet consumers are less timid in sending out personal information for online transactions, but they may also be worried about threats of improper use and distribution of this information. As such, the majority of PC users may have a vested interest in the protection of Internet privacy.

H11: *The higher the number of PC users in a city, the more favorable the coverage of Internet privacy regulation.* (Lifestyle Market Analyst, 2000)

Political Partisanship. Under President Clinton, Democrats primarily sided with Internet companies self-regulating their privacy policies. Republicans by contrast tended to agree with the FTC's assessment that "self-regulation alone [is] not enough to protect consumers' online privacy" (Rosen, 2000, p. 3). They typically evoke four distinct principles when discussing the need for privacy legislation: notice, choice, access, and security. Republicans often view legislation as the most logical remedy for Internet privacy issues. As a result:

H12: *The higher the percentage of Democrats in a city, the less favorable the coverage of Internet privacy regulation.* (Lifestyle Market Analyst, 2000)

H13: *The higher the percentage of Republicans in a city, the more favorable the coverage of Internet privacy regulation.* (Lifestyle Market Analyst, 2000)

Methodology

Twenty-one papers were examined over a 5-year period, ranging from January 1996 to January 2001 on coverage of Internet privacy regulation. All the articles included in the sample mentioned the words *privacy* and *Internet* or any synonym such as the World Wide Web, the Net, or information superhighway as the subject of discussion. Any article more than 350 words that dealt with Internet privacy was included in the sample, yielding 495 articles. If a paper's article count exceeded 25, then a random sample of the articles was taken, using a program[1] developed by Paul Houle on www.randomizer.org, to achieve the maximum number of 25.

---

[1]The Research Randomizer on www.randomizer.org uses an adaptation of the Central Randomizer program developed by Paul Houle.

For this sample, several newspapers were selected for their geographic dispersion and for their availability on the DIALOG Computer Information Program.

Prominence and direction scores were measured or coded. Each article's content was evaluated as "favorable," "unfavorable," or "balanced neutral" toward issues concerning privacy on the Internet:

- Coverage that was considered favorable toward Internet privacy regulation reported on existing dangers that currently threaten privacy on the Internet. These articles called for government legislation to protect privacy on the Web and expressed a general fear of private information falling into the wrong hands.
- Coverage unfavorable toward Internet privacy regulation did not support the idea of government regulation of the Internet. The tone of these articles suggested that the current measures taken to monitor information were satisfactory, and information currently transacted over the Web was relatively well protected.
- Coverage that was considered balanced or neutral toward Internet privacy gave basic information concerning the issue, emphasizing neither the positive or negative attributes of the Internet and the privacy concerns attached to it.

Results

Media Vectors ranged from +.211 to -.137. Of the 21 newspapers studied, the majority of the coverage on Internet privacy regulation were balanced/neutral. Only a handful of the cities could be considered significantly favorable/unfavorable. Both the *Boston Globe* and the *Cincinnati Enquirer* showed slightly positive coverage of the issue, whereas the *San Francisco Chronicle* had negative coverage of this topic. Table 4.4 lists the cities and their corresponding media vectors ranked from highest to lowest:

Thirteen city characteristics (See Table 4.5) were used as independent variables to assess the association between city structure and newspaper coverage of Internet privacy regulation. The most significant was percent of technical/professional occupations, linked to negative coverage of Internet privacy efforts ($r = -.372$; $p = .048$). Although not technically significant, most of the correlations regarding families with children revealed that, in a directional sense, the younger the children in a family, the more favorable the coverage of Internet privacy regulations.

Regression Analysis

In the case of the Internet privacy regulation, regression analysis (see Table 4.6) reveals that professional/technical occupational status accounts for 22% of the variance. No other variable is significant in the regression equation.

It may not be surprising that percent professional and percent families with children are negatively correlated, as illustrated in Table 4.7.

TABLE 4.4. Internet Privacy Media Vectors

NEWSPAPER	MEDIA VECTOR
Cincinnati Enquirer	0.211
Boston Globe	0.201
St. Louis Post-Dispatch	0.149
(Memphis) *Commercial Appeal*	0.101
(Portland) *Oregonian*	0.080
Detroit Free Press	0.072
San Jose Mercury News	0.060
Tallahassee Democrat	0.060
Milwaukee Journal Sentinel	0.048
Kansas City Star	0.046
Pittsburgh Post-Gazette	0.041
(Albany) *Times-Union*	0.037
Denver Post	0.022
Phoenix Gazette	0.017
Seattle Times	0.014
Charlotte Observer	0.010
Fresno Bee	0.003
Atlanta Journal/Constitution	0.000
Lexington Herald-Leader	−0.029
Philadelphia Inquirer	−0.039
San Francisco Chronicle	−0.137

TABLE 4.5. Internet Privacy Pearson Correlations

HYPOTHESIS	CORRELATION	PROBABILITY
Technical/professional	−0.372	0.048*
Families w/ children 8–10	0.334	0.070
Families w/ children 11–12	0.328	0.073
Income of $100,000+	−0.321	0.078
Families w/ children 13-15	0.295	0.097
Age (75 and over)	0.227	0.161
Families w/ children 5-7	0.198	0.195
Single parents	0.181	0.210
Republican	0.174	0.225
Computer users	−0.168	0.233
Families w/ any children	0.161	0.243
College educated	−0.131	0.286
Democrat	−0.102	0.330

*Significant at < .05

TABLE 4.6. Internet Privacy Regression Analysis

MODEL	R	CUMULATIVE R	R SQUARE	F CHANGE	SIG. F CHANGE
Percent professional/ technical	.47	22.09	22.09	8.139	.007

TABLE 4.7. Professional Occupations Negatively Linked to Families With Children

CITY CHARACTERISTIC	CORRELATION WITH PERCENT PROFESSIONAL	PROBABILITY
Percent families w/ children 11–12	-.532	.006
Percent over 75 years	-.468	.016
Percent families w/ children under 18	-.418	.030
Percent below the poverty line	-.312	.084

Violated Buffer Hypothesis Confirmed

The city characteristic of technical/professional occupations was significantly correlated with coverage opposing legislation on Internet privacy. Although not significant, a "directional" relationship was also similar. Like professional occupations, income level is associated negatively with Internet privacy regulation ($r = -.321$; $p = .078$). Together, these findings suggest that those who are of greater socioeconomic status are linked to media perspectives viewing government intervention in this area as a threat to their way of life, affirming the violated buffer hypothesis. This pattern may reflect a "lifestyle autonomy" hypothesis, suggesting that those in privileged occupations consider themselves capable of understanding the Internet as a system, with little need for government regulation. Perhaps professionals tend to be more familiar with the Internet and how it operates, including the risks involved as well as ways of avoiding them.

Although the connection is not direct, it supports other research concerning Magic Johnson and his positive HIV announcement (see chap. 8). In that study, a violated buffer also existed because the more privileged in a city no longer felt guarded or separate from the HIV virus. If it was possible for Magic Johnson to acquire this disease, then anyone could. In a similar fashion, the privileged in a city could feel intimidated by the government's role in Internet privacy regulation. Perhaps an "invasion" perspective emerges, suggesting that once government is able to control the Internet there is no limit to its ability to control personal information exchange, and those with professional status and high income may view this circumstance as threatening.

Three out of the six city characteristics concerning families with children yielded directional results. The specific categories that showed these results were families with children ages 8–10 years ($r = .334, p = .070$), 11–12 years ($r = .328, p = 073$), and 13–15 years ($r = .295, p = .097$). These directional findings are consistent with the "lifecycle" hypothesis that the higher the percentage of families with children, the more favorable the coverage of Internet privacy, suggesting support for shielding children in the form of strict Internet regulation regarding personal privacy and information exchange. These results resemble research conducted on the Elian Gonzalez story, in which the proportion of families with children ages 5–7, a life cycle measure, was linked strongly with favorable newspaper coverage of his proposed repatriation to his father in Cuba (Mink, Puma, & Pollock, 2001). Curiously, several city characteristics had no significant or directional relationship to coverage of Internet privacy, including, strikingly, percentage of computer users and political affiliation.

Conclusion

This study found a significant relationship between a particular city characteristic, occupational status, and coverage of Internet privacy regulation. Suggestions for further research include expanding the number of cities represented in the study and exploring other time frames. The stakeholder hypothesis could be expanded to include rate of Internet use, such as hours per week, as well as percentage subscribing to an Internet service provider (ISP). By broadening the spectrum of newspapers and cities and adjusting the sampled time frame, further studies may reveal other correlations between city characteristics and newspaper reporting.

BUSH VERSUS GORE: NATIONWIDE NEWSPAPER COVERAGE OF THE US SUPREME COURT DECISION "STOPPING THE VOTE COUNTING" IN FLORIDA IN THE 2000 PRESIDENTIAL ELECTION

Introduction

The U.S. Supreme Court made history in December 2000 by awarding Bush the presidency without acknowledging the validation of every citizen's vote. It is questionable whether the decision was a breach of justice. Al Gore supporters would say that the U.S. Supreme Court's partisan decision denied thousands of Florida citizens the right to exercise their vote. On the other hand, Bush supporters could argue that it was time for America to make a decision.

It is arguable that the 2000 presidential election between Gore and Bush was more a duel between Democrats and Republicans than an exercise in popular democracy. As a result of this division, a president assumed office who wasn't elected by popular vote. The U.S. Supreme Court made a ruling that will affect our nation for many years. Controversial court decisions such as *Roe v. Wade* could be affected with the newly elected conservative president. Major economic and foreign policy decisions have been influenced, especially in the areas of taxation, funding for programs that reduce inequality and a sea-change foreign policy shift approving pre-emptive war. Everyday lives have been irrevocably changed because of this controversial outcome.

It is worthwhile exploring the role of media in this controversy. Major media play a substantial role educating citizens about political parties, candidates, and their plans for the country and are key players in "framing" issues for public discussion and opinion formulation. It is especially useful to study how demographics are related to media coverage. It is reasonable, for example, to expect that cities with higher percentages of Republican voters would treat the ruling in Bush vs. Gore more favorably than cities with a majority of Democratic voters. It can also be predicted that cities with higher minority populations would manifest less favorable coverage of Bush vs. Gore.

This study compares newspaper coverage from different cities to measure how the same decision was reported in cities throughout the nation. This analysis will illuminate, according to one observer, "the Supreme Court's conservative majority, who were supposedly acting as referee in a race, stuck out a foot, tripped one of the contestants and then said, 'Too bad. You didn't cross the finish line in time'" (Levine, 2000, p. H5).

Scholarly Articles and Communication Literature: Results of Bush vs. Gore Search

Research was conducted in communication journals and online databases for articles dealing with the Supreme Court's decision in the case of the 2000 presidential election. However, little significant information concerning Bush vs. Gore and the media's coverage of the Supreme Court's final decision was documented in scholarly communication literature. The most pertinent information regarding the topic was found in sources indexed in political, economic, and business literature.

A search via the Communication Institute for Online Scholarship (CIOS) and other databases such as ComAbstracts, ComIndex and ComSearch, using key terms such as "media and court decisions," "media and politics" and "press and politics" resulted in little relevant information regarding the Supreme Court. Journals pertaining to communication research, such as *Journalism & Mass Communication Quarterly*, *Political Communication*, and *Southern Communication Journal* were also searched. Terms such as "media and supreme court," "media and politics," "politics and election," and "press and politics" provided little data. A useful article was written for *Political Communication* by Daron Shaw, titled 'The Impact of

News Favorability and Candidate Events in Presidential Campaigns" (1999). Some information was unavailable on Bush vs. Gore in communication journals because of its recent occurrence. These results were nevertheless unsettling due to the importance Bush vs. Gore has for the communication field.

Although information on the Supreme Court and media was scarce in communication literature, articles were readily available in electronic periodicals and political journals. Ebscohost is an online database that provides access to more than 2,100 electronic journals published in the past 4 years. A broad search with the key terms "press and politics," "media and politics," "judges and media," and "Supreme Court and count" revealed thousands of matches. A *Humanist* article titled "Media Myopia and the Future of Democratic Politics," like many articles found, faulted the media for confusion that coincided with the Bush vs. Gore case (Buell, 2001). The article suggested "Florida became almost as much of a badge of shame to the media mavens as it was a legal crisis for the Bush and Gore camps" (p. 35). Problems with the election were partially blamed on media.

A search with online political science databases and journals using key terms such as "media and politics" or "Supreme Court and media coverage" yielded seven matches. For example, the May 1998 edition of a political journal, *Current*, contained the article "Cast a Cautious Eye on the Supreme Court," suggesting that a journalist's duty is to emphasize the "wide separation of 'politics' and 'law'"; media should not act as the Supreme Court's publicist but rather as educators for the public (Kennedy, 1998).

Expansive background research on the media's role in the Supreme Court's final decision in Bush vs. Gore or the Supreme Court and media generally revealed little information in communication literature.

This case study is an effort to redress the imbalance by studying the relationship between city demographics and newspaper coverage of the Supreme Court decision in Bush vs. Gore. Political and social interest groups have exercised substantial power through their public involvement and have been important catalysts influencing the outcomes of highly debated issues. Influential "stakeholders" may include such groups as Republicans and Democrats, women, minorities, and homosexuals (Demers & Viswanath, 1999). By recognizing that many factors influence change on critical issues and by incorporating the community structure approach, this study maps the relation between local city characteristics and media coverage of the highly controversial Supreme Court ruling to stop counting votes in the 2000 presidential election.

Hypotheses

Community structure approach hypotheses fall into three cluster groups, including stakeholders, violated buffer, and vulnerability.

Stakeholders

The "stakeholder" categories of partisanship, age, gender, and ethnicity are relevant. For example, in previous research it has been shown that the larger the number of organizations or businesses marketing their products or services to the gay community in a city, the more favorable the newspaper coverage of the efforts to legalize same-gender marriage (Pollock & Dantas, 1998). Additionally, proportions of stakeholders such as senior citizens have been linked, respectively, with relatively positive coverage of Dr. Kevorkian, and negative coverage of legalization of physician-assisted euthanasia (Pollock, Coughlin et al., 1996; Pollock & Yulis, 2004).

Partisanship. It is obvious that Bush vs. Gore is a partisan issue. Florida's predominately Democratic Supreme Court declared that all the votes should be counted, a ruling that favored the Democratic candidate, Al Gore. Yet the Republican dominated U.S. Supreme Court ruled that time was up for the counting of hand ballots because the United States needed a president. That decision handed the presidency to Republican candidate George W. Bush.

Predictably, a key division of public opinion on the Supreme Court decision was between Bush supporters and Gore supporters. Ninety-three percent of Bush supporters agreed with the Supreme Court ruling, whereas 81% of Gore supporters disagreed (Moore, 2000). Partisanship was found an important factor in the community structure studies of Social Security reform and a Patients' Bill of Rights (Pollock, Tanner, & Delbene, 2000; Chapter 5). Consequently, it is reasonable to expect that there may be a correlation between the proportion of those citizens in a city who voted Republican or Democratic in the 1996 presidential election and favorable newspaper coverage of the decision. Thus:

H1: *The higher the percentage of those in a city who voted Republican in the 2000 presidential election, the more favorable the coverage of the Supreme Court's decision to halt the counting in Bush vs. Gore.* (County and City Extra, 2002)

H2: *The higher the percentage of those in a city who voted Democratic in the 2000 presidential election, the more unfavorable the coverage of the Supreme Court's decision to halt the counting in Bush vs. Gore.* (County and City Extra, 2002)

Age. Other differences in reaction to the Supreme Court decision are found regarding age. According to a Gallup Poll released December 14, 2000, Americans under age 50 disagreed with the Court's decision, whereas older Americans took the opposite point of view (Moore, 2000). Other studies linking community structure to reporting on social change have revealed that percent of a city population 75 or older can be associated with distinct reporting on Dr. Kevorkian, physician-assisted suicide, and trying juveniles as adults (Pollock, Coughlin et al., 1996; Pollock & Yulis, 2004; Chapter 7). Therefore:

> **H3:** *The higher the percentage of citizens age 75+ in a city, the more favorable the coverage of the Supreme Court's decision to halt the counting in Bush vs. Gore.* (Lifestyle Market Analyst, 2000)

Gender. Gender is another area where there may be different evaluations of Bush vs. Gore. Men tend to favor the ruling, whereas women are split evenly (Moore, 2000). Working women of 2000 might have been threatened by the GOP's conservative views on issues such as opposing legalization of the "morning after" abortion pill. Consistent with gender concerns, another community structure study confirmed a link between percent women in the workforce and relatively favorable newspaper coverage of human cloning (Pollock, Dudzak et al., 2000).

Independent working women tend to favor the more liberal presidential candidate to help ensure their rights as women. This has been seen in every presidential election since 1980. The gender gap is a relatively strong feature of contemporary politics (Bowman, 2000). Indeed, women, as a whole, tend more often to vote Democratic, whereas men are generally more likely to vote Republican (Bowman, 2000). Accordingly:

> **H4:** *The greater the percentage of working women in a city, the less favorable the newspaper coverage of the Supreme Court's decision to halt the counting in Bush vs. Gore.* (County and City Extra, 2000)

Ethnicity. The liberal views of the Democratic Party correspond with issues that many minorities face. For example, Pollock, Robinson, and Murray (1978) found a positive correlation between a high percentage of Black population in a city and pro-choice abortion coverage. Thus:

> **H5:** *The greater the percentage of African Americans in a city, the more unfavorable the newspaper coverage of the Supreme Court's decision to halt the counting in Bush vs. Gore.* (County and City Extra, 2000)

> **H6:** *The greater the percentage of Hispanics in a city, the more unfavorable the newspaper coverage of the Supreme Court's decision to halt the counting in Bush vs. Gore.* (County and City Extra, 2000)

Privilege: Violated Buffer

The violated buffer hypothesis predicts that the higher the percentage of privileged groups in a city, the less favorable the reporting on either biological threats or threats to an established way of life. Examining indicators of privilege—such as percent college educated, percent population with professional/technical occupational status, and percent of households with annual income over $100,000—suggests a relationship between these city characteristics and newspaper coverage of the Bush vs. Gore U.S. Supreme Court decision.

Since the U.S. Supreme Court decided to stop the counting of ballots in Florida, one could argue that the civil rights of voters throughout the United States were violated because all the votes in Florida were not acknowledged. According to a Gallup poll released January 16, 2001, only 42% of Democrats approved of the job the Supreme Court is doing, in comparison to a August 2000 poll, in which 70% of Democrats approved. These results suggest that Democrats thought differently about the U.S. Supreme Court after its controversial role in the 2000 presidential election and would argue that the decision was not based on sound legal reasoning, but on partisanship, because Republican appointees hold a majority on the U.S. Supreme Court 7–2. This is particularly evident in the knowledge that lower income areas, which tend to vote Democratic, tended to use punch-card ballots compared to the machine-read ballots available in higher income areas, which tend to vote Republican. Because the U.S. Supreme Court chose to stop the counting before a final decision was reached, it prevented a number of the punch-card ballots that needed to be recounted from being acknowledged.

The decision made by the U.S. Supreme Court led some to question the integrity of the institution. A number of newspapers and lawyers throughout the nation were shocked by the U.S. Supreme Court's intervention. Substantial numbers of citizens feared that the U.S. Supreme Court, an institution obligated to uphold justice, had manipulated the political system. If the U.S. Supreme Court itself could be so clearly partisan, then there was little hope for fairness elsewhere. Although the economically and educationally privileged may have voted for Bush, their faith in the system may have been somewhat shaken by the U.S. Supreme Court decision, leaving a sense of vulnerability and concern that the ruling posed a threat to a cherished way of life. Therefore:

H7: *The higher the percent college graduates, the more unfavorable the coverage of the Supreme Court's decision to halt the counting in Bush vs. Gore.* (Lifestyle Market Analyst, 2000)

H8: *The higher the percent employed in professional/technical operations, the more unfavorable the coverage of the Supreme*

Court's decision to halt the counting in Bush vs. Gore. (Lifestyle Market Analyst, 2000)

H9: *The higher the percent families with annual incomes of $100,000 or more, the more unfavorable the coverage of the Supreme Court's decision to halt the counting in Bush vs. Gore.* (Lifestyle Market Analyst, 2000)

Vulnerability

It is reasonable to expect that those living below the poverty line and the unemployed would generally oppose the U.S. Supreme Court's decision to stop the counting. Gore's liberal platform, which supported welfare and tax cuts for the middle to lower classes, would have directly benefited those "unbuffered" stakeholders. Bush's platform was economically conservative and favored tax cuts for the upper middle to upper classes. The partisanship of the U.S. Supreme Court decision threatened both the future of households that fall below the poverty line and the unemployed in a city. Thus:

H10: *The higher the percent of households that fall below the poverty level, the more unfavorable the coverage of the Supreme Court's decision to halt the counting in Bush vs. Gore.* (County and City Extra, 2000)

H11: *The higher the percent unemployed, the more unfavorable the coverage of the Supreme Court's decision to halt the counting in Bush vs. Gore.* (County and City Extra, 2000)

Methodology

Sample Selection

The Supreme Court decision on Bush vs. Gore was studied in 21 major newspapers nationwide (see Table 4.8). The time period ranged from December 9, 2000 to March 31, 2001, representing a period when the subject of Bush vs. Gore assumed major importance. This sample included all relevant articles of 150 words or more in length within the sampled time frame, collected from the DIALOG Classroom Information Program, yielding 494 newspaper articles. Newspapers in Florida or Texas were omitted because of the pro-Bush biases associated with those states, each of which had elected a son of George H. W. Bush, the 41st president, as governor. Even though Tennessee is the home state of Al Gore, it was included in the sample because the vice president failed to win it.

TABLE 4.8. Bush vs. Gore Media Vectors

NEWSPAPER	MEDIA VECTOR
Grand Forks Herald	.192
Baton Rouge Advocate	.082
Commercial Appeal (Memphis)	.036
Buffalo News	.011
Milwaukee Journal Sentinel	−.011
Arizona Republic (Phoenix)	−.013
Dayton Daily News	−.028
San Diego Union-Tribune	−.080
Seattle Times	−.100
Lexington Herald Leader	−.101
Pittsburgh Post	−.101
Albany Times Union	−.112
Denver Post	−.114
Detroit Free Press	−.116
Boston Globe	−.122
St. Louis Post Dispatch	−.133
Charleston Gazette	−.168
Augusta Chronicle (ME)	−.174
San Francisco Chronicle	−.186
Philadelphia Inquirer	−.206

Prominence, Direction, and Media Vectors

Prominence scores were calculated, and article directional scores were assigned by three different coders as favorable, unfavorable, or balanced neutral toward Bush vs. Gore. Coverage considered *favorable* to Bush vs. Gore included those articles viewing this decision positively. Articles were also deemed favorable when a majority of the text contained positive aspects and viewpoints concerning Bush vs. Gore. Coverage *unfavorable* to Bush vs. Gore included articles that focused on negative coverage of the Supreme Court's decision. Articles were also deemed unfavorable to the Bush vs. Gore decision when the majority of the text focused on negative consequences of the decision. *Balanced/neutral* coverage included articles that displayed both sides of the debate over Bush vs. Gore in approximately equal measure, or revealed a disinterested, unbiased outlook, raising issues about Bush vs. Gore without making a clear judgment. After the collected articles were assigned their directional scores, a Holsti's coefficient of inter-coder reliability was calculated at .92. After media vectors were calculated, Pearson correlations and multiple regressions were run.

Results

Varied Coverage, Mostly Negative

Media vectors ranged from +.192 to –.206, demonstrating that newspaper coverage of this issue varied throughout the nation. Most coverage of the Supreme Court decision was unfavorable. Of the 21 papers studied, 4 exhibited favorable coverage, whereas 17 scored negatively.

Violated Buffer Confirmed by Pearson and Regression Analysis; Partisanship Less Important

Pearson correlations yielded strong correlations linking negative newspaper coverage of the Supreme Court decision of Bush vs. Gore with several specific demographic variables (Table 4.9). The largest correlations confirm the violated buffer hypothesis, linking privilege to dissatisfaction with the Supreme Court: the percentage of college graduates in a city ($r = -.596$, $p = .002$), and families with annual incomes of over \$100,000 ($r = -.508$, $p = .009$). Other significant results follow partisan expectations: the percentage of people who voted Democratic in the 1996 election ($r = -.474$, $p = .015$), and the number of people who voted Republican in the 1996 election ($r =$

TABLE 4.9. Bush vs. Gore Pearson Correlations

VARIABLE	PEARSON CORRELATION	SIGNIFICANCE
College graduates	–.596	.002**
Income of \$100,000+	–.508	.009**
Democrats	–.474	.015*
Republicans	.414	.031*
Working women	–.304	.090
Professional/technical	–.272	.116
75+ years	–.206	.185
Poverty line	.166	.236
Hispanic	–.159	.246
Unemployed	–.138	.275
African American	–.045	.423

*Significant at .05 level; **Significant at .01 level

.414, p = .031). No other significant correlations were found using Pearson correlations. Using multiple regression, only one variable was significant: percent college graduates, accounting for 25% of the variance (Table 4.10).

Discussion: Privilege More Important Than Partisanship

Overall, the pattern in newspaper coverage was unfavorable to the Supreme Court's decision. Four significant results emerged, supporting the violated buffer and stakeholder hypotheses. The percentage of college graduates and percentage of households with annual incomes over $100,000 are linked to unfavorable coverage of the Supreme Court's decision to halt the counting, thus supporting the violated buffer hypothesis. Although the Supreme Court decision to halt the vote counting was widely regarded as a "partisan" event, reported as dividing Republican and Democrats nationwide in public opinion polls, newspaper coverage tended to reflect more precisely the concerns of relatively privileged groups.

The result is a curious paradox. Although privileged groups are widely regarded as favoring Bush and the Republican party generally, the very same groups are linked to relatively negative coverage of the Supreme Court decision that made Bush's ascension to office possible. Perhaps newspapers in this instance reflected less the obvious immediacies of political partisanship than long-term concerns with the perceived legitimacy of both presidential elections and Supreme Court proceedings generally. As a result, the community structure approach has illuminated a link between privilege and reporting previously unexplored or paid little attention in other media analyses. This reveals both community and media concern with the historic legitimacy of national institutions such as the presidency and the Supreme Court, suggesting that community structure studies can be useful in uncovering a wide range of less obvious links between city demographics and reporting on political and social change.

TABLE 4.10. Bush vs. Gore Multiple Regression Analysis

MODEL	R	R SQUARE	R SQUARE CHANGE	F CHANGE	SIG. F CHANGE
College graduate	.499	.249	.249	5.975	.025

5

THE VULNERABILITY HYPOTHESIS

Greater Proportion of Vulnerable Citizens Linked to Favorable Coverage of Critical Issues

"Vulnerability" is a city characteristic few communication scholars would associate automatically with coverage of critical events. Vulnerable populations might include the poor; the unemployed; perhaps those in high-crime areas; and some portions of the African-American, Hispanic, and other minority communities. None of these population segments is associated frequently with maximum newspaper readership. A market-driven analysis is therefore unlikely to connect reporting on critical events automatically to newspaper reporting reflecting the concerns of the less privileged.

Unlike a market perspective, the community structure approach expects media coverage to display some resonance with a wide range of publics. Previous research in this tradition confirms that newspapers can reflect the interests of vulnerable populations. In reporting on coverage before, during and after the *Roe v. Wade* Supreme Court decision legalizing abortion, for example, the higher the proportion of those below the poverty level in a city, the more favorable the coverage of abortion legalization—and the greater the incidence of abortion after the decision as well (Pollock et al., 1978). Similarly, regarding a 1971 uprising at New York's Attica prison, a second abortion legalization decision by the Supreme Court in 1976 and a referendum rescinding a Dade County, Florida ordinance protecting the rights of homosexuals in access to housing, reporting in some major U.S. papers reflected the interests of several "vulnerable" populations: prisoners, the economically disadvantaged, and homosexuals. Once again, the larger the proportion of those below the poverty level in a city, the more sympathetic the newspaper coverage of each vulnerable group's concerns (Pollock & Robinson, 1977). Another study using the community structure approach found that the higher the poverty or unemployment level in a city, the less inflammatory or ethnocentric the reporting on a widely reported conflict between Caribbean Americans and Hasidic Jews in Queens, New York, in 1978 (Pollock & Whitney, 1997). A related study on structural pluralism found ethnic pluralism associated with reporting variations (Hindman et al., 1999).

Many explanations could be offered for this pattern. Perhaps the messages of the civil rights and related movements have become internalized in a younger generation of journalists. Perhaps newsroom hiring and retention of journalists from more diverse backgrounds contributes. Perhaps journalists' professional norms and values are modified by long-term changes in social values regarding women and minorities and other historically disadvantaged groups. Whatever the engine of awareness for these groups "unbuffered" from uncertainty, newspaper reporting on critical events can reflect the interests of more vulnerable segments of society. Two case studies selected for this chapter focus on reporting on efforts to ban capital punishment and on a Patients' Bill of Rights. These two examples illuminate by what might be called "redistributive justice" issues, which represent a renewed effort to ensure equal access to benefits historically unevenly available to those with few economic resources and also to ensure survival.

NATIONWIDE COVERAGE OF CAPITAL PUNISHMENT

Introduction

The death penalty is a worthy topic for media research. By 1992, 44 countries had abolished the death penalty, whereas other countries such as Canada use it only for treason and war crimes. Many countries still hold the death penalty as law but have not carried out executions in several years. Although more than half of the countries in the world have abolished the death penalty in law or practice, the United States has increased its rate of executions and number of crimes punishable by death. Thirty-eight states including the District of Columbia continue to use the death penalty. Texas is the state with the most executions per year.

Critics charge that capital punishment violates the "cruel and unusual punishment" provision of the Eighth Amendment. Supporters say that this clause was not intended to prohibit legal executions. During 1972, in the case of *Furman v. Georgia*, the U.S. Supreme Court ruled that capital punishment was no longer legal. However, in the 1976 case of *Gregg v. Georgia* the court allowed capital punishment to resume in certain states. Some groups, such as Amnesty International, have been trying to abolish capital punishment. Many states have also called for moratoriums, which would temporarily suspend the death penalty while lawmakers examine its validity for the future. The death penalty is certainly one of the nation's most controversial issues. Yet little information on the death penalty is found throughout the communication field.

Literature Review

A review of communication journals revealed articles on the death penalty, but considering its controversial nature, not as many as one might expect. Journal indexes including *Communication Abstracts via EBSCOhost, ComIndex, CIOS* journals, *ComAbstracts* via *CIOS* and *WIL3* (Wilson online database) were all utilized during the search. Keywords "capital punishment" "death penalty," and "executions" yielded little. Adding the keyword "crime" yielded article matches, but almost all were outdated by more than 15 years. More recent articles illuminate: journalists' personal biases and opinions in reporting crime news (Pritchard & Hughes, 1997); growing support for "punishing" criminals (Shaw, Shapiro, Lock, & Lawrence, 1998); the ethics of televising executions (Shipman, 1995); premature pretrial publicity in capital cases (Sandys & Chermak, 1996); and the way media can "mold" public opinion on executions (Lipschultz & Hilt, 1999).

Because completing a search in the field of communication revealed few articles, other journals in the social sciences were reviewed. Some articles surfaced under key terms such as "racial discrimination and death penalty," "race discrimination and United States" and "capital punishment and deterrence." One article revealed a defendant was four to five times as likely to suffer the death penalty if the victim were White than if the victim was African American (Tabak, 1999). Another confirmed that from 1933 to 1980, the death penalty was not a deterrent to homicide in Texas (Sorenson & Wrinkle, 1999).

The death penalty is a controversial topic, generating extensive media coverage, but media studies appear to focus more on violent crime trials and public opinion than on capital punishment itself. This study begins to remedy that imbalance by exploring how city demographics are linked with coverage of the issue.

Hypotheses

Community structure hypotheses have been developed in three cluster groups: stakeholders, the buffer hypothesis, and vulnerability.

Stakeholders

Three subgroups of stakeholders are of interest regarding capital punishment: ethnicity, belief system, and partisanship.

Ethnicity. Blacks and Hispanics as stakeholders have received relatively little attention in community structure media studies. In communication literature, seldom will racial or ethnic minorities be regarded as indicators of community structure in relation to community "pluralism" (see Gandy, 1996, 1999; Goshorn & Gandy, 1995). Yet, ethnicity can play a crucial role for both the victim and the murderer when determining if the death sentence should be imposed. Groups such as Amnesty International believe that minorities are at an unfair advantage for capital punishment sentencing. Those convicted of killing a White victim are more likely to receive the death penalty, and there are a disproportional number of blacks on death row. Therefore:

H1: *The greater the percentage of Blacks in a city, the less favorable the coverage of the death penalty.* (County and City Extra, 1999)

The same principles should hold true for the Hispanic community. Texas has the greatest number of executions per year, as well as the greatest percentage of Hispanics of any state in the United States. Because Hispanics, like African Americans, are also vulnerable to criminal legislation, it is expected that the presence of Hispanics will be linked to relatively negative reporting on the death penalty. Accordingly:

H2: *The greater the percentage of Hispanics in a city, the less favorable the coverage of the death penalty.* (County and City Extra, 1999)

Belief System. Catholics were certainly influential stakeholders regarding reporting on abortion. The higher the percentage of Catholics in a city, the less favorable the coverage of the *Roe v. Wade* decision to legalize abortion (Pollock et al., 1978) and of a subsequent 1976 decision upholding *Roe v. Wade* (Pollock & Robinson, 1977). More germane to the present inquiry, in 1974 the Catholic bishops of the United States declared the Church's opposition to capital punishment, and the Catholic community continues to do so in the belief that use of the death penalty can only lead to the further erosion of respect for life in society (*The Catholic Almanac*, 1999, p. 271). Accordingly:

H3: *The larger the percentage of Catholics in a city, the less favorable the coverage of the death penalty.* (Catholic Almanac, 1999)

Partisanship. Perspectives on the death penalty may be linked to political party affiliation. The percent of the population identifying itself as either Democratic or Republican could be associated with variations in newspaper coverage of capital punishment. The more Democrats in a community, it is expected a newspaper would run articles with a more liberal view or, considering the exoneration of so many on death row via advances in DNA testing, a viewpoint that considers arbitrariness in the administration of the death penalty. Consequently:

H4: *The higher the percentage voting for a Democratic presidential candidate in a city, the less favorable the coverage of the death penalty.* (World Almanac, 1999)

H5: *The higher the percentage voting for a Republican presidential candidate in a city, the more favorable the coverage of the death penalty.* (World Almanac, 1999)

Privilege: The Buffer Hypothesis

The buffer hypothesis, described in detail in chapter 3, proposes that the greater the proportion of a city's population privileged or buffered from financial and occupational uncertainty, the more favorable a city's newspaper will be toward those who are less privileged, or to those making human rights claims. Having a college education could correlate with a better understanding of multiple issues surrounding the death penalty. Educated citizens would have better access to literature on capital punishment and are more likely to consider both sides of the argument. Similarly, high family income or occupational status can be associated with greater access to media and a wide, pluralistic range of viewpoints. Therefore:

H6: *The greater the percentage of annual family incomes of $100,000+ or more the less favorable the coverage of the death penalty.* (Lifestyle Market Analyst, 1999)

H7: *The greater the percentage with a college education, the less favorable the coverage of the death penalty.* (Lifestyle Market Analyst, 1999)

H8: *The greater the percent with professional/technical occupational status, the less favorable the coverage of the death penalty.* (Lifestyle Market Analyst, 1999)

Vulnerability

When a city has a greater population below the poverty level, citizens who suffer from poverty may be more likely either to resort to crime, including violent crime, and therefore become more vulnerable to capital punishment. The same can be expected for cities with high unemployment rates. For these reasons, to the extent that media reflect the concerns of those below the poverty level and the unemployed, newspapers may report unfavorably on the death penalty.

Traditionally, newspaper reporting may have had little or no relation to the proportion of those in poverty because citizens below the poverty level are less likely to be educated or to buy or read a newspaper (Marger, 1991). As the introduction to this chapter reveals, however, some community structure studies have revealed newspapers can legitimize the plight of the less privileged, specifically those below the poverty level and those who are unemployed.

Therefore:

H9: *The greater the percentage below the poverty level, the less favorable the coverage of the death penalty.* (Lifestyle Market Analyst, 1999)

H10: *The greater the unemployment rate, the less favorable the coverage of the death penalty.* (County and City Extra, 1999)

Apart from economic disadvantage, another indicator of vulnerability is crime rate. Those cities with a high crime rate, especially violent crime, may be expected to favor strict crime legislation. Proponents of capital punishment claim capital punishment deters crime and ensures that dangerous criminals are not reintroduced to society. Favorable coverage of the death penalty is reasonable to expect in communities that support lowering the crime rate and decreasing the number of violent crimes. Accordingly:

H11: *The greater the overall crime rate* (excluding arson) *in a city, the more favorable the coverage of the death penalty.* (Uniform Crime Reports, 1998)

H12: *The greater the violent crime rate per 100,000 in a city, the more favorable the coverage of the death penalty.* (County and City Extra, 1999)

Methodology

Utilizing the DIALOG newspaper database, 15 newspapers from a variety of cities nationwide were surveyed. All articles of 150 words or more mentioning "death penalty," "capital punishment," "execution," "death row," or "death sentence" were selected from the 2-year period 1997 through 1999, yielding 305 articles. The search began during 1997, the year New Jersey Governor Christie Todd Whitman announced the creation of a commission to make recommendations on speeding up the death penalty.

The newspapers were chosen in order to provide a diverse cross-section of the United States (see Table 5.1). Articles were coded for prominence and direction. An article was coded as "favorable" if the content within the article seemed to support or favor the death penalty. The article was coded as "unfavorable" if the content within the article was against or opposing the death penalty. The article was coded as balanced/neutral if the content within the article made no effort to side one way or the other, or if it contained an approximately equal proportion of both favorable and unfavorable material concerning the death penalty. Comparing the evaluations of two coders, Holsti's coefficient of intercoder reliability was .88. After using the combined prominence and direction scores from each newspaper to calculate media vectors, Pearson correlations and regression analyses were run.

Results

Newspaper Scores and Rankings

Media vectors varied from one paper to another in covering the death penalty, ranging from a +.283 to –.128. Overall, the coverage was favorable, with 60% of the newspapers reporting favorably on capital punishment. Only six had negative coverage on the matter. Phoenix had the most favorable coverage with a coefficient of .238. New Orleans was on the other end of the spectrum with a coefficient of -.128. Because Texas leads the nation in number of executions each year, it was striking that Houston displayed a negative media vector.

One city characteristic has a clearly significant relationship to reporting on capital punishment: percent below the poverty level (Table 5.2).

Regression Analysis

Results from the regression analysis show that poverty rate accounts for 26% of the variance in reporting on capital punishment, associated with negative coverage. In the regression equation, no other variable is significantly linked to coverage of the issue.

TABLE 5.1. Capital Punishment Media Vectors

NEWSPAPER	MEDIA VECTOR
The Arizona Republic (Phoenix)	.283
Rocky Mountain News (Denver)	.127
Pittsburgh Post-Gazette	.127
The Oregonian (Portland)	.072
The Philadelphia Inquirer	.065
The Atlanta Journal/ Constitution	.061
The Sacramento Bee	.029
The Democrat (Tallahassee)	.019
The Times Union (Albany)	.011
The Charlotte Observer	−.003
St. Louis Post-Dispatch	−.018
Houston Chronicle	−.025
Boston Globe	−.035
Detroit Free Press	−.103
Times-Picayune (New Orleans)	−.128

TABLE 5.2. Capital Punishment Pearson Correlations

HYPOTHESES	PEARSON CORRELATIONS	SIGNIFICANCE
Poverty rate	−.509	.026
Percent Black	−.431	.055
Percent Democrat	−.355	.097
Percent Republican	.355	.097
Unemployment rate	−.334	.112
Violent crime rate (/100,000)	−.265	.170
College education	.244	.190
Crime rate	−.240	.195
Percent Catholic	−.153	.294
Families with incomes $100,000+	.137	.313
Percent Hispanic	.122	.339
Percent professional/technical status	.104	.354

TABLE 5.3. Capital Punishment Multiple Regression Model Summary

MODEL	R (EQUATION)	R-SQUARE (CUMULATIVE)	R-SQUARE CHANGE	F CHANGE	SIG. F CHANGE
Poverty rate	.509	.260	.260	4.556	.051

Discussion of Results

Vulnerability: Strong Correlations with Poverty, Percent African American

Poverty is the variable in the vulnerability cluster with the strongest results. Poverty rate, associated with negative coverage of the death penalty, has the most significant Pearson correlation ($r = -.509$; $p = .026$) and is the only significant factor in the regression analysis, accounting for 26% of the variance. Percent African American was almost significant and negative ($r = -.431$; $p = .055$), consistent with expectations. Conventional wisdom would assume that historically those below the poverty level and African Americans are more vulnerable to criminal legislation and are often underrepresented in the court system. Groups in this situation are unlikely to favor capital punishment or media reporting enhancing its value.

Similar in direction, although not significant, were results found with city unemployment rates ($r = -.334$; $p = -.112$). This is consistent with a study of reporting on ethnic conflict in Crown Heights, Queens, New York City, revealing that the higher the unemployment rate in a city, the more likely a newspaper's reporting will demonstrate concern for less privileged groups (Pollock & Whitney, 1997). Another finding that was not significant in the power of its association but linked in an unexpected direction was rate of violent crime ($r = -.265$; $p = .17$). In this case, although poverty and violent crime coexist in large measure in the cities studied ($r = .458$; $p = .043$), poverty, a long term measure of resource impoverishment, is more clearly linked to coverage than is level of violent crime, which may vary substantially from one year to the next. These findings suggest that newspaper coverage can be sensitive to those who are more vulnerable to an issue, especially if these groups are more highly represented in a city. In general, "vulnerability" is a major factor associated with reporting unfavorable to the death penalty.

A Directional Stakeholder Finding: Partisanship

Partisanship as represented by the percent Democrat in a city (r=-.355; p =. 098), and percent Republican in a city (r = .355; p = .098) is not strictly significant, not meeting the .05 level of significance. From a "directional" perspective, however, findings are consistent with expectations: If a city has a high percent voting Democratic, reporting on capital punishment will tend toward an unfavorable direction, whereas higher percentages voting Republican are linked to reporting directed toward favoring capital punishment.

Conclusion

Acknowledging the importance of poverty level and percent African American, this case study of capital punishment can be retested using different samples of cities, in particular cities of widely different sizes. Although city size was not strictly significant in this sample, a wider range of cities might allow its potency to be examined more exhaustively.

NATIONWIDE COVERAGE OF A PATIENTS' BILL OF RIGHTS

Introduction

The "Patients' Bill of Rights Act of 1999," sponsored by Representative Charles Norwood (R, Georgia) and Representative John Dingell (D, Mich.) (Pear, 1999, p. A1), sought to permit all citizens to seek professional health services and receive high-quality care at reasonable costs (Weiss, 1999). By defining a standard of care, the bill promoted the development of innovative, cost-effective organizations focusing on clinical quality improvements, patient satisfaction, and access to information (Weiss, 1999). More specifically, the new plan included universal coverage, access to specialists, continuity of care, access to emergency care, and allowance of appeals to health coverage decisions (Shalala, 1999). Despite its apparent benefits, the bill was controversial.

During a memorandum on federal agency compliance with the Patients' Bill of Rights, President Clinton (1998) stated that, "it is possible and desirable to ensure that patients have the tools they need to navigate through an increasingly complex health care delivery system" (pp. 298–299). Opposition to the bill came from the Republican Party and health insurance corporations. Opponents contended that it was a "recipe for inflation" and that it would prompt health maintenance organizations (HMOs) to drop coverage for the elderly and poor, swelling the ranks of the uninsured due to increased insurance premiums (Patients, 1999). On October 7, 1999, the House of Representatives passed a bill giving patients a wide range of new rights (Pear, 1999). These rights would guarantee patients access to emergency care and medical specialists, to appeal coverage decisions to an independent board, prohibit HMOs from retaliating against doctors who fight for the needs of their patients, and make it easier for patients to sue health plans in state courts (Pear, 1999). Because of its importance, debate on the Patients' Bill of Rights drew substantial media coverage. Exploring this topic can provide insight into the ways media cover controversial health-related issues and measure coverage variation from one place to another.

Scholarly Articles and Communication Literature: Little Concerning a Patients' Bill of Rights

Many communication journals as well as online communications databases were searched. Although little specific information concerning a Patients' Bill of Rights appears in communication literature, some relevant sources concerning the topic are indexed in medical, political, and economic literatures.

Online database *ComIndex* was searched, using key terms such as "patient and bill and rights," as well as "health-care reform," "patient and physician," and "health-care," revealing little or no relevant information addressing a Patients' Bill of Rights. Other leading communication collections and journals, such as *Communication Abstracts*, the *Communication Institute for Online Scholarship* (CIOS), *Journal of Health Communication, Health Communication,* and *Political Communication* were also searched, with few results. This paucity of information is surprising because the rights of the patient deserve serious attention in the field of communication. For example, passage of a Patients' Bill of Rights would empower doctors to communicate freely about treatment options, alternative risks, benefits, and consequences without "gag rules" in their contractual agreements (Shalala, 1999).

Although relevant information in the communication literature was scarce, articles concerning a Patients' Bill of Rights in medical and hospital journals were easily found. Articles such as "A Patients' Bill of Rights: The Medical Student's Role" (Shalala, 1999) and "Defining a 'Patients Bill of Rights' for the Next Century" (Weiss, 1999) were located in the *Journal of the American Medical Association,* and an article "The Subtext is Reform" in

Hospitals and Health Network highlighted difficult issues such as rights to consumer choice and the right to specific health care benefits (Greene, 1997). Furthermore, several articles were found in business and political periodicals and journals such as *The New Republic, The Economist, Industry Week*, and *Business Week* (McNamee & Dunham, 1998). One article, "To the Hustings," suggested that although most Americans do not want their health managed, they surely recognize the economic pressures that produced HMOs in the first place ("To the Hustings," 1998). A recurring theme throughout these articles compared the costs of a Patients'Bill of Rights with the benefits.

Political news articles concerning the Patients' Bill of Rights were also readily available because the bill itself was passed in the House of Representatives on October 7, 1999. An article from *The New York Times* called "House Passes Bill to Expand Rights on Medical Care," stated that the bill "would set uniform standards for health insurance, which has been regulated mainly by the states" (Pear, 1999, p. A1). Representative Norwood said, "Managed-care insurance plans have enjoyed a near total immunity from any legal accountability for injuring and killing the citizens of this country for monetary gain," and that "no thinking, feeling American can agree to let that stand" (Pear, 1999, p. A1). More political implications were found in the July 1998 edition of *The Economist*. The article, "To the Hustings," stated, "polls constantly show that around 80% of Americans are happy with the reality of their managed care," but the same article quoted President Clinton claiming "Millions of Americans are looking to us for the right kind of action. They want us to pass a strong, bipartisan patients' bill of rights" ("To the Hustings," 1998, p. 33).

In addition to articles on medical, political, and economic issues concerning the Patients' Bill of Rights, a sociological article is pertinent. In an article called "Harry and Louise Go to Washington: Political Advertising and Health Care Reform," the *Journal of Health Politics, Policy and Law* suggests that the impressions of not only the public, but also news reporters and Washington elites were altered by ads attaching negative connotations to key elements of Clinton's health care reform plan for 1993/1994 (West, 1996). The article clearly compares media coverage with public policy and public opinion, a tripartite comparison experienced health communication scholars have asked colleagues to pursue.

By extensively researching different communication literatures in databases and journals, it is apparent that there is a need for more research on health care policy, specifically a Patients' Bill of Rights, in the field of communication. By contrast, relevant information was found in medical, political news, and economic literatures, suggesting a gap between the health communication field and other health-related fields. Exploring coverage of a Patients' Bill of Rights is an effort to begin closing that gap.

Hypotheses

Eleven individual hypotheses can be placed into four cluster groups including the following: health care access, the violated buffer hypothesis, vulnerability, and stakeholder clusters.

Access to Health Care

Health care access is a key feature of the Patients' Bill of Rights. The bill articulates a need for health care coverage for all Americans, access to specialists, as well as access to emergency care (Pear, 1999), Newspaper coverage of the Patients' Bill of Rights is possibly related to the percentage of municipal spending on health care, the number of physicians per 100,000 residents, and the number of hospital beds per 100,000 residents in a city. A study concerning legalization of physician-assisted euthanasia revealed a positive correlation between access to health care (physicians per 100,000 residents) and favorable newspaper coverage (see chap. 3). Therefore, the greater the access to health care generally, the more likely coverage of the Patients' Bill of Rights will be favorable, specifically:

H1: *The greater the percentage of municipal spending on health care in a city, the more favorable the coverage of the Patients' Bill of Rights.* (Lifestyle Market Analyst, 1999)

H2: *The greater the number of physicians per 100,000 residents in a city, the more favorable the coverage of the Patients' Bill of Rights.* (County and City Extra, 1999)

H3: *The greater the number of hospital beds per 100,000 resident population, the more likely the coverage of the Patients' Bill of Rights is favorable.* (County and City Extra, 1997)

Violated Buffer

Buffer and violated buffer hypotheses have been described in detail in chapters 3 and 4. These hypotheses are useful in our study of coverage of a Patients' Bill of Rights. Considering indicators of privilege such as the percentage of the population with professional/technical occupational status or the proportion of city residents with annual family incomes of $100,000 or more, it is possible that there may be a relationship between these city characteristics and newspaper coverage of the Patients' Bill of Rights. Rather than being "buffered" by the problem of patients' rights, privileged groups, many of whom now use HMOs, are increasingly as vulnerable as previously less privileged groups to the arbitrary decisions of HMO healthcare gatekeepers. This, in turn, supports a violated buffer hypothesis because privileged groups are growing to view HMO performance as a life-threatening or certainly quality-of-life-threatening issue. Therefore, it is believed that high proportions of professionals, as well as families with incomes over $100,000, in a city will be linked to relatively favorable coverage of the Patients' Bill of Rights. Violated buffer expectations were confirmed for media coverage of Magic Johnson's HIV announcement, in which his announcement created a new perceived health vulnerability for economically successful Americans (see chap. 8).

It is expected that the educationally privileged have the same relationship to coverage of the Patients' Bill of Rights as the economically and professionally privileged. Those with 16 or more years of education are likely to support rights claims and to oppose acts that violate human rights. Regarding health-related issues, the violated buffer hypothesis has been confirmed for reporting on efforts to ban tobacco ads targeting children (Pollock, Nisi, & McCarthy, 1999), the FDA's effort to regulate nicotine (Caamaño, Pollock, Virgilio, & Lindstrom, 2001) and the MSA, discussed in chapter 4. Therefore:

> **H4:** *The higher the percentage of population in a city with professional or technical status, the more likely the reporting on the Patients' Bill of Rights will be favorable.* (Lifestyle Market Analyst, 1999)

> **H5:** *The higher proportion of city residents with annual family incomes of $100,000 or more, the more likely a city newspaper is to report favorably on the Patients' Bill of Rights.* (Lifestyle Market Analyst, 1999)

> **H6:** *The higher the proportion of college graduates, the more favorable the reporting on the Patients' Bill of Rights.* (Lifestyle Market Analyst, 1999)

Vulnerability

It is reasonable to expect that community dwellers who are below the poverty level or unemployed will have positive views toward legislation concerning patients' rights. Nationwide community structure approach studies cited in the introduction to this chapter revealed that the higher the percentage below the poverty level, the more favorable the coverage of the 1973 *Roe v. Wade* decision and a subsequent 1976 abortion decision by the US Supreme Court, as well as respectful, noninflammatory coverage of different ethnic groups in conflict (Pollock & Robinson, 1977; Pollock et al., 1978; Pollock & Whitney, 1997). Conventional wisdom suggests a positive association between the proportion of those in a city who are unemployed or below the poverty level and favorable coverage concerning what is presumably a clear benefit for the economically marginalized, a Patient's Bill of Rights, specifically:

H7: *The greater the proportion of city residents below the poverty level, the more favorable the coverage of the Patients' Bill of Rights will be.* (County and City Extra, 1999)

H8: *The greater the proportion of unemployed residents in a city, the more favorable the coverage of the Patients' Bill of Rights will be.* (County and City Extra, 1999)

Stakeholders: Age and Political Partisanship

Although "stakeholders" are not as organized as traditional "interest groups," the communication literature on protest groups illuminates stakeholder links to media coverage, discussed in chapter 7. Previous research using the community structure approach has revealed that the greater the proportion of recognized stakeholders in a city, the more newspaper coverage is likely to vary accordingly to their concerns. For example, senior citizens have a great deal at stake in efforts to legalize physician-assisted euthanasia. One study of newspaper coverage revealed that the greater the proportion of those 75 or older in a city, the less favorable the newspaper reporting on legalization of physician-assisted euthanasia (Pollock & Yulis, 2004). It is therefore reasonable to expect that there may be a correlation between the proportion of those 75 or older in a city and favorable newspaper coverage of patients' rights. Thus:

H9: *The greater the proportion of those in a city 75 years of age or older, the more likely the reporting of the Patients' Bill of Rights will be favorable.* (County and City Extra, 1999)

Age stakeholders apart, the Patients' Bill of Rights has clearly been a partisan issue. It was passed by a House of Representatives vote of 275 to 151, in which 206 of the votes for the approving of the bill were from Democrats (Pear, 1999). Recognizing that the Patients' Bill of Rights has strong support from the Democratic Party, it is highly possible that newspaper coverage would be relatively favorable in communities that have high proportions of Democrats, and conversely, unfavorable where there are high proportions of Republicans. Democrat and Republican votes during the 1996 presidential election can be used to gauge the proportion of those affiliated with the Democratic or Republican parties or partisan stakeholders in a city. Therefore:

H10: *The greater the proportion of Democrats in a city, the more favorable the newspaper coverage of the Patients' Bill of Rights will be.* (County and City Extra, 1999)

H11: *The greater the proportion of Republicans in a city, the more likely that newspaper coverage of the Patients' Bill of Rights will be unfavorable* (County and City Extra, 1999)

Methodology

Sample Selection

This study explored coverage of the Patients' Bill of Rights in 21 major newspapers nationwide (see Table 5.4.). All articles of 150 words or more were sampled for the period January 1 to October 31, 1999. This range represented a time when the subject of patients' rights and reforming health care assumed major importance. The beginning of the year was a natural inflection point for the issue because it had only recently gained national prominence. The resulting 387 newspaper articles, chosen from cities representing a national cross-section of the United States, were collected from the DIALOG Classroom Information Program newspaper database.

After prominence scores were calculated, "direction" coding was conducted according to the following criteria:

Coverage considered *favorable* to the Patients' Bill of Rights included those articles viewing this bill an essential right, in which all Americans deserve health benefits such as universal coverage, access to specialized care and access to emergency care. Articles were also deemed favorable when a majority of the text contained positive aspects and viewpoints concerning the Patients' Bill of Rights. In many articles, it was argued that there was a need to set a better standard of health care to promote the development of innovative, cost-effective organizations that focus on clinical quality improvements, patient satisfaction, and access to more information.

Coverage *unfavorable* to the Patients' Bill of Rights included articles that focused on the high costs and high taxes that coincide with the health coverage issue. Some unfavorable articles also directly opposed the Patients' Bill of Rights with topics such as lawsuits against HMOs and citizens against government regulation for health care.

Balanced/neutral coverage included articles that displayed both sides of the debate over the Patients' Bill of Rights in approximately equal measure, or revealed a disinterested, nondirectional outlook, raising issues about the Patients' Bill of Rights without making a clear judgment. After the collected articles were assigned their directional scores, three researchers coded a systematic subsample of one third of the articles, yielding a Holsti's coefficient of intercoder reliability of .85

Results

Media vectors, Pearson correlations, and regression analysis revealed the following: Media Vectors ranged from .504 to –.034. Of 21 newspapers studied, most of the coverage on the Patients' Bill of Rights was slightly favorable or balanced/neutral. Only one newspaper, *The Lexington Herald Leader*, showed slightly negative coverage of the issue. Table 5.4 presents a list of city newspapers and their media vectors.

TABLE 5.4. Patients' Bill of Rights Media Vectors

NEWSPAPER	MEDIA VECTOR
Philadelphia Inquirer	.504
Akron- Beacon Journal	.465
Albany Times Union	.377
New Orleans Times Picayune	.340
Charlotte Observer	.230
Cleveland Plain Dealer	.201
Atlanta Journal/ Constitution	.159
Sacramento Bee	.128
San Francisco Chronicle	.114
Seattle Times	.090
Houston Chronicle	.072
Memphis Commercial Appeal	.071
Phoenix Gazette	.053
Pittsburgh Post-Gazette	.052
Baltimore Sun	.050
Wichita Eagle	.035
Boston Globe	.023
St. Louis Post- Dispatch	.019
Portland Oregonian	.014
Denver Rocky Mountain News	.011
Lexington Herald Leader	–.034

One city characteristic, poverty level ($r = .451$; $p = .026$), had a significant relationships (.05 or better) to newspaper coverage. Three additional city characteristics had a "directional" relationship, significant at the .10 level or better: Percent voting Democratic, percent unemployed, and percent voting Republican (see Table 5.5). Percent voting Democratic and percent voting Republican were linked in predictable ways to support for a Patients' Bill of Rights (Democratic voting, positively; Republican voting, negatively). Oddly enough, the variable of age (75 years or older) did not show any significant results, contrary to how important the issue is to senior citizens. Perhaps a Patient's Bill of Rights has moved out of the category of a concern associated only with age to become a "universalized" concern of interest to all citizens. This study's results support the "universalization" hypothesis.

TABLE 5.5. Patients' Bill of Rights Pearson Correlations

HYPOTHESIS	CORRELATION	PROBABILITY
Poverty	.451	.026*
Democratic voting	.355	.057
Unemployment	.352	.059
Republican voting	−.294	.098
Age (75 and older)	.195	.199
Education	−.138	.276
Income	−.108	.321
Hospital beds/100,000	−.078	.368
Physicians/100,000	−.076	.371
Professional/tech status	.051	.413
Percent health funding in municipal budget	−.029	.450

*Significant at .05 level

Regression Analysis

In the case of the Patients' Bill of Rights, one variable correlated significantly with the media vectors in the multiple regression analysis: Percent below the poverty level accounted for 20% of the variance (Table 5.6).

TABLE 5.6. Patients' Bill of Rights Multiple Regression Summary

MODEL	R (EQUATION)	R-SQUARE (CUMULATIVE)	R CHANGE SQUARE	F CHANGE CHANGE	SIG. F
Percent below poverty level	.451	.203	.203	4.329	.052

Discussion of Results

Vulnerability: Associated With Positive Coverage of the Patients' Bill of Rights; Challenging the Media "Guard Dog" Hypothesis

The city characteristic of poverty was the strongest variable in the Pearson correlation ($r = .451, p = .029$), and the amount of variance in the regression analysis was .203. This result confirms the hypothesis that the greater the proportion below the poverty level, the more favorable the coverage of the Patients' Bill of Rights.

These findings suggest that newspaper coverage can be sensitive to those who experience relatively limited access to health care. These results are consistent with the study on "Media Agendas and Human Rights: The Supreme Court Decision on Abortion," published in *Journalism Quarterly*. Multi-newspaper research conducted by Pollock, Robinson, and Murray (1978) on *Roe v. Wade* revealed that varied city poverty levels had a similar positive link to relatively favorable newspaper coverage of the U.S. Supreme Court decision legalizing abortion. To find that media can reflect the views or concerns of non-elites or those unlikely to be considered newspaper "markets" challenges the view of Olien et al., (1995) in their assertion that media usually function as "guard dogs," protecting the interests of established elites. Links between relatively "vulnerable" groups and media reporting on social change clearly deserve further study.

Conclusion: Access and Stakeholders

The debate over creating legislation supporting patients' rights is controversial and reveals nationwide variations in newspaper coverage. Overall, the study found most city newspaper coverage of the Patients' Bill of Rights to be favorable or balanced/neutral. This may suggest that, on the whole, the nation's major newspapers support improved health care.

Nationwide city newspaper coverage of the Patients' Bill of Rights seemed connected to the interests of those below the poverty level. The higher the percentage of individuals below the poverty level in a city, the more favorable the newspaper coverage of the Patients' Bill of Rights. It is possible to conclude that an issue as important as the Patients' Bill of Rights would give a rise to a public interest, in which newspapers reach beyond typical readership markets to precise stakeholders for this issue: those with little access to health care. This finding reveals clearly a link between the proportion of "vulnerable" populations in a city and sympathetic newspaper coverage.

Finally, the research supports further research concerning the influence of partisan politics. The issue of the Patients' Bill of Rights lines up along political and social cleavages. This research reveals a sharp disagreement in viewpoints along party lines. It is curious that in this study, and contrary to other research on coverage of health care issues, demographics measuring "privilege" such as income, education level, and professional status are not linked as clearly to healthcare legislation as are poverty levels with the Patients' Bill of Rights issue. The possibilities for future research connecting the community structure approach and media coverage of health care issues are extraordinary and deserve serious attention.

6

THE ECONOMIC PROTECTION
HYPOTHESIS

One of the most traditional expectations about any link between social structure and reporting on political and social change is that there is some relation between economic power and media coverage. In their work on the hypothesis that media often function as guard dogs, Olien et al. (1995) argued that media often serve not as first amendment watchdogs for the community as a whole, but rather as guard dogs for "groups having the power and influence to create and command their own security systems" (p. 305). The authors contend that media should not be considered some sort of disembodied Fourth Estate, separate from society, not independent agencies, but rather are "subject to system controls as are government, the courts, the schools or education" (p. 303). The authors suggest that because media, in their view, are controlled by dominant powers in business and government, media often serve as "sentries" for established groups in social conflict. Examples of this include media concentration on quoting administrative sources when covering scientific and technological issues (Tichenor, Donohue, & Olien, 1970); and the work of Shoemaker (1984) and Herman (1985) finding media concentrating on powerful groups, "marginalizing" the less powerful (Olien, Donohue, & Tichenor, 1995).

It is one thing to assert the primacy of economic interests. It is another thing to explore more extensively how economic interests and reporting on political or social change are linked, in particular because economic interests do not exist in a vacuum: they may conflict or coincide with other strategic or political interests. Additionally, economic interests may vary even within small communities. For example, the economic interests of business owners in a community may differ from the broader community's economic interests in maintaining a fairly high level of employment. This chapter explores the way community economic interests and reporting on political and social change can be linked by focusing on two critical events: the 1997 handover of Hong Kong to China and the congressional decision to pass the NAFTA. Each critical event represented a potential threat to or reinforcement of economic interests and therefore a challenge to the "protection" of those interests.

THE 1997 HANDOVER
OF HONG KONG TO CHINA

Introduction

On July 1, 1997, the British colony of Hong Kong was handed over to the People's Republic of China. This historical event signified the end of Great Britain's 156 years of imperial rule, turning over this booming capitalist city and its residents to one of the largest centrally managed economic and political systems in the world.

Under the Sino-British Joint Declaration of 1984, China agreed to allow Hong Kong to maintain a high degree of autonomy as a Special Administrative Region (SAR) for 50 years after the July 1, 1997 handover. Thirteen years later, the event raised several political, economic, and cultural concerns. Would the People's Republic of China (PRC) honor the terms of the 1984 agreement? Would the economy of Hong Kong continue to succeed under Chinese rule? Should China's history of human rights violations and political oppression be a major concern to the people of Hong Kong?

These questions became focal points for the media in their coverage of the transition. Many human rights activists and financial investors saw the handover of Hong Kong as having severe economic and political implications. Conversely, others viewed the transition as the return of Hong Kong to its rightful owner and believed that the independence and entrepreneurial trajectory of the city would not only remain intact but would eventually spread into mainland China.

This case study examines aggregate data from several American cities and compares this information with variations in coverage of the Hong Kong handover. Three questions were addressed: How much attention did communication scholars pay to the Hong Kong transition issue? How much variation occurred in newspaper coverage throughout the United States? How strongly was that variation linked with measures of economic privilege?

Review of Communication Literature: A Research Gap

A review of several major communication journals revealed little information on the subject of the handover of Hong Kong from Great Britain to China. *Communication Research, Communications Studies, Critical Studies in Mass Communications, Communication Quarterly, Journal of Applied Communication Research, Journalism & Mass Communication Quarterly,* and *Communication Abstracts* entries between 1991 and 1995 provided few articles containing relevant subject matter on media coverage of the Hong Kong handover. Multiple keyword searches were performed including: Hong Kong, China, "human rights," "transition," "international business," and "land rights." Although articles were retrieved with these key words, most focused on either the role of mass media or business communication in East Asian countries. A few articles have been written about media coverage of political and social issues in Hong Kong (Chan, 1988/1989; Chan, 1994; Chan & Lee, 1988; Chu & Lee, 1995; Lee, 1993; Martin, Wilson, & Meng, 1994). A few articles have also dealt with Tiananmen Square and politics or government (Chen, 1993; McIntyre, 1993; He & Zhu, 1994; Pepper, 1995, 1996; Waller & Ide, 1995), others with education or student demonstrations (Hertling, 1997; Kobland, du, & Kwon, 1992; Lee & Chan, 1990), and still others with business and commercial interests (Chen, 1993; Coplin, 1995; Halpern, 1983; Jellicorse, 1994, Zhu, 1991).

One particular article from *Journalism & Mass Communication Quarterly* discussed press coverage of the Tiananmen Square massacre, the 1989 incident that clearly exposed human rights violations on the part of the Chinese government. Zhang and Krauss (1995) wrote:

> Images of Tiananmen Square received and inspired global responses. The United States, Canada, Australia, Japan, The European Community, and some international organizations applied various economic and political sanctions against the Chinese government. The communist countries of Yugoslavia, Vietnam, and the Soviet Union also expressed their shock of the military suppression. China was isolated in the international community. (p. 412)

The Tiananmen Square incident seriously damaged other nations' views of the Communist PRC.

Another article from *Communication Quarterly* primarily discussed the difference in dialects and ethnic identities of the people of Hong Kong and mainland China, but it did note the political impact of the territory's transition once under Chinese sovereignty. Pierson (1992) claimed the following:

Putonghua (the language) and the radically different political culture of
mainland China, will be challenging the hybrid Hong Kong Chinese
culture and the dominance of Cantonese. Although the outcome is far
from certain, it is likely that there will be a significant shift in language
loyalties as a result of the territory's political changes. (p. 382)

Although little was found in communication journals regarding Hong
Kong's transition, leading economic and political science journals as well as
foreign publications *Far Eastern Economic Review* and *Asian Survey* manifested substantial interest. An article in *Current History* addressed fears that
rights and freedoms of the people of Hong Kong might be endangered.
Frank Ching (1996) commented, "The controversies that have arisen
between Hong Kong and China—and between Britain and China—have
occurred largely in the political sphere. One centers on the extent to which
democracy will be allowed to grow" (p. 273). Under the Sino-British Joint
Declaration of 1984, Hong Kong was given a high degree of autonomy,
allowing the people of the territory to have separate executive, legislative,
and political powers. With Hong Kong now under Chinese sovereignty,
many wonder whether or not such autonomy will continue. The article
states that "Chinese officials have warned Hong Kong against transforming
itself from an economic city into a political city" (p. 273).

Other political science journals also express similar concerns. Of particular interest is an article in entitled "A Looming Greek Tragedy in Hong
Kong." Similarly, referring in *Foreign Policy* to the handover of Hong Kong,
former *New York Times* correspondent Tad Szulc (1997) commented, "It is
likely to mark the beginning of the end of the most political freedoms and
the respect for human rights that the 6.3 million inhabitants of Hong Kong,
now enjoy—to say nothing of the prospects for democracy" (p. 77). The
article drew attention to a meeting by a special Beijing policy panel on
January 20, 1997 to repeal or rewrite several Hong Kong legal provisions
and restore the British colonial police powers to ban peaceful demonstrations (p. 79). "All indications are that the Chinese are determined to act as
they please, regardless of international opinion" (Szulc, 1997, p. 79).

An article in *World Today* discussed the economic significance of Hong
Kong:

It has provided directly and indirectly 60-70 percent of China's commercial investment and acted as a gateway for China's access to international trade and international finance. Without the technological, managerial and marketing know-how of Hong Kong, China would not have
been able to penetrate so rapidly into sophisticated Western markets.
(Yahuda, 1996, p. 261)

Many economists worried that political pressures from mainland China could prove detrimental to Hong Kong's economic success. If China did interfere and was unable to carry out the policy of "one country, two systems" in Hong Kong, problems would arise. Yahuda explained, "In short, China's relations with the key countries of the Asia-Pacific would take a profound turn for the worse. Foreign investors would take fright. China's chances of joining the World Trade Organization would suffer a decisive setback" (p. 262). Another article from *Journal of Small Business Management* added an additional economic dimension, stating, "Worried about the impact that China's communist policies may have on Hong Kong's capitalist economy, many entrepreneurs have emigrated" (Dana, 1996, p. 80).

In contrast to the Cassandras, some articles published in *Far Eastern Economic Review* projected a more favorable view of the transition. Finding comfort in Beijing's permitting Hong Kong to maintain its autonomy as an SAR for 50 years after 1997, one article offered optimism: "One (possibility) is that Hong Kong will not merely survive as a center of economic and other freedoms, but will become a pilot project for an increasingly free China and a forcing house of libertarian practices" (Johnson, 1997, p. 16). In another article from *Far Eastern Economic Review*, Gilley (1997) wrote, "The region's tycoons see Hong Kong's reversion to China as a huge opportunity to gain access to mainland markets and build up an international presence" (p. 22). Newspapers gave extensive coverage to this July 1, 1997 historical event.

Hypotheses Linking Privilege With Concerns About the Hong Kong Handover

At least two aggregate indicators of privilege in a city, education level and percent of families with relatively high incomes, are expected linked to newspaper coverage of the Hong Kong handover.

Education

Regarding education, cities with more college-educated residents will have a better opportunity to be informed about China, the takeover, and the history or the British occupation of Hong Kong. Furthermore, better educated citizens can adopt a more global view of the situation. Hong Kong, previously a democratic state, could face major obstacles when returned to the PRC. A major power in trade and business, Hong Kong could be abused by China in an effort to take advantage of financial resources. The more highly educated will be more familiar with incidences of human rights violations and the confrontation in Tiananmen Square.

H1: *The higher the percentage of people within a city who have had 16 or more years of education, the less favorable the coverage of the Hong Kong handover.* (Lifestyle Market Analyst, 1996)

Economic Privilege

Consistent with concerns about the potential loss of Hong Kong's entrepreneurial freedom and energetic trading success, relatively privileged groups are likely to be more concerned about the loss of access to economic resources than are the less privileged. Families earning more than $100,000 per year may be less likely to favor the transition because gainfully employed individuals in such families are more likely to be employed in businesses or sectors that may be adversely affected by any negative results of the handover and may also hold bonds and stock in affected companies. Whether through greater awareness or direct economic interest, the prospect of symbolic or expected financial loss could lead privileged individuals to manifest more guarded or negative perspectives on the handover. Accordingly:

H2: *The higher the percentage of people earning $100,000 or more per year in a city, the less favorable the coverage of the Hong Kong handover.* (Lifestyle Market Analyst, 1996)

Sample Design, Definitions of Favorable and Unfavorable Reporting

A national cross-section of 20 newspapers, each representing a separate major metropolitan area, was surveyed for content regarding the handover of Hong Kong to the PRC. The search, which utilized the DIALOG Classroom Instruction Program, was conducted by using keywords such as "Hong Kong" and "handover" and selected all articles of 150 words or more on the topic that appeared from January 1, 1996 to October 28, 1997. The newspapers were chosen in order to provide a diverse cross-section of the United States (see Table 6.1).

After coding for article prominence, articles were sorted for content, classified in one of three groups. *Favorable* articles took an optimistic or positive stance on the Chinese takeover of Hong Kong. They stressed the future benefits of the handover and chose not to significantly criticize China on a number of issues. *Unfavorable* coverage took a more cautious approach and stressed some of the more controversial issues involved in the event. *Balanced/neutral* coverage was characterized by either relatively similar amounts of both positive and negative coverage or generally nondirectional coverage. After all articles were coded, Holsti's coefficient of intercoder reliability was calculated at .81.

TABLE 6.1. Hong Kong Handover Media Vectors

NEWSPAPER	MEDIA VECTOR
St. Louis Post-Dispatch	.231
Memphis Commercial Appeal	.160
Chicago Tribune	.082
Seattle Post-Intelligencer	.0534
Atlanta Journal/Constitution	.0527
Denver Rocky Mountain News	.0515
New Orleans Times Picayune	.049
Charlotte Observer	.044
Albany Times-Union	.043
Houston Chronicle	−.002
Pittsburgh Post-Gazette	−.010
Orlando Sentinel	−.035
Portland Oregonian	−.038
Boston Globe	−.055
Baltimore Sun	−.059
Cincinnati Inquirer	−.082
San Francisco Chronicle	−.100
Philadelphia Inquirer	−.210
Phoenix Gazette	−.282
Detroit Free Press	−.359

Results: Nationwide Variation in Reporting on Hong Kong Handover

There was noticeable variation among the calculated media vectors. The range between the media vector scores was nearly .6, with St. Louis (+.231) the most favorable newspaper and Detroit (−.358) the most unfavorable.

Protection Hypothesis Confirmed: Income Clearly Linked to Opposition to Hong Kong Handover

As Table 6.2 indicates, revealing Pearson correlations between city characteristics and media vector scores, the higher the family income level, the

TABLE 6.2. Hong Kong Handover Pearson Correlations

HYPOTHESIS	PEARSON CORRELATION	SIGNIFICANCE
$100,000+ income	−.395	.043
College education	−.093	.349

more negative (or less positive) the coverage of the Hong Kong handover (r = −.395; p = .043). Education level, by contrast, is not significantly related to media coverage of the transition (r = −.093; p = .349). For this case study, the proportion of families with relatively high incomes in a city is linked to level of media unfavorability to the Hong Kong transition. Economic "protection" interests corresponded with coverage opposed to the Hong Kong handover.

NATIONWIDE COVERAGE OF THE NORTH AMERICAN FREE TRADE AGREEMENT

Introduction

Because so many citizens identified with employment/unemployment issues, this critical event is an ideal opportunity for studying the association between citizen/influential concerns and newspaper coverage. NAFTA took effect on January 1, 1995. Consistent with the post-World War II effort to develop more integrated, open markets, NAFTA, a 2000-page extension to the 1988 U.S.–Canada free trade agreement, removes tariffs, trade barriers, and restrictions on foreign markets to increase the flow of products, agricultural goods, and services among the three countries. Its provisions were to go into effect over the next 15 years.

With so much historic and bipartisan support, NAFTA nonetheless became the most controversial free trade agreement in recent decades. A variety of business journalists and publications reassured U.S. citizens that the agreement was in the national interest in the long run, leading to strengthened exports (Dowd, 1993; Marshall, 1993). Some groups remained opposed, nevertheless, including labor unions, the textile industry and environmentalists, concerned about loss of certain industries, jobs, and what by U.S. standards appear to be lenient environmental protection laws.

Although passing NAFTA presented President Clinton with substantial dilemmas, the controversy, as reported in the mass media, represents an opportunity for communication scholars to craft serious questions. Asking the question that Bennett and Manheim (1993) posed about coverage of the Gulf War, how well did the media "frame" or "cue" events so that mere facts being reported were given attention and broader meanings?

In their Gulf War report, Bennett and Manheim argued that "the public defines an issue as it is cued by media, and the media as they are cued by policy elites." The authors also argued that unless policy elites debate matters early and vehemently in the course of a developing news story, opportunities to cue the public may be lost. Unlike reporting on the Gulf War, policy elites had multiple opportunities to debate NAFTA *early and vehemently* in the course of a developing news story, so that few opportunities to cue the public were lost.

The NAFTA debate is also an excellent example of a critical event evoking employment issues because, according to an August 1993 Gallup poll, the American public was concerned about it as an employment/jobs issue, with 68% surveyed saying they thought jobs would be lost because U.S. businesses would move to Mexico. Only 22% believed NAFTA would create jobs in America because Mexico would buy more U.S. exports. Furthermore, the public was almost evenly split on NAFTA, with 44% opposed, 41% in favor. (Gallup & Moore, 1993). NAFTA was clearly controversial.

With the public so divided, even disapproving, newspapers had many options in covering the NAFTA debate. To the extent papers varied, what factors present in their communities are associated with that variation? And are the factors associated with variation linked to relatively short- or long-term community concerns or characteristics?

Employment Issues Scarce in Communication Literature

A review of the communication literature reveals few articles focusing on the association between the umbrella issue of employment/unemployment and mass or public communications regarding it. Some attention has been paid to the use of information technologies by populations employed in the rural sector and by telecommuters, working from home (Abbott, 1989; Kraut, 1989; LaRose, 1989). Three articles do focus directly on media and unemployment as a political or social problem, noting that television for schooling in developing countries can strain government capabilities to absorb employment demands (Arnove, 1975); television reports offer few explanations of the reasons for unemployment (Barkin & Gurevitch, 1987); and as a city's unemployment level rose, local coverage of the issue increased (Shaw & Slater, 1988).

Given this "information gap" or "attention gap" between public or scholarly concerns (among economists, political scientists, and sociologists) about unemployment and the dearth of concern displayed in the communication literature, it is worthwhile focusing on NAFTA coverage in particular because the issue was universally discussed in the United States, Ross Perot demonized it, and there was a win–lose vote on NAFTA in the Congress.

Two Hypothesis Clusters: Privilege and Economic Disadvantage

Economic Privilege

It is anticipated that in cities with relatively high proportions of the economically advantaged and well educated, in particular where the service sector is comparatively large, reporting on NAFTA may be relatively receptive to the changes it can introduce because such groups are "buffered" from many of the uncertainties accompanying large-scale social or economic change. Economic self-interest may be present as well. High proportions of privileged residents may be linked to relatively pro-NAFTA reporting in a city because economically and socially dominant groups, according to Smith (1984b) and Tichenor et al. (1980), can be associated with news reports articulating those groups' interests, which are likely to favor the economic benefits offered by NAFTA. These umbrella expectations lead to an overall economic advantage hypothesis. Accordingly:

H1: *The greater the percentage with annual family incomes of $100,000 or more, the more favorable the newspaper coverage of NAFTA.* (Lifestyle Market Analysis, 1993)

H2: *The higher the proportion of college-educated, the more favorable the newspaper coverage of NAFTA.* (Lifestyle Market Analysis, 1993)

Community Protection or Economic Disadvantage

In contrast, in cities with relatively high levels of economically disadvantaged (high proportions of unemployed or residents below the poverty level) or high proportions of employees in manufacturing, whose jobs would presumably be more at risk than would those of service workers once NAFTA was passed, reporting on NAFTA is predicted to be less favorable. Therefore:

H3: *The higher the percentage of unemployment or poverty in a city, the less likely media are to report favorably on NAFTA.* (County and City Extra, 1993)

H4: *The higher the percentage of the civilian labor force employed in manufacturing in a city, the less likely media are to report favorably on NAFTA.* (County and City Extra, 1993)

Sample and Coding Categories

For this analysis, 553 articles printed from September 1, 1993 to December 31, 1993 (averaging more than 20 articles per paper) were measured and evaluated using the DIALOG newspaper database. All articles on NAFTA activities or their implications more than one paragraph in length printed in the stated time frame were sampled in 20 newspapers, representing a geographic cross-section of the United States (see Table 6.3.). After prominence scores were calculated, directional measurements were assigned to each newspaper article.

Coverage *favorable* to NAFTA included articles describing it or its supporters as "gigantic agreement," "winners," "help world trade," and "results

TABLE 6.3. NAFTA Media Vectors

NEWSPAPERS	MEDIA VECTORS
Lexington Herald	.232
Wichita Eagle	.225
Philadelphia Inquirer	.210
Akron Beacon Journal	.199
Seattle Times	.156
Atlanta Journal/Constitution	.125
Orlando Sentinel	.120
Rocky Mountain News (Denver)	.095
Phoenix Gazette	.060
Dayton Daily Press	.040
Los Angeles Times	.039
Portland Oregonian	.029
Boston Globe	.020
Chicago Tribune	.020
Houston Post	.018
Allentown Morning Call	.009
Detroit Free Press	.004
St. Petersburg Times	−.090
Sacramento Bee	−.110
Pittsburgh Gazette	−.140

oriented." Other terms coded as favorable included "mature economic partnership," "dynamic era of growth," "enlarge the pie," "seize the moment," and "rejecting NAFTA would be an international disaster."

Coverage *unfavorable* to NAFTA included articles containing such phrases as "pro-NAFTA propaganda," "republicrat," "orgy," "bully pulpit," and "depressed wages." Unfavorable articles also tended to focus on such terms as "jobs are disappearing," "trigger a stampede," "cheap labor," "will kill American jobs," "one giant sting," "twilight of unionism," "bill of bads," and "good deal for the rich only."

Balanced/neutral coverage either contained material that made no effort to legitimize or delegitimize NAFTA, or it contained an approximately equal proportion of both favorable and unfavorable material.

After evaluating article direction with this threefold classification, a systematic random subsample of 50% of the articles was coded by two researchers and yielded Holsti's coefficient of intercoder reliability of .84. Each article's prominence score and its directional score (favorable, unfavorable, or balanced/neutral) were then used to calculate a media vector for each newspaper. To test the two umbrella hypotheses correlation and regression analyses were used.

Results: A Major Disconfirmation

Positive media vector scores indicated the legitimizing of NAFTA, whereas negative scores revealed the delegitimizing of the international agreement. Table 6.3 shows that media vector scores ranged from .232 for the *Lexington Herald* to –.14 for the *Pittsburgh Gazette,* with the majority of scores (17 out of 20) favorable or balanced/neutral regarding NAFTA.

Contrary to prediction, correlation analysis yields directional disconfirmation of the manufacturing hypothesis. As Table 6.4 reveals, the higher the

TABLE 6.4. NAFTA Pearson Correlations (Selected)

Variable	INCLUDING DETROIT		WITHOUT DETROIT	
	Correlation	Significance	Correlation	Significance
Percent in manufacturing	.372	.11	.465	.045*
Percent below poverty level	–.223	.34	–.229	.345
Percent unemployed	–.222	.35	–.118	.440
Percent in services	–.221	.35	–.230	.342

*$p < .05$

percentage of city employees in manufacturing, the more favorable media are toward NAFTA. Curiously, this finding was not significant at less than the .05 level of significance until Detroit was removed from the sample. Scatterplot analysis revealed that Detroit was not typical but somewhat deviant among cities with considerable numbers in manufacturing.

Perhaps Detroit was different because it still represents one of the most highly organized areas of unionized labor, the United Auto Workers. Furthermore, Detroit's core industry, automobiles, is especially sensitive to foreign competition. Whatever the reason, when Detroit was removed from the sample a clear, significant finding surfaced in Table 6.4; high levels of manufacturing were associated with newspaper coverage relatively favorable to NAFTA ($r = .46$; $p = .045$).

Little or No Correlation Between Other City Characteristics and Coverage of NAFTA

Although multiple regression analysis confirms that percent in manufacturing is the only variable that can explain any variance (22%) at a significant level (.045), in its association with favorable reporting on NAFTA, none of the other tested hypotheses yielded significant results. Contrary to the hypotheses, there are no significant relationships between newspaper coverage of NAFTA and long-term indicators of personal advantage or disadvantage accrued over a lifetime, such as education level, income level, unemployment level or even poverty level.

Percent Employed in Manufacturing Linked to Reporting Favorable to NAFTA

Occupational sector, specifically percent employed in manufacturing, outweighs the factors of education, income and occupational status in its association with reporting on NAFTA. Contrary to positions taken by organized labor, the higher the proportion of the labor force employed in manufacturing in a city, the more *positive* that city's reporting on NAFTA is likely to be. A possible umbrella explanation for the positive association of media coverage and manufacturing is the "guard dog" conception of media as sentries for established groups in social conflict, suggesting that news is primarily about those at or near the top of power hierarchies and those low in the hierarchies who threaten the top. In this case, media coverage was more consistent with the interests of owners and senior managers in manufacturing than with the interests of hourly wage-earners. Mapping coverage of the NAFTA debates demonstrates that archival data comparing newspaper databases and city characteristics can reveal significant variations in reporting on political and economic policies.

The Value of a Community Structure Approach

Finding that a high percentage employed in the manufacturing sector is related positively with media support for NAFTA suggests that in this case newspapers may have functioned less as public interest watchdogs, skeptical of official pronouncements, than as "economic protection" guard dogs for groups having "the power and influence to create and command their own security systems" (Olien et al., 1995, p. 305). Because the NAFTA debate is linked so specifically to only one city characteristic, however, this study evokes two cautions for the community structure approach. One limitation is that individual newspapers may have well-identified histories or positions—in the case of the *Detroit Free Press*, strongly pro-labor—that may exist or persist independent of a city's demographic configuration. Scatterplot analysis can reveal whether a particular city's characteristics are consistent with, dissociated from or contrary to predominant patterns. In a similar fashion, the *Rocky Mountain News* was removed from a sample of coverage of China's bid for the 2000 Olympics because Denver is the only U.S. city to mount a successful referendum to reject a Winter Olympics after the city's organizers had made a successful bid before the International Olympic Committee (Pollock et al., 1997). With the *Detroit Free Press*, its contrary pattern justified close examination and, given its relatively idiosyncratic history, exclusion from a revised sample.

A second caution focuses on how many citizens an issue appears to affect. The handover of Hong Kong raised political and economic issues of essentially universal importance. It was not unexpected that a broad measure of privilege, percent families with high incomes, was linked significantly to reporting on the future of Hong Kong. NAFTA, by contrast, appears most relevant to very specific economic interests. It may not be surprising, therefore, that only one city characteristic—percent labor force in manufacturing—varies strongly with NAFTA reporting because of a high degree of issue specificity. Nevertheless, although a particular newspaper's special history or a concrete issue's specificity can constrain the use of the community characteristic approach, it remains a valid tool.

Evidence from this study of reporting on the NAFTA debate confirms that newspapers reporting positively on NAFTA was proportional to each city's workforce employed in manufacturing. Because so much of labor was clearly against NAFTA, the reporting pattern is precisely contrary to the presumed interests of labor and congruent with the interests of manufacturing management. Analysis of newspaper NAFTA coverage reveals a substantial amount of evidence consistent with the economic protection dimension of the guard dog conception of media as "sentries for established groups in social conflict" (Olien et al., 1995, p. 306).

7

THE STAKEHOLDER HYPOTHESIS

Higher Proportions of Issue Stakeholders Are Linked to Favorable Coverage

INTRODUCTION

Tichenor, Donohue, and Olien (1973, 1980) found that the larger the city size, the greater the plurality of viewpoints presented by the media. Beyond city size, however, the size of particular stakeholder groups may have a great deal to do with reporting on issues that affect those groups. Although stakeholders are not as organized as traditional "interest groups," the communication literature on protest groups can illuminate the stakeholder concerns of senior citizens. Both conventional wisdom and empirical research suggest that the greater the size of a protest group, the more attention and favorable coverage that group will receive in mass media (McLeod & Hertog, 1992, 1999). This expectation is consistent with examinations of major newspaper and television network coverage of protest marches in Washington, DC, between 1982 and 1991, where the most powerful predictor of whether the media covered a demonstration was the size of the protest (McCarthy, McPhail, & Smith, 1996).

The presence of stakeholders may contribute to variation in media coverage from city to city. As cited in a literature review, Swisher and Reese (1992) found that in pro-tobacco regions, media coverage of tobacco-related issues was more favorable than in other regions. Additionally, Powers and Andsager (1999) found that media coverage of silicone breasts implants was more favorable after Dow Corning's public relations campaign, and in 2000, Andsager concluded that media framing of the late-term abortion debate of 1996 was influenced by the lobbying efforts of pro-choice and pro-life groups. Similarly, previous research using the community structure approach has shown that the greater the proportion of businesses or organizations marketing to the gay community in a city, the more favorable the coverage of efforts to legalize same-sex marriage (Pollock & Dantas, 1998). Consistently, researchers found that the higher the percentage of women in the workforce, the more favorable the coverage of cloning and of the Eappens, the parents of the child who was shaken to death by a nanny (Pollock, Dudzak et al., 2000; Pollock, Morris, Citarella, Ryan, & Yulis, 1999). A related study found women given more newspaper attention in ethnically diverse communities (Armstrong, 2002). An anomalous study found that in the year after the attacks on New York and Washington, DC of September 11, 2001, the percent of foreign born and number of Arabic and Farsi speakers in cities were linked not, as expected to favorable coverage of Islam, but rather to reverse, unfavorable coverage of one of the world's largest religions. In that case, however, much of the entire population of the United States may have become converted into "stakeholders in fear" (Pollock, Piccillo, Leopardi, Gratale, & Cabot, 2005).

In similar fashion, other nationwide city newspaper samples using the community structure approach have confirmed the link between stakeholder size and relatively favorable coverage of stakeholder concerns. Percent below the poverty level is linked to favorable coverage of *Roe v. Wade* (Pollock et al., 1978); and percent 75 and over is linked to relatively favorable coverage of Dr. Kevorkian (Pollock, Coughlin et al., 1996). With a precision that might surprise event the most market-oriented researchers, it was also found that the higher the percent families with children between the ages of 5 and 7 in a city, the more likely coverage of Elian Gonzalez, the Cuban boy whose mother drowned carrying him to the United States, favored repatriating Elian to his father in Cuba. Elian turned age 7 while in the United States (Pollock, Mink, & Puma, 2001). The three case studies in this chapter focus on stakeholders associated with diverse policy concerns: efforts at gun control, Arctic drilling, and proposals to try juveniles as adults.

NATIONWIDE NEWSPAPER COVERAGE
OF GUN CONTROL SINCE COLUMBINE

Introduction

The Second Amendment states that "The right of the people to keep and bear arms should not be infringed." As society has evolved, so have the uses, needs, and varieties of guns. What was once used for the primary purpose of survival has now become a major tool in modern crime. This development has led to two extreme positions on gun control.

The central issue with proposed gun control laws is that some citizens believe their Second Amendment rights would be violated, convinced they should be able to own guns for protection and hunting purposes. Since the Constitution clearly protects the right to bear arms, they see little justification for gun restrictions. Groups like the National Rifle Association (NRA) and those in the gun lobby do not believe that guns are the reason for violence. Second Amendment purists passionately assert that "Guns don't kill people, People kill people."

Others believe guns are to blame for much of the violence in the United States; they consider the Second Amendment outdated and deserving reform. There are occasional movements in Congress for more gun control legislation, especially limiting the availability of handguns. Understandably, legislation has become a more intense topic since the 1999 Columbine school shootings. Indeed, gun control laws have been a serious debate topic since the 1981 assassination attempt on President Ronald Reagan, which left his press secretary, James Brady, severely paralyzed (Kahane, 1999). Those in favor of gun control see such incidents as the Littleton, Colorado, Columbine High School shooting of April 1999, as just one of many disasters prompting demand for stricter control over the buying and use of guns. The community structure approach can be used to explore links between city demographics and reporting on efforts at gun control.

Communication Literature Has Not "Hit the Target"

Investigating communication journals, few articles were found on "gun control and media." In the years following such tragedies as the attempted assassination of Ronald Reagan and the Columbine shootings, it is extraordinary to learn that using keywords "gun control and media" and "Brady Bill," little could be found in scholarly journals such as *Communication Research, Critical Studies in Mass Communication, Journal of Communication, Journalism Quarterly, Quarterly Journal of Speech, Mass Communication and Society,* and *Newspaper Research Journal.* An online search in CommAbstracts using keywords "Brady Bill" and "gun control and media," yielded four articles.

Although *Public Opinion Quarterly* featured an article on public opinion of gun control laws and regulations, it dates to 1977 (Schuman & Pressor, 1977–1978). *Political Communication* also yielded a story about public opinion, in April 1992 (Mauser & Kopel, 1992), suggesting that polls mislead the public into answering more favorably toward gun control laws legislation. Although public opinion is important to gun control, neither article asked why media report what they do. A third article criticized the media for being "biased, careless, and in error in its discussion of weapons" (Gest, 1992). A fourth article discussed legislation before Congress (Moore,

1994). Evaluating communication journal offerings, it is clear that the communication field not only lacks substantial current research, but it also lags behind such fields as business and criminal justice.

A general search on Ebscohost using keywords "gun control and media" yielded 41 journal articles, with 10 focusing on media coverage of gun control. These articles question whether or not the media maintained a bias toward gun control and its effects on the exposed public, but none was published in communication journals. An Ebscohost search using keyword "Brady Bill and media" yielded only one article exploring TV and media biases toward gun control legislation (Dickens, 1997).

A criminal justice database search on "gun control and media" uncovered an article titled suggesting that "the mass media have a potent impact on the public's fear of crime" (Stalans & Lurgio, 1996, p. 365), but the influence of society on media (the reverse question) was not considered. Furthermore, this article takes its information from a citywide (Cincinnati) study, as opposed to a state or even national focus. Another article maintains that "pro-gun groups and the mass media have exaggerated recent increases in the rate of gun ownership by women" (Zimring, 1995, p. 1). Little on media and gun control beyond these two articles was found in criminology or law and justice articles.

Conducting a search in leading business, intellectual, and political science journals, several relevant articles were also found. In some cases, a few journals, such as *Reason, National Review*, and *The American Politics Quarterly*, had printed more articles regarding the media and gun control than in all of the communication journals combined. This evidence confirms the supposition that the topic is a major public issue, but one seldom addressed in communication literature. The main questions raised are whether media are biased about gun control and could media coverage of the issue be fair after incidents such as the Columbine shootings. The most discussed issue, overall, in articles found in business journals, was how much media coverage could sway public opinion on gun control. In an article in *The American Politics Quarterly*, a survey was conducted to measure any slant. Of 653 newspaper articles reviewed, articles supporting gun control outnumbered those opposed by a 10–1 margin (Smith, 2000).

The other noteworthy observation when comparing communication literature and other literature is the dates published. Before and after Columbine, little, if anything, was published in communication journals. In the business databases and journals, by contrast, most of the material found was printed after Columbine. This clear discrepancy among journals suggests that more studies on contemporary gun control legislation deserve attention in the communication field. Indeed, President Clinton met with Congress in March 2000 to discuss legislation on media coverage and gun control (FDCH Political Transcripts, 3/16/2000).

Hypotheses

Community structure hypotheses can be combined in three cluster categories: stakeholders (life-cycle position and political partisanship), violated buffer, and vulnerability.

Stakeholders

Although the right to bear arms is granted to each American citizen, gun control is doubtless a more important issue for certain stakeholders than for others. Other community structure studies have found that the larger the size of groups in a given city, the more likely newspapers are to report favorably on issues pertinent to these groups (see the introduction to this chapter).

Life Cycle Position. There is evidence suggesting that "identification" with a certain incident or public figure is associated with empathy and positive regard, as shown in the study of Magic Johnson's HIV announcement (see chap. 8). Those most affected by this event were those psychologically "involved" with him. This involvement was linked to personal concern about AIDS and the risk of AIDS in the heterosexual community (Basil & Brown, 1994; see also Flora & Maibach, 1990).

Likewise, certain groups are more likely to "identify" with the fight for gun control. Specifically, parents with children are expected to experience more horror at the Columbine tragedy and empathize with the loss of children. Parents with children, in general, are more likely to look favorably on parent concerns generally, as in the return of Elian Gonzalez to his father (Mink, Puma, & Pollock, 2002), which was covered quite favorably in cities with high proportions of families with children about the same age (5–7) as young Elian. Accordingly:

H1: *The higher the percentage of households with children under 2 years of age, the more favorable the newspaper coverage of gun control.* (Lifestyle Market Analyst, 2000)

H2: *The higher the percentage of households with children ages 2–4, the more favorable the newspaper cover of gun control.* (Lifestyle Market Analyst, 2000)

H3: *The higher the percentage of households with children ages 5–7, the more favorable the newspaper coverage of gun control.* (Lifestyle Market Analyst, 2000).

H4: *The higher the percentage of households with children ages 8–10, the more favorable the newspaper coverage of gun control.* (Lifestyle Market Analyst, 2000)

H5: *The higher the percentage of households with children ages 11–12, the more favorable the newspaper coverage of gun control.* (Lifestyle Market Analyst, 2000)

H6: *The higher the percentage of households with children ages 13–15, the more favorable the newspaper coverage of gun control.* (Lifestyle Market Analyst, 2000)

H7: *The higher the percentage of households with children ages 16–18, the more favorable the newspaper coverage of gun control.* (Lifestyle Market Analyst, 2000)

Additionally, because they don't have spouses with whom to share an identity or "protective" responsibilities, single parents may be likely to identify strongly with the need to protect their children. Yet because of their relatively solitary duties, single parents may feel safer in their own homes if a gun is accessible for emergencies. Accordingly:

H8: *The higher the percentage of single parents in a city, the less favorable the coverage of gun control.* (county and City Extra 2000)

Hunters and Shooters. Citizens involved in an activity are more likely to have a strong attachment to issues surrounding that pursuit. Hunting and shooting have been routine activities in several areas, especially in regions where citizens use guns for leisure or food purposes as opposed to strictly household protection. Those who frequently participate in these activities are more likely to display a negative reaction toward the issue of gun control, and it is predicted that media will reflect this perspective. Accordingly:

H9: *The higher the percentage of people in a city who hunt frequently, the less favorable the newspaper coverage of gun control will be.* (Lifestyle Market Analysis, 2000)

Political Partisanship. Perhaps the most obvious of the opinionated stakeholders are the two major political parties: the Democrats and the Republicans. Republicans are notoriously more supportive of less restrictive gun usage, whereas Democrats generally fight for stricter gun legislation. For example, the Brady Bill of 1993, under the Clinton administration, implemented a mandatory waiting period in order to purchase a handgun (Kahane, 1999). NRA spending confirms this polarization. The NRA allots 83.4% of its funding to the Republican party whereas only 16.6% is given to the Democrats (Center for Responsive Politics, 2004). Media may reflect these differential political perspectives, and therefore:

> H10: *The higher percentage voting Democratic in a city, the more favorable the coverage of gun control will be.* (County and City Extra, 2000)

> H11: *The higher percentage voting Republican in a city, the less favorable the coverage of gun control will be.* (County and City Extra, 2000)

Violated Buffer

The violated buffer hypothesis expects that the greater percent of privileged who believe their way of life threatened, the more unfavorable the coverage of the perilous issue. For example, because the Columbine tragedy made it evident that the privileged are also at risk, and even relatively affluent, suburban high schools can experience gun eruptions, it is expected that privilege will be linked correspondingly with more favorable coverage of gun control. By extension, it can be hypothesized that:

> H12: *The larger the proportion of households in a city with an income of $100,000 or more, the more favorable the coverage of gun control.* (Lifestyle Market Analyst, 2000)

> H13: *The larger the percent who have 4 or more years of college education, the more favorable the coverage of gun control.* (Lifestyle Market Analyst, 2000)

> H14: *The larger the proportion of those with professional or technical status in a city, the more favorable the coverage of gun control.* (Lifestyle Market, Analyst)

Vulnerability

The higher the percentage of disadvantaged populations in a city, the greater the chance that media perspectives may be more sympathetic toward selected issues (see chap. 5). Because the socially marginalized in a city are more likely to become victims of crime, especially violent crime, one might expect their presence linked to favorable coverage of gun control. Relatively disadvantaged groups might include those who are unemployed or living below the poverty level, those who are denied certain opportunities based on historical ethnic factors or lack of access to a relatively new culture (African Americans or Hispanics), and those living in high crime areas. Based on these considerations, the following hypotheses are suggested:

H15: *The higher the percent unemployed in a city, the more favorable the coverage of gun control.* (County and City Extra, 2000)

H16: *The larger the percent below the poverty level, the more favorable the coverage of gun control.* (County and City Extra, 2000)

H17: *The larger the percent African Americans in a city, the more favorable the coverage of gun control.* (Lifestyle Market Analyst, 2000)

H18: *The greater the percent Hispanics in a city, the more favorable the coverage of gun control.* (Lifestyle Market Analyst, 2000)

H19: *The larger the number of police reported offenses in a city, the more favorable the coverage of gun control.* (Uniform Crime Reports, 2000)

H20: *The higher the homicide rate in a city, the more favorable gun control coverage will be.* (Uniform Crime Reports, 2000)

Methodology

Sample Selection

This study explores coverage of gun control in a cross-section of 21 major newspapers nationwide (see Table 7.1). All of the articles of more than 150 words in length were sampled from each newspaper from the period April 20, 1999, the day of the Columbine shootings, through November 2000, a period of almost 1.5 years. The resulting 420 newspaper articles were collected from the DIALOG Classroom Information Program newspaper database available to college libraries. The *Denver Post* was excluded from the sample because of event proximity biases that might have been introduced by the Columbine massacre.

After coding for prominence, each article also received a "directional" score. Coverage considered *favorable* toward gun control included articles viewing gun control as a safety precaution, as in after the Columbine shootings. Articles were also coded as favorable when a majority of the text praised viewpoints accommodating or receptive to gun control.

TABLE 7.1. Gun Control Media Vectors

NEWSPAPER	MEDIA VECTOR
The Arizona Republic/The Phoenix Gazette	0.500
Detroit Free Press	0.484
The Charlotte Observer	0.472
The Boston Globe	0.390
The Seattle Post-Intelligencer	0.347
The Atlanta Journal/The Atlanta Constitution	0.293
San Francisco Chronicle	0.288
St. Louis Post-Dispatch	0.218
The Oregonian	0.195
The Philadelphia Inquirer	0.192
Denver Post	0.182
Milwaukee Journal Sentinel	0.182
Pittsburgh Post-Gazette	0.149
The Plain Dealer	0.123
Tallahassee Democrat	0.111
Lexington Herald-Leader	0.068
The Times-Picayune	0.050
The Times Union	0.021
The Cincinnati Enquirer	−0.022
The Commercial Appeal	−0.056
The Fresno Bee	−0.058

Unfavorable coverage of gun control included articles that focused on the constitutional right to bear arms as well as the issue of guns as protection. *Balanced/neutral* coverage included articles that gave both viewpoints on gun control in approximately equal measure, presenting an overall nondirectional perspective. Two researchers read each article independently, yielding a Holsti's coefficient of intercoder reliability of .91.

Results

Media vectors, Pearson correlations, and regression analyses were calculated. As predicted, the media vectors of newspaper coverage varied greatly nationwide, ranging from .500 (Phoenix) to –.058 (Fresno). Most city papers were favorable: Of the 21 cities studied, 18 showed favorable coverage of gun control, whereas 3 exhibited negative coverage. Table 7.1 reveals the media vectors for each newspaper, whereas Table 7.2 tabulates Pearson correlations between city characteristics and the media vector.

TABLE 7.2. Gun Control Pearson Correlations

HYPOTHESES	PEARSON CORRELATION	SIGNIFICANCE
Households w/kids 16–18	–.681	.000**
Households w/kids 13–15	–.552	.005**
Percent single parents	–.538	.006**
Percent income over $100,000	.519	.008**
Households w/ kids 11–12	–.512	.009**
Households w/ kids 8–10	–.505	.010*
Percent college 4+ years	.399	.037*
Percent professional/ technical	.388	.041*
Percent hunting as an activity	–.374	.047*
Percent households w/kids 5–7	–.340	.066
Percent unemployed	–.333	.070
Percent women in workforce	.326	.074
Household w/ kids 2–4	–.306	.089
Below poverty level	–289	.102
Police reported offenses	.260	.128
Percent African American	–.176	.223
Percent voted Republican	–.165	.238
Percent voted Democrat	.135	.280
Households w/kids <2	–.103	.329
Percent Hispanics	–.176	.223
Homicide rate	.043	.426

*Significant at .05 level
**Significant at .01 level.

Analysis and Discussion

Stakeholder (Life-cycle Position) Hypotheses Confirmed, But in Opposite Direction, Suggesting a Possible "Vigilante" Hypothesis

Overall, this study on gun control revealed that newspapers report favorably on the issue to some degree. Correlation analysis yielded multiple significant results, almost all falling into the life-cycle position, and violated buffer hypotheses, with one in the stakeholder category. The most significant finding was the percentage of households with children ages 16–18 correlating negatively with the media vector, thus disconfirming the original hypothesis (Table 7.2).

Regression analysis confirms the same city characteristic as the only significant variable, accounting for 46% of the variance, shown in Table 7.3.

Within the "life-cycle position" cluster, almost all Pearson correlations proved highly significant at the 1% level (see Table 7.4). The variables pro-

TABLE 7.3. Gun Control Multiple Regression of City Characteristics

VARIABLE	R	R-SQUARE	F CHANGE	SIGNIFICANCE F CHANGE
Households with children ages 16-18	.681	.463	15.731	.000

TABLE 7.4. Gun Control Life Cycle Position Significant Findings

CHARACTERISTIC	PEARSON SCORE	SIGNIFICANCE
Households w/ kids 16–18	−.681	.000**
Households w/ kids 13–15	−.552	.005**
Percent single parents	−.538	.006**
Households w/ kids 11–12	−.512	.009**
Households w/ kids 8–10	−.505	.010**

**Significant at the .01 level or better

ducing these findings included households with children, ages 8–10, 11–12, 13–15, 16–18, as well as percent of single parents in a city. The table compares each life–cycle finding significant at the .01 level.

Children's ages were deconstructed into small, discrete categories to yield the most specific results. Although it was predicted that percentage of single parents would correlate negatively with newspaper coverage of gun control, it was expected that families with children would be associated with favorable coverage of gun control. It is striking that the exact opposite results were yielded and, in fact, households with children correlate highly *unfavorably* with newspaper coverage of gun control. Households with teens probably most at risk of being victims of gun violence (the 16–18 age group) are linked strongly with opposition to gun control.

A possible explanation is that these variables also correlate positively with the "vulnerability" cluster, which includes percentage below the poverty line and percentage unemployed. Although percent unemployed in a city was only directionally linked to negative coverage of gun control ($r = -.333$; $p = .07$), associating households with children and the "vulnerability" variables—in particular regarding low-income and high crime rate—generates an explanation resembling a "vigilante hypothesis."

More specifically, when examining which variables correlate positively with core indicators of economic "vulnerability" (poverty level and percent unemployed), it was found that homicide rate per one thousand correlated significantly with poverty level ($p < .01$) and with the percentage unemployed ($p < .05$). It is not surprising that highly vulnerable social segments experience a higher crime rate. This could reasonably correspond with families perceiving a need for self-protection. The vigilante hypothesis, in which individuals or groups take the law into their own hands, suggests that households with children living within this environment may regard gun possession as an important part of personal protection, and any effort at gun control a threat to that effort to maximize family safety. Additionally, the percent who hunt and shoot yielded significant results ($r = -.374$; $p = .047$). People who enjoy hunting and shooting are confirmed linked to media coverage opposed to legislation that would make it more difficult for them to purchase what they consider to be recreational devices.

Violated Buffer Confirmed: Partisanship, Other Measures Not Significant

All three variables within the violated buffer cluster proved significant, including: percent households with incomes of $100,000 or more ($r = .519$; $p = .008$); percent with 4 or more years of college education ($r = .399$, $p = .037$), and percent professional/technical workers ($r = .388$, $p = .041$). As predicted, those with higher levels of privilege may perceive their way of life as threatened and are associated with promoting measures to maximize safety

Measures of partisanship failed to produce significant results. The disparity of NRA targeting more than 80% of its political funding toward the Republican Party did not manifest itself in newspaper coverage of gun control. Nor did the Million-Mom March, on May 14, 2000, supported by the Democratic Party, a rally backing stronger gun legislation, illuminate partisan alignments. These disparities in funding and mobilization did not manifest themselves in significantly divergent newspaper reporting on gun control aligned with different voting patterns. Other variables, including percentage below poverty level, percentage African American, percentage Hispanic, number of police reported offenses, and homicide rate per 100,000 yielded no significant correlations with coverage of gun control.

Conclusion

There are strong correlations between city characteristics and newspaper coverage on the issue of gun control. This study found significant relationships between newspaper coverage and variables within the stakeholder (especially lifecycle) and violated buffer clusters. In total, the study yielded nine significant results.

The most surprising findings were in the life-cycle position stakeholder cluster. Households with a higher percentage of children ages 8–10, 11–12, 13–15, 16–18 revealed a negative association with the issue of gun control. This pattern disconfirmed the original hypotheses. After the Columbine incident in 1999, it was expected that families with children would generally view new gun control legislation favorably. However, when comparing the cluster with measures of "vulnerability," there were noticeably high correlations between families with children and measures of underprivilege. These findings buttress a "vigilante hypothesis," suggesting that the disadvantaged may perceive a need to protect themselves.

Results may have been affected somewhat by two specific circumstances: a shooting and a national mobilization event. With the highest media vector supporting gun control, Detroit was home to Kayla Rolland, a 6-year-old shot to death at school. Prior to this tragedy, articles were coded less favorably in comparison to after the school shooting. Second, the Million-Mom March on May 14, 2000, fostered positive public perceptions of gun control legislation. A large percentage of the articles read dealt with this event and thus could have affected findings. Any of these incidents could have contributed to both public perception of gun control and newspaper coverage. Further studies of gun control coverage over time will test the consistency of the life-cycle findings that emerged so strongly from this study.

NATIONWIDE NEWSPAPER COVERAGE OF DRILLING IN THE ARCTIC NATIONAL WILDLIFE REFUGE

Introduction

With the election of George W. Bush in January 2001, drilling for oil in the Arctic National Wildlife Refuge (ANWR) became a real possibility. Since 1960, the ANWR has been protected from development under law, except for a small segment set aside in 1980 for future exploration into oil reserve potential known as Section 1002. In the U. S. quest for increased energy, we must decide how that energy will be produced. By not drilling in the ANWR, the "Last Great Wilderness" could be preserved for generations to come. However, any oil mined could ease the country's reliance on foreign fuel, especially from the unstable Middle East. If increased oil is still required, then the ANWR holds some reserves; however, is the destruction of the land and ecosystem worth the value of the oil? By "framing" issues in various ways, newspapers can help present some environmental or energy positions as more reasonable or attractive than others. This study analyzes the role of newspapers in discussions about the ANWR, exploring connections between newspaper coverage and city demographics.

Literature Review

An extensive search of communications journals, online databases, and related scholarly journals yielded a paucity of results focusing on drilling for oil in the ANWR, or even energy policy and production. Although little information was directly linked, several articles helped construct a foundation to understand better the debates and controversies related to drilling in the ANWR.

The scientific community, especially those in the biological and ecological arenas, has paid considerable attention to the consequences of oil exploration on one of the last wilderness areas in the United States (Gibbs, 2001; Niiler, 2000; Strieker, 2000). The conclusions of all these authors are not optimistic. The consensus is that the exploration or drilling for oil in the ANWR would cause "permanent, irreversible damage" (Strieker, 2000, p. 47), and Gibbs (2001) stated, "Some habitat will be damaged or destroyed" (p. 66). Why is it important to keep this area pristine? This question has at least four different answers, each worth careful consideration.

First, the ANWR serves as a "control area against which [scientists] can compare the environmental effects of human development" (Gibbs, 2001, p. 69), such as measuring global warming and effects on wildlife. Related to the "control area" goal for the ANWR is the concept of "wilderness." In his study, *The Human Experience of Wilderness*, Tony Murphy (1999) posited that there is a common definition of wilderness in U.S. culture. Wilderness is seen as "a place for withdrawal from modern life, for physical and spiritual renewal and as a connection to the environment." Perhaps even more notably, "these meanings were shared by visitors and non-visitors to wilderness" (p. 36). Although most of us may never visit the ANWR it is important to society that this kind of wilderness be preserved.

A second issue is how drilling will affect area residents. According to Faith Gemmill (1999), there are approximately 7,000 Gwich'in people, a Native American tribe that will be affected dramatically by any drilling. This tribe's main lifeline is the porcupine caribou, who migrate through the proposed drilling area. If the caribou's migratory pattern were altered, it could destroy the way of life of the Gwich'in people.

A third issue concerns the question of how much oil is trapped beneath the ANWR's costal plain. Oil supply has been the target of numerous studies and the results of the studies have been contradictory. A 1991 study published in *Energy Journal* states the prospects for drilling in the ANWR are uncertain. "First there is the fundamental difference in interpretation of the basic geology of the region, which changes the geological potential by 100%" (Powell, 1991, p. 12). Powell explained that the way the soundings and preliminary geologic tests are interpreted could vary greatly. Another observation of Powell's report is that the ultimate profitability of any oil exploration depends on the price of oil. If the price is high, then the exploration may be profitable, but with prices low, "almost no foreseeable discoveries will be economic" (p. 12). This concern over profitability is shared among many researchers and those in the oil business (Holdren, 2001).

Even more important than the discussion over drilling in Alaska is a larger, fourth issue: the debate over the future of our nation's energy production and policy. President Bush's current energy plan calls for increased production of power to meet growing needs. Is this the best plan for the future of the country, or should we focus more on conservation, alternative energy, and reducing our power consumption?

If conservation and reduction of power consumption were the future path of the nation, then drilling in the ANWR would not be an issue. The aforementioned environmental concerns would undoubtedly take precedence over the extraction of a finite amount of oil in a finite area of wilderness. However, our current needs for energy are real, evident in the uncertainties of global politics after September 11, 2001.

Is oil the answer? In the long run, any oil raised from below the Arctic tundra may not make much difference. According to one source, "Whatever the ANWR might bring in the way of a modest and temporary reduction in oil import requirements, it would buy nothing against the parallel problem of climate change risks and little if anything against the electrical supply problems such as those plaguing California" (Holdren, 2001, p. 51).

Although this topic has been thoroughly discussed in Congress as well as in multiple media outlets, communication research on this topic is scarce. Furthermore, communication research seldom focuses on issues pertaining to the environment or energy. The majority of communications research done on energy usage or oil consumption is decades old (Anderson & Lipsey, 1978; Kepplinger & Roth, 1979). The primary reason for the research at that time was the energy crisis of 1973-1974. Since then, conditions have improved. As Holdren (2001), put it, "Real energy prices were falling. Gasoline lines and electricity blackouts were absent. Urban air quality was generally improving" (p. 43). This is no longer the case. Electricity blackouts were daily occurrences in California in late 2001, heating oil and natural gas prices increased dramatically in the winters of 1999–2001, and the United States currently imports over half its oil. These energy and environmental issues may have played a role in the 2000 presidential election. If a topic is part of a set of presidential election issues, surely it is worthy of more research in the communications field. It is expected that opinions will vary from city to city based on demographics.

Hypotheses

Hypotheses cluster within four umbrella groups, including stakeholders (especially political partisanship), protection, violated buffer, and vulnerability.

Stakeholders

A variety of stakeholder categories might be connected to reporting on arctic drilling, including political partisanship, environment-friendly lifestyles, union membership and commitments to public land.

Political Partisanship. McLeod and Hertog (1999) proposed that the interests of a specific group would be reflected in newspaper coverage, and the larger the group, the more intense the coverage as well as the more propitious for the group's interests. Other studies have revealed correlations between many different interest groups, or stakeholders, and the newspaper coverage of group ideals; Pollock et al. (1997) showed more favorable coverage of China's offer to host the Olympic Games of 2000 in cities with a larger percentage of Asian Americans. A study on nationwide newspaper coverage of a Patients' Bill of Rights, reported in chapter 5, revealed a sharp disagreement reflecting different political party agendas. Coverage varying with party strength was also apparent in newspaper accounts of the effort by the FDA to regulate nicotine, blocked ultimately by the U.S. Supreme Court (Caamaño, Pollock, Virgilio, & Lindstrom, 2001).

Republicans are generally in favor of the drilling prospect, evident in President Bush's proposal. Democrats are generally opposed to drilling in the wildlife refuge, hence former President Clinton's veto of a bill proposing the drilling, spurring a government shutdown (Erfle, McMillian, & Grofman, 1990). As a result, the larger the percentage of either party in a city, the more likely media coverage will reflect the dominant party's position, therefore:

H1: *The higher the percentage voting Republican in the last presidential election, the more favorable the coverage of drilling in the ANWR.* (County and City Extra, 2000)

H2: *The higher the percentage voting Democratic in the last presidential election, the less favorable the coverage of drilling in the ANWR.* (County and City Extra, 2000)

Environment-Friendly Lifestyle. It is reasonable to assume that some specific leisure lifestyles correspond closely with awareness or interest in environmental issues. Because of their frequent immersion in the outdoors, at least two groups of stakeholders are likely to manifest substantial interest in the quality of outdoor life: hunters and campers. It is further expected that these stakeholders are interested in preserving the existing environment as much as possible. In addition, those who in surveys say they are "very interested" in the environment can be anticipated unfavorable toward arctic drilling. Accordingly:

H3: *The higher the proportion of those in a city who hunt frequently, the less favorable the coverage of drilling in the ANWR.* (Lifestyle Market Analyst, 2000)

H4: *The higher the proportion of those in a city who camp frequently, the less favorable the coverage of drilling in the ANWR.* (Lifestyle Market Analyst, 2000)

H5: *The higher the proportion of those who are "very interested" in the environment, the less favorable the coverage of drilling in the ANWR.* (Lifestyle Market Analyst, 2000)

Union Membership. Other groups also hold or are believed to hold stakes in the drilling debate. Newspaper coverage of the debate has often framed drilling with an increase in jobs. Examples of this framing can be seen in *The Washington Post* and *The Boston Globe*, respectively: "Bush's plan to drill in the Arctic National Wildlife Refuge, a project that unions expect to create 25,000 jobs in Alaska" (Allen, 2001, p. A02); "the issue for labor is plain: Is it worth supporting Bush's drilling proposal—and the jobs that it would create" (Jordan, 2001, p. F4). These reports on drilling aligned with jobs have persuaded some union members to agree on this specific oil exploration, therefore:

> **H6:** *The higher the percentage of union members in a city, the more favorable the coverage for drilling in the ANWR.* (Lifestyle Market Analyst, 2000)

Commitments to Public Land. It is reasonable to theorize that cities that have already embraced qualities associated with conservation and preservation will not only have a larger population against drilling in the refuge, but will also show less favorable coverage of the issue. Cities that already spend large amounts on public lands will logically have a large, environmentally concerned populace. Therefore:

> **H7:** *The larger the percentage of a city's budget devoted to public lands, the less favorable the coverage for drilling in the ANWR.* (County and City Extra, 2000)

Economic "Protection" Hypothesis

Newspapers are often referred to as "watchdogs" for the public. However, it is quite possible that they can act as "guard dogs" of those in power, giving favorable coverage to elite economic interests and, therefore, shielding established powers (Olien et al., 1995). One community structure study showed that, despite opposition toward NAFTA from labor, cities with higher percentages of the "civilian labor force employed in manufacturing in a city" displayed more favorable coverage of NAFTA in newspapers (see chap. 6). Perhaps this correspondence of employment in manufacturing and coverage favoring NAFTA reflects the role newspapers can play as guard dogs, supporting powerful economic interests, in this case manufacturing owners. In the case of drilling in the Arctic refuge, it is expected that newspapers might act as guard dogs toward owners and managers, or "privileged" groups, because it would protect their interests.

> **H8:** *The higher the percentage of the population employed in manufacturing in a city, the more favorable the coverage for drilling in the ANWR.* (County and City Extra, 2000)

Violated Buffer Hypothesis

In sharp contrast with the protection hypothesis, the violated buffer hypothesis expects a negative correlation between "privileged" groups and media coverage of drilling in the ANWR. The violated buffer hypothesis suggests that privileged groups could believe their lifestyles and their children's well being are threatened by environmental dangers such as the destruction of protected lands. The Chapter 4 case study on newspaper coverage of the tobacco industry's MSA found a positive correlation between cities with higher populations of "privileged" groups and favorable coverage of the MSA, part of an effort to protect children from tobacco advertising, presumably in part because such advertising "violates" the health and well being of all children, including those of privileged groups. In relation to the ANWR, "privileged" groups may be "buffered" from economic shifts, like upward changes in oil prices, but they could also experience a "violation" of a cherished way of life and potential violation of the health and safety of their children. Therefore, from a violated buffer perspective:

H9: *The higher the percentage of families earning $100,000 or more per year in a city, the less favorable the coverage for drilling in the ANWR.* (Lifestyle Market Analyst, 2000)

H10: *The higher the percentage of the population that is college educated in a city the less favorable the coverage for drilling in the ANWR.* (Lifestyle Market Analyst, 2000)

H11: *The higher the percentage of the population with professional occupations in a city, the less favorable the coverage for drilling in the ANWR.* (Lifestyle Market Analyst, 2000)

Vulnerability

Newspaper coverage is not limited to portraying the values of the privileged but can also reflect the concerns of the less privileged. In the chapter 5 study of national newspaper coverage of the Patients' Bill of Rights, a high correlation was found between positive reporting on the issue and percent unemployed and below the poverty level. This finding suggests newspapers could function in this scenario as watchdogs, concerned about the needs and concerns of the less fortunate.

Newspaper coverage of the ANWR debate has often framed drilling with an increase of jobs. Put bluntly, higher unemployment and poverty levels suggest that jobs are needed. Thus, because drilling means more employment, the more favorable the expected coverage of drilling in the ANWR, therefore:

H12: *The higher the percentage of those in a city below the poverty level, the more favorable the coverage for drilling in the ANWR.* (County and City Extra, 2000)

H13 *The higher the percentage of those unemployed in a city, the more favorable the coverage for drilling in the ANWR.* (County and City Extra, 2000)

Methodology

Sample Selection

This study examined the coverage of drilling in the ANWR systematically in 13 major newspapers throughout the United States, representing a geographical cross-section of the nation (see Table 7.5.). All articles 150 words or more in length printed in each of the papers were sampled from the period of September 1, 2000 through September 10, 2001 (*N* = 241 articles), a period when drilling in the ANWR was emotionally debated nationwide and prominent on media agendas. Although discussions were conducted prior to this time, it was not until George W. Bush and Al Gore revealed their energy policies that debate over this issue surfaced consistently on a nationwide level. After September 11, 2001, national priorities were understandably changed in response to terrorist threats. The articles were collected via Lexis Nexis and the DIALOG Classroom Information Program newspaper databases.

Measures and Dependent Variables

After prominence scores were calculated, article direction was evaluated using the criteria described here.

Articles were coded as *favorable* if they exhibited content that was determined to be generally pro-drilling in the ANWR. These articles included discussion of the need for more oil production and more energy; an increase in jobs associated with oil production; and new, safer drilling technologies. Articles that framed the political figures associated with pro-drilling attitudes in a positive way, put a favorable perspective on the union's stance toward drilling were coded as favorable, as were articles describing drilling as a solution for the nations' energy woes, ridding the United States of dependence on foreign oil.

Articles coded as *unfavorable* generally were pro-conservation regarding the ANWR. These articles framed favorably conservation over production, often claiming oil production is a short-term solution. Some articles would include praise of fuel saving measures like stricter fuel efficiency standards for sport utility vehicles. Unfavorable articles also described the importance of preserving one of the last untouched wildernesses and generally took pro-environmental positions. Some articles also attacked political leaders who promoted drilling. Other articles included nationwide polls showing many against drilling, sometimes including studies suggesting the number of expected additional jobs to be much lower than previously thought. In general, articles promoting long-term solutions to national energy needs were coded as "unfavorable."

Articles that reported on the ANWR debate evenhandedly were coded as *balanced/neutral*. These articles offered statistics allowing readers to come to their own conclusions. Some of these articles related coverage of the congressional debates and accurate reporting of voting. Facts that aid the arguments of several different interests regarding drilling were fully represented in balanced/neutral articles, including the perspectives of oil firms, conservationists, politicians or everyday citizens. For two coders per article, Holsti's coefficient of intercoder reliability was .89.

Results

Newspaper coverage of drilling for oil in the ANWR during the period of September 2000 to September 10, 2001 indeed varied nationwide. The media vectors ranged from +.056 to −.187, revealing divergent opinions among city newspapers, with most media vectors (11 out of 13) balanced/neutral or negative. Table 7.5 displays media vector variation. After calculating media vectors, Pearson correlations were run (see Table 7.6).

TABLE 7.5. Arctic Oil Drilling Media Vectors

NEWSPAPER	MEDIA VECTOR
The Houston Chronicle	0.056
The Seattle Times	0.035
The Denver Post	0.001
The Atlanta Journal/ Constitution	0.000
The Times-Picayune (New Orleans)	−0.010
The Pittsburgh Post-Gazette	−0.016
The Lexington Herald-Leader	−0.021
The San Diego Union-Tribune	−0.024
The Philadelphia Inquirer	−0.028
The Milwaukee Journal-Sentinel	−0.046
The Arizona Republic/The Phoenix Gazette	−0.055
The Boston Globe	−0.147
The San Francisco Chronicle	−0.187

TABLE 7.6. Arctic Drilling Pearson Correlations

HYPOTHESIS	PEARSON CORRELATION	SIGNIFICANCE
Percent voting Democratic	−.709	.003**
Percent voting Republican	.705	.004**
Percent families earn $100,000+	−.677	.006**
Percent college educated	−.583	.018*
Percent of population that hunts	.553	.025*
Percent unemployed	.495	.043*
Percent professional/technical	−.474	.051*
Percent employed in manufacturing	.403	.086
Percent poverty level	.296	.163
Public land budget	.241	.214
Number of union members	−.227	.239
Percent of population that camps	.078	.399
Percent of population interested in environment	.012	.485

*Significant at .05 level, one-tailed.
**Significant at .01 level, one-tailed

Stakeholder "Partisanship" Hypothesis Confirmed: Percent Voting Democratic or Republican Keys to Coverage

The political partisanship hypotheses expected that cities with larger populations voting Democratic in the 1996 Presidential election would have less favorable coverage of drilling in the ANWR, whereas cities with more Republican voters in the same election would have more favorable coverage. Both hypotheses proved highly significant, as Democratic voting corresponded with unfavorable news coverage ($r = -.709$, $p = .003$), while Republican voting corresponded with favorable news coverage ($r =. 705, p = .004$). Another stakeholder hypothesis with significant results was percent population that hunts, unexpectedly correlating positively with coverage favoring drilling ($r = .553, p =. 025$). Remaining stakeholder hypotheses linking environment-friendly lifestyles to coverage, including camping or self-reported interest in the environment, were not supported. Other stakeholder variables such as union membership or city commitment to public land were likewise not significantly connected to arctic drilling coverage.

Violated Buffer Linked to Negative Coverage, Vulnerability to Pro-Drilling Articles

The violated buffer hypothesis expected less favorable coverage of drilling in the ANWR among cities in direct proportion to the percentage of citizens who are more privileged economically, educationally, and professionally. Although drilling could affect fuel prices and threaten the lifestyles of all people, results confirm the violated buffer hypothesis, showing that higher percentages of a population with income over \$100,000 indeed correlate with less favorable newspaper coverage of drilling in the ANWR ($r = -.677$; $p =.006$), as does percent population with a 4-year college education ($r = -.583$; $p =.018$) and percent employed in professional/technical occupations ($r = -.474$; $p = .051$). As predicted, city characteristics were also linked significantly to economic vulnerability. Although a long-term measure of vulnerability, poverty level, is not associated with drilling coverage ($r = .296$; $p = .163$), a more variable measure of vulnerability, percentage unemployed, is indeed linked as predicted to favorable coverage of ANWR drilling ($r = .495$, $p = .043$). In contrast to the violated buffer and vulnerability results, the "protection" hypothesis was not supported. Percent of the population employed in manufacturing proved to be only directional with favorable coverage of ANWR drilling ($r = .403$; $p = .086$).

Regression Analysis

Multiple regression analysis revealed that two variables—percentage voting Democratic in the 1996 presidential election and percent unemployed—accounted for 74% of the variance in their association with the media vector. Specifically, the percentage voting Democratic in the 1996 presidential election accounted for 50.3% of the variance, illustrating the strongest relationship, as shown in Table 7.7.

Conclusions and Implications for Further Research

As predicted, Pearson correlation and regression analysis showed strong support for the stakeholder hypothesis, in particular political affiliation. As expected, unfavorable coverage was linked to percent voting Democratic in the 1996 election, whereas percent voting Republican showed a near equal but opposite connection. Regression analysis further demonstrates the strong link between political affiliation and newspaper coverage; percent voting Democratic accounted for over half of the variance in coverage.

Percent of the population earning more than \$100,000, 4-year college educated, and professional or technical all were linked to unfavorable cover-

TABLE 7.7. Arctic Oil Drilling Multiple Regression Analysis

MODEL	R (EQUATION)	R SQUARE (CUMULATIVE)	R SQUARE CHANGE	F CHANGE	SIGNIFICANCE OF F CHANGE
Percent voting Democratic	.709	.503	.503	11.140	.007
Percent voting Democratic, percent unemployed	.861	.741	.238	9.160	.013

age of drilling. This association illustrated the violated buffer hypotheses, suggesting that, although privileged groups were buffered from increases in fuel prices, they may also have considered themselves threatened by the destruction of the refuge.

Another stakeholder hypothesis showed a positive correlation between hunting and favorable coverage of drilling, contrary to expected results. Although it is natural to believe that hunting may be associated with protection of the environment, it is logical to assume a link with gun control issues as well. Republicans tend to favor less gun control than Democrats; therefore, it is reasonable to expect many hunters to be aligned with the Republican Party. Both Pearson and regression analysis showed political party affiliation a more powerful factor than hunting.

Also as expected, the percentage of the population unemployed was positively linked with pro-drilling views, in agreement with the "vulnerability" hypothesis. The unemployed may see drilling as an opportunity for more jobs and lower fuel prices. The percent unemployed in a city also proved significant in the regression analysis, accounting for nearly 24% of the variance.

These findings confirm the usefulness of the community structure approach. Further research could include a wider range of newspapers to improve sample size. In addition, following the tragic events of September 11, 2001, and increased instability in Middle Eastern oil-producing countries, the public may display burgeoning concerns about oil availability. This could be reflected in more positive coverage of drilling in the future. Environmental, energy and drilling issues are ongoing and would benefit from further extensive research.

NATIONWIDE NEWSPAPER COVERAGE
OF TRYING JUVENILES AS ADULTS

Introduction: The Debate Over Juvenile Sentencing

Since the state of Illinois formed the nation's first juvenile court in 1899, juvenile (under 18) and adult crimes have been treated differently by the criminal justice system. However, with high-profile, violent juvenile crimes such as the school shootings in Columbine, Colorado and Jonesboro, Arkansas, many wonder if young people should once again be held accountable for their actions according to adult standards of justice. Those who favor trying juveniles as adults believe the potential of much harsher treatment and sentences will serve as a deterrent, whereas the opposition argues that the primary purpose of the juvenile justice system is rehabilitation, not retribution.

Curiously, a surge in media coverage of crimes by juveniles comes at a time when the juvenile crime rate is actually *decreasing*. The potential exists, therefore, for the creation of significant misperception concerning the seriousness and extent of crimes by juveniles. It is therefore reasonable to pose the following question: Is media reporting on the issue of juvenile crime framed in a way that fosters or promotes misperceptions?

The debate on the issue of whether or not to try juveniles as adults has sparked discussion across the nation. Since 1992, at least 47 states have expanded their laws to allow more juveniles to be tried and sentenced as adults for an expanding number of felony crimes such as weapons possession, drug crimes, and burglary ("Black Youths Treated More Harshly," 2000; Coupet, 2000). This may suggest a nationwide trend holding young people more accountable for criminal actions, supporting prison time, as opposed to time in a juvenile detention center, as a deterrent to juvenile crime. However, those who oppose laws lowering the age of adult accountability say these new laws shift the focus of the juvenile justice system from rehabilitation to punishment. Critics claim that if "you put (a child) in with older, smarter, bigger criminals, he'll only become a bigger, meaner criminal" (Nirode, 2000, p. 8E).

Perhaps surprisingly, studies show that juvenile crime is decreasing. A recent National Crime Victimization Survey, tracking crime trends in the United States since 1973, reports juvenile crime at its lowest rates since tracking began. The FBI also reports that the number of children under age 13 committing homicides is at its lowest since that statistic was first registered in 1964 (Shiraldi, Sept. 5, 2000). Most media, however, do not seem to mention these statistics, especially in the wake of violent school shootings such as Columbine. According to Shiraldi, in his article "Exorcising School Shootings," nearly two-thirds of Americans believe juvenile crime is on the increase. There is a significant gap between perception and reality.

From these statistics, it is appropriate to ask if media coverage of juvenile crime is skewed. Varying reports of juvenile crime could encourage the public to view the subject of trying juveniles as adults in diverse ways. Comparing media coverage on this controversial topic among a national cross-section of cities in the United States, researchers can map variations in reporting framing trying juveniles as adults as well as differences in city demographics, income and education, political partisanship, religious affiliation, gun laws, and family structure.

Communication Literature Seldom Addresses
Trying Juveniles as Adults

Although the subject of reforming the juvenile justice system has been high on media agendas for the greater part of the 1990s, there has not been a corresponding level of concern reflected in communication research literature. Databases such as *ComAbstract* through the CIOS homepage and *ComIndex* provided few results when searching for terms such as "trying juveniles as adults," "juvenile crime," and "juvenile sentencing." Most of the articles found were only loosely related to the topic. The lack of scholarly research in the communication field suggests that few serious inquiries have been made examining national media coverage of trying juveniles as adults. One article found in the 1997 *Journal of Communication*, "Patterns of Deviance in Crime News," focused on why journalists opt to cover the news (particularly crime news) in the manner they do in Milwaukee, focusing on journalists' frames of reference regarding race/ethnicity, gender, and age (Pritchard & Hughes, 1997). The study is similar to the community structure approach in the research questions it poses, but does not focus on media coverage of trying juveniles as adults.

However, other, non-communication databases have provided literature on this controversial subject. Criminal Justice Abstracts from 1968 to 2000 yielded three articles on "trying juveniles as adults." One study in the Criminal Justice Abstracts noted that from 1992 to 1995, 40 states and the District of Columbia adopted legislation to allow juveniles to be tried in adult courts (Torbet et al., 2000). A second study explored the outcomes for juveniles tried as adults in New Mexico using 49 cases between 1981 and 1990, finding that trying juveniles as adults was a rare phenomenon in that state (Mays & Houghtalin, 1992).

Broader searches of the *Criminal Justice Abstracts* yielded more scholarly articles. "Juvenile sentencing" returned 24 articles, whereas the keyword "juvenile crime" returned 760 articles in the database. *PsychInfo*, a resource in citing psychology literature, returned 103 articles searching by "juvenile crime" and 5 articles under "juvenile sentencing," but once again returned no articles on "trying juveniles as adults." Still, these results are much larger than those found in communication literature. Similar searches of scholarly databases EbscoHost and newspaper/magazine/journal database Lexis-Nexis revealed many articles on juvenile crime, but almost nothing on sentencing juveniles. These searches suggest that more research is focused on juvenile crime itself rather than on sentencing juveniles as adults. With such a controversial and widespread topic, it is surprising that communication scholars have overlooked media coverage of trying juveniles as adults and other related subjects.

Articles found in the previously mentioned *Criminal Justice Abstracts* do, however, highlight recent trends of growing support for trying juveniles as adults, suggesting the topic merits further inquiry. Preliminary results of the 1995 National Prosecutor's Survey suggested "strong support emerged for trying juveniles as adults as a deterrent to gang crime" (Knox, Martin, & Tromanhauser, 1995, p. 1). Today, 15 states try juveniles in adult courts without restriction (Gibeaut, 1999). Forty states release information such as the juvenile's name and picture to the media. Juvenile sex offenders must be registered in 39 states. Michigan allows kids under age 14 to have adult trials for specific crimes, and both Vermont and Wisconsin have children as young as 10 in adult trials ("Should Children Be Tried," 1999). In 2000, 62% of Californian voters cast their ballots for Proposition 21, mandating that children over 14 years old be tried as adults (DiIulio, 2000). With an overwhelming number of states passing legislation to try juveniles as adults and highly publicized school shootings, it is reasonable to expect growing public support for stiffer penalties for juvenile offenders, including trying juveniles in the adult court system.

Although public opinion and recent legislation may support trying juveniles as adults, some literature in scholarly journals and periodicals opposes placing adolescents in adult prison system. Both the *Christian Science Monitor* and the *University of Pennsylvania Law Review* published articles against trying juveniles as adults (Coupet, 2000; Van Slambrouck, 2000). A lead story in *The New York Times Magazine* (Talbot, 2000) criticized modern practices, highlighting juveniles tried as adults now serving time in adult prisons. In "The Maximum Security Adolescent," Margaret Talbot (2000) depicted several adolescents "doing serious time" in adult prison systems, narrating, for example, the odyssey of a 14-year-old girl jailed in an adult prison for robbing and assaulting her grandparents, framing the story of these juvenile offenders as "victims" of an unforgiving system. Talbot quoted Donna Bishop, a professor of criminology at Northeastern University, who concludes that instead of rehabilitation, youths in adult prisons "spend most of their time talking to more skilled and experienced offenders who teach them new techniques of committing crime and methods for avoiding detection" (p. 58).

Although respected psychologists, criminologists, journalists, and politicians have taken the time to research and publish literature on trying juveniles as adults, communication scholars have not focused on the topic as central to the field of communication. If media act substantially to protect economic and political elites, in what Olien et al. (1995), and later Bishop (2000) referred to as the guard dog function of the media, how accurately can newspapers reflect the concerns of entire communities, including those groups with few advantages?

Hypotheses

Community structure hypotheses have been collected in three major cluster groups including stakeholders (partisanship, life-cycle position, age, marginality), privilege (buffer hypothesis), and vulnerability.

Stakeholders

Stakeholders are those most directly affected by issues of public policy or have the most influence over such issues. This study will consider groups affected by public policy outcomes of juvenile sentencing in four categories: partisanship, life-cycle position, age, and marginality.

Partisanship. Political affiliation is arguably one of the most influential stakeholders concerning public policy. Partisanship was found as an important factor in community structure studies of coverage of Social Security reform (Pollock, Tanner, & Delbene, 2000), a Patients' Bill of Rights (chap. 5) and environmental issues such as whether to permit oil drilling in the Arctic (chap. 7). Cities with high percentages of Democratic voters are expected to support legislation that rehabilitates juvenile offenders rather than incarcerates them and should resist attempts to sentence juveniles in the adult court system. Accordingly:

> **H1:** *The higher the percentage voting Democratic in the 1996 Presidential election, the less favorable the coverage of trying juveniles as adults.* (County and City Extra, 1998)

In cities with high percentages of Republican voters, the opposite is expected, with Republicans favoring "get-tough" measures against juvenile offenders. Republicans have traditionally supported tougher penalties for any criminal action, including sentencing juveniles in the adult court system. Accordingly:

> **H2:** *The higher the percentage voting Republican in the 1996 Presidential election, the more favorable the coverage of trying juveniles as adults.* (County and City Extra, 1998)

Life-Cycle Position. Possible hypotheses developed under life-cycle position include ages of various children and retired persons. It is unlikely that media sources tailor their coverage to children, however it may be reasonable to predict that media will recognize the interests of parents, many of whom do read newspapers. The percentages of families with children in certain age ranges may be a critical factor in media coverage of sentencing juveniles as adults. Presumably parents may be concerned about the prospects of their own children were they incarcerated with adults. Therefore:

H3: *The higher the percent families with children from 5 to 7 years old, the less favorable the coverage of trying juveniles as adults.* (Lifestyle Market Analyst, 1998)

H4: *The higher the percent families in a city from 8 to 10 years old, the less favorable the coverage of trying juveniles as adults.* (Lifestyle Market Analyst, 1998)

H5: *The higher the percentage of families with children from 11 to 12 years old, the less favorable the coverage of trying juveniles as adults.* (Lifestyle Market Analyst, 1998)

H6: *The higher the percentage of families with children from 13 to 15 years old, the less favorable the coverage of trying juveniles as adults.* (Lifestyle Market Analyst, 1998)

A high correlation with unfavorable coverage is expected especially for high percentages of families with children in the 16- to 18-year-old age categories. Juvenile offenders in these age ranges are the most at risk to be tried as adults and are the most questionable candidates for adult court. Psychologist Laurence Steinberg of Temple University, head of a research project on adolescent development and juvenile justice, concludes that "most people older than sixteen are not greatly distinguishable from adults on the relevant competencies . . . on the other hand, people thirteen and under really do not have these abilities. For them, adult court should not be an issue. The tricky ages are fourteen, fifteen, and sometimes sixteen" (Talbot, 2000, p. 88). Accordingly:

H7: *The higher the percentage of families with children in a city from 16 to 18 years old, the less favorable the coverage of trying juveniles as adults.* (Lifestyle Market Analyst, 1998)

Age. The presence of senior citizens in a community could play a role in reporting (Pollock, Coughlin et al., 1996; Pollock & Yulis, 2004). In communities with high percentages of retired persons, coverage of trying juveniles as adults could be favorable if senior citizens believe they are threatened by juvenile crime. Accordingly:

H8: *The higher the percentage of retired persons in a city, the more favorable the coverage of trying juveniles as adults.* (Lifestyle Market Analyst, 1998)

H9: *The higher the percentage of persons from 65 to 74 years old in a city, the more favorable the coverage of trying juveniles as adults.* (Lifestyle Market Analyst, 1998)

H10: *The higher the percentages of persons 75 years old or older in a city, the more favorable the coverage of trying juveniles as adults.* (Lifestyle Market Analyst, 1998)

Ethnicity: African Americans and Hispanics have a special "stake" in the issue of juvenile sentencing. According to a report published by the Urban League, three out of four youths imprisoned with adults are minorities. Blacks also account for 40% of the youths sent to adult courts and 58% of the youths sent to adult prison ("Black Youths Treated More Harshly," 2000). To the extent newspapers "mirror" the concerns of a wide range of community stakeholders, the discrepancy in the proportion of minority children sentenced as adults could understandably result in less favorable coverage in communities with high populations of African Americans or Hispanics. Therefore:

H11: *The higher the percentage of African Americans in a city, the less favorable the coverage of trying juveniles as adults.* (Lifestyle Market Analyst, 1998)

H12: *The higher the percentage of Hispanics in a community, the less favorable the coverage of trying juveniles as adults.* (Lifestyle Market Analyst, 1998)

The Buffer Hypothesis

The buffer hypothesis expects that the greater the proportion of privileged groups in a city, the more favorable newspaper coverage of issues concerning human rights claims. In applying this concept to trying juveniles as adults, it is possible that if privileged groups consider themselves or their children at risk of juvenile crime, prompted by events such as the

Columbine shootings, which occurred in a relatively prosperous suburb, the violated buffer perspective may prevail. But if the community structure studies on Anita Hill, legalization of physician-assisted suicide and embryonic stem cell research (documented in chap. 3) are useful guides, the privileged in a city are more likely to consider sentencing juveniles in adult courts as a violation of human rights. Privileged groups may consider juveniles the best candidates for rehabilitation within the justice system, thus showing the same sympathy often shown towards human rights claims made by other disadvantaged groups. Therefore:

H13: *The higher the percentage of citizens with 4 years of college, the less favorable the coverage of trying juveniles as adults.* (Lifestyle Market Analyst, 1998)

H14: *The higher the percentage of families making $100,000 or more, the less favorable the coverage of trying juveniles as adults.* (Lifestyle Market Analyst, 1998)

H15: *The higher the percentage of those with professional/technical occupational status, the less favorable the coverage of trying juveniles as adults.* (Lifestyle Market Analyst, 1998)

Vulnerability

Like stakeholders, groups represented by the vulnerability hypothesis (percent below the poverty level or percent unemployed) could be affected by trying juveniles as adults (Pollock & Robinson, 1977; Pollock et al., 1998; Pollock & Whitney, 1997). Those who live in impoverished areas or cities with high unemployment rates are relatively vulnerable to criminal legislation and have diminished access to legal representation. Therefore:

H16: *The higher the percentage of citizens below the poverty line in a city, the less favorable the coverage of trying juveniles as adults.* (County and City Extra, 1998)

H17: *The higher the percentage of unemployment in a city, the less favorable the coverage of trying juveniles as adults.* (County and City Extra, 1998)

In contrast, cities with high crime rates may be vulnerable to juvenile crime and are more likely to fear crime committed by juveniles. Accordingly:

H18: *The higher the crime rate in a city, the more favorable the coverage of trying juveniles as adults.* (Uniform Crime Reports, 1998)

Methodology

A cross-section nationwide sample of 25 newspapers was collected, sampling all articles 150 words or more (403 articles) printed on trying juveniles as adults between January 1, 1996 and December 1, 2000, a span of almost 5 years (see Table 7.8). Owing to more national and state legislation favoring trying juveniles as adults, this period has revealed an increase in the number of juvenile defendants appearing for sentencing in adult courts. After articles were scored for "prominence," they were coded for "direction" as discussed below.

TABLE 7.8. Trying Juveniles as Adults Media Vectors

NEWSPAPER	MEDIA VECTOR
Fort Worth Star Telegram	.409
Lexington Herald-Leader	.240
Atlanta Journal/ Constitution	.212
Wichita Eagle	.165
Cincinnati Post	.164
Pittsburgh Post-Gazette	.081
Albuquerque Journal/Tribune	.044
Memphis Commercial Appeal	.019
Seattle Times	.004
Detroit Free Press	.001
Tallahassee Democrat	−.003
Denver Post	−.010
Charlotte Observer	−.023
Kansas City Star	−.029
Philadelphia Inquirer	−.053
Portland Oregonian	−.054
Saint Louis Post-Dispatch	−.054
Milwaukee Journal Sentinel	−.064
Phoenix Gazette	−.127
Cleveland Plain Dealer	−.135
San Francisco Chronicle	−.140
Boston Globe	−.160
New Orleans Times-Picayune	−.167
Columbia (SC) The State	−.235
Albany Times Union	−.294

Favorable coverage of sentencing youth as adults was assigned to articles that supported trying juveniles as adults. This coverage suggested that rehabilitative measures are not effective with juveniles. Additionally, these articles viewed sentencing juveniles to prison time in adult facilities as appropriate and necessary.

Unfavorable coverage of youth being tried as adults was assigned to articles that rejected the idea of sentencing juveniles as adults. This coverage contended that juveniles are not candidates who are mature enough for the harsher environment of the adult prison system, and therefore should be given a second chance in the rehabilitative environment of a juvenile prison.

Neutral/Balanced coverage of trying youths as adults presented both sides of the controversy or provided information without trying to persuade the reader. The coverage was "undirected" and provided the reader with current events regarding juveniles in the prison system. With two coders for each article, Holsti's coefficient of intercoder reliability was calculated at .93.

Results

Media vectors ranged widely in newspapers throughout the nation from .409 to −.294, with 17 out of 25 newspapers neutral or at least slightly negative. Newspapers in Albany, New York and Columbia, South Carolina, had the most unfavorable coverage of this topic with media vectors of −.294 and −.235, respectively. Only about one third of the newspapers surveyed demonstrated favorable coverage. Fort Worth yielded the highest media vector score for favorability at .409, and the three newspapers most favorable to trying juveniles as adults were in the south.

Pearson Correlations

Four of the city characteristics had significant correlations (at the .05% level or better) with media vectors. These hypotheses tested partisanship (percent voting Democratic or Republican in presidential elections), life-cycle position—families with young children (ages 5–7), and percent retirees in a city (See Table 7.9).

Regression Analysis

Multiple step-wise regression analysis determined the proportion of the variance accounted for by different city characteristics. Democrats voting in the 1996 presidential election and number of retired persons in a city accounted for 43% of the variance in newspaper media reporting. As with the Pearson correlation, the number of Democrats maintained its high level of significance, accounting for 29% of the variance alone. Retired persons accounted for another 14% of the variance (See Table 7.10).

TABLE 7.9. Trying Juveniles as Adults Pearson Correlations

HYPOTHESIS	CORRELATION	SIGNIFICANCE
Voting Democratic	−.539	.003**
Children age 5 to 7	.387	.028*
Retired	−.384	.029*
Voting Republican	.340	.048*
Sixty-five to seventy-four	−.268	.098
Seventy-five plus	−.260	.105
Children age 8 to 10	.237	.127
Children age 11 to12	.216	.149
Children age 13 to 15	.153	.232
College 4+ years	−.132	.265
Unemployment	−.115	.293
Children age 16 to 18	.109	.303
Poverty	−.100	.318
African American	−.097	.323
Professional/Technical	.079	.354
Hispanic	.070	.370
Income over $100,000	−.035	.434
Crime Rate	.003	.493

*Significant at .05 level
**Significant at .01 level

TABLE 7.10. Trying Juveniles as Adults Multiple Regression

MODEL	R (EQUATION)	R SQUARE (CUMULATIVE)	R SQUARE CHANGE	F CHANGE	SIGNIFICANCE OF F CHANGE
Democratic	.539	.290	.290	9.395	.005
Democratic, Retired	.655	.429	.139	5.334	.031
Democratic, Retired, Republican	.685	.469	.040	1.521	.222

Discussion of Results

Stakeholders: Partisanship Plays an Important Role in Media Coverage

More than any other characteristic, partisanship was a decisive factor in coverage of trying juveniles as adults. Corresponding with expected negative newspaper coverage of trying juveniles as adults, percentage voting Democratic was discovered highly significant at the .003 level and accounted for 29% of the variance, rendering this the strongest variable in both the Pearson correlations and regression analysis. Republicans were also statistically powerful at the .048 level of significance. These findings show the influence of partisanship in reporting. Political affiliation can be clearly linked to the way media portray public policy issues.

Life-cycle Position: Families with Children Ages 5–7 Correspond With Positive Coverage, Retired With Negative Coverage of Trying Juveniles as Adults

Two variables with significant connections to coverage of trying juveniles as adults, both measuring position in the life-cycle, disconfirmed their expected hypotheses. For example, contrary to prediction, the greater the percentage of children between the ages of 5 and 7 in a city, the *more favorable* the coverage of trying juveniles as adults, significant at the .028 level. Additionally, all of the other family/children age segments (families with children ages 8–10, 11–12, 13–15, 16–18) were also positively related, although not significantly, to trying juveniles as adults. Indeed, Pearson correlation (Table 7.9) reveals a linear progression with age of children. The younger the children in a family, the higher the correlation between proportion of families with children and favorable coverage of trying juveniles as adults.

Perhaps the younger the children in a family, the more likely parents, and indeed entire communities, try to protect their children from older juvenile offenders. Five to seven is a sensitive age, when most children will begin formal schooling and spend considerable time away from parents, leaving them open to "societal dangers." If parents view older juveniles who commit crimes as threats to the safety of their own younger children, then it is reasonable to conclude they might favor harsher adult penalties. This finding buttresses a media function reflecting not so much a direct "market" as the concerns of distinct community groups, in particular parents of younger children.

Another life-cycle variable, percent retirees in a city, was also significantly linked to unfavorable reporting on the topic (significant at the .029

level), and accounted for 14% of the variance, making it the second most powerful variable in the regression analysis. This finding of presumed retiree empathy for convicted juveniles contradicts the original hypothesis that senior citizens fear juvenile crime and believe that juveniles should serve adult time for adult crime.

Consistent with the findings about retirees, the percent of those age 65–74 in a city ($p = .098$) and percent 75 or older ($p = .105$) also have a negative relationship (although not quite significant) with trying juveniles as adults. Perhaps many retirees, more than but not unlike other older citizens, are linked significantly with opposition to trying juveniles as adults because they contact children as "grandchildren." Because grandparent responsibilities for young children are generally not as "protective" as duties parents assume, grandparents may demonstrate more "compassion" for young people generally than parents who have specific children to guide and defend. Grandparents, buffered from more direct parenting responsibilities, may be able to "afford" opposition to trying juveniles as adults more than parents can. Data collected on percent "grandparents" in each city could have tested directly the grandparent "buffer" hypothesis.

Another factor might be what Erik Erikson called "generativity," the tendency to want to "give back" for what one has received as one grows older, confirmed in a national survey the author conducted in the early 1990s (American Board of Family Practice, 1991). Perhaps retirees and other seniors are better than others at taking the "long view," understanding through experience what social scientists have found in several studies, that many legal offenders "outgrow" their disruptive behaviors with age. In any case, retirees and families with young children are linked differently to proposals to try juveniles as adults.

No Significant Findings for Access, Privilege, Ethnicity, or Vulnerability

There were no significant correlations for the city characteristics of privilege, ethnicity, or vulnerability. Curiously, ethnic identity did not play a role in this study, although Black and Hispanic youths are more likely to be tried and sentenced as adults. Additionally, vulnerability also had little relation to media reporting on the issue. Perhaps the most surprising result is that there was no significant correlation with crime rate, considering that the issue of trying juveniles as adults is inherently part of the larger issue of crime and how society deals with it. Indeed, of all the variables tested, crime rate had the weakest correlation with coverage of trying juveniles as adults. These findings suggest strongly that media coverage of public policy is filtered through various prisms, in this case the filters of partisanship and position in the life cycle. There is clearly no "kneejerk," automatic correspondence between level of crime and reporting on policy proposals connected to it, such as trying juveniles as adults.

Implications for Further Research

Trying juveniles as adults has become an issue high on the agenda of juvenile justice reform. Although juvenile crime is statistically decreasing, several school shootings have heightened public awareness of juvenile sentencing, prompting inquiries into the most effective punishment and treatment for juvenile offenders. Owing to the importance of this issue at the present juncture, further studies of the topic's evolution in the media should be conducted using the community structure approach. Because of the tremendous strength of both partisanship and life-cycle position, further exploration should be made of the relation of these variables to reporting on other public policies. Media are clearly capable of reflecting the views of diverse population segments, from Democrats to Republicans, from retirees to families with small children.

Additionally, city characteristics that lacked significance should be further considered. Crime rate was not significant in this study, but an exploration using data on juvenile crime rates presents an opportunity for the discovery of additional results. Finally, new hypotheses can be developed for percent voting Democrat and Republican in different presidential election years. Multiple further research possibilities have the potential to yield significant results in future research on trying juveniles as adults.

SECTION III

SHIFTING FRAMES,
MULTIPLE METHODOLOGIES
AND FUTURE RESEARCH

8

SHIFTING COVERAGE OF THOSE WITH HIV/AIDS (RYAN WHITE TO 1995)

Turning on the Pendulum of Privilege

INTRODUCTION: EFFICACIOUS GROUPS AND COMMUNITY NORMS

Most studies on media agenda-setting start with media content analysis as the point of departure and then test the association between media coverage and either public opinion or public policy. The key question is usually "How much do media agendas 'set' the agendas found in public opinion or public policies?" A 1995 study, for example, concluded that press coverage does have an impact on social beliefs regarding HIV transmission (Hertog & Fan, 1995). The studies on this topic are important and significant, because they help us understand just how much impact media agendas have on agendas in other domains.

Curiously, however, although media themselves are often viewed as the "first cause" or "causal" agent in the chain of agenda-setting, a previous question is seldom asked: "Who or what influences the agenda-setters?" Yet, scholars occasionally focus on that question, asking, for example, how much the biographical histories of journalists might reveal about their perspectives on reporting (see Johnstone, Slawski, & Bowman, 1976; Pollock, 1981; Weaver & Wilhoit, 1988). Or how much do journalists mirror the interests of influential elites, functioning perhaps less as watchdogs skeptical of official pronouncements than as guard dogs for established interests (see Olien et al., 1995)? This interest in what happens "prior" to agenda-setting allows researchers to move from asking how media influence public opinion or policy to queries about how media frames or agendas are "built." From whom or what do media agenda-setters take their cues about the significance and direction of news events?

This special attention to influentials who may affect journalists' perspectives on social change has begun to yield specific scholarly interest among health communication researchers. For example, Dearing and Rogers (1992) in a study of newspaper agenda-setting and HIV/AIDS urged the following:

> Mass media organizations are far from autonomous actors in the determination of which issues become news. . . . Research on media agenda-setting should conceptualize the output of mass media organizations as being closely responsive to the *perceived attitudes and values* held by *efficacious groups* of people within their relevant environment. . . . Interpersonal networks of concerned individuals, governments, community groups, scientific findings and political leaders stand out in the present case as important determinants of news coverage about AIDS. (p. 191, italics added)

The perceived attitudes and values of efficacious groups are therefore worth examining as important "determinants" of news coverage on AIDS.

This focus on efficacious groups that might influence AIDS reporting converges with the findings of a group of health communication scholars who urge looking at community "norms" as factors affecting the way citizens with HIV/AIDS are viewed by journalists. Community norms have been given serious attention by Keith Stamm (1985) in *Newspapers and Community Ties*. Similarly, a scholarly panel recommended to the Office of AIDS, National Institute of Mental Health (NIMH), that scholars map media coverage of HIV/AIDS victims and families in an effort to measure both the impact of media on community perceptions and norms, as well as the impact of those same norms on media coverage (Panel for NIMH, 1995, p. 1). Both community norms and efficacious groups are capable of influencing HIV/AIDS coverage.

CITY CHARACTERISTICS AND REPORTING ON HIV/AIDS: USEFUL IN MEASURING VARIATION

In general, newspapers are viewed by media scholars as closely linked to the communities they serve. To ask questions about the relation of community or city characteristics and media is to pose an issue that researchers on AIDS and mass communication have not addressed very much. A great deal of the scholarly work on HIV/AIDS, especially pre-Magic Johnson announcement reporting, focused on the way the disease-infected were portrayed as victims, and which groups (especially nonmainstream groups) were most likely to be associated with that label (see, e.g., Albert, 1986; Fee & Fox, 1989; Grube & Boehme-Duerr, 1988; Johnson & LaTour, 1991; Lester, 1992; MacNair, Elliott, & Yoder, 1991; Perloff, 2001; Poirier, 1991; Reardon & Richardson, 1991; Serovich & Greene, 1993; Serovich, Greene, & Parrott, 1992; Singer, Rogers, & Glassman, 1991.

Some studies underscored the importance of media in forming perceptions and called for less "sensational" reporting and more attention to "educational communication" regarding HIV/AIDS (see Atkin & Arkin, 1990; Davidson, 1991; Druschel, 1991; Kalichman & Hunter, 1992; Lester, 1992; Reardon, 1989; Reardon & Richardson, 1991; Rogers & Chang, 1991; Rogers, Singer, & Imperio, 1993). And other studies directly called for more systematic mass communication research on the role of mass media in forming attitudes toward HIV/AIDS, reaching beyond "descriptive" attempts to more experimental and scientific efforts (see Stroman & Seltzer, 1989 on the role of age and race; Brown, 1991; Bush, 1990; Bush & Bolter, 1991; Zimet, 1993 on the role of education).

After Magic Johnson's announcement in particular, scholarly articles focused less on nonmainstream groups than on the public as a whole and on HIV/AIDS as a national issue. This research included work on knowledge about the disease, AIDS in celebrities, AIDS testing, and personal risk (Engelberg, Flora, & Nass, 1995; Gelert et al., 1992; Lowry & Shidler, 1993; Maibach & Flora, 1993; Snyder & Rouse, 1995; Williams, 1995). Other research confirmed that no matter the education level, groups tested prior to Magic Johnson's announcement knew less about HIV/AIDS than groups tested afterward. The suggested difference: Magic Johnson's celebrity status (Kalichman, Russell, Hunter, & Sarwer, 1993; Wanta & Elliot, 1995; see also Kennamer & Honnold, 1995). In general, prevention campaigns became a major theme after the 1991 announcement (Biddle, Conte, & Diamond, 1993; Cawyer & Smith-Dupre, 1995).

One systematic study of coverage of Magic Johnson after his November 7, 1991 announcement documented variations in tone among five of the nation's major papers as the story was explored further, changing from unadulterated heroism to more serious questioning about HIV/AIDS transmission generally (Payne & Mercuri, 1993). That study relied on a highly targeted sample of the first month of coverage in five major papers, documented amounts of coverage and overall shifts in topic, tone and "mediated reality," and found overall "similar" coverage. Major questions remain unanswered, however. First, exactly how much variation exists in widespread newspaper coverage of the HIV celebrity-victim, and are some characteristics of cities more closely associated than others with varied coverage of the knowledge about infection?

Existing studies have mapped the "what" of reporting on HIV/AIDS, tracing shifts in coverage. These studies have seldom developed "explanations" for those shifts. A focus on city characteristics as indicators of "efficacious groups" or "community norms" can help answer "how" and "why" coverage of HIV/AIDS has changed over time. To what extent does coverage in key cities vary with the specific characteristics and circumstances of those cities? How much does coverage of those with HIV/AIDS represent a social "mirror" of the demographics surrounding newspapers?

TWO CLUSTERS OF HYPOTHESES

A review of the theoretical and empirical literature on ties between community structure and newspaper reporting, as well as the literature on social responses to plagues, yields two key clusters of hypotheses in this exploration of reporting on Magic Johnson, concerning media access and distribution of privilege.

Media Access

Circulation Size

In the series of Minnesota studies conducted by Tichenor et al. (1980), partially summarized in *Community Conflict and the Press*, larger cities or communities are believed (and found) to display a wider range of group interests and perspectives than smaller communities because of the greater social differentiation and stratification found in larger cities. This "structural pluralism" is also presumed associated with a wide range of viewpoints expressed in relatively large newspapers, which Tichenor et al. find are more likely than smaller papers to serve as crucibles for the negotiation of community concerns and conflicts.

Other studies, moreover, link the number of media outlets not simply with a plurality of viewpoints, but more explicitly with media viewpoints generally accommodating political or social change. Concurring with these observations, Hindman (1999) urged that the more society has access to information and knowledge, the greater the ability for social actors to initiate projects that promote social change or challenge those in power. It seems as though the greater the number of media or media "reach," the more effectively media might shape public opinion or even threaten the interests of powerful groups. A proposition articulated by Gaziano and Gaziano (1999) asserts that collectivities acquiring relatively more knowledge through the media can be expected to be more effective in challenging elite groups and in using power to effect change that benefits them. Furthermore, in *Newspapers and Community Ties: Toward a Dynamic Theory*, Stamm (1985) advocated the perspective that cities with high quality of life will be more likely to have newspapers that will evaluate new issues from a plurality of perspectives. Consistently, Lowrey, Becker, and Punathambekar (2003) found that larger newspaper circulation is associated with greater diversity in staff expertise. Therefore, in the expectation that larger leading newspapers are associated with a greater "tolerance" for diversity:

> **H1:** *The larger the number of newspapers, or the larger a leading newpaper's circulation size, the more likely coverage of those with HIV/AIDS will be favorable.* (Gale Directory of Publications and Media Sources, 1992)

Media Saturation

Similarly, Tichenor et al., expect media abundance to be associated with a plurality of perspectives on critical events. The greater the number of media outlets, the greater the opportunity for the expression of a variety of viewpoints on important issues. The same assumption can be applied to cable television stations as well (Baldwin, Barrett, & Bates, 1992). If the number of media outlets in city can be considered measurement of the "role" of media in a community, then the greater the role of media in a community, the greater the stimulation of social capital and political pluralism (Friedland & McLeod, 1999). This assertion is supported by a study on coverage of environmental issues, concluding that the more diverse a community, the greater the opportunity media had to challenge the legitimacy of the existing power structure (Dunwoody & Griffin, 1999). By extension, the greater access to cable television in a city, the more likely newspapers will report favorably on social change. Because a wider range of viewpoints will likely include greater empathy for a variety of behaviors and circumstances, applying these perspectives to coverage of those with HIV/AIDS:

> **H2:** *The greater the number of cable television stations in a city, the more favorable the expected newspaper coverage of those with HIV/AIDS.* (Gale Directory of Publications and Media Sources, 1992)

When an issue is new or just emerging on the media agenda, and when audiences have relatively little alternative experience with an issue, then media are likely to exert substantial influence on public opinion. For example, Pfau and Kendall (1997) found that radio exposure is a primary source of information on unfamiliar or recently emerging political candidates, more important than interpersonal experiences. It is therefore reasonable to suggest that the more media outlets available allowing an issue further debate or development, the greater the likelihood of shifts in coverage accommodating social or political change.

In a collection of articles compiled by Dennis and Pease (1995) in their book *Radio: The Forgotten Medium,* it was revealed that radio is very much alive, remaining "the world's most ubiquitous medium, certainly the one with the widest reach and greatest penetration" (p. xvi). Radio remains an excellent media source, as it is accessible to almost everyone, inexpensive, and portable. Specifically, talk radio offers an exchange of ideas that is not present in other forms of media, (Owen, 1997). According to a 1993 survey of 1,507 randomly selected Americans by the Times Mirror Center for the People and the Press "talk radio represents the widest window on the world of politics and issues for the vocal minority" (Dennis & Pease, 1995, p. 46). In a study conducted by Pollock and Dantas (1998), a positive correlation was revealed between access to FM stations in a city and favorable coverage of same-sex marriage. Accordingly, expecting that radio can function as a vibrant transmitter of innovative ideas:

H3: *The greater the number of FM radio stations in a city, the more favorable a paper's coverage of those with HIV/AIDS.* (Gale Directory of Publications and Media Sources, 1992)

H4: *The greater the number of AM radio stations in a city, the more favorable a paper's coverage of those with HIV/AIDS.* (Gale Directory of Publications and Media Sources, 1992)

Privilege: The "Buffer " and "Violated Buffer" Hypotheses

The more individuals in a city who are "buffered" from scarcity and uncertainty, the more likely a city newspaper is to report favorably on human rights claims, and the less likely a paper is to manifest traditional political and social values that have denied refugees, minorities and women access to economic and political advancement. The buffer hypothesis has been confirmed in recent studies and is the focus of chapter 3.

In the case of Magic Johnson, the buffer hypothesis was likely to be turned on its head, because his announcement created a new vulnerability for economically and socially successful Americans. According to Nelkin and Gilman (1991), in a chapter in a book titled *In Time of Plague: The History and Social Consequences of Lethal Epidemic Disease,* the threat of AIDS, similar to the threats of other contagions in the past, spawned efforts to place blame on someone or some group because: "Blaming has always been a means to make mysterious and devastating diseases comprehensive and therefore possibly controllable. . . . In a situation of communal anxiety, locating blame for disease is in effect a strategy of control. If responsibility can be fixed, perhaps something—discipline, prudence, isolation—can be done" (Nelkin & Gilman, 1991, pp. 40-41).

Drawing the connection between blame's quest for certainty and deep social-class biases, Nelkin and Gilman noted that it represents a way for individuals to feel safer and "distant" from the threat of contamination:

> Categories of blame often reflect *deep social-class biases*. Illness is frequently associated with poverty and becomes a justification for social inequities. But blaming is also a way to create psychological as well as social boundaries. For the individual, blame is a way to draw a boundary between the self and the diseased, and thereby to release anxiety. To make stereotypical definitions of who is at risk is, of course, to fantasize. But disease is frequently associated with the "other," be it the other race the other class, the other ethnic group. (See the carefully documented case of venereal disease by Allan Brandt, *No Magic Bullet*, 2nd ed., 1987.) Inevitably, the locus of blame is also tied to specific ideological, political and social concerns. Blame is in effect a social construct, a reflection of the worldviews, social stereotypes and political biases that prevail at a given time. (Nelkin & Gilman, 1991, p. 141, italics added)

Magic Johnson's circumstances, however, changed the ease with which relatively privileged groups could blame the "other." For Mr. Johnson was clearly very successful and had access to multiple privileges. If someone like him were at risk from HIV/AIDS (his promiscuous lifestyle notwithstanding), then privileged groups in general might also be at risk. In this context, Magic Johnson pierced any "buffer" that might have shielded the privileged from the threat of HIV contamination so long associated with marginal groups.

As a result, cities with relatively high proportions of privileged people could be predicted to display newspaper reporting reflecting a violated buffer, unfavorable coverage for someone who had so much going for him and who behaved with what Fred Bruning (1991) wrote in *MacLean's* as "astonishing disregard in this precarious age." Violated buffer rationales, hypotheses and case studies are the focus of chapter 4. Several hypotheses follow logically:

H4: *The higher the percentage of professionals or executives/managers in a city, the less favorable the coverage of those with HIV/AIDS.* (County and City Extra, 1992)

H5: *The higher the percentage of college-educated in a city, the less favorable the coverage of those with HIV/AIDS.* (County and City Extra, 1992)

H6: *The higher the proportion of those with annual family incomes of $100,000 or more, the less favorable the coverage of those with HIV/AIDS.* (Lifestyle Market Analyst, 1992)

METHODOLOGY

The period studied included the time frame from 1984, when Ryan White was first diagnosed with HIV/AIDS, through most of 1995. Two kinds of newspaper sampling were completed. One was a focus on "critical events," or better stated "critical people" such as Ryan White, Magic Johnson, and Arthur Ashe. All three were or became celebrities whose coverage represented key opportunities to study coverage of those with HIV/AIDS. A second kind of sampling simply examined coverage of HIV/AIDS in general from the year immediately prior to Magic Johnson's announcement (1990) through selected years until 1995, the year Magic Johnson announced he would return to the Lakers. All articles over 200 words were eligible and analyzed. Newspapers were selected for their geographic dispersion and for their availability either on the DIALOG Computer Information Program or on microfilm (see Table 8.1).

The resulting sample included the following newspapers in all but one sampling period: *The Atlanta Constitution, The Boston Globe, The*

TABLE 8.1. HIV/AIDS Sample Periods and Article Totals

CELEBRITY OR TIME PERIOD	NUMBER OF ARTICLES SAMPLED (NO. OF NEWSPAPERS IN PARENTHESIS)
Ryan White (January 1984, through December 1989)	278 (15)
1990	225 (14)
Magic Johnson (Nov.-Dec., 1991)	435 (21)
1992	305 (15)
Arthur Ashe (April 8, 1992 [announcement] to September 27, 1994, HBO special on Ashe)	251 (15)
1994	309 (15)
1995	274 (15)
TOTAL ARTICLES SAMPLED	2,059

Charlotte Observer, The Chicago Tribune, The Detroit Free Press, The Houston Post, The Madison (WI) Capital Times/State Journal, The Miami Herald, The New Orleans Times-Picayune, The Philadelphia Inquirer, The Phoenix (Arizona) Republic/Gazette, The Rocky Mountain News, The St. Louis Post-Dispatch, The San Francisco Chronicle and *The Seattle Times.* The Ryan White sample was slightly different because some major papers gave him little or no coverage. As a result, *The Los Angeles Times, The New York Times,* and *The Washington Post* were substituted for papers offering little coverage.

After coding each of the resulting 2,059 articles for "prominence," each article was also coded for "direction" according to one of the following three categories:

1. *Legitimizing or favorable.* This meant the dominant content of the article described celebrities or noncelebrities with HIV/AIDS as essentially people worthy of empathy. In the case of celebrities, coverage might even portray them as: heroic (even if a "fallen" hero, a major role model, candid in facing and describing his "plight"), educational (new social role as activist), a leader ("good" people can get sick), able to overcome new challenges and generally lovable.

2. *Delegitimizing or unfavorable.* In articles coded with this designation celebrities or noncelebrities with HIV/AIDS were portrayed as meriting blame for their condition or otherwise characterized them as leading undesirable lifestyles. In the case of celebrities, in particular Magic Johnson, the negative designations might extend to "predatory" (consider the many women infected by Magic Johnson), a bad example, "womanizer" (promiscuity), thoughtless (endangering other players by playing on the All-Star team and returning to basketball), lacking in leadership (quitting the AIDS commission), and reinforcing fear and intolerance (his message discriminates against gays and women, who face a double standard compared to the tolerance displayed toward his sexual exploits).

3. *Balanced or neutral.* The dominant content of an article was neither clearly favorable nor unfavorable, or contained a roughly equal amount of both favorable and unfavorable material.

All articles were selected for intercoder reliability tests, and the overall Holsti's coefficient of intercoder reliability ranged from .85 to .94. Prominence and direction scores were combined for each newspaper to calculate media vectors.

RESULTS

An overview of media vectors for each newspaper for each time period or celebrity sampled is found in Table 8.2, ranked from highest to lowest average media vector. The variation in reporting for each sample frame and for each newspaper is apparent. The paper with the least amount of variation range (.31 out of 2.0 possible) is the (Madison, WI) *Capital Times.* The paper with the most variation (1.31) is the *Arizona Republic (Phoenix Gazette).*

Although no single city characteristic was confirmed significant throughout the entire time period studied, two major hypothesis clusters were confirmed for discrete periods of time or "critical events."

Media Saturation Associated With Reporting on Ryan White

The following rank-order correlations comparing level of favorable coverage of Ryan White with city characteristics reveal that number of FM stations and number of total radio stations are strongly associated with favorable coverage of the hemophiliac boy. Number of television channels is less clearly linked to coverage, and indicators of privilege are not associated at all with variations in coverage of Ryan White. It is reasonable to conclude, therefore, that as initial public awareness about HIV/AIDS began to build in the mid and late 1980s, the relative number of radio channels available may have provided opportunities for a plurality of viewpoints on a hemophiliac child, and perhaps on others with HIV/AIDS as well. This finding is consistent with the Tichenor et al. (1980) assertion that the greater the number of media in a city, the greater the opportunity for diverse viewpoints to be presented in the media (See Table 8.3).

Buffer Hypothesis Confirmed for Periods When Disease Seems "Contained"

Because the buffer hypothesis anticipates that cities with high proportions of privilege will manifest greater media empathy for disadvantaged groups, it is reasonable to expect that privilege will be linked to relative high levels of sympathy for those with HIV/AIDS. This was confirmed clearly in 1994, more than 2 years after Magic Johnson's announcement in November 1991 failed to auger a surge of the disease into the privileged sectors of society. That is, concerns about a quickly burgeoning epidemic that would suddenly invade high status groups were quelled after 2 years. The other year that the buffer hypothesis was confirmed slightly was 1990, in the wake of national empathy for Ryan White and prior to Johnson's famous announcement.

TABLE 8.2. Media Vectors for Reporting on Those With HIV/AIDS

NEWSPAPER	1990	MAGIC JOHNSON	1992	ASHE	1994	1995	RANGE (VARIATION)	AVERAGE MEDIA VECTOR
Charlotte Observer	.02	.58	.20	—	.02	.22	.56	.208
Boston Globe	.64	.05	.03	.25	.09	.18	.68	.206
New Orleans Times-Picayune	.08	.23	-.01	.60	.04	.26	.67	.200
Philadelphia Inquirer	.03	.56	.10	.29	.11	.01	.55	.183
Rocky Mountain News	.02	.20	.18	.58	.06	-.01	.59	.172
San Francisco Chronicle	-.19	.07	.36	.50	.11	.00	.69	.142
Madison (WI) Capital Times	.04	.30	.04	.35	.06	.06	.31	.142
Seattle Times	.27	.16	-.34	.56	.13	.05	.90	.138
Detroit Free Press	-.17	.21	.11	.54	.15	-.11	.71	.12
Chicago Tribune	-.01	.46	-.14	.29	.04	.08	.60	.12
Atlanta Journal-Constitution	.16	.19	-.21	.34	.10	-.02	.55	.093
Arizona Republic	.13	.69	-.62	.13	.07	.14	1.31	.086
Houston Post	.09	.21	-.17	.22	.11	.03	.39	.08
St. Louis Post-Dispatch	.02	.15	-.26	.41	.03	.11	.67	.076

TABLE 8.3. Ryan White Spearman Rho Correlations

HYPOTHESES	SPEARMAN RHO CORRELATION	SIGNIFICANCE
FM radio stations	+.59	$p < .025$
Number of radio stations	+.52	$p < .05$
Number of newspapers	+.48	$p < .05$
Number of cable TV stations	+.43	$p < .10$
Newspaper circulation	+.40	$p < .10$
Number of TV stations	+.39	$p < .10$
Percent professionals	+.08	$p > .25$
Education 4+ years of college	+.06	$p > .25$
Family income $100,000 plus	+.03	$p > .25$

Specifically, as Table 8.4 reveals, in 1994 the higher the proportion of relatively privileged citizens in a city—professionals ($r = .586$; $p < .025$); college educated ($r = .593$; $p < .01$); relatively affluent ($r = .654$; $p < .005$)—the more favorable the coverage of those with HIV/AIDS. Indicators of media access were not significant after their earlier association with coverage of Ryan White. In 1990, one measure of privilege—percent with family income $100,000 or more ($r = .44$; $p < .05$)—was associated with relatively favorable coverage of those with HIV/AIDS. Examining the content of reporting in both years, what both 1994 and 1990 have in common is reporting that considers the epidemic somewhat "contained" so that a massive outbreak affecting every segment of society is highly unlikely.

TABLE 8.4. Spearman Rho Correlations and Significance Levels (in parentheses) 1990, Magic Johnson (Nov/Dec 1991) and 1994

HYPOTHESIS	1990	MAGIC JOHNSON	1994
Percent professionals	.30 (<.25)	-.650 (<.005)	.586 (<.025)
Education 4+ years of college	.37 (<.10)	-.659 (<.005)	.593 (<.01)
Family income $100,000 plus	.44 (<.05)	-.19 (>.25)	.654 (<.005)

Violated Buffer Hypothesis Confirmed
for Coverage of Magic Johnson

As expected, Magic Johnson's announcement in 1991, after Ryan White and before massive education campaigns were initiated to educate the public about the disease, changed the ease with which relatively privileged groups could blame (or indeed feel sorry for) the "other." Because Johnson was clearly very successful, then privileged groups in general might also be at risk. Any buffer that might have shielded the privileged from the threat of HIV contamination was immediately pierced.

Accordingly, as the preceding table reveals, the greater the proportion of privileged groups in a city—college educated ($r = -.66$; $p =.001$); percent professionals ($r = -.65$; $p = .001$)—the *less favorable* the coverage of Magic Johnson. The very privileged groups associated with empathic coverage of those with HIV/AIDS in 1990, and especially in 1994, are the very "efficacious groups" linked to less favorable coverage of Magic Johnson in 1991. Although virtually all newspapers studied revealed positive media vectors in reporting on Magic Johnson, specific indicators of relative privilege in cities are linked strongly to less favorable coverage of the athlete.

Media Vectors Can Reveal Shifts and Levels
of Consensus Over Time

Two kinds of shifts can be observed in coverage of those with HIV/AIDS over time. One is a shift in the direction of city characteristics as factors associated with coverage variation. The most dramatic shift is between the association of privilege with *less favorable* reporting on Magic Johnson in 1991 and the mirror opposite, the association of privilege with *empathic* reporting on those with HIV/AIDS in 1994.

The other shift is from wide variations in media vectors both among cities and from one time period to another. Although the range in media vectors was rather large from Ryan White through 1992, as the following table reveals, in 1994 and 1995 the range was much smaller (in bold in Table 8.5), suggesting an emerging consensus on HIV/AIDS coverage over time— much less variation from paper to paper.

TABLE 8.5. Ranges of City HIV/AIDS Media Vectors Across Critical
Events and Time Frames

TIME FRAME OR CRITICAL EVENT	HIGHEST AND LOWEST MEDIA VECTORS		RANGE
Ryan White	.37 -	-.14	.51
1990	.64 -	-.19	.83
Magic Johnson (Nov.- Dec. 1991)	.69 -	.05	.64
1992	.36 -	-.62	.98
Arthur Ashe	.60 -	.13	.47
1994	.15 -	.02	.13
1995	.26 -	-.02	.28

DISCUSSION

City Characteristics Can Influence Media Agenda—Setting in a Crisis

The hypothesis that media saturation and multiplicity matter in coverage of HIV/AIDS is confirmed in a special sense. The only time frame or critical event for which number or penetration of media was associated significantly with coverage was regarding newspaper reporting on Ryan White, at the inception of public awareness about the disease. The greater the number of FM radio stations, or the greater the number of newspapers, the more favorable the coverage of Ryan White. One proposition that might be derived from these findings is that: *The number and penetration of media outlets matter most at the inception of a crisis, before either the public generally or even "efficacious groups" in particular acquire substantial information about the substance of the crisis.*

A second proposition is more obvious. *Coverage of a crisis (in this case, an epidemic) is likely to vary with precise degrees of privilege during periods of transition.* In this case study of reporting on HIV/AIDS, privilege mattered most under two conditions: (a) when a highly regarded sports hero (Magic Johnson) made it clear that privilege is no "buffer" from a disease that is relentlessly democratic in its affinity for all high risk-takers; and (b) when a national effort at education, including massive media educational efforts, yielded a new, more accurate understanding about the risks of HIV/AIDS and the likelihood of privileged sectors themselves contracting the disease (1994). In both cases, whether reacting sharply with "distancing" or with "understanding," the relative presence of high occupational status

professionals and well-educated citizens was associated with precise variations in coverage of those with HIV/AIDS. Overall, coverage of those with
HIV/AIDS varied along a "privilege pendulum," swinging from sympathetic coverage of Ryan White and others prior to Magic Johnson's announcement, to less sympathetic coverage during and after the basketball star's rev-
elation, then back to sympathetic coverage with the news about Arthur
Ashe's condition. Coverage shifted along an axis of privilege.

A Few Key Circumstances Can Transform Coverage Dramatically

Coverage of both heroism and mobilization may have played major roles in
shifting coverage from fear of massive contamination to one of empathy and
understanding. Coverage of both clear heroism (Arthur Ashe) and mobilization of HIV/AIDS victims was made possible by a special circumstance that
may distinguish HIV/AIDS-diagnosed citizens from the victims of all previous plagues. Unlike their predecessors in other lethal epidemics, those
with HIV/AIDS are sometimes able to live many years with the disease, an
opportunity that some have taken to educate the public not only about risks,
but also about chances for constructive lifestyles.

"Buffered" Groups Have Usually "Distanced" Themselves From Plague Victims

Examining the historical literature on plagues and lethal diseases, it is
clear that relatively "buffered" sectors of society—those with better educations, incomes or jobs—have usually "distanced" themselves strongly from
those who carried fatal diseases. Surveying historical materials, and whether
referring to the Black Death, smallpox, bubonic plague, cholera, the worldwide flu epidemic after World War I or AIDS itself, five similar "distancing"
stages appear to emerge, stages that can overlap. These are followed, in the
case of HIV/AIDS, by a stage of victim mobilization and public compassion. (See footnote 1 for sources on histories of plagues.)[1]

---

[1]Sources consulted in the search for common historical "stages" of social reaction to plagues
include the following: Astruc (1754); Bethel (1995); Beveridge (1977); Black (1986); Brandt
(1985); Camus (1948); Cartwright (1972); Clark (1988); Conrad and Schneider (1992); Douglas
and Wildavsky (1970); Durey (1973); Farmer (2005); Gilman (1988); Grmek (1991); Gussow
(1989); Hopkins (1963); Kinsella (1989); Krieg (1992); Langone (1991); Marks and Beatty
(1976); Martin (1994); McNeill (1977); Morris (1987); Rosenberg (1962); Shilts (1987);
Shrewsbury (1970); Sontag (1977); Stine (1995); Swenson (1988); Ziegler (1969).

Five Stages of "Distancing": A Historical Model

Before comparing coverage of HIV/AIDS with social reaction to other plagues, the historical stages and their most likely sequence deserve explanation. The first stage is usually "denial" that a major pestilence exists, during which the disease is usually called something much milder than the epidemic it truly represents. The second stage is often "segregation" and "stigmatization" of the growing number of victims through negative metaphors and quarantine. When the malady makes an initial transition to the "general" population, a third stage of "intimate fear" may develop as many individuals are faced with their own mortality for the first time. A possible fourth stage, "blaming" the victims, and, in addition, "distrust of authority," may serve to alleviate guilt from the population by fixing a locus of responsibility on "undesirable" social groups (such as minorities and foreigners), powerful groups such as the government, individual lifestyles, and/or divine retribution from God. "Blame" may surface as it becomes clear that established authorities and institutions can't hold back the plague.

The fifth stage, a "hierarchy of victims," might be observed if the disease is finally "universalized," when members of the social elite and "innocent" individuals like women and children become infected. Four distinct groups emerge, from most to least "legitimized": child victims (such as Ryan White, a child hemophiliac); martyrs—spouses and/or lovers of the infected and hemophiliacs; "redeemed sinners"—athletes and celebrities who appear forgiven for their moral crimes in exchange for Olympic medals and funding educational programs; and finally, "unredeemed sinners"—drug addicts and homosexuals, who cannot easily muster public sympathy.

An additional, or sixth stage in this model of public reaction to epidemics might appear only in the case of HIV/AIDS, a "mobilization of the infected" or "victims in the spotlight" phase. Since this disease is one of the few that does not completely immobilize its victims at the outset, some of those who are HIV positive have had time to organize on behalf of all victims to draw attention to the way society, business and government treat those diagnosed with the disease. With the exception of this last phase, all phases of public reaction are often historically associated with segregation, ostracism and social and physical banishment for the victims of lethal disease. What is fascinating about HIV/AIDS, however, is that victims can live long enough, are approachable enough to make a contribution through mobilization or example (Johnson, Ashe) and through the power of modern media to personalize and humanize all those with the disease.

Reporting "Frames" Can Shift:
Can Community Norms Be Connected?

The media can play a constructive role in mass education about an epidemic. In 1994, the percentage of those with HIV/AIDS in a city (Center for Disease Control and Prevention, 1993) was linked to relatively empathic reporting on those with the disease ($r =. 60; p < .01$). There was no significant link between incidence of HIV/AIDS in a city and reporting on Magic Johnson's HIV/AIDS announcement. What clear media "frames" existed at the inception of public awareness about HIV/AIDS, and how did they shift over time?

Table 8.6 illustrates that although clear frames in coverage of HIV/AIDS may not have followed the six-stage historical model exactly as predicted, the prominence of three distinct frames varied over time in rather understandable ways. The table is based on a content analysis of the same articles used to calculate media vectors (coding simply for the "presence" of a theme), and Holsti's coefficients of intercoder reliability varied from .88 to .93. Any given article can clearly contain more than one frame.

Newspaper reporting on the segregation of those with HIV/AIDS and the stigma attached to the disease were highest in 1992. Similarly, reporting on "intimate fear," the fear that everyone, including relatively "mainstream" populations might be at risk, reached its maximum coverage in the same year, 1992. The probable reason for the prominence of both issues in 1992 is that this was the year immediately following Magic Johnson's HIV announcement the previous November, late in 1991. That announcement unleashed a barrage of coverage about him, fear of contagion and of efforts to educate the public about sexually risky behavior. Consistently, the lowest media vectors or least favorable reporting on HIV/AIDS in all the samples

TABLE 8.6. Three Prominent Frames Vary Over Time: Percentage of Articles Where Theme Appears

YEAR	SEGREGATION AND STIGMA %	INNATE FEAR %	MOBILIZATION OF VICTIMS %	(NUMBER OF ARTICLES)[a]
1990	14.3	21.9	7.1	(225)
1992	**35.7**	**29.6**	19.6	(305)
1994	22.1	18.2	**47.5**	(309)
1995	21.7	16.3	27.4	(274)

Note: Highest figure in column in bold.
[a]Any article can contain more than one theme.

was indeed found in 7 out of 14 papers in 1992, the year after Magic Johnson's vulnerability was publicized.

Perhaps partly in response to concerns about segregation and stigma associated with HIV-positive citizens, and partly in response to the widespread intimate fear that mainstream populations were at risk, many efforts were subsequently made (and given prominence in news stories in 1994) to mobilize those with HIV/AIDS. By making those with HIV/AIDS highly visible, reporting on their concerns helped demonstrate that their rights were in jeopardy and that a substantial segment of HIV/AIDS-positive citizens were at least as articulate and as apparently "mainstream" in their lifestyles and workstyles as most other citizens. Congruently, at the same time that articles on those with HIV/AIDS in 1994 made major mention of "mobilization" (47.5%), the proportion of articles mentioning "intimate fear" that almost everyone was at risk dropped from 29.6% in 1992 to 18.2% in 1994 and 16.3% in 1995. Mobilization may, therefore, have had at least some of the educational effect it was intended to have.

Consistently, for 9 out of 14 papers, the highest media vectors recorded were for reporting on Arthur Ashe, who may have evoked more favorable reporting than Magic Johnson because he was viewed as a "victim" of a blood transfusion rather than as a risk-taker, and perhaps because of his prominence within the Black community as someone who found many ways to "give back." There may have existed a "hierarchy of victims," in which some of those with HIV/AIDS were viewed as having more "acceptable" or "legitimate" lifestyles than others. The norm that "exemplary citizens" are given more favorable consideration than "uneven" citizens is clear and unavoidable. Expressed in more scientific terms, it is tempting to speculate that the higher the social or economic status of someone with HIV/AIDS, the more favorable the expected coverage. Yet reasons for contracting the disease matter. Magic Johnson's lifestyle left him with less favorable coverage, whereas Arthur Ashe's medical reasons for his diagnosis earned him sympathy. Not all those with high or celebrity status are awarded similar coverage.

The frames of "segregation and stigma," intimate fear, and "mobilization of victims" were so clear and present in reporting on those with HIV/AIDS across so many newspapers across the nation that is reasonable to consider them candidates for "community norms." Their prominence and persistence in so many news articles would not have been logically possible without some level of resonance with the communities the newspapers serve. Widespread concerns about segregation and stigma, intimate fear, and legitimacy granted the mobilization of victims were doubtless necessary for so much about these topics to have been written for so long.

CONCLUSION

City characteristics appear capable of guiding, shaping or framing reporting in specific circumstances: at the inception of a crisis (Ryan White) or during periods of transition such as the sudden vulnerability of a successful hero (Magic Johnson), or the effort to educate citizens about the limits of risk and our shared humanity (Arthur Ashe and mobilization of those with HIV/AIDS). Community norms that reflect traditional, historical tendencies to segregate and stigmatize or to display intimate fear can shift over time, most likely the result of educational efforts, media attention, the tragedy of a clear hero (Ashe) and the mobilization efforts by victims to demonstrate our shared humanity. City characteristics deserve to be compared with content analyses of other health issues and social and political issues generally to test their potency during crises and critical events.

9

CONVERGING EXPLANATIONS FOR COVERAGE OF HOMOSEXUALS IN THE BOY SCOUTS OF AMERICA

Community Structure, Public Opinion, and Ownership Patterns

On my honor I will do my best
*To do my duty to God and my country
and to obey the Scout Law;
To help other people at all times;
To keep myself physically strong,
mentally awake, and morally straight.*

—*Boy Scout Oath*

For years, the Boy Scouts of America (BSA) have lived by this oath. In July 1990, Eagle Scout and Scout Master James Dale received word that his lifestyle did not comply with the oath of the Boy Scouts of America (BSA) because he was homosexual. In August 1999, Dale took his case to the NJ Supreme Court and won on grounds that the BSA had discriminated against him based on his sexual orientation. On appeal, regardless of evidence that Dale had previously devoted 11 honorable years of his life to the Boy Scouts, the U.S. Supreme Court decided on June 28, 2000, that the organization had the right to restrict membership if a person's actions contradicted the its set of moral standards. This chapter's analysis reaches beyond other case studies' Pearson correlations and preliminary regressions to include factor analysis, regression of factors, regional comparisons with public opinion, investigation of secondary/circulation papers in each city, and comparisons of locally owned and corporate-(elsewhere) owned coverage. These multiple analyses demonstrate the versatility, richness, and power of the community structure approach.

The issue of allowing gays in the Boy Scouts can be framed in several ways. Newspaper articles positively framing the issue favor allowing homosexuals to remain members of the BSA. Generally, those holding a positive view believe that banning gays from the BSA is discriminatory and violates one's civil rights. Articles framing the issue negatively view homosexuality as morally wrong and gay scout leaders as imperfect role models for young scouts. These negatively framed articles may also emphasize that private organizations have a right to restrict membership, and the BSA, a private organization, can set membership standards that scouts and leaders must be "clean" and "morally straight."

The U.S. Supreme Court decision in *Dale vs. The Boy Scouts of America* warranted extensive media coverage because the opposing sides hold such strong opinions and because the Boy Scouts are a long admired institution with strong ties to local communities. This case study examines differences in media coverage in different cities focusing on variations in levels of affluence, voting patterns, religious identity, lifecycle position, ethnic identity, and other relevant demographics. Another factor possibly affecting media coverage is the percentage of families with primary school-age children in a given city. These parents may represent interested stakeholders because of parental concern, which may be linked to newspaper coverage unfavorable to gays in the Boy Scouts. By contrast, cities with higher proportions of organizations marketing to gays may reveal relatively favorable coverage of gays in the Boy Scouts. This examination links different community configurations and coverage of homosexual membership in the BSA.

LITERATURE REVIEW

Although many communication journals, as well as online databases, were searched for articles concerning the issue of gays in the Boy Scouts, it was striking that little or no information had been published regarding this or related issues. Because the BSA affects the lives of so many young boys and their families all over the country, the lack of information about this issue is puzzling.

Ebscohost, Communication Abstracts, and *CommIndex* were searched with little result. A search of *Communication Abstracts,* an authoritative listing of scholarly communication articles, using key terms such as "boy scouts and gay," "scouts and homosexual," and "boy scouts and supreme court" was conducted, but few articles were found. When broadening the search with general subject headings such as "gay" or "boy scout," little more surfaced. These articles dealt mainly with different aspects of homosexual issues, such as gays' portrayal on television and gays in the military. One article entitled "Journalism and News Media" dealt with a study that "analyzes the way in which television news organizations selected and used unofficial sources in covering the 1992–1993 controversy over homosexuals and military service" (Steele, 1997, p. 537). Using the same subject headings, other communication journals were searched, including *Political Communication*, and *Journalism and Mass Communication Quarterly*, resulting in little relevant information. One exception is a paper on cultural indicators of social change, focusing on homosexuality (Nisbet & Shanahan, 2004). Another exception is the television industry, where debates over gay rights, including the gays in the Boy Scouts debate, are of interest to industry. Becker believes that incorporating homosexual material into lineups will attract a more liberal, college-educated, intellectual audience (Becker, 1998).

It is possible that the paucity of information in communication journals results from the issue's recency, making headlines only a few years ago. The rights of both homosexuals and private organizations should be compelling topics for the communication field. The Supreme Court's decision to permit the Boy Scouts to choose whom they allow to become members sends a strong message to those the BSA dismisses, especially those in the gay community. The case not only involves a "deep-rooted conflict" regarding acceptance of gays within communities, but also a serious dispute concerning basic constitutional rights (*Boy Scouts: Discrimination and the Law*, 2000).

Although information was scarce in communication journals, articles concerning gays in the Boy Scouts, and gays in particular, were easily found in social science sources such as *Sociological Abstracts* and *Political Science Abstracts*. A search of *Sociological Abstracts* revealed two relevant articles entitled "Culture War against the Boy Scouts" (Donohue, 1994) and "The Boy Scouts Under Siege" (Salzman, 1992). Both articles were written before the Supreme Court case, indicating sustained interest in this important issue. "The Boy Scouts Under Siege" examines the defensive position the Boy Scouts took in the 1990s, pointing out that the Boy Scouts "refuse to permit atheists, homosexuals, and girls to become members based on their interpretation of the oath, and they feel legally entitled to exclude them because they are a private organization" (p. 594).

Because the issue of gays in the Boy Scouts has warranted a Supreme Court decision, it would seem an essential issue for communication scholars. Finding clearly relevant information outside the communication field in sociological and political science journals suggests a gap between the communication discipline and other social sciences. Issues that invoke group mores and norms also affect newspaper coverage. Because cities with a significant homosexual population may have different views from cities with large numbers of families of Boy Scout age, it is reasonable to expect the Supreme Court ruling to be reported differently in newspapers of different cities.

HYPOTHESES

Community structure hypotheses can be placed in three cluster groups including the stakeholder hypothesis, buffer hypothesis, and vulnerability hypothesis.

Stakeholder Hypotheses

Gays and Lesbians

Previous community structure research discussed in chapter 7 revealed that the greater the proportion of specific stakeholders in a city, the more newspaper coverage is likely to vary according to their concerns. When seeking a correlation between stakeholders in a city and how that city covers gay rights issues, it seems obvious that the number of gays and lesbians residing in the city should be taken into account. However, the difficulty of measuring gay and lesbian presence has posed a dilemma.

Pollock and Dantas (1998) found significant results by creating a Gay Market Index (GMI). Using an encyclopedia of gay resources in the United States, Dantas and Pollock collected data for this study from the 1995–1996 national edition of the Gayellow Pages. Fashioning a "GMI," it was found that the greater the proportion of businesses or organizations marketing to the gay community in a city, the more likely city newspapers were to report favorably on efforts to legalize same-sex marriage. Using the 1999–2000 Gayellow Pages, the GMI was updated for this study (Cronbach's alpha coefficient of scale reliability = .782; see Table 9.1).

Therefore:

> **H1:** *The larger the number of gay businesses and organizations marketing primarily to gay and lesbian clientele in a city, the more favorable the expected coverage of gays in the Boy Scouts.*
> (Gayellow Pages, 2000)

Political Partisanship

Broad political identities and voting preferences may be linked to views about gays in the BSA. Previous studies documented in chapters 6 and 7 confirm the power of percent voting Republican or voting Democratic in their association with a wide range of issues such as a Patients' Bill of Rights (chap. 5), drilling in the Arctic, or trying juveniles as adults (chap. 7). It is also reasonable to assume that partisanship may be associated with the coverage of homosexuals in the BSA. Members of both the Democratic and

TABLE 9.1. Gay Market Index

Cities	Accomodations Hotels, B&Bs	Bars, Clubs, Discos	Bookstores	Religious Groups	Organizations and Resources	AIDS/HIV Health Care	Gay Publications	TOTAL
San Francisco	26	69	10	14	69	19	13	220
Seattle	7	32	12	6	52	11	2	122
Boston	11	16	10	4	65	7	2	115
Fort Worth	4	37	2	8	47	8	3	109
Philadelphia	6	18	4	7	46	13	6	100
Atlanta	5	40	3	11	26	10	3	98
Denver	4	29	4	6	29	10	3	85
San Diego	10	26	3	5	29	9	3	85
Tampa	6	34	3	5	19	8	3	78
Detroit	0	30	2	6	25	6	3	72
Phoenix	5	29	2	10	20	5	1	72
Pittsburgh	2	18	3	8	28	9	2	70
Milwaukee	0	22	5	4	31	4	2	68
Saint Louis	3	23	5	5	19	7	4	66
Buffalo	1	11	3	4	23	4	2	48
Memphis	0	20	0	4	14	2	1	41
Cincinnati	1	14	4	3	15	1	0	38
Albany	2	12	2	3	12	6	0	37
Albuquerque	7	7	4	4	7	2	4	35
Charlotte	0	12	4	3	12	4	0	35
Omaha	0	9	2	2	11	0	2	26
Wichita	0	10	0	4	7	3	1	25
Dayton	0	11	1	3	5	0	2	22
Lexington	0	4	2	2	8	1	0	17
Baton	1	6	1	4	3	1	0	16
Fort Wayne	0	5	1	3	3	2	0	14
Columbia	0	6	1	3	3	0	0	13
Fresno	0	5	1	0	7	0	0	13
Tallahassee	0	3	0	1	2	1	1	8

Copyright Pollock and Dantes (1998–2007). Updated by Pollock, DuRoss, Moscatello, and O'Rouke (2001).

Republican parties hold strong opinions regarding gay rights. The Clinton Administration proposed the "Don't ask, Don't tell" policy as a compromise to the Republican party's position seeking to ban gays from the military. According to Sue Kirchhoff in the July 1998 issue of *CQ Weekly*, over the years top congressional Republicans have taken an increasingly tough stance against homosexual rights. Thus:

> **H2:** *The higher the percentage of Republicans in each city, the less favorable the coverage of gays in the Boy Scouts.* (Country & City Extra, 2000)

> **H3:** *The higher the percentage of Democrats in each city, the less favorable the coverage of gays in the Boy Scouts.* (County & City Extra, 2000)

Religious Identity/Belief System

It is also clear that some churches and other religious organizations have taken strong stances on the issue. According to *The New York Times*, "The Vatican calls homosexual practice a serious moral disorder" (Niebuhr, 1996, p. A1). Pollock et al. (1978) found a strong correlation between the percentage of Catholics within a city and negative coverage of *Roe v. Wade*. It seems logical, then, that certain religious beliefs, in particular those that emphasize literal interpretations of a Bible, might play a large role in the newspaper coverage of *Dale vs. The Boy Scouts of America*. Therefore:

> **H4:** *The larger the proportion of Catholics in each city, the less favorable the coverage of gays in the Boy Scouts.* (Catholic Almanac, 2000)

> **H5:** *The larger the percentage of families participating in Bible/devotional readings in a city, the less favorable the coverage of gays in the Boy Scouts.* (Lifestyle Market Analyst, 2000)

Position in LifeCycle

A study conducted by Mink, Puma, and Pollock (2001) on the custody battle over Elián Gonzalez, found that nationwide newspaper coverage favoring the repatriation of Gonzalez to his biological father in Cuba was directly linked to the proportion of families in cities with children of similar age, 5–7. Coverage generally supported the rights of natural parents who play an active, attentive role in the rearing of offspring. Coverage of gun control and trying juveniles as adults is also linked to life-cycle position (chap. 7). It seems reasonable to assume that families with young children of approximately elementary school age or younger might be concerned with the safety and morality of the BSA and newspapers might reflect those stakeholder concerns. Therefore:

> **H6:** *The greater the percentage of families with children ages 12 and under (just prior to and at entry level of Boy Scout age), the less favorable the coverage of gays in the Boy Scouts.* (Lifestyle Market Analyst, 2000)

Ethnic Identity

Although one may assume that minorities, who often suffer from oppression and prejudice, would strongly support gay rights, seeing homosexuals as allies in a civil rights battle, some evidence suggests otherwise. Some African Americans have expressed resentment toward gays and lesbians, arguing that ethnic identity is a cause for equal rights, unlike homosexuality, which in their eyes is a lifestyle choice (Pollock & Tobin, 2000). According to John Sibley Butler, in the November/December 1993 issue of *Society*, "Comparing homosexuals to blacks is comparing a lifestyle with a race: an achieved characteristic with one that is ascribed; a choice in expressed lifestyle with one that is by and large not a choice" (p. 18). Some members of minority groups may not view favorably gays who make a decision to live a particular lifestyle, whereas minorities typically have fewer lifestyle choices. Therefore:

> **H7:** *The larger the percentage of African Americans in each city, the less favorable the coverage of gays in the Boy Scouts.* (Lifestyle Market Analyst, 2000)

> **H8:** *The greater the percentage of Hispanics in each city, the less favorable the coverage of gays in the Boy Scouts.* (County and City Extra, 2000)

Buffer Hypothesis

The buffer hypothesis predicts privilege linked to specific perspectives favoring human rights claims. The buffer hypothesis was confirmed in chapter 3 for coverage of Anita Hill during the Clarence Thomas hearings, the right to physician-assisted suicide, and the "right" to embryonic stem cell research. It is possible that there may be a relationship between these city characteristics and favorable newspaper coverage of gays in the Boys Scouts.

H9: *The larger the percent college educated, the more favorable the coverage of gays in the Boy Scouts.* (Lifestyle Market Analyst, 2000)

H10: *The larger the percent with professional or technical status, the more favorable the coverage of gays in the Boy Scouts.* (Lifestyle Market Analyst, 2000)

H11: *The larger the percent of families with an income of $100,000 or more, the more favorable the coverage of gays in the Boy Scouts.* (Lifestyle Market Analyst, 2000)

Vulnerability

It is reasonable to expect that some in a community who are below the poverty level may have negative views on gays in the Boy Scouts. Those living below the poverty line may be less empathic with those who appear to "marginalize" themselves voluntarily. Therefore:

H12: *The larger the percent living below the poverty level, the less favorable the coverage of gays in the Boy Scouts.* (County and City Extra, 2000)

METHODOLOGY

Sample Selection

This case study tracks coverage of gays in the Boy Scouts systematically in a geographic cross-section of 21 major newspapers throughout the nation (see Table 9.2). All articles 150 words or more in length printed in each newspaper were sampled from the period of January 1, 1998 to March 1, 2001, a time frame when debate over gays in the Boy Scouts surfaced and developed. The resulting newspaper articles were collected from the DIALOG Classroom Information Program newspaper database and Lexis-Nexis Academic Universe, both available to college libraries.

Article Prominence and Direction

After prominence scores were calculated for each article, the directional measurements of favorable, unfavorable, or balanced/neutral toward gays in the Boy Scouts were assigned to each article by two different coders.

Coverage *favorable* to allowing gays in the Boy Scouts included articles that considered this decision a violation of one's civil rights. These articles

TABLE 9.2. Gays in the Boy Scouts of America Media Vectors

NEWSPAPER	MEDIA VECTOR
San Francisco Chronicle	.256
Philadelphia Inquirer	.221
Boston Globe	.217
Denver Post	.211
St. Louis Post Dispatch	.137
Atlanta Journal	.122
Times Union-Albany	.121
Buffalo News	.092
Dayton Daily News	.070
Charlotte Observer	.038
Seattle Times	.033
Tallahassee Democrat	.033
Pittsburgh Post Gazette	.024
Cincinnati Enquirer	.019
Fort Worth Star Telegram	.006
Wichita Eagle	−.007
Columbia State	−.009
Phoenix Gazette	−.014
Memphis Commercial Appeal	−.015
Milwaukee Journal Sentinel	−.078
Lexington Herald Leader	−.188

stressed that a group such as the BSA should promote tolerance of all types of people. Favorable articles were directly opposed to the verdict of *Dale vs. BSA*, claiming that such a decision was discriminatory.

Coverage deemed *unfavorable* to allowing gays in the Boy Scouts included articles that framed homosexuality as immoral or perhaps against the moral code of the BSA that boy scouts should be "morally straight" and "clean." Articles coded unfavorable also emphasized that private organizations have a right to restrict their membership. In some cases, these articles suggested that homosexuality is a lifestyle or personal choice, not an innate quality, thereby buttressing the prerogative of the Boys Scouts to exclude this group on moral grounds.

Balanced/neutral coverage included articles that recorded both sides of the debate over homosexuals in the Boy Scouts in approximately equal measure, or revealed a disinterested, nondirectional perspective on the issue. Finally, articles that dealt solely with James Dale or other individual homosexual members of the Boy Scouts and did not render a clear opinion on the more general topic of homosexuals in the Boy Scouts were coded balanced/neutral. After the resulting 322 articles were assigned their directional scores by at least two coders, a Holsti's coefficient of intercoder reliability was calculated at .89.

Multiple Procedures and Methodologies: Media Vectors, Pearson Correlations, Regression Analysis, Factor Analysis, Regional Comparisons With Public Opinion, Ownership Patterns

Prominence and directional scores were combined to calculate a media vector for each newspaper. An exploration of the relation between city characteristics described in the hypothesis section and media vectors was carried out using multiple statistical procedures.

1. Pearson correlations were run to measure which city characteristics were most strongly associated with each dependent variable.
2. City characteristics were subjected to regression analysis in order to isolate a few key city dimensions providing the highest degree of explanatory power in their association with coverage of homosexuals in the Boy Scouts.
3. Factor analysis clustered city characteristics into distinct, key city dimensions to improve the explanatory power of the independent variables.
4. Regression of factors correlated the significant dimensions of the factor analysis with the media vectors.
5. Public opinion measures collapsed in four regional categories were compared with media vectors averaged for each region.
6. Primary and secondary newspaper circulations for each city were examined for potential comparisons.
7. Ownership patterns were explored by comparing locally owned and nonlocally (corporate)-owned newspaper media vectors.

RESULTS

Newspaper coverage of gays in the Boy Scouts from January 1998 to March 2001 was indeed varied. Media vectors ranged from .256 to −.188, revealing divergent perspectives among city newspapers. Most of the coverage (17 out of 21 papers) was favorable or neutral toward homosexuals in the BSA.

Pearson Correlations

Newspapers were ranked according to each city's media vector, and Pearson correlations were run to explore the association between city characteristics and variation in reporting on gays in the Boy Scouts. The buffer hypothesis and three stakeholder hypotheses were supported (see Table 9.3).

Of 12 hypotheses tested, 6 resulted in a significance level of .01 or better. Another two hypotheses tested resulted in significance levels of .05 or better.

Buffer Hypothesis Supported

The buffer hypothesis expected more favorable coverage of gays in the Boy Scouts in direct proportion to the percentage of citizens in a city who are more privileged economically, educationally, and professionally. Indeed, results show that higher percentages of a population with family incomes

TABLE 9.3. Gays in the Boy Scouts Pearson Correlations

HYPOTHESIS	CORRELATION	SIGNIFICANCE
Family income $100,000+	.671	.000**
Republican	−.602	.002**
Gay market index	.599	.002**
Democratic	.596	.002**
College education	.593	.002**
Bible/devotional readings	−.588	.003**
Catholic	.492	.012*
Below poverty level	−.474	.015*
Children 12 and under	−.198	.195
Hispanics	.170	.230
African Americans	.044	.425
Professional/tech occupational status	.040	.432

*Significant at .05 level, one-tailed
**Significant at .01 level, one-tailed

greater than $100,000 correlated strongly with more favorable newspaper coverage of homosexuals in the Boy Scouts ($r = .671; p = .000$), as did percentage of population with a college education ($r = .593; p = .002$). These results pertaining to the buffer hypothesis support previous research documented in chapter 3, as does other research substantiating a connection between privilege and reporting favoring same-sex adoption (Pollock & Tobin, 2000).

Stakeholder: Gay Market Index
Hypothesis Supported

This study also strongly confirms the expectation that the higher the total number of businesses owned by or serving the gay and lesbian community in a city, the more favorably newspapers will cover the issue of gays in the Boy Scouts ($r = .599; p = .002$). Using the GMI, these results suggest that the relative presence of gays and lesbians in a city has an influence on print media. According to HKR, a research firm working on gay and lesbian marketing projects, a major reason mainstream businesses, and possibly the media in general, recognize gay and lesbian consumers is as follows:

> Gay men and lesbian women show their gratitude to marketers who have the courage to serve them. In return for what they see as acceptance and respect, gay consumers will go out of their way to patronize these companies. Furthermore, they will actively spread the word through an amazingly efficient network that circulates not only through word of mouth, but through 200 electronic bulletin boards and 105 local and national publications dedicated to America's gay and lesbian population. (Kahan & Mulrya, 1995, p. 46)

These results also confirm previous research conducted by Pollock and Dantas on same-sex marriages (1998) and Pollock and Tobin (2000) on same-sex adoption. Each set of results showed a correlation between a high GMI score and favorable newspaper coverage of gay rights issues.

Stakeholder: Political Partisanship
Hypotheses Supported

It was expected that cities with larger populations voting Democratic would have more favorable coverage of gays in the Boy Scouts, whereas cities with greater Republican populations would have less favorable coverage. Both correlations proved very significant, as Republican voting corresponded with negative news coverage ($r = -.602; p = .002$), whereas Democratic voting corresponded with favorable news coverage ($r = .596; p$

= .002). This partisan finding confirms research conducted on a Patients' Bill of Rights (chap. 5), possible Arctic oil drilling, and trying juveniles as adults (chap. 7).

Stakeholder: Religious Identity Hypotheses Significant

Both religious identity hypotheses, concerning percentage of Catholics and percentage of people engaging in Bible/devotional readings, proved significant. The greater the percent in a city participating in Bible/devotional readings, the less favorable the coverage of gays in the Boy Scouts ($r = -.588$; $p = .003$). Strikingly, however, the percentage of Catholics in a city correlated *positively* with favorable coverage of gays in the Boy Scouts ($r = .492$; $p = .012$).

This result directly contradicts the hypothesis that a greater percentage of Catholics in a city would be associated with negative newspaper coverage. Regarding same-sex marriage, Pope John Paul II not only reiterated the Church's refusal to recognize same-sex unions, but also called on Catholics to oppose the legal recognition of such marriages on the grounds that they were serious threats to family and society and conferred inappropriate institutional approval for deviant behavior (Eskridge, 1996). For these reasons, a positive correlation between percentage of Catholics and favorable coverage of a gay rights issue is surprising. Perhaps these results suggest that, as with birth control, U.S. Catholics may be more prepared to change than official church doctrines might suggest.

Vulnerability: Poverty Level Significant

As hypothesized, it was found that the greater the percent living below the poverty level in a city, the less favorable the coverage of gays in the Boy Scouts ($r = -.474$; $p = .015$). This supports the expectation that vulnerability may be linked to negative perspectives on gay lifestyle choices, consistent with a study finding that the greater the percent living below the poverty level, the less favorable the coverage of same-sex adoption (Pollock & Tobin, 2000).

Regression Analysis

Multiple regression revealed that two variables—percent family income over $100,000 and percentage Catholic—accounted for 58% of the variance in their association with the media vector. Specifically, the percent families with incomes greater than $100,000 accounted for 45% of the variance, illustrating the strongest relationship, as shown in Table 9.4.

TABLE 9.4. Gays in the Boy Scouts Regression Analysis

MODEL	R	R SQUARED	R SQUARED CHANGE	F CHANGE	SIG. F CHANGE
Income over $100,000	.671	.450	.450	15.522	.001
Income over $100,000 and Catholic	.758	.575	.125	5.316	.033

Factor Analysis

To refine results further, a factor analysis of city characteristics isolated clusters of city characteristics that occur frequently together. Factor analysis of city characteristics for the 21 cities sampled yielded four factors, all with component Eigenvalues of 1.00 or greater: privilege/choice, political partisanship, Catholics/professional status, and African American. Beneath each factor heading in Table 9.5 are its specific variable components.

Regression of the Factors: Privilege/Choice Most Significant

The four factors were themselves subjected to further multiple regression against the media vector with results shown in Table 9.6, yielding two significant factors accounting for 56% of the variance: "privilege/choice"

TABLE 9.5. Gays in the Boy Scouts Factor Analysis

	COMPONENT	FACTOR LOADING
Factor 1: *Privilege/choice*	Family income $100,000+	.825
	Gay market index	.725
	Percent college educated	.632
Factor 2: *Political partisanship*	Percent Republican	.923
	Percent Democrat	.917
Factor 3: *Catholics/professional status*	Percent Catholic	.780
	Percent with professional/ technical status	.776
Factor 4: *African American*	Percent African American	.860

TABLE 9.6. Gays in the Boy Scouts Regression of Factors

MODEL	R	R SQUARED	R SQUARED CHANGE	F CHANGE	SIG. F CHANGE
Privilege/choice	.574	.329	.329	9.331	.007
Privilege/choice plus political partisanship	.750	.563	.233	9.599	.006

(composed of college educated, income over $100,000, and GMI) 33% of the variance; and "political partisanship" (Republican, Democratic), 23% of the variance.

Regional Newspaper Coverage Consistent with Variations in Public Opinion

Table 9.7 compares average media vectors for each of four regions—reflecting level of favorable or unfavorable newspaper coverage of gays in the Boy Scouts—and regional comparisons of public opinion relatively favorable to gays in the BSA. Our findings suggest that average media vectors coincide closely with regional public opinion.

The strongest correlation between negative reporting and public opinion on gays in the Boy Scouts is found in the midwestern region of the United States. The first public opinion question, based on a Harris poll national survey of 1,248 people ages 18 and older, conducted in October

TABLE 9.7. Gays in the Boy Scouts: Regional Comparisons Between Media Vectors and Public Opinion

REGION	AVERAGE MEDIA VECTOR FOR REGION	PERCENT HAVING FRIENDS WHO ARE GAY OR LESBIAN	PERCENT WHO FEEL STRONGLY ABOUT THE ISSUE OF GAY RIGHTS AS A POLITICAL ISSUE IN A PRESIDENTIAL ELECTION
East	.135	31	25
South	−.002	23	21
Midwest	.028	19	34
West	.122	27	20

1992, was: "How strongly do you feel about the issue of gay rights as a political issue in a presidential election?" The results of this poll show that the midwest feels the strongest about the issue of gay rights. Consistently, the midwest also has a low average media vector, revealing that newspaper coverage in this region tends to be unfavorable toward gays in the Boy Scouts. These results, along with the average media vectors, tend to confirm the conventional wisdom of a more conservative south and midwest and a more liberal east and far west. These findings also coincide with the results of the 2000 presidential election, in which the south and midwest tended to vote for the more conservative Republican candidate.

The second public opinion question, based on a Harris survey conducted in October 1992 of 1,248 people ages 18 and older, was: "Do you have any close personal friends who are gay or lesbian, or not?" These results indicate that the midwest's low average media vector (.028) correlates with a low percentage (19%) of midwesterners polled having close friends who are gay or lesbian. Similarly the south's low media vector (–.002) also corresponded with a relatively low percent of residents (23%) reporting having friends who are gay or lesbian. Whatever the reason, regional comparisons suggest some degree of congruence or correspondence between regional newspaper reporting perspectives on gays in the BSA and regional public opinion regarding the issue.

Comparison of Primary and Secondary Newspapers: Not Statistically Useful

If the community structure approach is a powerful explanatory tool, then both leading newspapers and other significant newspapers might be expected to align themselves with city demographics. In order to test that expectation, an effort was made to go beyond the leading paper to identify the paper with the second highest circulation in each city, using a standard reference, *Gale's Directory*.

Yet investigation revealed that circulation sizes for the second largest papers in most cities were so small that they could not be construed to be broadly representative of city demographics. Few cities studied have comparable or near comparable papers. The clear exceptions are *The Denver Post* (circulation: 1,006,518) and *The Rocky Mountain News* (circulation: 956,146), both in Denver, and the *Seattle Times* (circulation: 943,698) and *Seattle Post Intelligencer* (circulation: 836,683). Comparing coverage of papers within these specific cities might be useful. Because leading and second largest newspapers in the newspapers studied are rarely comparable in scope or market nationwide, however, statistical comparisons of such papers in each city are not recommended on a nationwide basis because they are not expected to yield useful results.

Locally Owned Papers More Open and Accepting
of Gays in the Boy Scouts

Conventional wisdom expects that there is a distinct difference between reporting from corporate newspapers owned elsewhere and reporting from local newspapers. One would expect corporate, nonlocally owned newspapers to allow relatively liberal reporting on social and political change, as they are more concerned with bottom-line profit. In contrast, locally owned newspapers, although somewhat concerned with bottom-line profit, are presumably more concerned with newspaper content that does not discomfort local elites. That expectation has been confirmed by Demers (1996a) in his empirical work comparing locally owned and chain-owned newspapers, demonstrating the relatively conservative reporting of locally owned papers whose publishers are themselves part of local elite networks.

In this study, however, just the opposite was found. A *t*-test comparing media vectors of locally owned and chain-owned papers found that local papers are actually more liberal and accommodating regarding the issue of gays in the Boy Scouts, whereas the corporate-owned chains whose owners reside elsewhere seem to be more conservative (see Table 9.8).

What may account for the unexpected finding that locally owned papers are more accommodating toward homosexuals in scouting is that the Boy Scouts are such a cherished *local* institution. As anyone who has been part of an active troop is aware, the Boy Scouts are an intrinsic part of many communities, highly regarded as a valuable resource. Local publishers and journalists may be reluctant to interfere with the autonomy of a deeply admired institution. For example, the same year the U.S. Supreme Court upheld the right of the BSA to exclude gays, some individuals urged that the annual sale of Christmas trees by a local Boy Scout troop be boycotted in Princeton, New Jersey (where the author lives), to protest the national BSA's discriminatory policies. In sharp reaction, several Princeton residents responded by buying two trees instead of one to show their support for the local troop, the members and parents of which were well known through-

TABLE 9.8. Gays in the Boy Scouts: Locally and Chain-Owned
Newspaper *t*-Test

LOCALLY OWNED	CHAIN-OWNED	*T*-TEST SIGNIFICANCE
Mean media vector .113	Mean media vector -.010	+3.07
N = 11	*N* = 9	significance < .005 (one-tailed)

out the community, and the sales of trees by scouts reached an all-time revenue record.

CONCLUSION

Gays in the Boy Scouts has only recently arrived as a prominent topic on
media agendas. The issue of gays in the Boy Scouts, however, transcends
previous related issues such as same-sex marriage or same-sex adoption.
Decisions made involving this case will affect all families with children
involved in the Boy Scouts and private organizations setting membership
standards. As more incidents involving homosexuals in the Boy Scouts arise,
and as media coverage increases, further research will be useful. Studies of
the perceptions of different religious groups, such as Baptists, on this subject may prove insightful. Several religious groups do not agree with the
lifestyles homosexuals live, and these perspectives could significantly influence newspaper coverage of the issue. By striking contrast, because percent
of Catholics correlates positively with favorable coverage of gays in the Boy
Scouts, further research may indicate how much the views of Catholic laity,
if not the Catholic clergy, may be shifting. Community structure analysis of
city characteristics and newspaper coverage of gays in the Boy Scouts provides evidence that this supposedly "marginal" issue taps more "mainstream" social and political dimensions than might be expected.

10

TILTED MIRRORS

Media Alignment with Social Control And Social Change

REPORTING PATTERNS, LINKS TO PUBLIC BEHAVIOR, AND IMPLICATIONS FOR THEORY

Comparing all of the case studies, this chapter documents both variation among newspapers reporting on critical issues and newspaper consistency across distinct issues, illuminating enduring links between community structure characteristics—privilege, political partisanship, and vulnerability—and reporting connected to social change. Focusing on the theoretical implications of this research, this chapter confirms that media are often "tilted mirrors," aligned with community structure along an axis of inequality, inequality not simply linked to reporting perspectives reinforcing "social control." Inequality is also associated with media frames accommodating social and political change. Additionally, media can become aligned with specific stakeholders concerned with change, such as the number or ages of children in families, age (in particular senior citizens), partisan voters, and organizations/establishments marketing to key stakeholders. Drawing further theoretical connections between media and society, this chapter documents alignments between media patterns and social patterns: public opinion, public behavior, and public policy, comparing the theoretical potency of the community structure approach with that of two other established theories. Finally, several propositions are offered for future community structure research, exhorting communication scholars to study the process that connects journalist frame-building with city characteristics in reporting on critical issues.

CLUSTERED REPORTING PATTERNS

Greatest Reporting Variation in Reporting on Health, Children, and Teens

Using the media vector measure of newspaper issue "projection" permits researchers to compare newspaper variation from one issue to another. The maximum variation measured by the media vector is from +1 to −1, or a maximum difference of 2. Because most issues will rarely manifest anything approaching even a difference of 1, it is useful to set a difference threshold that distinguishes issues that have a "great deal of newspaper variation" from those that manifest only "some variation." If .50 is set as the threshold for "great deal of difference," the issues cited in Table 10.1 (putting HIV/AIDS momentarily aside), listed with the differences between their most extreme media vectors, qualify for the category of substantial difference;

Two patterns are apparent in the issues registering maximum newspaper projection variation across the nation, regarding health-related issues and issues linked to children or teens.

First, four of the maximum variation issues, including the two issues with the most varied coverage, focus on health issues: physician-assisted suicide, embryonic stem cell research, a Patients' Bill of Rights and the MSA. All of these issues focus on health concerns. Second, at least three of the issues focus on issues of concern to children or teens: trying juveniles as adults, gun control and the MSA. The first issue—trying juveniles as adults—is of obvious consequence to teens; gun control is a major issue among teenagers because so many teens purchase guns and are both perpetrators and victims of violent crime; and the MSA was fashioned in part as

TABLE 10.1. Substantial Differences in Some Media Vector Ranges

SOCIAL OR POLITICAL ISSUE	DIFFERENCE IN EXTREME MEDIA VECTORS
Physician-assisted suicide	1.123
Embryonic stem cell research	.792
Trying juveniles as adults	.703
Hong Kong transferred to People's Republic of China	.590
Gun control	.558
Patients' Bill of Rights	.538
Master Settlement Agreement on Tobacco	.500

an effort to restrict tobacco advertising to citizens under the age of 18. Finally, although only one of the issues manifesting maximum newspaper variation around the nation deals with foreign policy—the handover of Hong Kong to the PRC, a larger sampling of foreign policy issues (beyond Hong Kong's handover and NAFTA) might have yielded more events with maximum reporting variation. In summary, from the sample of issues studied in this exploration, topics linked to health and children display substantially varied newspaper coverage throughout the United States.

Indeed, as Table 10.2 makes clear, until the period after Arthur Ashe's announcement that he had contracted HIV/AIDS, coverage of that topic manifested substantial variation in newspapers throughout the United States.

Some Newspapers More Geographically Consistent Than Others: Coastal Versus Interior (River) Pattern

The papers in this study represent a national cross-section of large cities, unrepresentative of all cities of different sizes. Yet a survey of these cities can reveal patterns if our analysis examines evidence of geographic consistency in supporting or opposing change. Listing specific cities is less important than the search for broad patterns. Out of 14 case studies explored (postponing consideration of the HIV/AIDS studies), issues dealing with foreign or international affairs (Hong Kong, NAFTA) were excluded in order to focus on clear national issues. Of the remaining 12 issues, papers that were included in at least 9 (or 75%) of the case studies were selected for further analysis.

Despite substantial variation from one newspaper to another in coverage of critical events, in particular health and child-related issues, some newspapers were more consistent than others at either accommodating or opposing social and political change. Adjusting for "direction" accommo-

TABLE 10.2. Substantial Differences in HIV/AIDS Media Vector Ranges

TIME PERIOD/CRITICAL EVENT	DIFFERENCE IN EXTREME MEDIA VECTORS
1990	.81
Magic Johnson's announcement	.74
1991	.82
Arthur Ashe's announcement	.73
1994	.17
1995	.37

dating or resisting change in each case, those cities in the top half (7 out of 13 or 14 papers sampled) or at least the top one third (7 out of 20 or more papers sampled) were defined as accommodating change. Conversely, those cities in the bottom half or one third were defined as most skeptical about change. Table 10.3 illustrates the cities that were most consistent at either accommodating or opposing social and political change.

Two patterns are immediately visible: a coastal pattern and an interior river pattern. First, four out of the five cities with papers most often accommodating social or political change across several issues are located on the coasts: Boston, Philadelphia, San Francisco, and Seattle. The other city is Atlanta, one of the most rapidly growing and cosmopolitan cities in the south and home to the 1996 summer Olympics. The second pattern is an interior river pattern. Three of the four cities with newspapers most resistant to change are located on either the Ohio or the Mississippi rivers: Pittsburgh, St. Louis, and Memphis. Both coastal and interior river patterns, coinciding with newspapers relatively open to or opposed to sociopolitical change, are

Table 10.3.   Cities With Newspapers Consistently Accommodating or Opposing Social and Political Change

CITIES	NUMBER OF ISSUES (out of 12 maximum) MOST ACCOMMODATING SOCIOPOLITICAL CHANGE (among the seven cities with the *most positive* media vectors for each issue)	PERCENT ISSUES ACCOMMODATING CHANGE
San Francisco	8 of 10 issues	80
Boston	8 of 11 issues	73
Atlanta	5 of 9 issues	56
Philadelphia	6 of 11 issues	54
Seattle	5 of 10 issues	50

CITIES	NUMBER OF ISSUES (12 maximum) MOST SKEPTICAL ABOUT CHANGE (among the seven cities with the *least positive* media vectors for each issue)	PERCENT ISSUES SKEPTICAL ABOUT CHANGE
Lexington	5 of 9 issues	56
Pittsburgh	6 of 11 issues	54
Memphis	5 of 10 issues	50
St. Louis	4 of 11 issues	36

not surprising to students of politics, in particular to observers of the 2000 and 2004 presidential elections, in which the coastal states (the northeast and the west) tended to favor the Democratic candidate, whereas large portions of the interior of the country tended to favor the Republican contender.

Patterns of HIV/AIDS Coverage Somewhat Different From Other Issues

Although coverage patterns were somewhat consistent across the 12 issues that comprise most of the case studies in this volume, coverage of those with HIV/AIDS did not display such consistent patterns. Regarding regional patterns, newspaper coverage most favorable to those with HIV/AIDS was found in all four major regions of the United States: east (Boston, Philadelphia); south (New Orleans, Charlotte); midwest (Madison, Wisconsin); and west (Phoenix, Seattle). By this measure, the midwest had only one city's coverage (Madison, Wisconsin) in the "most favorable" category, whereas other regions of the nation revealed at least two cities in each region recording coverage "most favorable" to those with HIV/AIDS.

In a similar fashion, coverage least favorable to those with HIV/AIDS was also found in all four major regions of the United States: east (Philadelphia); south (Atlanta, Houston); midwest (Chicago, Detroit, St. Louis); and west (Denver, Phoenix, Seattle). By this measure, however, only Philadelphia (northeast) displayed coverage "least favorable" to those with HIV/AIDS. Indeed, unlike coverage of the 12 general social and political topics, in which there was substantial consistency for numerous cities across several of the 12 issues, coverage of HIV/AIDS revealed extreme oscillations. Three cities (Philadelphia, Phoenix, and Seattle) manifested coverage—for the six time periods/events studied—that was both extremely favorable for three of the time periods/events and yet extremely unfavorable for the other three. Extreme pendulum swings in coverage may have reflected swings in public opinion or official perceptions of those with HIV/AIDS.

Comparing Table 10.4 on coverage of HIV/AIDS with preceding tables on coverage of 12 other social and political issues, few immediate similarities are found. Only three of the seven cities with the most sympathetic coverage of those with HIV/AIDS are found among the six cities most accommodating to broad political and social change: Boston, Philadelphia, and Seattle. Only one of the nine cities with coverage least sympathetic to those with HIV/AIDS (St. Louis) is also among the four cities least accommodating, or most opposed to comprehensive change. Yet, these differences found in a city-by-city analysis of media vectors are probably imbedded in a few key patterns that describe the way city characteristics are linked systematically to newspaper coverage of political and social change, patterns discussed in the preceding chapters.

TABLE 10.4. Cities With Newspapers Most or Least Sympathetic to Those
With HIV/AIDS

CITIES	NUMBER OF ISSUES (out of 6) MOST SYMPATHETIC TO THOSE WITH HIV/AIDS (among the seven cities with the *most positive* media vectors for each issue)
New Orleans	4 of 6 issues
Madison, WI	4 of 6 issues
Boston	3 of 6 issues
Charlotte	3 of 6 issues
Philadelphia	3 of 6 issues
Phoenix	3 of 6 issues
Seattle	3 of 6 issues

CITIES	NUMBER OF ISSUES (out of 6) LEAST SYMPATHETIC TO THOSE WITH HIV/AIDS (among the seven cities with the *least positive* media vectors for each issue)
St. Louis	4 of 6 issues
Atlanta	4 of 6 issues
Chicago	4 of 6 issues
Denver	4 of 6 issues
Detroit	3 of 6 issues
Houston	3 of 6 issues
Philadelphia	3 of 6 issues
Phoenix	3 of 6 issues
Seattle	3 of 6 issues

THE POWER OF PRIVILEGE

For so many of the issues examined in this book, "privilege" is a central
dimension corresponding with precise levels of support for or opposition to
social change. In addition, a few indicators of privilege—for example, percent college educated, percent with professional/technical occupational status, or percent families with incomes of $100,000 or more—consistently link
city characteristics with reporting on political and social change. A small
number of key indicators form patterns that persist across reporting on
diverse issues.

Percent College Educated Significant, as Are Family Incomes of $100,000 Plus and Professional/Technical Occupational Status

For the buffer hypothesis—linking privilege with reporting relatively favorable toward human rights claims, and the violated buffer hypothesis—linking privilege with reporting relatively unfavorable toward issues that threaten a cherished or healthy way of life, education level is persistent in its association with coverage variation. Cities with higher levels of college educated citizens are likely to display: favorable coverage of Anita Hill, physician-assisted suicide and admitting gays in the Boy Scouts; less favorable coverage of tobacco advertising (and therefore favorable coverage of the MSA) and of the U.S. Supreme Court decision to stop the vote counting in Florida that awarded the presidential election to George W. Bush.

As with education levels, cities with high levels of families with incomes of $100,000 or more are also likely to reveal newspaper coverage favorable toward physician-assisted suicide, the MSA, and admitting gays in the Boy Scouts; less favorable toward the Bush vs. Gore decision. Consistently, cities with high proportions of professional/technical occupational status are further likely to display reporting favorable toward Anita Hill, embryonic stem cell research, and Internet privacy (and therefore less favorable to Internet censorship). High proportions of citizens who are college educated or with family incomes of $100,000 or more or with professional/technical occupational status are all strongly associated, in congruent directions, with both buffer and violated buffer hypotheses.

Additionally, stakeholder issues, although linked primarily with such city characteristics as position in the family lifecycle and partisanship (percent voting Democratic or Republican), are also associated with indicators of privilege. For example, the larger the proportion of those with high family incomes in a city, the less favorable the coverage of capital punishment, a violated buffer pattern. Coverage of both gun control and drilling in the Arctic are linked primarily to life-cycle position or partisanship. They are also linked, nevertheless, to education, income levels, and occupational status, all in predicted directions. The larger the proportions of those with high education, income, or occupational status levels in a city, the more favorable the coverage of gun control. Because relatively uncontrolled gun access can be seen as a threat to physical health or a cherished way of life, these findings fit a violated buffer pattern. Consistently, but in the opposite direction, the larger the proportions of those with high education, income or occupational status levels in a city, the less favorable the coverage of drilling in the ANWR. Because drilling would represent a destruction of a cherished way of life for animals and vegetation and Native Americans in Alaska, these findings also fit a violated buffer pattern. Different levels of privilege are linked strongly to coverage concerned with human rights and stakeholder issues.

Vulnerability (Poverty or Unemployment Levels)
Are Also Significant

Conventional wisdom suggests that newspaper coverage is expected to reflect a newspaper "market" of well-educated or privileged citizens, those most likely to purchase or read newspapers. That finding is confirmed partly in this analysis, described in both the buffer and violated buffer reporting patterns. Yet for several issues, measures of vulnerability—city level of poverty or level of unemployment—are linked to reporting variations.

If populations relatively buffered from economic uncertainty are often linked to coverage supporting human rights claims, then it is reasonable to expect that relatively unbuffered or vulnerable populations might be linked to coverage of human rights claims in a different way, if they are linked at all. From a market perspective, newspaper coverage should presumably have little relation to the proportion of vulnerable elements in a city because those with low incomes are least likely to buy or read newspapers. Curiously, however, this analysis finds links between coverage of some issues and the proportion of vulnerable population in city.

Specifically, the higher the poverty level in a city, the less favorable the coverage of Anita Hill, complementing the buffer hypothesis linking favorable coverage of Hill to privilege. Similarly, the higher the poverty level, the less favorable the coverage of physician-assisted suicide, complementing the buffer hypothesis linking favorable coverage of the proposal to privilege. The higher the poverty level, the less favorable the coverage of admitting gays into the Boy Scouts. The rationales for such links could vary considerably. High poverty levels might be associated with sympathy for a member of a historically disadvantaged group, African-American Clarence Thomas, having an opportunity to serve on the U.S. Supreme Court and therefore with less sympathy toward the damaging testimony of Anita Hill. Or high poverty levels might have been linked to less favorable coverage of physician-assisted suicide because its legalization might be associated with a presumed compulsion to accept early death. Or high poverty levels might be linked to a conviction that those who have a "choice" about sexual orientation might merit less compassion than those whose poverty offers few choices about their economic or social circumstances.

Parallel explanations might be offered for similar findings on other issues. The higher the poverty level, the more favorable the newspaper coverage of a Patients' Bill of Rights and the less favorable the coverage of capital punishment. The higher the unemployment level, the more favorable the coverage of proposed drilling in the ANWR (perhaps because drilling represents new employment opportunities). Whatever the rationales, the significant finding for this analysis is that newspaper reporting on these important issues reflects in part the precise proportions of those below the poverty level or unemployed in different cities. To suggest that newspapers reflect the perspectives of groups unlikely to read or buy newspapers is to ask that researchers reach beyond the view of newspapers as "businesses" serving particular markets to embrace a broader perspective of newspapers as "community" institutions negotiating interests and viewpoints of many different stakeholders.

Protection Hypothesis: A Special Case of Coverage Reflecting Economic Advantage

The protection hypothesis expects that there is a connection between economic interests in a city and reporting on economic issues. For example, it was expected that, because the North American Free Trade Agreement (NAFTA) represented a threat to export manufacturing jobs outside the United States, the higher the percent employed in manufacturing in a city, the less favorable the coverage of NAFTA. Curiously, the opposite results surfaced. Finding that higher percents employed in manufacturing were linked to coverage favorable to NAFTA, it is reasonable to conclude that newspaper coverage reflected less the economic interests of entire communities (jobs) than the more narrow economic interests of the owners and managers of manufacturing industries.

Similarly, regarding the handover of Hong Kong to the PRC, coverage was framed far more often as an economic issue than a human rights issue, representing a loss for open markets and free trade generally. The most significant finding was that the higher the percent families with incomes of $100,000 or more, the less favorable the coverage of Hong Kong's transfer to the PRC. Once again, economic privilege is associated with coverage favorable to the economic interests of the most privileged.

Stakeholder Interests: Position in the Lifecycle and Partisanship

The link between stakeholders and reporting favoring their interests is in some sense expected. Consistent with conventional wisdom, the higher the proportion of those engaged in hunting and shooting, the less favorable the coverage of gun control (although higher proportions of hunters and shooters in a city are linked to favorable coverage of drilling in the ANWR). Also consistent with conventional expectations, the higher the proportion of devotional readers in a city, the less favorable the coverage of gays in the Boy

Scouts. The types of stakeholder characteristics that surface most promi-
nently in this analysis, however, are political partisanship and position in the
lifecycle.

It will not be surprising to those who follow national news closely that
the higher the proportion voting Republican in either the presidential elections of 1996 or 2000 in a city, the more favorable the newspaper coverage
of oil drilling in the ANWR and of trying juveniles as adults, and the less
favorable the coverage of gays in the Boy Scouts. Support for the oil industry, harsh treatment for offenders and skepticism toward gays are all parts of
some segments of various Republican political agendas. In sharp contrast,
the higher the proportions voting Democratic in either the presidential elections of 1996 or 2000, the less favorable the newspaper coverage of oil
drilling in the ANWR and of trying juveniles as adults, and the more favorable the coverage of gay admission to the Boy Scouts. For each of these
issues, political partisanship was the key dimension associated with variations in coverage nationwide. Many commentators have noted the rise in
political partisanship in Washington, DC, beginning in particular with the
ascendancy of Newt Gingrich among the Republicans in the early 1990s,
continuing through the impeachment of President Clinton and in the examination of potential judicial nominations, environmental issues, and all sorts
of criminal justice issues connected with Attorney General Ashcroft in the
first years of the George W. Bush presidency, not to mention the Supreme
Court decision that threw the presidential election to Bush. It is therefore,
not surprising that political partisanship is linked so closely to newspaper
reporting on several prominent political and social issues.

Although political partisanship is a straightforward stakeholder category, a clear element of conventional wisdom, the other major stakeholder category, position in the lifecycle, is less obvious. Previous research has uncovered a curious relationship. The higher the proportion of families with children between the ages of 5 and 7 in a city, the more favorable the newspaper
coverage urging repatriation of Elian Gonzalez (the boy who survived his
mother's attempt to flee Cuba for Florida) to the boy's father in Cuba
(Mink, Puma, & Pollock, 2001). At least two aspects of this finding merit
attention. First, what kind of connection can there be between a life-cycle
category generally (families with children of particular ages) and precise differences in reporting on a critical political or social event? Second, why is
there such a strong connection (significant at the .03 level) between the precise proportion of families with children the same age as Elian (who turned
7 while in the United States) and similarly precise levels of newspaper coverage favoring his return to his father in Cuba? Other variables studied,
including percent speaking Spanish at home or percent Hispanic, were not
at all significantly linked to reporting on the issue. These questions about the
relation between position in the family lifecycle (percent families with chil-

dren in different age ranges) and newspaper reporting on critical events is important, yet few clear answers emerge.

The case study on coverage of gun control in this volume offers further evidence for the importance of position in the lifecycle. The proportions of families with children in different age ranges are all linked significantly with newspaper coverage of efforts at gun control. The older the children (in particular, the larger the proportion of families with children ages 16–18 in a city) the less favorable the coverage of gun control. Although families with children 16–18 were very significantly associated with unfavorable coverage of gun control ($p = .000$), even the proportion of families with children ages 8–10 was also strongly linked with unfavorable coverage of the issue ($p = .01$). Similarly, regarding a different critical issue, trying juveniles as adults, the proportion of families with children 5–7 were significantly tied to reporting "favorable" to regarding juveniles as adults ($p = .028$), whereas at the other end of the life-cycle spectrum, the proportion of retired persons in a city was linked to reporting "opposed" to trying juveniles as adults ($p = .029$). This study has been able to map a connection, but "how" and "why" this connection between life-cycle position and newspaper reporting occurs deserves more elaborate study.

IMPLICATIONS FOR THEORY

Tilted Mirrors: Media Alignment on an Axis of Inequality

The centrality of privilege as a pivot around which newspaper coverage rotates or tilts is a key finding of this media alignment study. Privilege in this study has been measured primarily by education, family income, and professional economic status. At least two of these indicators—education and occupational status—must be "earned." Additionally, although family income may be the product of either birthright or earned economic advantage, high correlations among family income, education, and professional occupational status suggest that, whatever the fortunes of their ancestors or parents, a large portion of those in the privileged family income category also worked to attain high levels of education and professional achievement.

As a result, privilege as measured in this study resembles less the manifestation of a rigid social class than of a managerial, technical, or professional cluster that may have collective interests but that nevertheless is capable of selective flexibility and tilted coverage. Thus, when issues are clearly framed as human right issues—workplace harassment regarding Anita Hill, legalization of physician-assisted suicide or embryonic stem cell research, social and economic privilege can be associated with reporting sympathetic to rights claims, a pattern this study calls *the buffer hypothesis*: Privilege and distance from economic uncertainty are linked to reporting essentially favorable to those whose concerns are framed as "rights claims."

These same measures of inequality—education, professional status, family income—can nevertheless also link privilege to reporting *unfavorable* to challenges to biological existence or a cherished way of life. Examples include reporting unsympathetic to Magic Johnson when making his HIV announcement (suggesting that HIV/AIDS could clearly threaten mainstream, upscale citizens), tobacco company advertising to minors, efforts to censor Internet access and the Supreme Court decision (Bush vs. Gore) stopping the vote counting in Florida in the 2000 presidential election. In each case, the higher the proportion of privileged groups in a city, the less favorable the reporting on either recognized health issues (regarding HIV/AIDS or tobacco use) or issues challenging a valued way of life (including virtually unlimited access to information on the Internet or the belief that votes should have paramount importance in determining election outcomes). These examples confirm what this study calls a *violated buffer* hypothesis, in which privilege is expected to be linked to unfavorable reporting on biological/health threats or threats to a cherished way of life for privileged groups.

Consistent with the buffer and violated buffer hypotheses, confirming that inequality is aligned with both favorable and unfavorable coverage of social change, is the expectation that economic privilege, in particular, is linked to coverage favoring specific economic interests. For example, the percent employed in manufacturing in a city is linked to favorable coverage of NAFTA, suggesting that the interests of the owners and managers of manufacturing entities, rather than the interests of rank and file employees, are closely linked to coverage. Similarly, the higher the proportion of privileged groups in a city, the less favorable the coverage of the handover of Hong Kong to the PRC. This suggests that the loss of unfettered economic access to China is somehow reflected in reporting through the filter of a city's proportion of privileged groups.

Indeed, this exact alignment of reporting with equally precise measures of privilege is striking. What each of the case studies in this book reveals, across a wide range of topics and critical events reflecting efforts at social and political change, is the curious, measured incremental change in coverage "projection" exactly meshed with incremental differences in levels of privilege across distinct cities. If this exploration were to stop with these observations, however, it would often mainly offer an umbrella confirmation of the Tichenor, Donohue, and Olien guard dog hypothesis. From this perspective, media essentially function, most of the time, as guard dogs protecting the stability of the existing social order, in particular the interests of economic, political, and social elites.

Even if media guard elite interests, however, this exploration also confirms that "social control" may not be a consistent goal. Coverage supporting Anita Hill, legalization of physician-assisted suicide, and embryonic stem cell research was aligned with social change or defending certain "rights," found in reporting supporting the MSA on tobacco or Internet privacy, or opposing the Supreme Court's Bush vs. Gore decision. Additional case studies suggest a more varied model of reporting on political and social change, one that takes into account a wide range of stakeholders, and in particular, some of the more "vulnerable" segments of society.

Inequality for Whom? Media Alignment Tilted Toward "Vulnerable" Non-Elite Population Segments

Reporting reflecting social inequality may not necessarily be aligned with elite segments. Coverage of selected critical events can also be aligned with precise proportions of "vulnerable" groups in communities. For example, the higher the proportion below the poverty line, the more favorable the coverage of *Roe v. Wade* in the immediate aftermath of that decision (Pollock et al., 1978). In parallel fashion, poverty level is linked to unfavorable coverage of capital punishment, accounting for about 23% of the variance, and poverty level is also associated with favorable coverage of a Patients' Bill of Rights.

Curiously, the higher the poverty level, the less favorable the coverage of Anita Hill's testimony, perhaps in part because that testimony damaged the occupational mobility of Clarence Thomas, someone from an economically disadvantaged family. Similarly, the higher the poverty level, the less favorable the coverage of physician-assisted suicide, the mirror opposite of the buffer hypothesis. That is, those "unbuffered" from economic uncertainty are sometimes linked to media coverage on rights claims at variance from the coverage associated with privileged groups. For example, the higher the percent below the poverty level, the more favorable the coverage of drilling in the ANWR, associated not with environmental "rights" but with an increase in jobs.

Beyond Inequality: Media Tilt Coverage to Align With Multiple Stakeholders

Although media alignment along a fulcrum of inequality is confirmed abundantly in this exploration, another pattern is apparent as well. A wider range of alignments are uncovered, in particular linking coverage with family size (number of families with children of specific ages), age distribution (in particular senior citizens), partisan voting patterns (Democratic or Republican), or number of establishments serving stakeholders (such as those marketing to gays).

Regarding family size or family position in the lifecycle, the larger the number of families with children under age 18 in a city, the less favorable the coverage of efforts at gun control. This finding was contrary to expectation because it was presumed that families with children might wish to protect their offspring from the risk of gun violence. Yet, under circumstances where authorities are not considered sufficiently effective in controlling gun violence, it is not unreasonable for those with children to wish to give themselves the option of gun ownership for personal protection, a kind of "self-protection" or perhaps "vigilante" hypothesis. This finding was also consistent with research on trying juveniles as adults, in which high proportions of families with relatively "vulnerable" children between the ages of 5 and 7 were linked to reporting favoring punitive perspectives, considering juveniles as adults in the court system.

Regarding age, illuminated in the study on legalization of physician-assisted suicide, the number of those age 75 or more in a city is linked strongly to coverage of the issue. In previous research, the number of seniors age 75 or older was associated with relatively favorable coverage of Dr. Kevorkian's activities, apparently a refection of his ability to dramatize a dilemma faced by considerable numbers of seniors. But in subsequent research, it became clear that the higher the proportion of those age 75 or older is also linked strongly with relatively unfavorable coverage of actual legalization of physician-assisted suicide, perhaps because legalization implies social approval and therefore pressure on seniors to engage in what is obviously terminal activity.

Regarding political partisanship, considerable evidence suggests that the higher the proportion voting either Democratic or Republican in the most recent presidential election, the more newspaper reporting is aligned with those voting patterns when covering environmental issues, efforts to try juveniles as adults and, predictably, the Bush vs. Gore decision by the Supreme Court. For example, the larger the proportion voting Republican in either the 1996 or 2000 presidential elections, the more favorable the coverage of drilling in the ANWR, the more favorable the coverage of trying juveniles as adults and the more favorable the coverage of the Supreme Court decision to stop the counting in Florida that effectively awarded George W. Bush the 2000 presidential election. Political partisanship can play a major role in reporting on political and social change.

Regarding establishments serving particular groups, an index measuring a "GMI," based on the number of profit-making and nonprofit establishments marketing to gays in a city has been created specifically for this set of community structure studies. The GMI is linked strongly to reporting favoring legalization of same-sex marriage (Pollock & Dantas, 1998) and to reporting favoring same-sex adoption (Higgins, Dudich, & Pollock, 2003). Additionally, as chapter 9 reveals, the GMI is linked positively to favorable coverage of gays in the BSA, and therefore to unfavorable coverage of the Supreme Court decision allowing the BSA to exclude gays from membership or leadership.

In each of the preceding case studies, the relative presence of stakeholders is linked to coverage reflecting the apparent interests of those stakeholders. Whether the stakeholder measure is based on number of multiple community media channels (such as cable, FM or AM stations), family size, age, political party strength, number of establishments serving a particular group, or group "vulnerability," it is clear that a variety of stakeholder interests can find clear reflection in reporting on political and social change. It is also clear that media can function in more complex ways than guard dogs, reinforcing social control.

Rather, papers can resemble tilted mirrors, reflecting or refracting impulses toward change and the concerns of a broad range of publics and stakeholders. Like mirrors, newspapers can illuminate some visible features of their surroundings, leaving other events or issues outside their "frames" in penumbras or shadows. To extend the visual metaphor, *The New York Times'* Public Editor Daniel Okrent once quoted Richard Avedon as saying: "There is no such thing as inaccuracy in a photograph. All photographs are accurate. None of them is the truth" (Okrent, 2005, p. 2). In media coverage of the war in Iraq, for example, U.S. reporting on American troop casualties is probably accurate, but the "truth" of the war in Iraq is not illuminated because other casualties, in particular Iraqi civilian casualties, are typically ignored. In a similar fashion, because papers appear to frame social change in accordance with key community characteristics, they often "tilt" their coverage or reflections in alignment with variations in those characteristics. "Tilting" may be accurate for what media choose to frame, but tilted coverage is by no means a comprehensive understanding or narrative of "truth."

MEDIA ALIGNMENT WITH ATTITUDES, BEHAVIOR, AND PUBLIC POLICY

Media Alignment With Attitudes/Public Opinion: Regional Congruence

Media projection on critical issues can be aligned not only with community characteristics but also with public attitudes. As measured in public opinion surveys, public attitudes are available on a wide range of issues, but these attitudes are typically found collected and aggregated at national or regional levels. In order to compare media projections with public opinion, media vectors have been averaged for each of four regions as defined by the U.S. Census Bureau, then compared for comparable regional level public opinion data.

Overall, regional newspaper coverage of critical events closely parallels regional public opinion measures of the same or related issues, although a few discrepancies merit mention. Proximity between media coverage and public opinion is perhaps greatest in the west and least in the midwest, for reasons that may warrant exploration elsewhere. At the risk of issuing generalizations that appear to reinforce widely held stereotypes about each region, the following patterns emerge.

Western Coverage and Public Opinion Are Somewhat more Favorable to Ethical and Scientific Innovation.

As Tables 10.5 and 10.6 reveal, western media vectors and public opinion are most favorable toward legalization of physician-assisted suicide and to federal funding of embryonic stem cell research.

Physician-Assisted Suicide. Although all regions manifest clear, positive majorities of public opinion favoring physician-assisted euthanasia (from 61.5% in the south to the most positive in the west, 75.2%), the media vectors display more variation. Only the west is positive (.203), whereas the east is the most negative (–.187). Two propositions appear reasonable: First, where public opinion and newspaper coverage of an issue are both relatively positive (as in the west), a coherent, consensual public policy on an issue such as physician-assisted suicide may have an opportunity to form (as in Oregon or Washington). Second, where public opinion and newspaper coverage diverge the most (as in the east), the likelihood of a coherent, consensual public policy on an issue (such as physician-assisted suicide) is less likely.

TABLE 10.5. Physician-Assisted Suicide: Regional Media Vectors
            and Public Opinion

REGION	AVERAGE MEDIA VECTORS	PERCENT ANSWERING "YES"
NORTHEAST	–.187	68.1
SOUTH	–.141	61.5
MIDWEST	–.049	69.6
WEST	.203	75.2

General Social Survey, N = 5,009

Question: "Do you favor or oppose physician-assisted death?" Polls conducted over the period 1990–1994.

TABLE 10.6. Embryonic Stem Cell Research: Regional Media Vectors and Public Opinion

REGION	AVERAGE MEDIA VECTOR	PUBLIC OPINION POLL
WEST	.253	62%
NORTHEAST	.221	56%
MIDWEST	.129	53%
SOUTH	.059	50%

Question: "Do you think the federal government should or should not fund embryonic stem cell research, or don't you know enough to say?" Poll taken July–August 2001. All polling information was obtained directly from the Gallup Organization, Inc., Princeton, New Jersey.

Embryonic Stem Cell Research. The mean media vectors are highest in western newspapers and lowest in southern papers. Consistently, public support for federal funding of stem cell research is also strongest in the west (62%) and weakest in the south (50%), reinforcing the concept that reporting on critical issues can "mirror" public opinion. Additionally, the rank order of media vectors corresponds exactly with the rank order of public opinion, from highest to lowest, approving federal funding for embryonic stem cell research. From highest to lowest, approving funding, the regions are west, east, midwest, south (see Table 10.6).

Western Reporting and Public Opinion Are Relatively Unfavorable to Government Regulation

Regarding proposed (censorship) of the Internet and changes abolishing capital punishment, Western reporting is typically the most unfavorable, and public opinion is generally consistent. The "rugged individualism" of the west is alive and well in newspaper reporting.

Censoring the Internet. Two patterns are clear in Table 10.7. First, the regional newspaper coverage *least favorable* to Internet privacy regulation (an average media vector of -.041) is in the west, and consistently, the lowest levels of public opinion favorable to regulation are also in the west. Second, the *most favorable* regional newspaper coverage of the privacy regulation (an average media vector of .105) is in the midwest, and again, the highest levels of public opinion favorable to regulation are in the midwest. Whatever the reason, regional comparisons suggest some degree of congruence or correspondence between regional newspaper reporting perspectives on Internet privacy regulation and regional public opinion regarding the topic.

TABLE 10.7. Internet Regulation: Regional Media Vectors and Public
            Opinion

REGION	MEDIA VECTOR	(a) Would you be more likely to use the Internet, or not, if the privacy of your personal information was protected?	(b) How concerned would you be that content of what you would send over the Internet, would be read by some other person or organization?		
		Yes	Very Concerned	Somewhat Concerned	Total
MIDWEST	0.105	78.7%	68.9%	26.2%	95.1%
NORTHEAST	0.060	76.1%	73.4%	20.3%	93.7%
SOUTH	0.028	78.3%	67.5%	20.2%	87.7%
WEST	-0.041	74.2%	61.8%	20.0%	81.8%

[a]Question 1050D Harris Poll 2/24/98: "Would you be more likely to use the Internet, or not, if the privacy of your personal information and communications would be protected?" (Percentage answering "yes")

[b]Question 1060 Harris Poll 2/24/98: How concerned would you be that content of what you would communicate by electronic mail, through the Internet would be read by some other person or organization without your knowledge or consent? Would you be *very concerned, somewhat concerned, not very concerned,* or *not at all concerned?* (Percentage is total who answered either *very concerned* or *somewhat concerned.*)

Abolishing Capital Punishment. Along with the nation generally, the west displays favorable public opinion toward capital punishment (72.6%; See Table 10.8). Yet compared with other regions, the west displays media coverage most favorable to capital punishment. By extension, western coverage is least amenable to regulating or constraining the application of the death penalty.

The South Displays Media Coverage and Public Opinion Least Favorable to Tobacco Regulation and Gun Control

The Master Settlement Agreement Limiting Tobacco Advertising to Minors. Three patterns are clear (see Table 10.9). First, the regional newspaper coverage least favorable to the MSA (an average media vector of –.085) is in the south, and consistently, the lowest levels of public opinion unfavorable to tobacco companies are also in the south (regarding whether tobacco companies should be allowed to sell and advertise cigarettes however they want). This is consistent with a related study of nationwide coverage of the

TABLE 10.8. Capital Punishment: Media Vectors and Public Opinion

REGION	AVERAGE MEDIA VECTOR	FAVORABLE PUBLIC OPINION TOWARD CAPITAL PUNISHMENT
MIDWEST	-.061	74.5%
SOUTH	-.015	75.4%
NORTHEAST	.042	67%
WEST	.128	72.6%

Source of public opinion data: Harris Poll (September, 2000)

FDA's effort to regulate nicotine and a March 2000 Supreme Court decision denying the FDA that authority. Regional newspaper coverage least favorable to the FDA regulation of tobacco (an average media vector of –.105) was in the south (Caamaño, Pollock et al., 2001).

Second, the *second most favorable* regional newspaper coverage of the MSA (an average media vector of .11) is in the west, and the highest levels of public opinion unfavorable to tobacco companies (consistent with support for the MSA) are also in the west. Third, the east has the highest average newspaper support for the MSA (a media vector average of .142), but public opinion in the east is second from the south in weak opposition to tobacco corporations, or second from the bottom in opposition to tobacco companies doing whatever they wish. That is, the discrepancy between newspaper perspectives on tobacco companies — perspectives that favor the MSA

TABLE 10.9. Tobacco's Master Settlement Agreement: Regional Media Vectors and Public Opinion

REGION	AVERAGE MEDIA VECTOR	PERCENT DON'T BELIEVE TOBACCO COMPANIES SHOULD SELL OR ADVERTISE HOWEVER THEY WANT
SOUTH	-.085	54.2
MIDWEST	-.019	59
WEST	.11	62.7
EAST	.142	56.2

*Source: Harris Poll, 1006-person National sample, March 1997. Question: "Do you believe tobacco is a legal product so tobacco companies should be allowed to sell and advertise cigarettes however they want?"

and therefore restricting the power of such companies—and public opinion are greater in the east than in any other region. One possibility is that journalists in the east are either far more concerned about smoking than is public opinion in the east, or perhaps journalists in the east are more likely than counterparts elsewhere to exercise "leadership" on social or political issues independent of public opinion. Whatever the reason, regional comparisons suggest some degree of correspondence between regional newspaper reporting perspectives and regional public opinion regarding the MSA.

Gun Control. Two propositions derived from this primitive comparison appear worth examining. First, the southern region displays the least favorable reporting on gun control legislation, with a media vector of .156. Indeed, were it not for Charlotte (media vector = .472) and Atlanta (media vector = .293), the average media vector for the south would be .043. This low favorability among newspapers mirrors public opinion: the south is statistically tied for the region with the least favorable public opinion towards the requirement of gun permits (69.7%). Secondly, the northeast region is almost tied for second or third place as most favorable newspaper coverage of gun control legislation, with a media vector of .188. This mirrors somewhat the northwest's highest regional level of public opinion favoring gun permits (86.8%) (see Table 10.10).

The Northeast Displays Both Coverage and Public Opinion Supporting Several Issues Associated With Social Change

As with support for gun control by both media and public opinion, there is a correspondence in the northeast between media coverage and public opinion regarding a Patients' Bill of Rights and the rights of gays to join the BSA. In addition, the northeast, along with the west, were the two regions where both coverage and public opinion were most opposed to the Supreme Court decision allowing the BSA to exclude gays.

TABLE 10.10. Gun Control: Regional Media Coverage and Public Opinion

REGION	AVERAGE MEDIA VECTOR	PERCENT FAVOR REQUIRING GUN PERMITS
WEST	.242	68.5%
MIDWEST	.197	75.4%
NORTHEAST	.188	86.8%
SOUTH	.156	69.7%

General Social Survey 1998. Valid cases over several years = 25,616

A Patients' Bill of Rights. The results reveal some modest consistencies between the coefficients of imbalance and public opinion data. The northeast has both the highest average coefficient of imbalance and the highest percentage of favorable public opinion. This suggests that there is a positive relationship between reporting on the Patients' Bill of Rights and public opinion in that region. The midwest region displays similar results: Both the average coefficient of imbalance and public opinion data reveal the second highest favorable scores in the midwest region. The south and west regions both have lower coefficients of imbalance and lower percentages of favorable public opinion concerning the Patients' Bill of Rights (See Table 10.11).

Gays in the Boy Scouts of America. Average media vectors tend to confirm the conventional wisdom of a more conservative south and midwest and a more liberal east and far west. The northeast has the highest average media vector registering favorable coverage (.135), as well as the highest percentage saying they have friends who are gay or lesbian (31%). Asked in 1992 "How strongly do you feel about the issue of gay rights as a political issue in a presidential election?", the results show that the midwest feels strongest about the issue of gay rights. Consistently, the midwest (along with the south) also has a low average media vector, revealing that newspaper coverage in this region tends to be unfavorable towards gays in the Boy Scouts (see chap. 9).

Bush vs. Gore. Regarding Bush vs. Gore (see Table 10.12), two patterns are clear. First, regional newspaper coverage least favorable to the Supreme Court's decision (an average media vector of –.106) is in the northeast as well as the west (an average media vector of –.099). Consistently, the lowest levels of public opinion favorable to Bush being awarded the presidency are

TABLE 10.11. Patients' Bill of Rights: Regional Media Coverage and Public Opinion

REGION	AVERAGE MEDIA VECTOR	FAVORABLE PUBLIC OPINION TOWARD HEALTH CARE LEGISLATION
NORTHEAST	.239	51%
MIDWEST	.180	50.1%
SOUTH	.127	40.9%
WEST	.068	48.2%

Source for public opinion data: General Social Survey, 1996

TABLE 10.12. Bush vs. Gore Decision: Regional Media Vectors and
               Public Opinion

REGION	AVERAGE MEDIA VECTOR FOR REGION	PERCENT THINK BUSH WOULD HAVE WON
NORTHEAST	-0.106	16
WEST	-0.099	21
SOUTH	-0.065	36
MIDWEST	-0.019	26

Question:[a] "If everyone who tried to vote in Florida had their [sic] votes counted for the candidate who they thought they were voting for with no misleading ballots and infallible voting machines—who do you think would have won the election, George W. Bush or Al Gore?"

[a]This public opinion question was conducted by the Harris Poll in December 2000 on an adult sample.

also in the northeast and west. Second, the regional newspaper coverage most favorable to the Supreme Court's decision to stop the counting (an average media vector of −.019) is in the midwest as well as in the south (an average media vector of −.065). Accordingly, the highest levels of public opinion favorable to Bush becoming president are also found in the midwest and south. Therefore, regional comparisons suggest a strong correspondence between regional newspaper reporting on the Supreme Court's decision and public opinion regarding the rightful winner of the presidency.

There are clearly many parallels beyond regional media "projection" as measured by the media vector and regional measures of public opinion: In many of the case studies documented in this exploration, newspaper coverage "mirrors" public opinion. In addition to observations about the convergence of coverage and public opinion in the west, south, and northeast, the midwest also manifests some parallels. For example, support for a Patients' Bill of Rights is high in the midwest both in reporting and public opinion (see Table 10.11), and support for Internet regulation is higher in both reporting and public opinion in the midwest than elsewhere (see Table 10.7).

At the same time, some large discrepancies between reporting and opinion merit attention in selected case studies. For example, the west manifests the highest level of *newspaper* support for gun control, but the west is also the region with *public opinion* most opposed to gun control. This gap suggests that public opinion in the west may manifest that region's abiding opposition to government regulation of many kinds, or also that media are exercising "leadership" on the issue of gun control, taking a position at some variance with regional public opinion.

Another discrepancy is found in the midwest, which reveals the lowest media support of any region for capital punishment, yet public opinion in the midwest supports capital punishment more strongly than elsewhere. Still another example is found in the northeast, where media opposition to physician-assisted suicide is strongest, yet public opinion is almost 70% favorable. In each of these cases, media may depart from public opinion by exercising "leadership" on specific issues, or perhaps by representing stakeholders or interests other than public opinion broadly defined. In general, nevertheless, regional media coverage corresponds closely with regional public opinion regarding critical issues illuminating social and political change.

MEDIA ALIGNMENT WITH BEHAVIOR AND PUBLIC POLICY

Media alignment with city characteristics and public opinion are two ways media coverage and journalists connect with community context. Media coverage of critical events can also be connected with certain types of behavior and public policy as well, further confirmation of the way media are imbedded in social contexts. Media vector scores for different cities or regions converge with measures of such behavior as "demand" for abortion (abortion incidence), voting behavior and targeted marketing.

For example, the degree of favorable reporting in major city newspapers on *Roe v. Wade* at the time of that landmark decision legalizing abortion in 1973 corresponds rather closely with the incidence of lawful abortions performed after the decision. That is, the more favorable the coverage of legalized abortion, the higher the rate of abortion after the Supreme Court decision (see Alan Guttmacher Institution, 1974). Furthermore, media vectors and public opinion in Bush vs. Gore corresponded with regional voting patterns in the 2000 presidential election. The east and west coasts (and selected parts of the upper midwest) voted essentially for Gore, whereas most of the midwest and the south voted for Bush. Regional media coverage of Bush vs. Gore and public opinion matched the same regional voting patterns, a triple alignment of coverage, opinion, and votes. Moreover, coverage of several issues important to gays corresponds closely with the proportion of institutions marketing to gays in different cities. Coverage of same-sex marriage, same-sex adoption and gays in the BSA all corresponds closely with the proportion of different profit and nonprofit organizations marketing to gays as listed in the Gayellow Pages for each city (see, respectively, Pollock & Dantas, 1998; Higgins, Dudich, & Pollock, 2003; and chap. 10, this volume). The incidence of abortions, votes for president, and yellow page marketing listings are all forms of behavior that correspond closely with variations in media coverage of critical issues.

Beyond the behavior of individuals or institutions with marketing agendas, public policies can also correspond with variations in media coverage. Consider tobacco policies and policies designed to advance the rights of gays. In 1991, the American Stop Smoking Intervention Study (ASSIST) was initiated by the National Cancer Institute to prevent and reduce tobacco use primarily through policy-based approaches to alter the sociopolitical environment, such as encouraging policies and legislation or increasing coverage of tobacco-related issues in the media. In a study of nationwide newspaper coverage of the Supreme Court's decision in March 2000, denying the FDA the authority to regulate nicotine, newspaper articles on the topic were collected from throughout the United States (not simply from major cities), specifically from the ASSIST newspaper database. One of that study's observations was that high levels of newspaper support for FDA regulation of nicotine corresponded closely with newspaper locations in states that had passed laws regulating tobacco consumption (using an index measuring combinations of taxes on tobacco as well as laws on indoor and outdoor smoking). Thus, media support for FDA regulation matches a legal climate supporting regulation of tobacco use at the state level (Pollock, Stillman, & Yulis, 2002).

Tobacco policies apart, the proportion of laws passed protecting gay rights in a city can be shown to correspond strongly with levels of media support for same-sex adoption (Pearson $r = .687$; $p = .002$; Higgins et al., 2003). Table 10.13 reveals the construction of the Gay Legal Index (Cronbach's alpha = .866). It was striking that Pearson correlations revealed the community characteristic most highly correlated with favorable reporting on same-sex adoption was the Gay Legal Index ($r = .687$; $p = .002$) (Higgins et al., 2003).

The preceding observations about behavior—abortion incidence, voting behavior and marketing strategy—as well as public policy tobacco regulation and laws protecting gay rights—are only examples of patterns linking media coverage systematically with surrounding social and political contexts. Variations in media coverage of other critical issues can be compared systematically with variations in such behavior as changes in the incidence of HIV/AIDS, the number of firearms registered, or incidence of teenage tobacco uses. Differences in media coverage might also be compared systematically with variations in such public policies as legalization of physician-assisted suicide (sometimes on ballot initiatives in elections), laws either permitting or forbidding the trials of juveniles as adults, laws mandating stricter background checks for gun purchasers, or perhaps an Environmental Legal Index collecting a multiplicity of measures designed to maximize environmental protection. Media alignment with behavior and public policy is already clear for some critical issues. That alignment process deserves study for a far larger collection of political and social challenges.

TABLE 10.13. Gay Legal Index: Its Construction and Sources

CITY	LAWS FOR ADOPTION BY GAY INDIVIDUALS	LAWS FOR ADOPTION BY GAY COUPLES	LAWS FOR SECOND PARENT ADOPTIONS	LAWS BANNING DISCRIMINATION	LAWS ALLOWING FOR PARTNER BENEFITS	GAYS INCLUDED IN HATE CRIME LEGISLATION	TOTAL
Albany, NY	1	1	1	1	1	1	6
Atlanta, GA	0	-1	0	0	0	0	-1
Boston, MA	1	1	1	2	2	1	8
Chicago, IL	1	1	1	1	0	1	5
Cleveland, OH	1	-1	0	0	0	0	0
Denver, CO	1	1	-1	1	0	0	2
Houston, TX	1	-1	0	0	0	0	0
Memphis, TN	1	-1	-1	0	0	0	-1
Milwaukee, WI	1	1	-1	2	0	1	4
Omaha, NE	-1	-1	-1	0	0	1	-2
Pittsburgh, PA	1	1	1	1	0	0	4
San Diego, CA	1	1	1	2	2	1	8
San Francisco, CA	1	1	1	2	2	1	8
Seattle, WA	1	1	0	1	1	1	5
Tampa, FL	-1	-1	-1	0	0	1	-2

TABLE 10.13. Gay Legal Index: Its Construction and Sources *(continued)*

Sources: Lambda Legal Fund 2002, Gayellow Pages 2001-2002, Human Rights Campaign 2002. Copyright 2003-2007 Higgins, Dudich, and Pollock.

Note. "Laws for gay adoption by GLBT individuals, couples, and second parents" received scores based on analysis by Amnesty International's Human Rights Campaign Foundation. They rated laws state by state with the terms *Bad, Good,* or *Mixed* to describe the legislation and legal climate. Cities residing in states termed *Bad* received a score of -1, whereas those termed *Mixed* received a score of 0, and those termed *Good* received a score of 1.

"Laws banning discrimination" were documented by the Lambda Legal Fund, a legal resource for GLBT people. Cities received scores of 2 if they resided in a state that prohibited discrimination based on sexual orientation, and had an executive order protecting gays from dismissal from a job based on sexual orientation. A score of 1 was received if the state provided only one of the two, and a score of 0 was given if no laws were in place banning discrimination based on sexual orientation.

"Laws allowing for partner benefits" were documented by the Lambda Legal Fund. Cities received a score of 2 if the state offered domestic partner benefits to employees, and a domestic partner registry. The city received a score of 1 if the state provided only one of the two, and a score of 0 was received if the state offered neither domestic partner benefits to employees nor a domestic registry.

"Gays included in hate crime legislation" was recorded by the Lambda Legal Fund. Cities received a score of 1 if sexual orientation was included in Hate Crime legislation, and scores of 0 were received if they were not, or if no Hate Crime legislation existed, as in Tennessee.

"Total" was calculated by adding all of the values, for the comprehensive measure of "Gay Legal Index." (The measure of scale reliability for the index is .866).

COMPARING THEORIES: THE CONTRIBUTION OF THE COMMUNITY STRUCTURE APPROACH

A review of some major communication theories reveals at least two that might be compared with the community structure approach in exploring coverage of political and social change. This section identifies key elements of these theories, then compares their strengths according to four criteria useful in evaluating the explanatory power of the theories: causal pathways, units of analysis, scope, and explanatory simplicity/parsimony.

Agenda-Setting

Agenda setting, in the words of Maxwell McCombs, one of that approach's chief architects, is "a theory about the transfer of salience from the mass media's pictures of the world to those in our heads" (McCombs & Ghanem, 2001, p. 67). A key theoretical assertion for agenda-setting is that "the degree of emphasis placed on issues in the mass media influences the priority accorded these issues by the public" (p. 67). Agenda-setting has been effective in demonstrating parallels between issues high on media agendas and issues high on the list of public opinion priorities, making a case for media coverage affecting public perceptions of public policy issues. Additionally, agenda-setting research sometimes examines the antecedents of media agenda formation, exploring, for example, "agenda-building," investigating a wide range of factors that can influence media agendas, such as corporate press releases (in the case of breast implant controversies) (Powers & Andsager, 1999). In general, however, agenda-setting focuses primarily on the link between media agendas and public opinion, whether at the first or second level of agenda-setting, paying somewhat less attention to factors that might shape media agendas in the first place.

Diffusion Theory

As developed by Everett Rogers (1995) and elaborated by generations of colleagues and graduate students, diffusion theory expects that the impact of media on the diffusion of innovations will be uneven (with some embracing innovations earlier than others, called "early adopters") and will vary with several characteristics. Diffusion of innovations, for example, a cultural shift toward normative approval of nonsmoking, is time-consuming, and Rogers suggested that one of the purposes of diffusion research is to make the diffusion of innovations or health information a less lengthy process. Although mass communication channels may play a significant role in diffusion, interpersonal networks have been critical in a substantial amount of previous research. Yet for all the attention diffusion pays to networking and individual-level characteristics, the diffusion of policy or innovations can focus on mass media in at least three ways, with the innovation of nonsmoking behavior as an example:

1. *Awareness*: Individuals and groups can learn about alternatives to smoking, new options for quitting and possible alternatives to smoking through mass media.
2. *Interest*: Once aware of alternatives and options, information recipients may proceed from that level of information access to a higher level of interest, due in part to articles on the dangers of smoking or on the benefits of quitting smoking printed in newspapers.
3. *Evaluation*: By considering the experience of other people who have quit smoking, as relayed by mass media, individuals can evaluate whether they wish to adopt the "nonsmoking" innovation, knowing that quitting smoking has social support (categories reported in Vivian, 1995, p. 393).

Regarding ways to promote diffusion of the nonsmoking message, several channels can be used that reach beyond conventional channels such as television, radio, newspapers, and printed materials to include secondary minimedia (e.g., billboards, posters, and theater slides), entertainment-education materials (e.g., songs, program inserts, and comics) and interactive media (e.g., Web sites, CD-ROM disks, and computer games, Rice & Atkin, 2001).

Community Structure Approach

The community structure perspective, as outlined in this volume, proposes that demographic characteristics have a great deal of influence on coverage "projection" (the combined prominence and direction of coverage) of critical events. Community structure studies have several advantages. One is that the "community" level of analysis is quite flexible, allowing researchers to regard towns, cities, counties, entire states, regions, and even constructed "clusters" (such as high and low tobacco-dependent states) as "communities" for the purposes of research analysis (Pollock et al., 2002). Structural analyses have also illuminated cross-national communication issues (see S. Gratale et al., 2005; Wu et al., 2000). Another advantage is that, because community "structure" measures are relative stable and enduring (e.g., percent college educated, percent with family incomes of $100,000 or more), it is possible to fashion strong hypotheses about the "antecedents" of coverage, a topic that has received relatively little attention in scholarly communication studies or journalism literatures (Riffe et al., 1998; see also Noelle–Neuman, 1999).

The relatively fixed aspects of community structure clearly "precede" reporting on critical events. Other theories examining the relation between media reporting and public opinion, by contrast, are usually compelled to demonstrate substantial modesty in making causal assertions: Do media agendas affect public opinion? Or do public opinion and public agendas affect media agendas? Agenda-setting studies usually need to address that question in explicit fashion (Rogers & Dearing, 1988). Community structure studies, by contrast, are somewhat more secure in asserting that "structures," which by definition are relatively fixed and concretized, typically precede or predate media coverage or public opinion. As a result, community structure studies are capable of making robust claims about causal analysis of the "antecedents" of media coverage of tobacco control issues. At the same time, muscular claims about causality should be tempered with the recognition that much of reporting is a "negotiated" process involving a wide range of elements, including, of course, several characteristics belonging to journalists themselves and the journalism profession.

This exploration finds that several aspects of a community's social context are important in understanding the way media report on social change. Whatever the negotiation process, community structure studies on critical public issues suggest that news outcomes are far more patterned and systematic than bargaining at the individual level would evoke, and that there are relative consistent alignments between city configurations and reporting on emerging issues.

Three Theories Compared for Different Uses

Each of the three preceding communication theories can be usefully applied to the study of communication along at least four dimensions:

1. *Causal Pathways*: What types of causal assertions are typically associated with each theory? Are causal assertions usually relatively fixed, urging either that media typically "cause" shifts in public opinion, or the reverse, that public opinion affects media? By contrast, are multiple causal pathways suggested, exploring, for example, the "antecedents" of media coverage (e.g., the actions of institutions, the role of social or economic structure)?
2. *Units of analysis*. What units of analysis does each theory emphasize, if it emphasizes any particular one? Do some approaches move back and forth among multiple levels of analysis more fluidly than others?

3. *Scope.* Does a particular theory illuminate a wide range of attitudes, behaviors and outcomes, or rather something more specific?

4. *Explanatory Simplicity/Parsimony.* A theory should be as simple or parsimonious as possible. Generally, the fewer the number of propositions, the better the theory.

Comparing each of the three theories (see Table 10.14), diffusion and community structure theory have relatively flexible "causal pathways," with agenda-setting focusing more often on media themselves as relatively causal. Diffusion and community structure approaches both take into account the "antecedents" of media coverage and thus allow for the substantial influence of pre-existing conditions. Regarding "units of analysis," agenda-setting has special strength at the media channel and individual levels of analysis, the community structure approach at various macro-levels, whereas diffusion theory embraces multiple levels of analysis. With respect to "scope," all approaches are broad. Finally, regarding explanatory simplicity or parsimony, diffusion theory's maturity gives it unusual clarity, with agenda-setting also clear and community structure theory tightening its focus. Each of the preceding theories can be used for a variety of purposes. Their comparison is intended to highlight points of similarity and difference. In particular, the

TABLE 10.14. Comparing Theories of Communication and Social Change: Selected Characteristics*

THEORIES	CAUSAL PATHWAYS	UNITS OF ANALYSIS	SCOPE	EXPLANATORY SIMPLICITY/ PARSIMONY
Agenda-setting	Media often causal	Special strength at channel level (e.g., newspapers) and individual level	Broad	Clear
Diffusion	Media influential or catalytic/intervening effects on attitudes/ behavior	Multiple levels	Broad	Very clear
Community structure	Media antecedents influential, also public opinion	Special strength at macro-levels (e.g., city, county, state, region, cluster)	Broad	Emerging focus

*Copyright John C. Pollock (2007)

preceding models can be used to further understand the role of theory in public communication, especially communication advocacy efforts. (For an outline of the way the community structure approach and the media vector can be used in media advocacy, using physician-assisted suicide as an example, see the epilogue.)

COMMUNITY STRUCTURE AND FRAME-BUILDING: PROPOSITIONS FOR FUTURE RESEARCH

The preceding empirical summaries, case studies, and theoretical discussion permit the formation of several propositions for future research using the community structure approach.

Community Structure Studies Can Focus on a Few Key Characteristics Aligned Often With Reporting on Critical Events

Most of the case studies included in this volume document more than the influence of a single variable linking coverage to reporting on change. Yet, across multiple case studies, only a select group of variables demonstrate recurring significance. Similar clusters of a few key city characteristics shift slightly in their primacy when examining reporting patterns.

For example, percent professionals and college-educated are both linked strongly to reporting favoring Anita Hill's claims against Clarence Thomas, with the relative presence of professionals of foremost importance. For physician-assisted suicide, the tobacco MSA, and the Supreme Court decision allowing the BSA to exclude homosexuals, by contrast, family income was the most powerful link with favorable reporting perspectives. Education and percent professionals were significant or nearly so, but somewhat less important. For embryonic stem cell research and the Supreme Court's Bush vs. Gore decision, college education had the strongest relation with journalism either accommodating or opposing change. In the case of Bush vs. Gore, income was in a significant but secondary position. Different indicators of privilege may shift in rank and primacy, but only a few key characteristics, professionals, education, and family income, consistently emerge as significant.

Similarly, political partisanship in the form of party voting behavior in presidential elections was the key link with reporting on ANWR drilling and trying juveniles as adults, but it was also potent for other case studies as well. Party voting patterns were second or third most important (often after privilege indicators) in reporting on embryonic stem cell research, tobacco's MSA, Bush vs. Gore, and the Supreme Court decision allowing the BSA to exclude homosexuals.

Furthermore, indicators of vulnerability such as percent below the poverty level or percent unemployed are of paramount importance for other issues. Vulnerability characteristics are linked to variations in reporting on a Patients' Bill of Rights and Internet privacy and are also of some importance in reporting on Arctic oil drilling, legalization of physician-assisted suicide, and the Supreme Court Boy Scout decision. It is clear that a few key community structure indicators are linked to substantial variation in reporting. Measures of privilege and political partisanship are the two most powerful measures linked to reporting on change, along with, to a lesser extent, measures of vulnerability.

Community Structure Characteristics Are Most Closely Aligned When a Political Or Social Issue Is Newly Formed or Recently Emerging

The case study of reporting on those with HIV/AIDS over time in the early 1990s provides the clearest evidence that community structure characteristics (in this case, privilege) can be closely aligned with journalistic perspectives during the emergence and early development of an issue on the nation's news agenda. Yet that correspondence can drop to little at all (e.g., in reporting on those with HIV/AIDS in 1995) by the time an issue "matures."

Preliminary observations also suggest that issues can "progress" over time from association with a single, typically stakeholder city characteristic to broader issues of privilege distribution as issues ripen in public discussion. For example, in reporting on Dr. Kevorkian and legalization of physician-assisted suicide in the early and mid-1990s, percent age 75 and over was the city demographic most clearly linked to reporting on the pathologist's activities and the legalization issue. Yet, as chapter 3 clarifies, more recent reporting (1997–2002) on legalization of physician-assisted suicide is associated more strongly with a broader set of indicators, privilege and vulnerability, than with age alone.

Another example is reporting on issues of great interest to homosexuals. In the mid- to late-1990s, reporting on such topics as legalization of same-sex marriage and same-sex adoption were linked strongly to a stakeholder indicator, the magnitude of institutions marketing explicitly to a gay clientele in each city. By the time of the study on the Supreme Court decision allowing the Boy Scouts to exclude gays (sampling newspapers over 3 years, from January 1998 to March 1, 2001), reporting on homosexual exclusion was linked to a broader set of city characteristics, to political partisanship, and even more strongly to indicators of privilege. Other issues deserve the attention of researchers tracing the way reporting on some critical issues shifts from initial links to specific stakeholders to later associations with broader social constructs such as privileged social segments.

Variations in Newspapers Issue "Projection" Can Be Closely Aligned With Variations in Public Opinion, Public Behavior and Public Policy

In chapter 9 and this chapter are several illustrations of ways media "projection" as measured by media vectors can be linked closely with public opinion, public behavior, and public policy. For example, at a regional level of analysis, news coverage and public opinion are somewhat more favorable to scientific and ethical innovation, compared to other regions, in the western United States. At the same time, western reporting and public opinion are relatively unfavorable toward government regulation. Not unpredictably, the south displays both public opinion and media coverage least favorable to tobacco regulation and gun control. These matched observations approach classic stereotypes in their simplicity, but measurements of regional media projection and public opinion nevertheless confirm their general correspondence and veracity.

Public behavior and public policy can also be aligned closely to measures of issue "projection." Regarding behavior, city media vectors correspond closely with post-*Roe v. Wade* abortion incidence (Pollock et al., 1978), with voting patterns in the 2000 presidential election, and with the proportion of institutions in cities explicitly marketing their services to gays (measured by the GMI, as explained in chap. 9). Regarding public policy, media vectors linking different states together are aligned closely with different levels of legal support for regulation of tobacco use, and city media vectors regarding support for gay adoption are connected closely to a Gay Legal Index measuring each city's level of protection for gays. Media vectors should be compared with a wider range of public opinion issues and with multiple measures of public behavior and public policy.

Inequality Is Connected Not Simply to Reporting Aligned With the Status Quo, But Also to Reporting Accommodating Social and Political Change

Confirming traditional expectations, inequality can be linked with journalism supporting the status quo. Regarding existing economic arrangements, reporting on NAFTA and on the handover of Hong Kong to the PRC reflected either specific manufacturing interests or broad economic privilege in maximizing profit or economic access. Reporting on other critical issues, however, revealed that privilege (those buffered from uncertainty) can also be aligned with benevolent media perspectives on human rights and access to scientific innovation; as well as unfavorable reporting on issues representing challenges to health or a valued way of life.

Additionally, the absence of privilege ("vulnerable" or "unbuffered" population segments below the poverty level or experiencing high unemployment levels) can be linked strongly with reporting perspectives on issues reflecting challenges to health or value systems. Furthermore, stakeholders categorized by family size or children's age distribution, along with partisan voting, can be more powerful than privilege indicators in their association with journalism representing social change, exemplified by such issues as gun control, Arctic oil drilling, and trying juveniles as adult. Thus, a national cross-section of newspaper coverage suggests that media do not always report on critical events by reinforcing the status quo, functioning as vehicles of social control. Rather, journalists may also reflect other patterns: accommodating some human rights claims, opposing challenges to health or cherished ways of life, reflecting the claims or interests of the less economically powerful, or "mirroring" the concerns of specific stakeholders, be they families with children of certain ages or voters selecting particular party nominees for the presidency. Other case studies and patterns deserve attention to explore how many other social or systemic purposes media serve beyond the well-documented function of social control.

Community Structure Characteristics Are Not Rigid, Deterministic Indicators of Reporting, But Rather Are Linked to Fluid, Shifting Alignments and Choices About How to Frame Social and Political Change

To return to a question posed at the inception of this study: How do journalists make choices about framing social change? Implicit in that question is the conviction that journalists do have choices, especially when an issue is recently emerging on media agendas. Interpreted rigidly, the community structure approach might be presumed to support a highly deterministic epistemology, suggesting that "structure is all" in reporting on social change. Although community structure is clearly very important in coverage of critical events, this analysis raises serious questions about the way journalists interact with different community structures to produce the news they write. In particular, what impels journalists to frame events to yield one pattern rather than another, for example:

- Why did journalists write about Anita Hill's testimony regarding Clarence Thomas primarily from a buffer perspective, offering sympathy in direct proportion to levels of privilege, in particular percent professionals in a community, rather than from a violated buffer perspective, opposing an individual's testimony that could derail the legal process (and a hard-working individual's career) at the last moment? Both buffer and violated buffer perspectives are linked to community privilege levels, but why did journalists choose one frame over another? The simple association of privilege or community structure and reporting on a critical event gave no clear guide about frame selection and development processes adopted by journalists. How the dominant "sympathetic" frame was chosen or fashioned deserves exploration and suggests some fluidity in the association between community structure and reporting on social change.

- How do journalists choose to construct frames aligned with those who typically have little access to journalists, in particular with "vulnerable" groups, such as the poor or unemployed, or parents with children of various ages? Although the least economically advantaged citizens presumably may have relatively few ongoing ties to journalists, their interests were linked closely with reporting on *Roe v. Wade*, a Patients' Bill of Rights, and capital punishment. Journalists could have chosen to frame any of these critical issues from an alternative violated buffer perspective, suggesting perhaps that abortion violated a cherished way of life, a Patients' Bill of Rights could lead to runaway budget deficits, or capital punishment was an appropriate response to violent crime. Instead, journalists generally framed these issues in alignment with the proportion of vulnerable citizens in their communities. How did that process of frame selection work, and how did journalists arrive at a frame that is not aligned with the upscale, well-educated traditional market for newspapers?

- How do journalists select from among competing frames, in particular when one frame carries the weight of conventional wisdom or reflects conventional news routines and professional norms?

  ✦ How did journalists choose to frame Bush vs. Gore primarily in accordance with city levels of privilege (education and family income), and contrary to expectation, inversely with privilege (so that higher levels of education and income were linked with correspondingly negative levels of coverage of the Supreme Court decision favoring the 2000 Republican presidential candidate)? Rather than frame that high court decision traditionally, as a legitimate process and outcome, journalists generally framed it as a violated buffer pattern, a challenge to a cherished way of life. In particular when more conventional partisan politics frames were readily available (Democrats vs. Republicans), how did journalists decide to break the "spiral of silence" regarding high court legitimacy (see Shanahan & Jones, 1999; Shanahan, Scheufele, Yang, & Hizi, 2004) and adjust their issue frames so that reporting aligned precisely with education and income in somewhat counterintuitive ways?

✧ In a similar fashion, what led journalists to frame the issue of gun control after Columbine primarily in alignment with the family size and ages of children rather than in correspondence with more conventional party politics or partisan voting configurations? Or conversely, how did reporting on trying juveniles as adults come to be aligned primarily with partisan voting patterns rather than with the interests of those most affected by juvenile legal policies, families with children of particular ages, in particular citizens with few economic advantages?

In each of the preceding case studies, conventional assumptions about media frames and alignments are challenged by the findings. In each instance, the reporting of journalists reached beyond standard news conventions and routines to frame critical issues in ways that aligned reporting with unexpected community characteristics. What process led journalists to depart from presumed journalistic norms to fashion frames that aligned precisely with city characteristics reflecting privilege, family size, and voting patterns?

It is one thing to map patterns of media alignment. It is quite another to make intelligent guesses about the processes that bring about that alignment. How do city characteristics, which are relatively static, become translated into shifting media perspectives on critical social and political issues? Do different groups make their views known in predictable ways? Are newsroom recruitment patterns changing and linked to reporting shifts? Are journalists "socialized" to accommodate rather distinct city perspectives through some kind of long-term learning process? How do journalists balance the "social validation" of organizational or newsroom group orientations and reliance on wire services (Donsbach, 1995, 2003; Patterson & Donsbach, 1996) with the specifics of stakeholders and other groups in the geographic community outside the newsroom (Lowrey et al., 2003)? Why do journalists consider some sources more "legitimate" than others (Youngmin, 2005)? Or are there some kinds of reporting perspectives, professional norms or ground-level professional theory (such as "public journalism") that help journalists balance the traditional goals of "objective" reporting with a sensitivity to the specific interests of a city's residents or newspaper readers (see Donsbach, 1995; Glasser, 1999; Schudson, 1978, 2001)? A visual schematic of the potential influence of several of these factors that might intervene between the relatively stable qualities of community structure and the fluidity of reporting on social change is represented in Fig. 10.1.

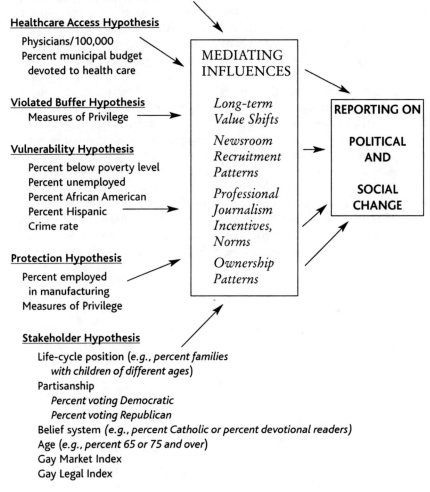

Buffer Hypothesis

Measures of Privilege:
College educated
Families with incomes $100,000+
Professional/technical occupational status

Healthcare Access Hypothesis

Physicians/100,000
Percent municipal budget
devoted to health care

<u>**Violated Buffer Hypothesis**</u>
Measures of Privilege ──────▶

Vulnerability Hypothesis

Percent below poverty level
Percent unemployed
Percent African American
Percent Hispanic ──────▶
Crime rate

Protection Hypothesis

Percent employed
in manufacturing
Measures of Privilege

Stakeholder Hypothesis

Life-cycle position (*e.g., percent families
with children of different ages*)
Partisanship
Percent voting Democratic
Percent voting Republican
Belief system (*e.g., percent Catholic or percent devotional readers*)
Age (*e.g., percent 65 or 75 and over*)
Gay Market Index
Gay Legal Index

MEDIATING
INFLUENCES

*Long-term
Value Shifts*

*Newsroom
Recruitment
Patterns*

*Professional
Journalism
Incentives,
Norms*

*Ownership
Patterns*

REPORTING ON

**POLITICAL
AND**

**SOCIAL
CHANGE**

**Fig. 10.1. Community structure model with hypotheses, city characteristics, and
mediating influences**

Some communication scholars have begun to draw attention to news coverage and framing as "negotiated" outcomes, the product of bargaining and balancing different interests. Zelizer (1993) and Berkowitz and TerKeurst (1999), for example, suggested that attention be paid to the concept of *interpretive community*, defined as a cultural site where meanings are constructed, shared, and reconstructed by members of social groups in the course of everyday life. Specifically, interpretive community proponents urge a focus on the "social mechanisms of the journalist-source relationship . . . as a struggle for determining meanings among groups of social actors" (p. 125).

These questions about the process that impels journalists to choose some frames over others are inherently important. They are especially so because the frames journalists select can be linked directly to precise variations in particular city characteristics. The way journalists go about making these framing choices, however, and how those framing choices are linked to community structure, remain significant, unresolved questions. The community structure approach helps uncover some of the patterns connecting social structure to reporting on social and political change. Yet the persistent questions it raises about the mysterious interaction between journalists and community, the precise process of making decisions to frame issues a particular way, remain elusive and deserve the enduring attention of communication scholars.

EPILOGUE

Community Structure Predictions,
Constraints and Uses

PREDICTIVE POWER

To be useful as an explanatory framework, the community structure approach should address at least two challenges. One is comparative, testing the power of the community structure approach against competing explanations. The other challenge is forward rather than backward-looking, prospective rather than retrospective, asking how well the approach goes beyond explaining the past to predicting the future (see Viswanath & Finnegan, 2002; Wallack, Dorfman et al., 1993).

Comparing Competing Explanations:
Frame-Building Has Multiple "Drivers"

Regarding the comparative challenge, the community structure approach can be compared with other explanations by focusing on one critical event or category of critical events. Consider the alternative explanation of "ownership patterns." Examining coverage of gays in the BSA, chapter 9 revealed that certain community structure characteristics (in particular the number of organizations or businesses marketing to gays, a stakeholder hypothesis) was a better predictor of coverage variation than were newspaper ownership patterns (locally owned or owned elsewhere). This type of comparison deserves elaboration. For example, comparing the relative predictive power of community structure and ownership factors might be extended beyond gays in community organizations to coverage of related issues such as same-sex marriage and same-sex adoption.

In addition to ownership patterns, another explanation competing for attention with the community structure approach is the role of political leadership. Policy-making leadership might be manifest in the passage of laws protecting either the rights of disadvantaged groups or the health concerns of most citizens. For example, community structure factors might be primary "drivers" of public opinion and public policy, encouraging both coverage sympathetic to gays and policy makers to pass laws protecting gays. Or the causal direction may be altered, with policy makers passing protective local legislation and creating a public opinion climate of acceptance that media in turn "mirror" rather than influence.

Similarly, regarding health issues, community structure factors may affect both local policy makers and laws forbidding smoking in public facilities as well as favorable news coverage of those laws. Conversely, local policymakers and environmental tobacco smoke laws may affect media coverage or public opinion independently of community structure predictions. Such comparisons of the influence pathways of community structure, media ownership patterns and policy making all deserve attention in order to illuminate the precise effect of community structure factors on media reporting on political and social change.

In any event, the "drivers" of increased issue coverage or frame-building may be quite diverse, ranging from a catastrophic event such as 9/11, to a celebrity "shock" such as Magic Johnson's HIV announcement, to the gradual accumulation of understanding leading to widespread sympathy for Arthur Ashe on the occasion of his HIV announcement, to long-term learning about the dangers of nicotine leading to widespread favorable coverage of the tobacco MSA of 1998, to the general media disappointment that the Supreme Court had intervened in the 2000 presidential election process in Florida. Drivers of frame building can vary from cataclysms to corporate or public policy or court decisions, from referenda or congressional bills to gradual shifts in public opinion. Multiple sources can energize frame-building, and it would be myopic to suggest that there is a "single" source of shifts in media frames.

Predicting the Future

Competing explanations aside, for the community structure approach to be convincing as a robust explanatory framework, it must also be prospective as well as retrospective, not only explaining the past, but also offering a model to predict the future. Responding to that challenge by examining contested frames in the case studies in the volume, several propositions can be advanced to further investigations by using the community structure approach and combining it with some elements of diffusion theory outlined in chapter 10. The "master" proposition derived from the exploration of multiple case studies is that as contested issues emerge, community structure connections and predictions become stronger. "Emergence" of issues can be operationalized by measuring increasing numbers of news reports, or increasing prominence of news reports on specific issues. Applying this umbrella perspective on community structure patterns, the following propositions can be offered:

Proposition 1: Buffer Hypothesis

As media reporting emphasizes expansion of human rights, in particular long-standing or scientific rights that expand choice (such as women's rights or medical innovations), the buffer hypothesis is a reasonable prediction, linking high proportions of privileged groups in communities with relatively expansive reporting legitimizing rights claims. Expressed more dynamically, as new human rights issues emerge (e.g., same-sex marriage, same-sex adoption), cities with higher proportions of privileged groups are likely to manifest favorable coverage of these claims earlier than cities with smaller proportions of privileged groups. In the language of diffusion theory, cities with higher proportions of privileged groups are more likely to be "early adopters" of favorable coverage of emerging rights claims.

Proposition 2: Violated Buffer Hypothesis

As media reports increasingly frame an expansive concept of rights "violations"—for example, the "right" of parents to protect children from the health threats of cigarette advertising targeting minors, the "right" of Internet users to unfettered Web access, or the "right" to have popular votes counted or recounted to decide presidential elections—the violated buffer hypothesis is a reasonable prediction, linking high proportions of privileged citizens in localities with relatively negative reporting on "rights" violations. In diffusion theory language, cities with higher proportions of privileged groups are more likely to be early adopters of unfavorable coverage of rights violations.

Proposition 3: Vulnerability Hypothesis

Increased media reporting on inequitable policies disadvantaging clearly vulnerable population segments—such as the death penalty affecting African Americans disproportionately, or limited access to health care affecting poorer citizens—is likely to associate high proportions of those vulnerable groups in communities with coverage opposing the policies. In diffusion theory terms, cities with higher proportions of vulnerable groups are more likely to be early adopters of unfavorable coverage of emerging or re-emerging issues expressing social inequality.

Proposition 4: Protection Hypothesis
Increased media reporting on policies advantaging or disadvantaging certain economic groups—such as those employed in manufacturing (e.g., the NAFTA) or economic elites generally (e.g., transferring control of Hong Kong to mainland China)—is likely to link high proportions of economically defined groups with coverage aligned with group economic interests. In the language of diffusion theory, cities with higher proportions of economically advantaged groups are more likely to be early adopters of coverage favoring those financial interests.

Proposition 5: Stakeholder Hypothesis
Increased media framing of policies substantially affecting distinct stakeholders is likely associated with high proportions of those stakeholders in a community. Because gun control efforts disproportionately affect families in a specific position in the lifecycle—those with high proportions of teens, families with children most likely to carry guns—coverage is predicted to vary with the proportion of such families. Because efforts to ban oil drilling in the Arctic are of special concern to Democrats, the proportion of such voters is expected aligned with coverage opposing the drilling. Because efforts to try juveniles as adults affect traditional Democratic voters disproportionately, reporting opposing such efforts is predicted to vary according to voter preference as well as position in the lifecycle: Families with small children may be most concerned, whereas retirees may be less involved. Whether groups are defined by position in the lifecycle, environmental orientation, or partisan political preferences, the proportion of all such groups is expected aligned with reporting on specific stakeholder issues. From the perspective of diffusion theory, cities with higher proportions of particular stakeholders are more likely to be early adopters of increased coverage favoring the interests of those stakeholders.

CONSTRAINTS ON THE COMMUNITY STRUCTURE APPROACH

As the preceding propositions imply, in order to test connections between community structure and reporting on change, it is essential to measure and explore contested frames. After dominant frames are identified, propositions linking structure and coverage can be tested. Yet at least two constraints on the predictive efficacy of the community structure approach deserve attention. One is the lack of consistent correspondence between community structure characteristics and the direction of reporting frames. The other constraint is difficulty in predicting, a *priori*, which hypothesis or proposition will govern a particular critical event.

One constraint is that there is no automatic, one-to-one correspondence between a particular set of community structure characteristics and the direction of reporting on specific critical issues. As outlined in chapter 8, reporting on those with HIV/AIDS shifted over time in the late 1980s and 1990s, with initial buffered, sympathetic reporting on those with HIV in 1990 associated with relatively high levels of privilege—significantly regarding family income (< .05) and directionally regarding education (< .10). That shifted dramatically with Magic Johnson's announcement that he had contracted HIV in 1991, and violated buffer, unsympathetic reporting toward those with HIV became linked with high levels of privilege. Then the pendulum swung back to sympathetic reporting on HIV-positive citizens during and after the period when tennis star Arthur Ashe announced he had contracted the condition from heart bypass surgeries, empathic reporting corresponding, once again, as in the pre-Magic Johnson period, to levels of privilege. Framing of a particular concern, in this case, a condition or disease considered incurable, shifted dramatically. Levels of privilege were strongly associated with each type of frame, but in essentially opposite directions. Specific community structure characteristics are not necessarily linked to a particular frame direction.

Additionally, it is difficult to determine, in advance, which hypothesis is likely to be most robust linking community structure characteristics to coverage frames. For example, political partisanship (percent voting Democratic or Republican in the last presidential election) is strongly associated with the direction of coverage of trying juveniles as adults, a stakeholder concern. Yet another type of stakeholder concern, "crime rate," is remarkably weak in its association with coverage of trying juveniles as adults. Presumably, those living in cities with relatively high crime rates may have relatively focused concerns about the issue of trying juveniles as adults, yet these stakeholders are not linked to coverage of the issue with any appreciable degree of strength. To say that stakeholders are linked to coverage of trying juveniles as adults does not specify which stakeholders are associated most strongly with that coverage.

Furthermore, prior to analyzing data collection and results for that issue, it might have been reasonable to suppose that a different hypothesis altogether would be somewhat muscular: The buffer hypothesis, suggesting that high levels of privilege in a city would be associated with negative coverage of trying juveniles as adults because such action might take away the rights of minors. Just as privilege is linked with supporting women's rights, the right of patients to request physician-assisted suicide and the right to engage in innovative medical research that could help millions (embryonic stem cell research), so too might privilege be linked to sympathy with the legal rights of minors. Yet this buffer hypothesis, although completely reasonable, did not prove significant. Thus, the buffer hypothesis confirms a link between privilege and coverage of "some" rights, but by no means "all" rights.

Indeed, as with reporting on those with HIV/AIDS, there is some evidence that the buffer hypothesis might not be completely consistent over time in reporting on long-standing rights issues. Regarding recent reporting on affirmative action, for example, a recent study found that, completely contrary to expectation, high levels of privilege in cities are associated with oppositional reporting on affirmative action, apparently because that concept may be less associated for some with compensation for historical inequities than with unfairly privileging some groups over others. Certain court decisions in recent years and discussions about racial or ethnic "quotas" may have contributed to this unexpected finding, resembling less a "buffer" than a "violated buffer" hypothesis, in which privilege is linked with negative coverage of a threat to what may have been a previously cherished way of life for at least some people (Lutkenhouse, Pollock, Smyth, & Dokus, 2006).

USES OF THE COMMUNITY STRUCTURE APPROACH FOR COMMUNICATION PRACTITIONERS AND ADVOCATES: AN EXAMPLE FROM THE COVERAGE OF PHYSICIAN-ASSISTED SUICIDE

Whatever its predictive power and constraints, the community structure approach exploring newspaper coverage of political and social change is a useful theoretical and methodological orientation helpful to communication practitioners in three types of research often used in public communication campaigns: formative, processual, and summative/evaluation research. Some examples from recent research on coverage of physician-assisted suicide are instructive.

Formative Research

In the formative research stage, prior to launching a communication campaign, the community structure approach can help identify the prominence of key stakeholders and measure the level of consensus about a given policy proposal—all with unusual efficiency.

Stakeholder Identification and Prominence. It is clear that senior citizens, for example, have a stake in any policy proposals regarding physician-assisted suicide. Less clear, however, until researchers begin measuring them, are the perspectives of other potential stakeholders—such as the medical and public health community, or privileged groups generally. By measuring the degree of media alignment with different potential stakeholders—using correlations, factor analysis, regression analysis and the media vector, the community structure approach helps assess the "prominence" of distinct stakeholders for a specific issue. This approach therefore helps communication practitioners learn which stakeholders are most prominent in fashioning a comprehensive public communication campaign.

Level of Policy Consensus. The community structure approach measures not only the prominence of different stakeholders in policy discussions but also the degree of directional consensus. For example, in the case of physician-assisted suicide, the perspectives of senior citizens are apparently completely at variance with the perspectives of citizens in communities with high proportions of physicians, medical facilities, and medical budgets, communities with predictably large proportions of highly privileged citizens with income, educational and occupational advantages. This approach measures directional differences among stakeholders so that practitioners can craft distinct messages taking into account these discrepancies.

Processual Research

The community structure approach, in particular the media vector media analysis scoring technique, can be used to track changes that occur during the implementation of a public communication campaign. The approach is especially helpful in longitudinal measures of the changing strength of different media "frames" regarding high-profile policies generally, in this case alternative framing of the physician-assisted suicide debate. Community structure analysis over time of Dr. Kevorkian's activities and then legalization of physician-assisted suicide did reveal a changing frame emphasis. Initial analysis of nationwide newspaper coverage of Kevorkian revealed a strong stakeholder association between relatively favorable newspaper coverage of the pathologist's euthanasia activities and the presence of larger percentages of citizens over age 75 (Pollock, Coughlin et al., 1996).

Yet the relatively favorable framing of the issue linked to the presence of senior citizens appeared to shift when efforts to legalize physician-assisted suicide arose on statewide ballots and referenda. Although legalization of the practice appears at first inspection to offer more choices for seniors, community structure analysis revealed new media frames suggesting that "choice expansion" may not be the way many seniors perceived the new legal possibility. Community structure approaches and media vector scores may therefore function as "early warning" devices, alerting practitioners to the emergence of new or alternative media frames that represent serious concerns for issues stakeholders and targeted population segments.

Additionally, by measuring media coverage of this and similar issues systematically, communication practitioners can sometimes track senior perspectives more efficiently than by commissioning expensive, cumbersome public opinion polls. Indeed, the Domke, Fan et al. (1997) media analysis scores and equations have done as well or better than sophisticated national public opinion polls at predicting the actual vote distribution in a presidential election. Polling data may not be readily available on citizen perspectives on critical events at the city level. In these circumstances, practitioners can use community structure analysis to reveal the emergence or prominence of key issues as newsworthy media agenda items.

Summative/Evaluation Research:
A Surveillance Tool

The community structure approach is also useful to practitioners as a "surveillance" tool, helping evaluate the policy or public opinion penetration of significant laws and regulations. For example, by measuring the degree of media "alignment" with referenda or ballot initiatives legalizing physician-assisted suicide, community structure analysis can measure variations in public consensus or approval regarding the issue. This is especially helpful when comparing different regions or state clusters. As this study reveals, both public opinion and media vectors often converge regarding a wide range of issues.

Community structure analysis and a modified media vector, relying on the National Cancer Institute's ASSIST multiyear database of nationwide newspaper coverage of tobacco-related issues, have been employed as surveillance tools to explore levels of media support for tobacco control, comparing coverage in states with relatively few efforts to regulate tobacco with reporting in states that enacted many regulations and taxes (Pollock, Stillman et al., 2002). Practitioners can therefore employ community structure analyses, comparing public opinion and media vectors, to map geographic variations in level of support for social advancement policies.

REFERENCES

Abbott, E. A. (1989, Summer). Electronic farmers' marketplace: New technologies and agricultural information. *Journal of Communication, 39,* 48–60.

Alan Guttmacher Institution. (1974). *Provisional estimates of abortion need and services in year following the 1973 Supreme Court decision.* New York: A Report by the Alan Guttmacher Institution, the Research and Development Division of Planned Parenthood Federation of America.

Albert, E. (1986). Acquired immune deficiency syndrome: The victim and the press. In T. McCormick (Ed.), *Studies in communication* (pp. 135–158). Greenwich, CT: JAI Press.

Allard, N. W. (1999). Privacy online: Washington report. *Hastings Communications and Entertainment Law Journal, 20,* 511–540.

Allen, M. (2001, August 27). Bush tries to forge bonds with steel, labor; Effort to reach unions continues. *The Washington Post,* p. A02.

Altman, D. G., Levine, D. W., Howard, G., & Hamilton, S. (1997). Tobacco farming and public health: Attitudes of the general public and farmers. *Journal of Social Issues, 53,* 113–128.

Altman, D. G., Schooler, C., & Basil, M. D. (1991). Alcohol and cigarette advertising on billboards. *Health Education Research, 6*(4), 287–490.

American Board of Family Practice. (1991). *American attitudes toward middle age.* Lexington, KY: Author.

Anderson, P. D., Jacobson, J., & Wasserman, J. R. (1997). Historical overview of tobacco legislation and regulation. *Journal of Social Issues, 53,* 75–95.

Anderson, R. W., & Lipsey, M. W. (1978). Energy conservation and attitudes toward technology. *Public Opinion Quarterly,* 17–30.

Andsager, J. L. (2000, Autumn). How interest groups attempt to shape public opinion with competing news frames. *Journalism & Mass Communication Quarterly, 77*(3), 577–592.

Armstrong, C. (2002, Fall). Papers give women more attention in ethnically diverse communities. *Newspaper Research Journal, 23*(4), 81–85.

Arnove, R. F. (1975). Sociopolitical implications of educational television. *Journal of Communication, 25,* 144–156.

Astruc, J. A. (1754). *A treatise of venereal disease*. London: Innis, Richardson, Davis.

Atkin, C., & Arkin, E. B. (1990). Issues and initiatives in communicating health information. In C. Atkin & L. Wallack (Eds.), *Mass communication and public health* (pp. 13–40). Newbury Park: Sage.

Baldwin, T. F., Barrett, M., & Bates, B. (1992). Uses and values for news on cable television. *Journal of Broadcasting and Electronic Media, 36*, 225–233.

Barkin, S. M., & Gurevitch, M. (1987). Out of work and on the air: Television news of unemployment. *Critical Studies in Mass Communication, 4*, 1–20.

Basil, M.D., & Brown, W. J. (1994, Summer). Interpersonal communication in news diffusion: A study of "Magic" Johnson's announcement. *Journalism Quarterly, 71*(2), 305–320.

Basil, M. D., Schooler, C., Altman, D. G., Slater, M., & Albright, C. L. et al. (1991). How cigarettes are advertised in magazines: Special messages for special markets. *Health Communication, 3*(2) 75–91.

Bate, B., & Self, L. S. (1983, Spring). The rhetoric of career success books for women. *Journal of Communication, 33*(2), 149–165.

Becker, R. (1998). Prime-time television in the gay nineties: Network television, quality audiences, and gay politics. *Velvet Light Trap, 36–47*.

Begley, S. (2001). In search of stem cells. *Newsweek*. Retrieved September 10, 2001, from: wysiwyg://11/http://www.msnbc.com/news/622832.asp.

Bennett, L. W. (1993). A policy research paradigm for the news media and democracy. *Journal of Communication, 4*(3), 180–189.

Bennett, L. W., & Manheim, J. B. (1993). Taking the public by storm: Information, cuing and the democratic process in the gulf conflict. *Political Communication, 10*(4), 331–351.

Bennett, L. W., & Paletz, D. L. (Eds.). (1994). *Taken by storm: The media, public opinion, and US foreign policy in the gulf war*. Chicago: University of Chicago Press.

Bergen, A., & Caporaso, N. (1999, August 18). Cigarette smoking. *The Journal of the National Cancer Institute, 91*, 1365–1375.

Berkowitz, D. (Ed.). (1997). *Social meaning of news*. Thousand Oaks, CA: Sage.

Berkowitz, D., & TerKeurst, J. V. (1999, Summer). Community as interpretive community: Rethinking the journalist-source relationship. *Journal of Communication, 49*(3), 125–136.

Bethel, E. R. (1995). *AIDS: Readings on a global crisis*. Boston, MA: Allyn & Bacon.

Beveridge, W. I. B. (1977). *Influenza: The last great plague*. New York: Prodist.

Biagi, S. (1999). *Media impact* (4th ed.). Belmont, CA: Wadsworth.

Biddle, N., Conte, L., & Diamond, E. (1993). AIDS in the media: Entertainment or infotainment. In S. C. Ratzan (Ed.), *AIDS: Effective health communication in the 90s* (pp. 151–172). Washington, DC: Taylor & Francis.

Bingham, S. G. (1991). Communication strategies for managing sexual harassment in organizations: Understanding message options and their effects. *Journal of Applied Communication Research, 19*, 88–115.

Bingham, S. G., & Burleson, B. R. (1989). Multiple effectives of messages with multiple goals: Some perceived outcomes of responses to sexual harassment. *Human Communication Research, 16*, 184–216.

Bishop, R. (2000). To protect and serve: The "guard dog" function of journalism in coverage of the Japanese-American internment. *Journalism & Communication Monographs, 2*(2), 65–95.

Black, D. (1986). *The plague years—A chronicle of AIDS, the epidemic of our time*. New York: Simon & Schuster.

Blumler, J., & Gurevitch, M. (1987). The personal and the public: Observations on agendas in mass communication research. In M. Gurevitch & M. Levy (Eds.), *Mass communication review yearbook 6* (pp. 16–21). Newbury Park, CA: Sage.

Boot, W. (1992). The Clarence Thomas hearings. *Columbia Journalism Review, 30*, 25–29.

Booth-Butterfield, M. (1989). Perception of harassing communication as a function of locus of control, work force participation, and gender. *Communications Quarterly, 37*, 262–275.

Borrus, A. (2000). Online privacy: Congress has no time to waste. *Business Week, 3699*, 54.

Bowman, K. (2000, September 19) The female vote. *Online NewsHour*. Retrieved February 16, 2000, from http://www.pbs.org.

Boy Scouts: Discrimination and the law. (2000, April 29). *The Economist*, pp. 29-32.

Boyd, M. J. (1991, Winter/1992, Spring). Collard greens, Clarence Thomas, and the high-tech rape of Anita Hill. *The Black Scholar*, 43–46.

Brandt, A. (1985). *No magic bullet: A social history of venereal disease in the United States since 1880*. New York: Oxford University Press.

Braun, K., Tanji, V., & Heck, R. (2001). Support for physician-assisted suicide: Exploring the impact of ethnicity and attitudes toward planning for death. *The Gerontologist, 41*(1), 51–60.

Brown, J. D., & Campbell, K. (1986, Winter). Race and gender in music videos: The same beat but a different drummer. *Journal of Communication, 36*(1), 94–106.

Brown, W. J. (1991). An AIDS prevention campaign: Effects on attitudes, beliefs and communication behavior. *American Behavioral Scientist, 34*, 666–678.

Brunet, J., & Proulx, S. (1989). Formal versus grass-roots training: Women, work and computers. *Journal of Communication, 39*(3), 77–84.

Bruning, F. (1991, December 9). The dishonesty of a magical life. *MacLean's*, p. 13.

Buell, J. (2001). Media myopia and the future of democratic politics. *Humanist, 61*, 35.

Bush, A. J., & Bolter, G. W. (1991). Rethinking the role of TV advertisement during a health crisis: A rhetorical analysis of the federal AIDS campaigns. *Journal of Advertisement, 20*, 28–37.

Butler, J. S. (1993, November/December). Homosexuals and the military establishment. *Society, 31*(1), 13–21.

Caamaño, A., Pollock, J. C., Virgilio, M., & Lindstrom, A. (2001, November). *Nationwide newspaper coverage of FDA regulation of tobacco: A community structure approach*. Paper presented at the annual conference of the National Communication Association, Atlanta.

Camus, A. (1948). *The plague*. New York: Vintage Books.

Carey, J. W. (1992). A republic, if you can keep it: Liberty and public life in the age of glasnost. In R. Arsenault (Ed.), *Crucible of liberty: 200 years of the Bill of Rights* (pp. 108–128). New York: The Free Press.

Carey, J. W. (1995). The press, public opinion and public discourse. In T. L. Glasser & C. T. Salmon (Eds.), *Public opinion and the communication of consent.* Mahwah, NJ: Erlbaum.

Carragee, K.M., & Roefs, W. (2004, June). The neglect of power in recent framing research. *Journal of Communication, 54*(2), 214–233.

Cartwright, F.F. (1972). *Disease and history.* London: Hart-Davis, MacGibbon.

Catechism of the Catholic Church. (1997, December 8). Retrieved February 17, 2002, from http://www.christusrex.org/www1/CDHN/ccc.html.

Catholic almanac. (1995-2004). Huntington, IN: Our Sunday Visitor.

Cawyer, C. S., & Smith-Dupre, A. (1995). Communicating social support: Identifying supportive episodes in an HIV/AIDS support group. *Communication Quarterly, 43,* 243–358.

Center for Responsive Politics. (2004, October 6). Gun control vs. gun rights: The issue. Opensecrets.org, para. 7.

Centers for Disease Control and Prevention. (1993, July). *HIV/AIDS surveillance report, Second quarter edition.* Atlanta, GA: U.S. Dept. of Health and Human Services.

Chaffee, S. (Ed.). (1975). *Political communication.* Beverly Hills: Sage.

Chan, A. B. (1988/1989). Gagging the Hong Kong press: Slippery road to 1997. *The International Journal of Mass Communication Studies, 42,* 161–175.

Chan J. M., & Lee C. (1988). Press ideology and organizational control in Hong Kong. *Communication Research, 15,* 185–197.

Chan, S. (1994). State press relationship revisited: A comparison of foreign policy coverage on the Hong Kong 1997 issue by three newspapers. *The International Journal for Mass Communication Studies, 53,* 135–145.

Chen, Y. (1993). Marketing China after Tiananmen: Marketing mix as applied to the promotion of international tourism. *Asian Journal of Communication, 3,* 75–93.

Ching, F. (1996). Hong Kong: The year before living dangerously. *Current History, 95,* 272.

Chu, L. L., & Lee, P. S. N. (1995). Political communication in Hong Kong: Transition, adaptation, and survival. *Asian Journal of Communication, 3,* 1–17.

Clark, M. (1988, May 8). Plagues, man and history: Lessons about AIDS from the Black Death. *Newsweek, 111,* 9.

Clegg Smith, K., Wakefield, M., Siebel, C., Szczypka, G., Slater, S., Terry-McElrath, Y., Emery, S., & Chaloupka, F.J. (2002, May). Coding the news: The development of a methodological framework for coding and analyzing newspaper coverage of tobacco issues. *ImpacTeen Research Paper No. 21.* Chicago: University of Illinois Chicago Circle.

Clinton, W. J. (1998). Weekly compilation of presidential documents. *Vale* [Online]. Available: www. valenj. org.

Coleman, R., & Wu, H. D. (2006, March). More than words alone: Incorporating broadcasters' nonverbal communication into the stages of crisis coverage theory—evidence from September 11. *Journal of Broadcasting & Electronic Media, 50* (1), 1–17.

Conrad, P., & Schneider, J. W. (1992*). Deviance and medicalization: From badness to sickness.* Philadelphia: Temple University Press.

Cook, T. (1998). *Governing with the news: The news media as a political institution.* Chicago: University of Chicago Press.

Coplin, W. D. (1995). Turning points in China over the next five years. *Planning Review, 23*, 23–37.

Coupet, S. M. (2000, April). What to do with the sheep in wolf's clothing: The role of rhetoric and reality about youth offenders in the constructive dismantling of the juvenile justice system. *University of Pennsylvania Law Review, 148*(4), 1303–1346.

D'Angelo, P. (2002) News framing as a multi-paradigmatic research program: A response to Entman, *Journal of Communication, 52*(4), 890–918.

Dana, L. P. (1996). Boomerang entrepreneurs: Hong Kong to Canada and back. *Journal of Small Business Management, 34*, 79–83.

Danzger, M. H. (1975). Validating conflict data. *American Sociological Review, 46*, 570–584.

Davidson, A. G. (1991). Looking for love in the age of AIDS: The language of gay personals, 1978–1988. *The Journal of Sex Research, 28*, 125–137.

Davis, J. C. (2000). Protecting privacy in the cyber era. *IEEE Technology & Society Magazine, 19*, 10, 13.

Dawson, G. (1992, October 13). PBS explores racial-sexual ideas in Hill–Thomas case. *The Orlando Sentinel*, p. 1E.

Dearing, J. W., & Rogers, E. M. (1992). AIDS and the media agenda. In T. Edgar, M. A. Fitzpatrick, & V.S. Freimuth (Eds.), *AIDS: A communication perspective* (pp. 173–194). Hillsdale, NJ: Erlbaum.

Dearing, J., & Rogers, E. (1996). *Agenda-Setting*. Thousand Oaks, CA: Sage.

Defrancesco, L. (2001, May 28). Stem cell researchers take on Parkinson's. *Scientist, 15*(11), 1, 18.

Demers, D. P. (1996a). Corporate newspaper structure, editorial page vigor and social change. *Journalism & Mass Communication Quarterly, 73*, 857–877.

Demers, D. P. (1996b). *The menace of the corporate newspaper: Fact or fiction?* Ames: Iowa State University Press.

Demers, D. P. (1996c, Summer). Does personal experience in a community increase or decrease newspaper reading? *Journalism & Mass Communication Quarterly, 73*(2) 304–318.

Demers, D. P. (1998, Autumn). Structural pluralism, corporate newspaper structure, and news source perceptions: Another test of . . . *Journalism & Mass Communication Quarterly, 75*(3), 572–592.

Demers, D. P., Craff, D., Choi, Y.-H., & Pessin, B. M. (1989, December). Issue obtrusiveness and the agenda-setting effects of national network news. *Communication Research, 16*(6), 793–712.

Demers, D.P., & Viswanath, K. (Eds.). (1999). *Mass media, social control, and social change: A macrosocial perspective* (pp. 159–181). Ames: Iowa State University Press.

Demers, D.P., & Viswanath, K. (1999). What promotes or hinders the role of mass media as an agent of social control or social change? In D. Demers & K. Viswanath (Eds.), *Mass media, social control, and social change: A macrosocial perspective* (pp. 419–424). Ames: Iowa State University Press.

Dennis, E., & Pease, E. (1995). *Radio: the forgotten medium*. New Brunswick, NJ: Transaction Publishers.

Dervin, B. (1987). The potential contribution of feminist scholarship to the field of communication. *Journal of Communication, 37*(4), 107–120.

Dickens, G. (1997. August 29). Gun-rights forces outgunned on TV. *Human Events, 53*(33), 20.

DiIulio, J. J. (2000, April 3). Young and deadly. *National Review.* Retrieved September 24, 2000, from http://web.lexis-nexis.com.

Dixon, R. D., Lowery, R. C., Levy, D. E., & Ferraro, K. F. (1991). Self-interest and public opinion toward smoking policies: A replication and extension. *Public Opinion Quarterly, 55,* 241–254.

Domke, D., Fan, D. P., Fibison, M., Shah, D. V., & Smith, S. S. et al. (1997, Winter). News media, candidates and issues, and public opinion in the 1996 presidential campaigning. *Communication Quarterly, 74*(4), 718–737.

Donohue, G. A., Olien, C., & Tichenor, P. J. (1985a). Leader and editor views of role of press in community development. *Journalism Quarterly, 62,* 367–372.

Donohue, G. A., Olien, C. N., & Tichenor, P. J. (1985b). Reporting conflict by pluralism, newspaper type and ownership. *Journalism Quarterly, 62*(3), 489–499, 507.

Donohue, G. A., Olien, C. N., & Tichenor, P. J. (1989, Winter). Structure and constraints on community newspaper gatekeepers. *Journalism Quarterly, 66*(4), 807–845.

Donohue, G. A., Tichenor, P. J., & Olien, C. (1995). A guard dog perspective on the role of media. *Journal of Communication, 45,* 115–132.

Donohue, W. (1994). Culture war against the Boy Scouts. *Society, 31,* 59–68.

Donsbach, W. (1995). Lapdogs, watchdogs and junkyard dogs. *Media Studies Journal, 9,* 17–30.

Donsbach, W. (2003). *Psychology of news decisions: Factors behind journalists' professional behavior.* Paper presented at the annual conference of the International Communication Association, San Diego, CA.

Douglas, M., & Wildavsky, A. (1970). *Purity and danger.* London: Penguin.

Dowd, A. R. (1993, November). Let's just say yes to NAFTA. *Fortune,* pp. 108–109.

Drushel, B.E. (1991). Sensationalism or sensitivity: Use of words in stories on Acquired Immune Deficiency Syndrome (AIDS) by Associated Press Videotext (part of a symposium on: Gay people, sex and the media). *Journal of Homosexuality, 21,* 47–61.

Dunwoody, S., & Griffin, R.J. (1999). Structural pluralism and media accounts of risk. In D. Demers & K. Viswanath (Eds.), *Mass media, social control, and social change: A macrosocial perspective* (pp. 139–158). Ames: Iowa State University Press.

Durey, M. (1973). *The return of the plague: British society and cholera in 1831-2.* Dublin: Gill & Macmillan.

Dutta-Bergman, M. J. (2004). An alternative approach to social capital: Exploring the linkage between health consciousness and community participation. *Health Communication, 16*(4), 393–409.

Dutta-Bergman, M. J. (2005, February). Access to the internet in the context of community participation and community satisfaction. *New Media & Society, 7*(1), 89–109.

Dworkin, G., Frey, R., & Bok, S. (1998). *Euthanasia and physician-assisted suicide: For and against.* New York: Cambridge University Press.

Dykstra, P. (1991, December). He who is without sin. *The Progressive, 55,* 11.

Eberl, J. T. (2000). The beginning of personhood: A Thomistic biological analysis. *Bioethics, 14*(2), 134–157.

Engelberg, M., Flora, J. A., & Nass, C. I. (1995). AIDS knowledge: Effects of channel involvement and interpersonal communication. *Health Communication, 7,* 73–91.

Entman, R. M. (1991). Framing U.S. coverage of international news: Contrasts in narratives of the KAL and Iran air incidents. *Journal of Communication, 41*(4), 6–25.

Entman, R. M. (1993a). Contestable categories and public opinion. *Political Communication, 10*(3), 321–242.

Entman, R. (1993b). Framing: Toward clarification of a fractured paradigm. *Journal of Communication, 43,* 51–55.

Entman, R. M., & Page, B. I. (1994). The news before the storm: The Iraq war debate and the limits to media independence. In W. L. Bennett & D. L. Paletz (Eds.), *Taken by storm: The media, public opinion, and U.S. foreign policy in the Gulf War.* Chicago: University of Chicago Press.

Entman, R.M., & Rojecki, A. (1993). Freezing out the public: Elite and media framing of the U.S. anti-nuclear movement. *Political Communication, 10*(2), 151–167.

Erbring, L., Goldenberg, E. N., & Miller, A. H. (1980, February). Front-page news and real-world cues: A new look at agenda-setting by the media. *American Journal of Political Science, 24*(1), 16–49.

Erfle, S., McMillian, H., & Grofman, B. (1990). Regulation via threats: Politics, media coverage, and oil pricing decisions. *Public Opinion Quarterly, 54,* 48–63.

Eskridge, W. (1996). *The case for same-sex marriage.* New York: The Free Press.

Fairchild, C. (2001). *Community radio and public culture.* Cresskill, NJ: Hampton Press.

Fan, D. (2002). Impact of persuasive information on secular trends in health-related behaviors. In R. Hornik (Ed.), *Public health communication: Evidence for behavior change* (pp. 251–264). Mahwah, NJ: Erlbaum.

Farmer, P. (2005, Winter). Global AIDS: New challenges for health and human rights. *Perspectives in Biology and Medicine, 43*(1), 10–16.

Fedler, F., Bender, J., Davenport, L., & Drajer, M. (2001). *Reporting for the media* (7th ed.). Fort Worth, TX: Harcourt.

Fee, E., & Fox, D.M. (1989). The contemporary historiography of AIDS. *Journal of Social History, 23,* 303–314.

Fico, F., & Cote, W. (2002, Spring). Partisan and structural balance of election stories on the 1998 governor's race in Michigan. *Mass Communication & Society, 5*(2), 165–182.

Fico, F., & Soffin, S. (1995). Fairness and balance of selected newspaper coverage of controversial national, state, and local issues. *Journalism & Mass Communication Quarterly, 72*(3), 621–633.

Finnegan, J. R., & Viswanath, K. (1988). Community ties and use of cable television and newspapers in a Midwest suburb. *Journalism Quarterly, 65*(2), 456–463, 473.

Fischer-Hubner, S. (1998) Privacy and security at risk in the global information society. *Information, Communication, & Society,.* 420–421.

Flora, J. A., & Maibach, E. W. (1990). Cognitive responses to AIDS information: The effects of issue involvement and issue appeal. *Communication Research, 17*, 759–774.

Florida, R. (2002). *The rise of the creative class: And how it's transforming work, leisure, community and everyday life.* New York: Basic Books.

Frey, L., Botan, C., & Kreps, G. (2000). *Investigating communication.* Needham Heights, MA: Allyn & Bacon.

Friedland, L. A., & McLeod, J. M. (1999). Community integration and mass media: A reconsideration. In D. Demers & K. Viswanath (Eds.), *Mass media, social control, and social change: A macrosocial perspective* (pp. 197–226). Ames: Iowa State University Press.

Friedrich, M. J. (2000, August 9). Debating pros and cons of stem cell research. *Journal of the American Medical Association, 284*(6), 681–682.

Gale Directory of Publications and Media Sources. Detroit, MI: Gale Research.

Gallup, A., & Moore, D. W. (1993, August). Public leery of new trade agreement. *The Gallup Poll,* pp. 2–3.

Gamson, W.A. (1989). News as framing. *American Behavioral Scientist, 33*(2), 157–161.

Gandy, O. (1996). If it weren't for bad luck: Framing stories of racially comparative risk. In V. Berry & C. Manning-Miller (Eds.), *Mediated messages and African-American culture: Contemporary issues* (pp. 55–75). Thousand Oaks, CA: Sage.

Gandy, O. (1999). Community pluralism and the "tipping point." In D. Demers & K. Viswanath (Eds.), *Mass media, social control, and social change: A macrosocial perspective* (pp. 159–181). Ames: Iowa State University Press.

Gates, H.L., Jr. (1994, March). Speech delivered during Black History Month, Trenton State College.

Gayellow Pages: The National Edition, USA and Canada 1999-2000. (2000). New York: Renaissance House.

Gaziano, E., & Gaziano, C. (1999). Social control, social change and the knowledge gap hypothesis. In D. Demers & K. Viswanath (Eds.), *Mass media, social control, and social change: A macrosocial perspective* (pp. 117–136). Ames: Iowa State University Press.

Gellert, G., Weismuller, P., Higgins, K., & Maxwell, R. (1992). Disclosure of AIDS in celebrities. *New England Journal of Medicine, 327,* 1389.

Gemmill, F. (1999). People of the Caribou Reborn. *Native Peoples, 13*(1), 50–54.

Gest, T. (1992). Firearm follies: How the news media cover gun control. *Media Studies Journal, 6*(1), 139–149.

Gibbs, N., & Duffy, M. (2001, August 20). In a 21st century speech on stem cell funding, Bush budges and finds compromise. Will it work? *Time,* pp. 15–16.

Gibbs, W. W. (2001). The Arctic oil and wildlife refuge. *Scientific American, 284*(5), 62–69.

Gibeaut, J. (1999, July). A jury question: Jurors should judge youths in juvenile court, some say. *American Bar Association Journal.* Retrieved September 24, 2000, from http://web.lexis-nexis.com.

Gilley, B. (1997). Regional politick. *Far Eastern Economic Review, 160,* 22–26.

Gilman, S.L. (1988). *Disease and representation: Images of illness from madness to AIDS.* Ithaca & London: Cornell University Press.

Ginsberg, B. (1986). *The captive public: How mass opinion promotes state power.* New York: Basic Books.

Gitlin, T. (1978). Media sociology: The dominant paradigm. *Theory and Society, 2,* 204–253.

Glasser, T. (1999). The idea of public journalism. In T. Glasser (Ed.), *The idea of public journalism* (pp. 3–18). New York: Guilford Press.

Golden, F. (2001, August 20). Before James Thomson came along, embryonic stem cells were a researcher's dream. *Time,* pp. 27–28.

Goshorn, K., & Gandy, O. (1995). Race, risk and responsibility: Editorial constraint in the framing of inequality. *Journal of Communication, 45,* 133–51.

Graber, D. A., & Smith, J. M. (2005, September). Political communication faces the 21st century. *Journal of Communication, 55*(3), 479–507.

Grahm, J. (1992). *Current biography yearbook: 1992.* New York: H.W. Wilson.

Gratale, D., Steer, C., Pollock, J.C. et al. (2002, November). *Nationwide newspaper coverage of embryonic stem cell research: A community structure approach.* Paper presented at the annual conference of the National Communication Association, New Orleans.

Gratale, S., Pollock, J., Hagert, J., Dey, L., D'Angelo, P., Braddock, P., D'Amelio, A., Kupcha, J., & Montgomery, A. (2005, May). *International coverage of United Nations' efforts to combat AIDS: A structural approach.* Paper presented at the annual conference of the International Communication Association, New York.

Greene, J. (1997, October 5). The subtext is reform. *Hospitals & Health Networks, 36,* p. 38.

Griffin, R. J., & Dunwoody, S. (1995, Summer). Impacts of information subsidies and community structure on local press coverage of environmental issues. *Journalism & Mass Communication Quarterly, 72*(2), 271–284

Grmek, M. D. (1991). History of AIDS: Emergence and politics of a modern pandemic. *The Wilson Quarterly, 15,* 105.

Grube, A., & Boehme-Duerr, K. (1988). AIDS in international news magazines. *Journalism Quarterly, 65,* 686–689.

Gussow, Z. (1989). *Leprosy, racism and public health.* Boulder, CO: Westview Press.

Halpern, J. W. (1983). Business communication in China, a second perspective. *Journal of Business Communication, 20,* 43–54.

Harry, J. (2001). Covering conflict: A structural-pluralist analysis of how a small-town and a big-city newspaper reported on environmental controversy. *Journalism & Mass Communication Quarterly, 78*(3), 419–436.

Hartman, A. (1992). It was not our finest hour (Clarence Thomas confirmation hearings). *Social Work, 37,* 3–4.

He, Z., & Zhu, J. (1994). The "voice of America" and China: Zeroing in on Tiananmen Square. *Journalism Monographs, 143,* 45.

Henderson, C. W. (2000). Researchers measure attitudes about death among terminally ill cancer patients. *Cancer Weekly,* 19–21.

Herbst, S. (1998). *Reading public opinion: How political actors view the democratic process.* Chicago: University of Chicago Press.

Herman, E. S. (1985, Spring). Marketplace of ideas revisited: Diversity of news: 'Marginalizing' the opposition. *Journal of Communication, 35*(3), 135–146.

Hertling, J. (1997). As huge changes loom in Hong Kong, many students appear to be oblivious. *The Chronicle of Higher Education, 43,* A49.

Hertog, J. K., & Fan, D. P. (1995, October). The impact of press coverage on social beliefs: The case of HIV transmission. *Communication Research, 22,* 545–574.

Higgins, K., Dudich, T., & Pollock, J. C. (2003, April). *Nationwide newspaper coverage of same-sex adoption: A community structure approach.* Paper presented at the annual conference of the New Jersey Communication Association, The College of New Jersey, Ewing, NJ.

Hindman, D. B. (1996). Community newspapers, community structural pluralism, and local conflict with nonlocal groups. *Journalism & Mass Communication Quarterly, 73*(3), 708–721.

Hindman, D. B. (1999). Social control, social change and local mass media. In D. Demers & K. Viswanath (Eds.), *Mass media, social control, and social change: A macrosocial perspective* (pp. 99–116). Ames: Iowa State University Press.

Hindman, D.B., Littlefield, R., Preston, A., & Neumann, D. (1999, Summer). Structural pluralism, ethnic pluralism, and community newspapers. *Journalism & Mass Communication Quarterly, 76*(2), 250–263.

Holdren, J. P. (2001). Searching for a national energy policy. *Issues in Science and Technology, 17*(3), 43–51.

Hopkins, D. R. (1963). *Princes and peasants: Smallpox in history.* Chicago: University of Chicago Press.

Hoyert, D. L., Arias, E., Smith, B. L., Murphy, S. L., & Kochanek, K. D. (2001). Deaths: Final data for 1999. *National Vital Statistics Reports, 49*(8), 1–113.

Hurst, J. (1993). *The history of abortion in the Catholic church: The untold story.* Washington DC: Catholics for a Free Choice.

Hurwitz, L., Green, B., & Segal, H. E. (1976) International press reactions to the resignation and pardon of Richard M. Nixon. *Comparative Politics, 9,* 107–123.

Hyde, M. (1993). Medicine, rhetoric, and euthanasia: A case study in the workings of a postmodern discourse. *Quarterly Journal of Speech, 79,* 201–219.

Hyde, M. J., & Rufo, K. (2000, February). The call of conscience, rhetorical interruptions, and the euthanasia controversy. *Journal of Applied Communication Research, 28*(1), 1–23.

Irving, D. (1999). When do human beings begin? *International Journal of Sociology and Social Policy, 19*(3-4), 22–46.

Iyengar, S. (1991). *Is anyone responsible? How television frames political issues.* Chicago: University of Chicago Press.

Iyengar, S., & Kinder, D. (1987). *News that matters: Television and American public opinion.* Chicago: University of Chicago Press.

Jamieson, K., & Cappella, J. N. (1995). *Media in the middle: Fairness and accuracy in the 1994 Health Care Reform debate.* Report of the Annenberg Public Policy Center of the University of Pennsylvania prepared for the Robert Wood Johnson Foundation.

Jamieson, K. H., & Waldman, P. (Eds.). (2002). *The press effect: Politicians, journalists and the stories that shape the political world.* New York: Oxford.

Janis, I. L., & Fadner, R. (1965). The coefficients of imbalance. In H. Lasswell (Ed.), *Language of politics: Studies in quantitative semantics* (pp. 153–160). Cambridge, MA: Harvard University Press.

Jankowski, N. W., & Prehn, O. (2002). *Community media in the information age: Perspectives and prospects.* Cresskill, NJ: Hampton Press.

Janowitz, M. (1952). *The community press in an urban setting.* New York: The Free Press.

Jansen, S.C. (1989, Summer). Gender and the information society: A socially structured silence. *Journal of Communication, 39*(3), 196–215.

Jeffres, L. W., Cutietta, C., Sekerka, L., & Lee, J-W. (2000). Newspapers, pluralism, & diversity in an urban context. *Mass Communication & Society, 3*(2/3), 157–184.

Jellicorse, J. L. (1994). Applying communication studies in Hong Kong. *Journal of the Association for Communication Administration, 86,* 23–40.

Johnson, C. B., Stockdale, M. S., & Saal, F. E. (1991). Persistence of men's misperceptions of friendly cues across a variety of interpersonal encounters. *Psychology of Women Quarterly, 15,* 463–475.

Johnson, K,, & LaTour, M. S. (1991) AIDS prevention and college students: Male and female responses to 'fear-provoking' messages. *Health Marketing Quarterly, 8,* 139–153

Johnson, P. (1997). A contrary view of colonialism. *Far Eastern Economic Review* [special issue], 8–16.

Johnson, T., Braima, M. A. M., & Sothirajah, J. (1999). Doing the traditional media sidestep: Comparing the effects of the internet and other nontraditional media with traditional media in the 1996 Presidential campaign. *Journalism & Mass Communication Quarterly, 76,* 99–123.

Johnstone, J., Slawski, E., & Bowman, W. (1976). *The news people: A social portrait of American journalists and their work.* Urbana: University of Illinois Press.

Jordan, R.A. (2001, August, 7). Labor's odd alliance with Bush. *The Boston Globe,* p. F4.

Kahan, H., & Mulrya, D. (1995). Attitudes towards homosexuality and attention to news about AIDS. *Journalism and Mass Communication Quarterly, 72*(2), 322–335.

Kahane, L. H. (1999). Gun lobbies and gun control: Senate voting patterns on the Brady Bill and the assault weapons ban. *Atlantic Economic Journal, 27*(4), 384–394.

Kalichman, C. S., & Hunter, L. T. (1992). The disclosure of celebrity HIV infection: Its effects on public attitudes. *American Journal of Public Health, 82,* 1374–1376.

Kalichman, S. C., Russell, R. L., Hunter, T. L., & Sarwer, D. B. (1993). Earvin "Magic" Johnson's HIV serostatus disclosure: Effects on men's perceptions of AIDS. *Journal of Consulting and Clinical Psychology, 61*(5), 887–891.

Kalwinsky, R. (1998). Framing life and death: Physician-assisted suicide and the *New York Times* from 1991-1996. *Journal of Communication Inquiry, 22*(1), 93–113.

Kennamer, J. D., & Honnold, J. A. (1995, Summer). Attitude toward homosexuality and attention to news about AIDS. *Journalism & Mass Communication Quarterly, 72,* 322–335.

Kennedy, R. (1998). Cast a cautious eye on the Supreme Court. *Current, 402,* 33–39.

Kepplinger, H. M., & Roth, H. (1979). Creating a crisis: German mass media and oil supply in 1973-74. *Public Opinion Quarterly, 3,* 285–296.

Kinsella, J. (1989). *Covering the plague—AIDS and the American media.* New Brunswick, NJ: Rutgers University Press.

Kirchhoff, S. (1998). GOP leaders' tougher stand against homosexual rights concerns some in party. *CQ Weekly, 56,* 1946.

Kissling, E. A. (1991). Street harassment: The language of sexual terrorism. In T.A. Van Dijk (Ed.), *Discourse and society* (Vol. 2, pp. 451–460). London, England: Sage.

Klandermas, B. (1997). *The social psychology of protest.* Cambridge: Blackwell.

Klandermas, B., Kriesi, H., & Tarrow, S. (Eds.). (1988). *International social movement research: From structure to action, Vol. 1.* Greenwich, CT: JAI Press.

Kline, K. N. (2006). A decade of research on health content in the media: The focus on health challenges and sociocultural context and attendant informational and ideological problems. *Journal of Health Communication, 11,* 43–59.

Knox, G. W., Martin, B., & Tromanhauser, E. D. (1995). Preliminary results of the 1995 national prosecutor's survey. *Journal of Gang Research, 2*(4), 59–71.

Kobland, C.E., Du, L., & Kwon, J. (1992). Influence of ideology in news reporting: Case study of *New York Times* coverage of student demonstrations in China and South Korea. *Asian Journal of Communication, 2,* 64–77.

Konrad, W. (1986). Women of CBS usher in a new day at Black Rock. *Working Woman, 11,* 115.

Kraus, S., & Davis, D. with Lang, G. E. & Lang, K. (1975). Critical event analysis. In S. Chaffee (Ed.), *Political communication* (pp. 189–121). Beverly Hills, CA: Sage.

Kraut, R. E. (1989). Telemarketing: The trade-offs of home work. *Journal of Communication, 39,* 48–60.

Krieg, J.P. (1992). *Epidemics in the modern world.* New York: Twayne Publishers.

Lacayo, R. (2001, August 20). How Bush got there. *Time,* pp. 17–23.

Lambro, D. (1991, October 18). Thomas: A new symbol for conservative blacks. *Atlanta Journal,* p. A/12.

Lang, K., & Lang, G. E. (1993). Perspectives on communication. *Journal of Communication, 43*(3), 92–99.

Langone, J. (1991). *AIDS, the facts.* Boston, MA: Little, Brown.

Lappe, M. (1991, December). Ethical issues in manipulating the human germ line. *The Journal of Medicine and Philosophy, 16*(6), 621–639.

LaRose, R., & Mettler, J. (1989). Who uses information technologies in rural America? *Journal of Communication, 39,* 48–60.

Larson, S. S. (1991). Television's mixed messages: Sexual content on *All My Children. Communication Quarterly, 39,* 156–163.

Lavery, J., Boyle, J., Dickens, B., Maclean, H., & Singer, P. (2001). Origins of the desire for euthanasia and assisted suicide in people with HIV-1 or AIDS: A qualitative study. *The Lancet, 358,* 362–366.

Lee, C., & Chan, J. M. (1990). The Hong Kong press coverage of the Tiananmen Square protests. *The International Journal for Mass Communication Studies, 46,* 175–195.

Lee, P. S. (1993). Press response to rapid social change in Hong Kong. *Asian Journal of Communication, 5,* 1–17.

Lester, E. (1992). The AIDS story and moral panic: How the Euro-African press constructs AIDS. *Howard Journal of Communications, 3,* 230–241

Levine, M. (2000, December 24). Court's ideological bias showed in Bush decision. *The Buffalo News,* p. H5.

Levine, R. (1997). Frail, elderly patients more opposed to physician-assisted suicide than younger relatives. Retrieved October 1997 from http://www.dukenews. due.edu/radio/elderly.html.

Lifestyle market analyst: A reference guide for consumer market analysis. (1997–2004). Wilmette, IL: Standard Rate and Data Service.

Linz, D., Donerstein, E., & Penrod, S. (1984). The effects of multiple exposures to filmed violence against women. *Journal of Communication, 34*(3), 130–147.

Lipschultz, J. H., & Hilt, M. L. (1999). Mass media and the death penalty: Social construction of three Nebraska executions. *Journal of Broadcasting & Electronic Media, 43*(2), 236–253.

Lowry, D. T., & Shidler, J. A. (1993, Autumn). Prime time TV portrayals of sex, "safe sex" and AIDS: A longitudinal analysis. *Journalism Quarterly, 70,* 628–637.

Lowrey, W., Becker, L.B., & Punathambekar, A. (2003). Determinants of newsroom use of staff expertise. *Gazette: International Journal for Communication Studies, 65*(1), 23–63.

Lutkenhouse, J., Pollock, J. C., Smyth, J., & Dokus, K. (2006, June). *Nationwide newspaper coverage of affirmative action in higher education: A community structure approach.* Paper presented at the annual conference of the International Communication Association, Dresden, Germay.

Lyon, D. (1998). The world wide web of surveillance: The Internet and off-world power-flows. *Information Communication & Society,.* 91–105.

MacNair, R. R., Elliott, T. R., & Yoder, B. (1991, August). AIDS prevention groups as persuasive appeals: Effects on attitudes about precautionary behaviors among persons in substance abuse treatment. *Small Group Research, 22,* 301–319.

Maibach, E., & Flora, J.A. (1993). Symbolic modeling and cognitive rehearsal: Using video to promote AIDS prevention self efficacy. *Communication Research, 20,* 517–545.

Mancini, P. (1993). The legitimacy gap: A problem of mass media research in Europe and the United States. *Journal of Communication, 43*(3), 100–111.

Manoff, R., & Schudson, M. (1987). *Reading the news.* New York: Pantheon Books.

Marger, M. N. (1991). *Race and ethnic relations* (2nd ed.). Belmont, CA: Wadsworth.

Marks, G., & Beatty, W. K. (1991). *Epidemics.* New York: Charles Scribner's Sons.

Marshall, P. G. (1993, January 29). U.S. trade policy. *CQ Researcher, 3,* 75–90.

Martin, E. (1994). *Flexible bodies: Tracking immunity in American culture from the days of polio to the age of AIDS.* Boston, MA: Beacon Press.

Martin, E. F., Wilson, G. B., & Meng, C. Y. (1994). Attitudes toward media freedoms in Hong Kong: A prelude to 1997. *The International Journal for Mass Communication Studies, 54,* 103–120.

Marwick, C. (2001). Embryonic stem cell debate brings politics, ethics to the bench. *Journal of the National Cancer Institute, 93,* 1192–1193.

Mauser, G. A., & Kopel, D. B. (1992). "Sorry, wrong number": Why media polls on gun control are often unreliable. *Political Communication, 9*(2), 69–92.

Mays, L. G., & Houghtalin, M. (1992). Trying juveniles as adults: A note on New Mexico's recent experience. *Justice System Journal, 15*(3), 814–823.

McAneny, L. (1992). One year later: Anita Hill now deemed more believable than Justice Thomas; Sharp change from last year. *Gallup Poll Monthly, 325,* 34–35.

McCarthy, J.D., McPhail, D., & Smith, J. (1996). Images of protest: Dimensions of selection bias in media coverage of Washington demonstrations, 1982 and 1991. *American Sociological Review, 61*, 478–99.

McCombs, M., Einsiedel, E., & Weaver, D. (1991). *Contemporary public opinion: Issues and the news.* Hillsdale, NJ: Erlbaum.

McCombs, M., & Ghanem, S. I. (2001). The convergence of agenda setting and framing. In S. D. Reese, O. H. Gandy, Jr., & A. E. Grant (Eds.), *Framing public life: Perspectives on media and our understanding of the social world* (pp. 67–81). Mahwah, NJ: Erlbaum.

McGinty, M. (2000). Surfing your turf. *Communications of the ACM, 43*, 19–21.

McGuire, W. J. (2001). Input and output variables currently promising for constructive persuasive communications. In R. E. Rice & C. K. Atkin (Eds.), *Public communication campaigns* (3rd ed., pp. 22–48). Thousand Oaks, CA: Sage.

McIntyre, B. T. (1993). Trust in media and government: A recursive model for natives of Hong Kong and mainland China. *Communication Research Reports, 10*, 203–208.

McKay, R. (2000 July 27). Stem cells—hype and hope. *Nature, 406*, 361–364.

McLeod, D. M., & Detenber, B. H. (1999, Summer). Framing effects of television news coverage of social protest. *Journal of Communication, 49*(3), 3–23.

McLeod, D. M., & Hertog, J. K. (1992) The manufacture of public opinion by reporters: Informal cues for public perceptions of protest groups. *Discourse and Society, 3*, 259–275

McLeod, D. M., & Hertog, J. K. (1999). Social control, social change and the mass media's role in the regulation of protest groups. In D. Demers & K. Viswanath (Eds.), *Mass media, social control, and social change: A macrosocial perspective* (pp. 99–116). Ames: Iowa State University Press.

McNamee, M., & Dunham, R. S. (1998, March 9). Patient's bill of rights: Business gets out the scalpel. *Business Week*, p. 47.

McNeill, W. H. (1977). *Plagues and peoples.* New York: Anchor.

Meier, D., Emmons, C., Wallenstein, S., Quill, T., Morrison, R., & Cassel, C. (1998, April 23). A national survey of physician-assisted suicide and euthanasia in the United States. *The New England Journal of Medicine, 338*(17), 1193–1201.

Merriam, J. E. (1989). National media coverage of drug issues. In P. Shoemaker (Ed.), *Communication campaigns about drugs: Government, media and the public* (pp. 21–28). Hillsdale, NJ: Erlbaum.

Merritt, D. (1996, August 23). Unconventional wisdom. *The New York Times*, p. A27.

Mink, M., Puma, J., & Pollock, J. C. (2001, May). *Nationwide newspaper coverage of the repatriation of Elian Gonzalez: A community structure approach.* Paper presented at the annual conference of the International Communication Association, Washington, DC.

Moore, D. (2000). *Gallup poll.* Princeton, NJ: The Gallup Organization.

Moore, M. P. (1994). Life, liberty, and the handgun: The function of synecdoche in the Brady debate. *Communication Quarterly, 42*(4), 434–447.

Moore, T. C., & Mae, R. (1987). Who dies and who cries: Death and bereavement in children's literature. *Journal of Communication, 37*(4), 52–64.

Morris, D. (1997). Older adults' perceptions of Dr. Kevorkian in Middletown, U.S.A. *OMEGA, 35*(4), 405–412.

Morris, R.J. (1987). *Cholera 1832: The social response to an epidemic.* New York: Homes & Meier.

Murphy, T. P. (1999). The human experience of wilderness. *Electronic Journal of Communications, 9*(2/4).

Myers, P. N., & Biocca, F. A. (1992). The elastic body image: The effect of television advertising and programming on body image distortions in young women. *Journal of Communication, 42*(3), 108–33.

Naisbitt, J.A. (1982). *Megatrends: Ten new directions transforming our lives.* New York: Warner Books.

Naisbitt, J.A. (1999). *Megachallenges.* San Jose, CA: toExcel.

National Institutes of Health. (2000a). *Stem cells: A primer.* Retrieved September 4, 2001, from http://www.nih.gov/news/stemcell/primer.html

National Institutes of Health. (2000b). *National Institutes of Health (NIH) update on existing human embryonic stem cells.* Retrieved September 5, 2001, from http://www.nih.gov/news/stemcell/082701list.html

Nelkin, D. (1987). The culture of science journalism. *Society, 24*(6), 17-25.

Nelkin, D., & Gilman, S. L. (1991). Placing blame for devastating disease. In A. Mack (Ed.), *In time of plague: The history and social consequences of lethal epidemic disease* (pp. 39–56). New York: New York University Press.

Niebuhr, G. (1996, February 8). Open attitude on homosexuality makes pariahs of some churches. *The New York Times,* p. A1.

Niiler, E. (2000). Awash in oil. *Scientific American, 283*(3), 21.

Nirode, J. (2000, May 26). Juvenile sentencing bill draws new foes. *The Columbus Dispatch,* p. 8E.

Nisbet, E. C., & Shanahan, J. (2004). *Developing cultural indicators of social change: The case of homosexuality.* Paper submitted to the Mass Communication Division of the 2005 annual meeting of the International Communication Association, New York, NY.

Nisbet, M. C. (2004). The polls: Public opinion about stem cell research and human cloning. *Public Opinion Quarterly, 68*(1), 132–155.

Nisbet, M. C. (2005, Spring). The competition for worldviews: Values, information, & public support for stem cell research. *International Journal of Public Opinion Research, 17*(1), 90–112.

Nisbet, M. C., Brossard, D., & Kroepsch, A. (2003). Framing science: The stem cell controversy in an age of press/politics. *Harvard International Journal of Press/Politics, 8*(2), 36–70.

Nisbet, M. C., Scheufele, D. A., Shanahan, J., Moy, P., Brossard, D., & Lewenstein, B. V. (2002). Knowledge, reservations, or promise? A media effects model for public perceptions of science and technology. *Communication Research, 29*(5), 584–608.

Noelle-Neumann, E. (1999). The effect of the mass media on opinion formation. In D. Demers & K. Viswanath (Eds.), *Mass media, social control, and social change: A macrosocial perspective* (pp. 51–76). Ames: Iowa State University Press.

Norris, P. (2000). *A virtuous circle: Political communications in postindustrial societies.* Cambridge, UK: Cambridge University Press.

Norris, P. (2004). Global political communication: Good governance, human development and mass communication. In F. Esser & B. Pfetsch (Eds.), *Comparing political communication: Theories, cases and challenges* (pp. 115–150). Cambridge, UK: Cambridge University Press.

Odorico, J. S., Kaufman, D. S., & Thomson, J. A. (2001). Multilineage differentiation from human embryonic stem cell lines. *Stem Cells, 19*(3), 193–204.

Okrent, D. (2004, January 9). No picture tells the truth: The best do better than that. *The New York Times,* p. 2.

Olien, C. N., Donohue, G. A., & Tichenor, P. J. (1995). Conflict, consensus and public opinion. In T.L. Glaser & C.T. Salmon (Eds.), *Public opinion and the communication of consent* (pp. 301–322). New York: Guilford.

Oregon Death With Dignity—Respect the Will of the People. (2002). Retrieved April 22, 2002, from http://www.dwd.org/law/safeguards.asp

Ota, A. (1999). FTC opposes federal regulation of Internet privacy. *Congressional Quarterly Weekly, 57*(29), 1733–1734.

Owen, D. (1997). Talk radio and evaluations of President Clinton. *Political Communication, 14*(3), 333–353.

Palley, M. L., & Palley, H. A. (1992). The Thomas appointment: Defeats and victories for women. *PS, 25,* 473–477.

Palmgreen P., & Clarke P. (1977). Agenda-setting with local and national issues. *Communication Research, 4*(4), 435–452.

Pan, Z., & Kosicki, G. M.. (1993). Framing analysis: An approach to news discourse. *Political Communication, 10,* 55–76.

Panel on Information Dissemination, Intervention Diffusion and Media Coverage. (1995). *NIMH effort to develop a consensus statement on research methods in behavioral research.* Rockville, MD: Office on AIDS, NIMH.

Papacharissi, Z., and Rubin, A. (2000). Predictors of Internet use. *Journal of Broadcasting & Electronic Media, 44,* 175–196.

Park, R. (1922). *The immigrant press and its control.* New York: Harcourt.

Patients bill of wrongs. (1999, September 14). *The Detroit News,* p. A8. *Lexis-Nexis* [Online]. Available: www.lexis-nexis.com

Patterson, T.E. (1995). *Out of order.* New York: Random House.

Patterson, T.E. (2002). *The vanishing voter: Public involvement in an age of uncertainty.* New York: Knopf.

Patterson, T. E., & Donsbach, W. (1996). News decisions: Journalists as partisan actors. *Political Communication, 13,* 455–68.

Payne, J., Ratzan, S., & Baukus, R. (1989). Newspaper coverage of the Harvard Medicare project: Regional distinction or discreet disregard. *Health Communication, 1*(4), 227–238.

Payne, J. G., & Mercuri, K. A. (1993). Crisis in communication: Coverage of Magic Johnson's AIDS disclosure. In S. C. Ratzan (Ed.), *AIDS: Effective health communication in the 90s* (pp. 151–172). Washington, DC: Taylor & Francis.

Pear, R. (1999, October 8). House passes bill to expand rights on medical care. *The New York Times,* pp. A1, A22.

Pederson, R. (1999, April). Cells for medicine. *Scientific American,* pp. 69–73.

Pepper, S. (1995). Hong Kong in 1994: Democratic human rights and the post colonial political order. *Asia Review, 35,* 48–60.

Pepper, S. (1996). Hong Kong in 1995: Institution building and citizenship between two sovereigns. *Asia Review, 36,* 25–32.

Perloff, R. M. (2001). *Persuading people to have safer sex: Applications of social science to the AIDS crisis.* Mahwah, NJ: Erlbaum.

Perry, D. (2000). Patient's voices: The powerful sound in the stem cell debate. *Science, 287*(5457), 1423.

Peterson J. L., Moore, K. A., & Furstenberg, F. F., Jr. (1991). Television viewing and early initiation of sexual intercourse: Is there a link? *Journal of Homosexuality, 21*, 93–118.

Pfau, M., & Kendall, K. E. (1997). Influence of communication during the distant phase of the 1996 Republican presidential primary campaign. *Journal of Communication, 47*(4), 6–26.

Pierson, H. D. (1992). Communication issues during a period of radical transition: The case of Hong Kong. *Communication Quarterly, 40*, 381–390.

Poirier, R. (1991). AIDS and traditions of homophobia. In A. Mack (Ed.), *In time of plague: The history and social consequences of lethal epidemic disease* (pp. 139–153). New York: New York University Press.

Pollay, R., Siddarth, S., Siegel, M., Haddix, A., Merritt, R. et. al. (1996, April). The last straw? Cigarette advertising and realized market share among youths and adults, 1979-1993. *Journal of Marketing, 60*, 1–16

Pollock, J. C. (1981). *The politics of crisis reporting: Learning to become a foreign correspondent.* Greenwood, CT: Praeger.

Pollock, J. C. (1995). Comparing city characteristics and newspaper coverage of NAFTA. *Mass Communication Review, 22*, 166–177.

Pollock, J. C. (1999). Reporting on political and social change: Asking the right questions. *The College of New Jersey Alumni Magazine, 3*, 26–31.

Pollock, J.C. (in press). The "communication commando" model creates a culture of research commitment. *Communication Teacher.*

Pollock, J. C., Awrachow, M., & Kuntz, W. J. (1994). *Comparing city characteristics and newspaper coverage of the Magic Johnson HIV announcement: Toward a national sample.* Paper accepted for presentation by the Health Communication Division for the annual meeting of the International Communication Association, Sydney, Australia.

Pollock, J. C., Coughlin, J., Thomas, J., & Connaughton, T. (1996). Comparing city characteristics and nationwide newspaper coverage of Dr. Jack Kevorkian: An archival approach. *Newspaper Research Journal, 17*(3/4), 120–133.

Pollock, J. C., & Dantas, G. (1998, July). *Nationwide newspaper coverage of same sex marriage: A community structure approach.* Paper presented at the annual conference of the International Communication Association, Jerusalem, Israel.

Pollock, J. C., Dudzak, M., Richards, K., Norton, S., & Miller, R. (2000, June). *Nationwide newspaper coverage of human cloning: A community structure approach.* Paper presented at the annual conference of the International Communication Association, Acapulco, Mexico.

Pollock, J. C., DuRoss, A., Moscatello, J., & O'Rourke, C. A. (2002, July). *Nationwide newspaper coverage of homosexuals in the Boy Scouts: A community structure approach.* Paper presented at the annual conference of the International Communication Association, Seoul, Korea.

Pollock, J. C., & Guidette, C. L. (1980). Mass media, crisis and political change: A cross-national approach. In D. Nimmo (Ed.). *Communication yearbook IV* (pp. 309–324). New Brunswick, NJ: Transaction Books.

Pollock, J. C., Kreuer, B., & Ouano, E. (1997, Winter). Comparing city characteristics and nationwide coverage of China's bid to host the 2000 Olympic games: A community structure approach. *Newspaper Research Journal, 18*, 31–49.

Pollock, J. C., Mink, M., & Puma, J. (2001, May). *Nationwide newspaper coverage of the repatriation of Elian Gonzalez: A community structure approach.* Paper presented at the annual conference of the International Communication Association, Washington DC.

Pollock, J. C., Mink, M., Puma, J., Shuhala, S., & Ostrander, L. (2001, November). *Nationwide newspaper coverage of women in combat: A community structure approach.* Paper presented at the annual conference of the National Communication Association, Atlanta.

Pollock, J. C., & Montero, E. (1998). Challenging the mandarins: City characteristics and newspaper coverage of the Internet 1993-1995. In B. Ebo (Ed.), *Cyberghetto or cybertopia: Race, class and gender on the Internet* (pp. 103–119). Westport, CT: Greenwood Press.

Pollock, J. C., Moran, B. et. al. (2001, May). *Nationwide newspaper coverage of hate crime legislation: A community structure approach.* Paper presented at the annual conference of the International Communication Association, Washington, DC.

Pollock, J. C., Morris, H., Citarella, R., Ryan, M., & Yulis, S. (1999, November). *The Louise Woodward "British Nanny" trial: Nationwide newspaper coverage of the Eappens; A community stakeholder approach.* Paper presented at the annual conference of the National Communication Association, Chicago.

Pollock, J. C., Nisi, V., & McCarthy, C. (1999, May). *Nationwide newspaper coverage of efforts to ban tobacco advertising toward children: A community structure approach.* Paper presented at the annual meeting of the International Communication Association, San Francisco.

Pollock, J. C., Piccillo, C., Leopardi, D., & Gratale, S., & Cabot, K. (2005, February). Nationwide newspaper coverage of Islam post-September 11, 2001: A community structure approach. *Communication Research Reports, 22*(1), 15–27.

Pollock, J. C., & Robinson, J. L. (1977). Reporting rights conflicts. *Society, 13*(1), 44–47.

Pollock, J. C., Robinson, J. L., & Murray, M.C. (1978). Media agendas and human rights: The Supreme Court decision on abortion. *Journalism Quarterly, 53*(3), 545–548, 561.

Pollock, J. C., Shier, L., & Slattery, P. (1995). Newspapers and the "open door" policy towards Cuba: A sample of major cities—community structure approach. *Journal of International Communication, 2*, 67–86.

Pollock, J. C., Shellenberger, J. & Fogerty, T. (2001, May). *Nationwide newspaper coverage of gun control since Columbine: A community structure approach.* Paper presented at the annual conference of the International Communication Association, Washington, DC.

Pollock, J. C., Spina, L., Dudzak, M., & Lemire, M. (2000, November). *Media alignment with social change: Nationwide newspaper coverage of the 1997 UPS strike.* Paper presented at the annual conference of the National Communication Association, Seattle, WA.

Pollock, J. C., Stillman, F. A., & Yulis, S. G. (2002, July). *Nationwide newspaper "framing" of the Supreme Court decision on FDA tobacco regulation: Testing a content analysis surveillance tool.* Paper presented at the annual conference of the International Communication Association, Seoul, Korea.

Pollock, J. C., Tanner, T., & Delbene, M. (2000, November). *Nationwide newspaper coverage of Social Security: A community structure approach.* Paper presented at the annual convention of the National Communication Association, Seattle, WA.

Pollock, J. C., & Tobin, B. (2000, April). *Nationwide newspaper coverage of same-sex adoption: A community structure approach.* Paper presented at the annual conference of the New Jersey Communication Association, Monmouth University, Long Branch, NJ.

Pollock, J. C., & Whitney, L. (1997, Fall). Newspapers and racial/ethnic conflict: Comparing city demographics and nationwide reporting on the Crown Heights (Brooklyn, NY) incidents. *The New Jersey Journal of Communication, 5*(2), 127–149.

Pollock, J.C., & Yulis, S. G. (2004, July-August). Nationwide newspaper coverage of physician-assisted suicide: A community structure approach. *Journal of Health Communication, 9*(4), 281–307.

Pomerantz, A. P. (1989). No film at 11: The inadequacy of legal protection and relief for sexually harassed broadcast journalists. *Cardozo Arts and Entertainment Law Journal, 8,* 309–324.

Powell, S. G. (1991). A risk analysis of oil development in the ANWR. *Energy Journal, 12*(3), 55–77.

Powers, A., & Andsager, J. (1999). How newspapers framed breast implants in the 1990s. *Journalism & Mass Communication Quarterly, 76*(3), 551–564.

Price, V., Tewksbury, D., & Powers, E. (1997). Switching trains of thought: The impact of news frames on readers' cognitive responses. *Communication Research, 24,* 481–506.

Pritchard, D., & Hughes, K. (1997) Patterns of deviance in crime news news. *Journal of Communication, 47*(3), 49–67.

Privacy on the Internet–Could try harder. (2000, May). *The Economist,* p. 65.

Putnam, R. (2000). *Bowling alone: The decline and revival of civic participation in America.* New York: W.W. Norton.

Rakow, L. F. (1986). Rethinking gender research in communication. *Journal of Communication, 36*(4), 11–26.

Ratzan, S. C. (1997). Editorial. *Journal of Health Communication, 2*(1), v–vi.

Ratzan, S. C. (Ed.). (1998). *The mad cow crisis: Health and the public good.* New York: New York University Press.

Ratzan, S. C. (2001). Mad cow crisis II: New casualties. *Journal of Health Communication, 6*(1), 1–2.

Reardon, K. K. (1989). The potential role of persuasion in adolescent AIDS prevention. In R. E. Rice & C. K. Atkin (Eds.), *Public communication campaigns* (pp. 273–289). Newbury Park, CA: Sage.

Reardon, K. K., & Richardson, J. L. (1991). The important role of mass media in the diffusion of accurate information about AIDS. *Journal of Homosexuality, 21,* 63–75.

Reber, B., Beaudoin, C., & Sanders, K. (2000, July). *Difficult newsroom decisions: Making editorial choices without guiding precedents.* Paper presented at the annual conference of the International Communication Association, Acapulco, Mexico.

Reese, S. D. (2001). Framing public life: A bridging model for media research. In S. D. Reese, O. H. Gandy, Jr., & A. E. Grant (Eds.), *Framing public life: Perspectives on media and our understanding of the social world* (pp. 7–31). Mahwah, NJ: Erlbaum.

Rheingold, H. (1993). *The virtual community: Homesteading on the electronic frontier.* Reading, MA: Addison-Wesley.

Rice, R., & Atkin, C. (Eds.). (2001). *Public communication campaigns* (3rd ed.). Newbury Park, CA: Sage.

Richmond, V.P. (1991). A communication perspective on sexual harassment: Affiliative non-verbal behaviors in synchronous relationships. *Communication Quarterly, 39,* 111–118.

Riffe, D., & Freitag, A. (1996, August). *Twenty-five years of content analysis in Journalism & Mass Communication Quarterly.* Paper presented to the annual convention of the Association for Education in Journalism and Mass Communication, Anaheim, CA.

Riffe, D., Lacy, S., & Fico, F.G. (1998). *Analyzing media messages: Using quantitative analysis in research.* Mahwah, NJ: Erlbaum.

Rivers, W. L., Miller, S., & Gandy, O. (1975). Government in the media. In S. Chaffee (Ed.), *Political communication.* (pp. 217–236). Beverly Hills, CA: Sage.

Roberts, M. L. (2000). Case study: Geocities (A) and (B). *Journal of Interactive Marketing, 14,* 60–72.

Rogers, E. M. (1986). *Communication technology: The new media in society.* New York: The Free Press.

Rogers, E. M. (1993). Looking back, looking forward: A century of communication study. In P. Gaunt (Ed.), *Beyond agendas: New directions in communication research* (pp. 19–40). Westport, CT: Greenwood.

Rogers, E. M. (1995). *Diffusion of innovations* (4th ed.). New York: The Free Press.

Rogers, E. M., & Chang, S. B. (1991). Media coverage of technological issues: Ethiopian drought of 1984, AIDS, Challenger and Chernobyl. In L. Wilkens & P. Patterson (Eds.), *Risky business: Communication issues of science, risk and public policy* (pp. 75–96.). Westport, CT: Greenwood.

Rogers, E. M., & Dearing, J. W. (1988). Agenda-setting research: Where has it been, where is it going? In J. A. Anderson (Ed.), *Communication yearbook 11* (pp. 555–594). Newbury Park, CA: Sage.

Rogers, T. F., Singer, E., & Imperio, J. (1993). The polls: Poll trends: AIDS—an update. *Public Opinion Quarterly, 57,* 92–96.

Rosen, C. (2000, October). Internet legislation. *Information Week, 807,* 92–94.

Rosenberg, C. (1962). *The cholera years.* Chicago: University of Chicago Press.

Rubin, A. D., & Geer, D. E. (1998). A survey of Web security. *Computer, 31,* 34–31.

Rusciano, F. (1998). *World opinion and the emerging international order.* Westport, CT: Greenwood Publishing Group.

Sabato, L. J. (1991). *Feeding frenzy: How attack journalism has transformed American politics.* New York: The Free Press.

Salzman, A. (1992). The Boy Scouts under siege. *The American Scholar, 61,* 591–597.

Sandys, M., & Chermak, S. M. (1996). A journey into the unknown: Pretrial publicity and capital cases. *Communication Law and Policy, 1*(4), 533, 541.

Scheufele, D. A. (1999). Framing as a theory of media effects. *Journal of Communication, 49,* 203–222.

Scheufele, D. A. (2000). Agenda-setting, priming and framing revisited: Another look at cognitive effects of political communication. *Mass Communication & Society, 3*(2/3), 397–316.

Schöenbach, K., & Becker, L. B. (1995). Origins and consequences of mediated public opinion. In T. L. Glasser & C. T. Salmon (Eds.), *Public opinion and the communication of consent* (pp. 323–347). New York: Guilford.

Schudson, M. (1978). *Discovering the news.* New York: Basic Books.

Schudson, M. (2001, August). The objectivity norm in American journalism. *Journalism, 2*(2), 149–170.

Schuman, H., & Presser, S. (1977–78). Attitude measurement and the gun control paradox. *Public Opinion Quarterly, 41*(41), 427–438.

Schweitzer, J. C., & Miller, J. (1991). What do newswomen cover? A first attempt to uncover subtle discrimination. *Newspaper Research Journal, 12,* 72–80.

Serovich, J. M., & Greene, K. (1993). Perceptions of family boundaries: The case of disclosure of HIV testing information. *Family Relations, 42,* 193–197.

Serovich, J. M., Greene, K., & Parrott, R. (1992, January). Boundaries and AIDS testing: Privacy and the family system. *Family Relations, 41*(1), 104–109.

Shalala, D. E. (1999). A patients' bill of rights: The medical student's role. *Journal of the American Medical Association, 281,* 857.

Shanahan, J., & Jones, V. (1999). Cultivation and social control. In D. Demers & K. Viswanath (Eds.), *Mass media, social control, and social change: A macrosocial perspective* (pp. 31–50). Ames: Iowa State University Press.

Shanahan, J., Nisbet, E. C., Diels, J., Hardy, B. W., & Besley, B. C. (2005, May). *Cultural indicators: Integrating measures of meaning with economic and social indicators.* Paper presented to the 2005 annual convention of the International Communication Association. New York, NY.

Shanahan, J., Scheufele, D., Yang, F., & Hizi, S. (2004, Fall). Cultivation and spiral of silence effects: The case of smoking. *Mass Communication & Society, 7*(4), 413–428.

Shaw, D. L. & Slater, J. W. (1988). Press puts unemployment on agenda. *Journalism Quarterly, 65*(2), 407–411

Shaw, D. R. (1999). The impact of news media favorability and candidate events in presidential campaigns. *Political Communication, 16,* 183–202.

Shaw, G. M., Shapiro, R. Y., Lock, S. J., & Lawrence, R. (1998). The polls-trends: Crime, the police, and civil liberties. *Public Opinion Quarterly, 62,* 405–426.

Sheffey, S., & Tindale, S. (1992). Perceptions of sexual harassment in the workplace. *Journal of Applied Social Psychology, 22,* 1502–1520.

Shilts, R. (1987). *And the band played on.* New York: St. Martin's Press.

Shipman, M. (1995). The ethical guidelines for televising or photographing executions. *Journal of Mass Media Ethics, 10*(2), 95–108.

Shiralidi, V. (2000, September 5). *Exorcising the ghosts of school shootings.* Retrieved October 17, 2000, from The Center on Juvenile and Criminal Justice, http://www.cjcj.org.

Shoemaker, P. (1984, Spring). Media treatment of deviant political groups. *Journalism Quarterly, 61*(1), 66–82

Shoemaker, P., & Mayfield, E. K. (1987). Building a theory of news content: A synthesis of current approaches. *Journalism Monographs No. 103.*

Shoemaker, P., & Reese, S.D. (1990, Winter). Exposure to what? Integrating media content and effects studies. *Journalism Quarterly, 67*(4), 649–652.

Shoemaker, P., &. Reese, S.D. (1996). *Mediating the message: Theories of influence on mass media content* (2nd ed.). Boston: Allyn & Bacon.

Should children be tried as adults? (1999). *Jet Magazine*, p. 52.

Shrewsbury, J. F. D. (1970). *Bubonic plague in the British Isles.* London: Cambridge University Press.

Sigal, L. V. (1973). *Reporters and officials.* Lexington, MA: DC. Heath

Singer, E., Rogers, T. F., & Glassman, M. B. (1991). Public opinion about AIDS before and after the 1988 U.S. government public information campaign. *Public Opinion Quarterly, 55,* 161–179.

Smith, C. (1991). Sex and genre on prime time. In M.S. Wolf & A. P. Keilwasser (Eds.), *Gay people, sex and the media* (pp. 93–118). Binghamton, NY: Haworth Press.

Smith, C., Fredin, E. S., & Nardone, C. A. F. (1989). Television: Sex discrimination in the newsroom: Perception and reality. *Sage Focus Editions, 106,* 227–246.

Smith, K. A. (1984a). Community perceptions of media impressions. *Journalism Quarterly, 61,* 164–168.

Smith, K. A. (1984b). Perceived influence of media on what goes on in a community. *Journalism Quarterly, 61,* 260–264.

Smith, K. A. (2000, June). Loaded coverage: How the news media miss the mark on the gun issue. *Reason, 32*(2), 38–44.

Snyder, L. B., & Rouse, R. A. (1995). The media can have more than an impersonal impact: The case of AIDS risk perceptions and behavior. *Health Communication, 7,* 125–145.

Solomon, D. (1991). A social marketing perspective on communication campaigns. In R. E. Rice & C. K. Atkin (Eds.), *Public communication campaigns* (2nd ed., pp. 87–104). Thousand Oaks, CA: Sage.

Sontag, S. (1977). *AIDS and its metaphors.* New York: Farrar, Strauss & Giroux.

Sorensen, J., Wrinkle, R., Brewer, V., & Marquart, J. (1999, October). Capital punishment and deterrence: Examining the effect of executions on murder in Texas. *Crime & Delinquency, 45*(4), 481–493.

Sparks, G. G., & Fehlner, C. L. (1986, Autumn). Faces in the news: Gender comparisons of magazine photographs. *Journal of Communication, 36*(4), 70–79.

Spindelman, M. S. (2000). Some initial thoughts on sexuality and gay men with AIDS in relation to physician-assisted suicide. *Georgetown Journal of Gender & the Law, 2,* 91–106.

Stalans, L., & Lurigio, A.J. (1996). Editors' introduction: Public opinion about the creation, enforcement, and punishment of criminal offenses. *American Behavioral Science, 39*(4), 369–378.

Stamm, K. R. (1985). *Newspaper use and community ties: Toward a dynamic theory.* Norwood, NJ: Ablex.

Stamm, K.R., & Fortini-Campbell, L. (1983). The relationship of community ties to newspaper use. *Journalism Monographs, 84,* 2-27.

Stark, S. (1992). Sexual harassment in the workplace: Lessons from the Thomas–Hill hearings. *Trial, 28,* 116–118.

Steele, J. E. (1997). Don't ask, don't tell, don't explain: Unofficial sources and television coverage of the dispute over gays in the military. *Political Communication, 14*(1), 83–96.

Steeves, L.H. (1993). Creating imagined communities: Development communications and the challenge of feminism. *Journal of Communication, 43*(3), 218–229.

Stempel, G., Hargrove, T., & Bernt, J. (2000) Relation of growth of use of the Internet to changes in media use from 1995 to 1999. *Journalism & Mass Communication Quarterly, 77,* 71–79.

Stencel, M., Lichter, S. R., & Sabato, L.J. (2000). *Peepshow: Media and politics in an age of scandal.* Lanham, MD: Rowman & Littlefield.

Stillman, F. A., Cronin, K. A., Evans, W. D., & Ulasevich, A. (2001, June). Can media advocacy influence newspaper coverage of tobacco: Measuring the effectiveness of the American stop smoking intervention study's (ASSIST) media advocacy strategies. *Tobacco Control, 10*(2), 137–144.

Stillman, F., Hartman, A., Graubard, B., Gilpin, E., Chavis, D. et. al. (1999, June). The American stop smoking intervention study: Conceptual framework and evaluation design. *Evaluation Review, 23*(3), 259–280.

Stine, G. J. (1995). *AIDS Update.* Englewood Cliffs, NJ: Prentice Hall.

Strieker, G. (2000, Sept./Oct.) Arctic odyssey. *Wildlife Conservation, 103*(5), 46–49, 68.

Stroman, C. A., & Seltzer, R. (1989, Winter). Mass media use and knowledge of AIDS. *Journalism Quarterly, 66,* 881–887.

Swenson, R. M. (1988). Plagues, history and AIDS. *American Scholar, 57,* 183.

Swisher, C., & Reese, S. (1992, Winter). The smoking and health issue in newspapers: Influence of regional economies, the Tobacco Institute and news objectivity. *Journalism Quarterly, 69*(4), 987–1000.

Szulc, T. (1997). A looming Greek tragedy in Hong Kong. *Foreign Policy, 106,* 76–89.

Tabak, R. J. (1999, Summer). Racial discrimination in implementing the death penalty. *Human Rights: Journal of the Section of Individual Rights & Responsibilities, 26*(3), 58–79.

Tabak, R., (2002). Striving to eliminate unjust executions: Why the ABA's individual rights and responsibilities section has issued protocols on unfair implementation of capitol punishment. *Ohio State Law Journal, 63*(1), 475–486.

Talbot, M. (2000). What becomes of the juvenile delinquent? *The New York Times Magazine, 6,* 41–47, 58–60, 88, 96.

Teinowitz, I. (1998). FTC chief asks Congress to ensure privacy on Web. *Advertising Age, 69*(23), 53.

The Election Data Book. Lanham, MD: Bernan Press.

Tichenor, P. J., Donohue, G., & Olien, C. (1973). Mass communication research: Evolution of a structural model. *Journalism Quarterly 50,* 419–425.

Tichenor, P. J., Donohue, G., & Olien, C. (1980). *Community conflict and the press.* Beverly Hills, CA: Sage.

To the hustings. (1998, July 11). *The Economist,* pp. 33–34.

Torbet, P., Griffen, P., Hurst, H., Jr., & Mackenzie, L. R. (2000). *Juveniles facing criminal sanctions: Three stats that changed the rules.* Washington, DC: Office of Juvenile Justice and Delinquency Prevention.

Tuchman, G. (1978). *Making news: A study in the construction of reality.* New York: The Free Press.

Tuchman, G., Daniels, A. K., & Benet, J. (Eds.). (1978). *Hearth and home: Images of women in the mass media.* New York: Oxford University Press.

Uniform Crime Reports: Crime in the United States. (1998). Washington, DC: Federal Bureau of Investigation.

Uniform Crime Reports: Crime in the United States. (1998–2000). Washington, DC: Federal Bureau of Investigation.

U.S. Bureau of the Census. (1992), *Statistical Abstract of the United States* (112th ed.). Washington, DC: Author.

U.S. Bureau of the Census. (1994). *1990 census of population: Social and economic characteristics.* Washington, DC: Department of Commerce.

U.S. Surgeon General's Report 1998: US Surgeon General. (1998, June 10). Tobacco use among US racial/ethnic minority groups. *The Journal of the American Medical Association, 279*(22), 1776.

Van Slambrouck, P. (2000). When is get tough too tough on teens? *Christian Science Monitor, 92*(51), 2.

Viswanath, K., & Finnegan, J. R., Jr. (2002). Reflections on community health campaigns: Secular trends and the capacity to effect change. In R. Hornik (Ed.), *Public health communication: Evidence for behavior change* (pp. 289–312). Mahwah, NJ: Erlbaum.

Vivian, J. (Ed.). (1995). *The media of mass communication* (3rd ed.). Needham Heights, MA: Allyn & Bacon.

Walker, G. C. (1997). The right to die: Healthcare workers' attitudes compared with a national public poll. *Omega Journal of Death and Dying, 35*(4), 339–345.

Wallack, L., Dorfman, L., Jernigan, D., & Themba, M. (1993). *Media advocacy and public health.* Newbury Park, CA: Sage.

Waller, W. P., & Ide, M. E. (1995). China and human rights. *Public Opinion Quarterly, 59*, 133–143.

Walsh-Childers, K., Chance, J., & Alley Swain, K. (1999, Spring). Daily newspaper coverage of the organization, delivery and financing of health care. *Newspaper Research Journal, 10*(2), 2–22.

Wanta, W., & Elliott, W. R. (1995). Did the "Magic" work? Knowledge of HIV/AIDS and the knowledge gap hypothesis. *Journalism and Mass Communication Quarterly, 72*, 312–321.

Wasserman, I. M., Stack, S., & Reeves, J. L. (1994). Suicide and the media: *The New York Times's* presentation of front-page suicide stories between 1910 and 1920. *Journal of Communication, 44*(2), 64–83.

Weaver, D., & Wilhoit, C. (1986). *The American journalist: A portrait of US news people and their work.* Bloomington: Indiana University Press.

Weaver, D., & Wilhoit, C. (1988, Summer). A profile of JMC educators: Traits, attitudes and values. *Journalism Educator,* 4–41.

Weaver, D., & Wilhoit, C. (1996). *The American journalist: A portrait of U.S. news people at the end of an era.* Mahwah, NJ: Erlbaum.

Weaver, J. B., III (1994). Pornography and sexual callousness: The perceptual and behavioral consequences of exposure to pornography. In D. Zillmann, J. Bryant, & A. C. Huston (Eds.), *Media, family and children: Social scientific, psychodynamic, and clinical perspectives* (pp. 215–228). Hillsdale, NJ: Erlbaum.

Weinstein, L., & Neumann, P. G. (2000). Internet risks. *Communications of the ACM, 43*, 71–79.

Weiss, S. C. (1999). Defining a "patients' bill of rights" for the next century. *Journal of the American Medical Association, 281*, 856.

West, D. M. (1996). Harry and Louise go to Washington: Political advertising and health care reform. *Journal of Health Politics, 21*, 35–68.

White, G. (2000 October). What we may expect from ethics and the law. *American Journal of Nursing, 100*(10), 114–118.

Williams, R. B. (1995). Ethical reasoning in television news: Privacy and AIDS testing. *Journal of Mass Media Ethics, 10*, 109–120.

Wilson, K., Scott, J., Graham, I., Kozak, J., Chater, S., Viola, R., de Faye, B., Weaver, L., & Curran, D. (2000). Attitudes of terminally ill patients toward euthanasia and physician-assisted suicide. *Archives of Internal Medicine, 160*, 2454–2460.

Winter, J. P., & Eyal, C. H. (1981). Agenda setting for the civil rights issue. *Public Opinion Quarterly, 45*(3), 376–383.

World Almanac and Book of Facts 1999. (1998, November). New York: Griffin.

World Almanac and Book of Facts. (2002). New York: Education Group.

Worthen, L.T., & Yeats, D.E. (1998) Assisted suicide: Factors affecting public attitudes. *Omega Journal of Death and Dying, 42*(2), 115–135.

Wu, H. D., Stevenson, R. L., Chen, Hsiao-Chi, & Güner, Z. N. (2002, Spring). The conditional impact of recessions: A time-series analysis of economic communication in the United States, 1987-1996. *International Journal of Public Opinion Research, 14*(1), 19–36.

Yahuda, M. (1996). The Tiananmen clock is ticking. *World Today, 52*, 261–263.

Yang, C. (2001, July 23). Pope meets Bush, condemns stem cell research. ABC news.com. Retrieved September 30, 2001,from wysiwyg://8/http://abcnews.go. com/secti...rld/DailyNews/italy010723_popebush.html

Youngmin, Y. (2005, December). Legitimacy, public relations, and media access: Proposing and testing a media access model. *Communication Research, 32*(6), 762–793.

Zelizer, B. (1993). Journalists as interpretive communities. *Critical Studies in Mass Communication, 10*, 219–237.

Zhang, G., & Krauss, S. (1995). Constructing public opinion and manipulating symbols: China's press coverage of the student movement in 1989. *Journalism & Mass Communication Quarterly, 72*, 412–425.

Zhu, J. (1991). Between the prescriptive and descriptive roles: A comparison of international trade new in China and Taiwan. *Asian Journal of Communication, 2*, 31–50.

Ziegler, P. (1969). *The black death.* New York: Harper & Row.

Zimet, G. D., Lazebnik, R., DiClemente, R. J., Anglin, T. M., Williams, P., & Ellica, E. M. (1993). The relationship of Magic Johnson's announcement of HIV infection to the AIDS attitudes of junior high school students. *The Journal of Sex Research, 3*(2), 129–134.

Zimring, F. E. (1995). Reflections on firearms and the criminal law: Guns and violence symposium. *Journal of Criminal Law and Criminology, 86*, 1–19.

AUTHOR INDEX

SUBJECT INDEX

Printed in the United States
88504LV00004B/70-144/A